Evidentiary Foundations

Second Edition

EDWARD J. IMWINKELRIED

Professor of Law
University of California at Davis
School of Law

THE MICHIE COMPANY
Law Publishers
CHARLOTTESVILLE, VIRGINIA

I would like to dedicate my work on this text to:

Cindy, Molly, and Kenny;
my parents, Mr. and Mrs. John Imwinkelried;
and my parents-in-law, Mary Jane Clark and
the late Lyman (Brownie) Clark.

PREFACE

In his classic text, *The Bramble Bush,* Professor Karl Llewellyn discusses the objectives of legal education. He explains that social policies dictate the substantive content of rules of law and that in turn, those rules of law dictate the historical facts the attorney must plead and prove to justify the result his or her client desires. The law student must learn to identify the social policies and legal rules implicated by the "raw facts" of the case.

Evidentiary Foundations is designed to help the law student appreciate how the policies underlying Evidence law translate into concrete lines of questions calculated to prove specific facts at trial. Each section of the text discusses an evidentiary doctrine which the student will probably study in the Evidence or Trial Practice course. The introductory part of each section describes the policies underlying the doctrine and the substantive content of the doctrine itself. The next part of the section demonstrates how the student can convert an abstractly worded provision of the Federal Rules of Evidence into a set of questions eliciting particular facts at trial.

Llewellyn viewed the development of the skill of precise, imaginative fact evaluation as the raison d'etre of legal education. I hope that this edition of *Evidentiary Foundations* will help law students develop that skill in their Evidence and Trial Practice courses.

Edward J. Imwinkelried

Davis, California

ACKNOWLEDGMENTS

The author would like to express his thanks to:

— Mr. Ronald Richards, class of 1989, University of California, at Davis Law School, who researched and proofread the manuscript for this edition;
— Helen Forsyth and Kathy Houston who typed the manuscript; and
— his colleagues, Richard C. Wydick and James E. Hogan. In 1988, Professors Wydick and Hogan helped the author prepare a special California edition of *Evidentiary Foundations*. Their comments on the manuscript for *California Evidentiary Foundations* were instrumental in preparing the second edition of *Evidentiary Foundations*.

SUMMARY TABLE OF CONTENTS

TABLE OF CONTENTS

Chapter 1

INTRODUCTION

A. INTRODUCTION

I have taught both Evidence and Trial Techniques for well over a decade. During that time I have identified some recurring complaints by my students. The primary complaint of the Evidence students is that they cannot develop a working understanding of the evidentiary doctrines we discuss in class. The students say that their Evidence casebooks and hornbooks do not explain how the doctrines operate in the courtroom. For their part, the Trial Techniques students complain that although they think they understand the abstract evidentiary doctrines, they cannot apply the doctrines. Specifically, they cannot convert the classroom theories into concrete lines of questioning for the courtroom.

Given those complaints, I began an experiment in the late 1970's. I browsed through such texts as the *American Jurisprudence Proof of Facts* set (Bancroft-Whitney Publishing Company) and *The Trial Manual of Predicate Questions* (National District Attorneys Association). I selected a set of sample foundations from these texts and encouraged my students to read the sample foundations during the course. At the end of the course, I solicited the students' comments on the experiment. On the one hand, the students responded that a set of sample foundations was an excellent idea. Several students remarked that as soon as they read a sample foundation, the abstract evidentiary doctrine made much more sense. On the other hand, most students felt that some of the sample foundations I had collected were too sophisticated or lengthy. That feeling is understandable. After all, the available sets of sample foundations are designed primarily for practitioners rather than law students.

At this point, I resolved to prepare a comprehensive set of simple foundations for law students and young trial attorneys. That set became the first edition of *Evidentiary Foundations* (1980). I have used the first edition in my own classes since its release. I think that the level of student performance in both Evidence and Trial Practice has improved since I began using the text, and I hope that the improvement is due in some small part to the use of the text. It has become clear to me that it is time for a second edition of *Evidentiary Foundations.* Developments in Evidence law have rendered some passages of the first edition inaccurate or misleading. Moreover, I understand the

1

structure of Evidence law better now; and I have reorganized this second edition to help students better appreciate that structure.

Most sections of the text use the following format. First, at the beginning of each section, there is a discussion of an evidentiary doctrine. The text discusses the modern common law and usually cites the applicable Federal Rule of Evidence as well. Since the principal purpose of this text is to teach trial technique rather than the evidentiary doctrine, the textual discussion of the doctrine is relatively short; and there are few case citations. The reader can find ample authority for this text's propositions of Evidence law in such hornbooks as C. McCormick, *Evidence* (West Publishing Company 1984) and E. Imwinkelried, P. Giannelli, F. Gilligan & F. Lederer, *Courtroom Criminal Evidence* (The Michie Company 1987). Second, the text breaks the doctrine down into a list of foundation elements. These elements are the historical facts and events which constitute the foundation. Each element is numbered. Finally, the section contains a sample foundation for the evidentiary doctrine. Each question in the body of the sample foundation is numbered; the number corresponds to the element of the foundation the question relates to. Thus, the numbered foundation shows the student how each element in the doctrine converts into concrete questions in the courtroom. I sincerely hope that this text will help Evidence students to understand evidentiary doctrine and assist Trial Techniques students to apply the doctrine. In the sample foundations,"J" means judge, "W" means witness, "P" the proponent of the evidence, "O" the opponent of the evidence, and "B" the bailiff or court reporter. The foundations assume that a jury is present. The procedure would be a bit more informal in a bench trial (a trial by judge alone).

B. LAYING A FOUNDATION — IN GENERAL

1. LEGAL RULES

For our purposes, the most important procedural rule is that the proponent of an item of evidence must ordinarily lay the foundation before formally offering the item into evidence. For example, the proponent of a letter must present proof of its authenticity before offering the letter into evidence. Proof of the letter's authenticity is part of the letter's "foundation" or "predicate." Substantive Evidence law makes proof of authenticity a condition precedent to the letter's admission into evidence. Whenever Evidence law makes proof of a fact or event a condition to the admission of an item of evidence, that fact or event is part of the foundation for the evidence's admission.

In most jurisdictions, the trial judge has discretion to deviate from this procedural rule; the judge may vary the order of proof and admit the evidence subject to the subsequent proof of the foundation. However, judges are reluctant to use this discretion. Proof of the foundation before the evidence's admission is usually the more logical order of presentation. Moreover, if the judge admits the evidence subject to subsequent proof of the foundation and the proponent later fails to present the proof, the judge will be in an awkward position. At the very least, the judge will have to instruct the jurors to disregard the evidence they have already heard. If the judge believes that the instruction will be ineffective and the jurors will be unable to put aside the evidence, the judge may have to grant a mistrial. Hence, whenever possible, the proponent should lay the foundation or predicate before formally offering the item of evidence.

2. PRACTICAL RULES

There are three cardinal rules for the draftsman of a line of questioning: simplicity, brevity, and preparation.

First, always use the simplest, most easily understood term. The trial attorney must communicate effectively with lay witnesses and jurors. Effective communication with lay persons requires that the trial attorney use lay diction. Jonathan Swift quite properly condemned the attorneys of his day for using "a peculiar Cant and Jargon of their own that no other mortal can understand ...." Sadly, many modern trial attorneys are guilty of the same literary sin. There is no need to resort to "prior" and "subsequent" if "before" and "after" will do quite nicely. There is no need to refer to "motor vehicle" when the word "car" is available. There is no justification for using "altercation" when the attorney could say "fight." Trial attorneys should realize that the examination of witnesses is a test of communicative skill rather than vocabulary.

Second, always make each question as short as possible. Rudolph Flesch has pointed out that there is an inverse relation between the length of a sentence and its comprehensibility; the longer the sentence, the lower the level of reader or hearer comprehension. Reading psychology studies document that the maximum length of a written sentence should be 25 words; if the sentence is any longer, reader comprehension drops off markedly. It is more difficult for a hearer to absorb a spoken sentence than it is for a reader to absorb a written sentence. Consequently, many experienced trial attorneys strive to limit their questions to ten or fifteen words in length. If the spoken question exceeds fifteen words, it can be very difficult for the witness and jurors to follow.

The third cardinal rule is preparation. Both the attorney and the witness must be well-prepared for trial. If the attorney falters or pauses too long during direct examination, the examination loses its flow and rhythm. If the witness appears uncertain during questioning, at the very least the jurors will doubt the quality of the witness's memory. The attorney must review the contemplated testimony with the witness before trial; the attorney should have the witness review the witness's deposition and other pretrial statements to refresh the witness's recollection.

C. LAYING A FOUNDATION ON DIRECT EXAMINATION

The general rules for laying foundations apply to direct examination. The direct examiner should lay a foundation before offering the evidence, and the examiner should observe the cardinal rules of simplicity and brevity. However, there are some additional rules the direct examiner must be familiar with.

1. LEGAL RULES

One rule the direct examiner should become familiar with is that in many jurisdictions, the technical evidentiary rules do not apply to some foundational questions. For instance, Federal Rule of Evidence 104(a) provides: "Preliminary questions concerning ... the admissibility of evidence ... shall be determined by the court .... In making its determination it [the court] is not bound by the rules of evidence except those with respect to privileges." Suppose that the proponent is offering a witness's former testimony at a prior trial. Part of the foundation for the former testimony exception to the hearsay rule is proof that the witness is unavailable at the present trial. In a jurisdiction where the hearsay rule does not apply to foundational evidence, the proponent could ask an investigator on the witness stand to relate a third party's statement that the former witness had moved to Sweden. The third party's statement would usually be inadmissible hearsay; the third party was outside the courtroom when he or she made the statement, and the proponent is offering the statement for the truth of its assertion. However, we are assuming now that the hearsay rule is inapplicable.

The second rule to bear in mind is that leading questions are usually forbidden on direct examination. Leading questions suggest the desired answer to the witness. Since the witness is presumably friendly to the direct examiner, the witness will probably follow the lead. Suppose that the plaintiff's brother was a witness to the accident. The plaintiff alleges that the defendant was speeding. The plaintiff calls her brother as a witness. It would be impermissibly leading for the plaintiff's attorney to ask, "Isn't it true that the defendant was going 80 miles an hour?" There is a serious risk that the witness, the plaintiff's brother, will simply follow the attorney's lead rather than attempting to give the most accurate testimony. On direct examination, the law prefers that the attorney use the non-leading question, "In your opinion, what was the defendant's speed?"

In addition to knowing the general prohibition of leading questions on direct examination, the direct examiner must realize that the prohibition is merely a norm rather than an absolute rule. There are numerous exceptions to the norm. One notable exception is that the direct examiner may use leading questions on preliminary matters. Most judges limit the scope of this exception to such matters as the witness' occupation and setting the scene for events. However, some judges construe "preliminary" very broadly and liberally permit leading questions on foundational matters. Another exception is that the direct examiner may use mildly leading questions to refresh the memory of a forgetful witness.

2. PRACTICAL RULES

Whenever possible, comply with the technical evidentiary rules. Even if the local law permits you to disregard those rules in laying a foundation, your disregard of the rules will often prompt an objection. The opponent may not realize that the technical rules are inapplicable, or in bad faith the opponent may be searching for any pretext to disrupt your direct examination. The ideal direct examination is flowing and uninterrupted; without distracting objections, the direct examiner gives the witness an opportunity to tell a story to the jurors. You want to minimize the risk that the opponent will interrupt your foundation with an objection. Every time you disregard the technical rules in your foundational questions, you risk a distracting objection.

The same practical considerations lead to the conclusion that whenever possible, you should use non-leading questions on direct examination. You want to reduce the risk that your foundation will be interrupted by a leading question objection. Moreover, if you have a good witness, you want the witness to do the talking. By using leading questions which must be answered "Yes" or "No," you restrict the witness' opportunity to speak; and the jurors may suspect that you are putting words in the witness's mouth. If the witness projects honesty and intelligence, you want to use open-ended, non-leading questions. The witness should be center stage. Juror psychology studies suggest a further reason to avoid leading the witness. One study found that the more acute jurors note the difference between leading and non-leading questioning. More importantly, when the jurors note that the attorney is leading a particular witness, they tend to infer that the attorney is doing so because the attorney lacks faith in the witness. Understandably, after drawing that inference, the jurors discount the witness' credibility. If you have a good witness, non-leading questions are tactically preferable on direct examination.

To ensure that your questions are non-leading, begin as many as possible with the words, "who," "what," "which," "when," "where," "how," and "why." If you begin a question with one of these words, you will find that it is very difficult to make the question leading. Indeed, many trial judges use the rule of thumb that questions beginning with these words are not leading. In this text, I have made a conscious effort to begin every question in the sample foundations for direct examination with one of these words. In the sample foundations, the word is in capital letters. My hope is that reading questions beginning with these words will help the student develop the skill and habit of phrasing non-leading questions.

I am not advocating beginning every sentence of direct examination with one of these words; that practice would make your direct examination annoyingly monotonous. As professional writers say, you want "elegant variation" in the phrasing of your questions. Sometimes you will not want an interrogatory sentence. When you elicit background information about your witness, you can use imperative sentences; for example, you may command the witness to "Please tell us where you work." To highlight the subdivisions of your direct examination, you may use declarative sentences such as "Now I want to ask you a few questions about what happened at the hospital." Even when you use interrogatory sentences, as we have seen, Evidence law sometimes permits you to use gently leading questions. However, most law students and new trial attorneys pay insufficient attention to the phrasing of their questions on direct examination. This text uniformly uses non-leading phrasing to help the reader develop a habit of consistently phrasing non-leading questions.

D. LAYING A FOUNDATION ON CROSS-EXAMINATION

The general rules for laying a foundation also apply here. Most of the general rules apply with even greater force on cross-examination. On cross, many judges are very reluctant to permit the examiner to introduce an item of evidence before presenting the foundational proof. On cross-examination, the witness is often hostile to the examiner; and the judge is more skeptical of the examiner's assurance that the witness will give favorable testimony at a later point in the examination. The norms of simplicity and brevity also apply with greater force on cross-examination. The hostile witness will often strain to misinterpret the question. The cross-examiner wants to frame questions that are so clear and so short that they cannot be misinterpreted. However, in addition to knowing the general rules for laying foundations, the cross-examiner must be cognizant of several special rules for cross.

1. LEGAL RULES

You will occasionally encounter a trial judge who believes that an attorney may not introduce an exhibit during the cross-examination of an opposing witness. That belief is erroneous. J. Tanford, *The Trial Process: Law, Tactics and Ethics* 388 (1983). It is true that Federal Rule of Evidence 611(b) confines cross-examination to "the subject matter of the direct examination." But if the exhibit relates to a matter raised on direct examination, "new exhibits properly may be introduced during cross-examination." Tanford, *supra*. Rule 611(a) gives the judge discretionary control over the order of proof; the permissibility of introducing exhibits during the cross-examination "lies in the discretion of the trial judge." Tanford, *supra*.

Since the witness is often hostile to the cross-examiner, the law permits leading questions on cross-examination. While leading questions are permissible on cross, argumentative questions are objectionable. An argumentative question challenges the witness about an inference from the facts in the case. Assume that the witness testifies on direct examination that the defendant's car was going 80 miles an hour just before the collision. You want to impeach the witness with a prior inconsistent statement. It would be permissible, leading cross-examination to ask, "Isn't it true that you told your neighbor, Mrs. Ashton, at a party last Sunday that the defendant's car was going only 50 miles an hour?" The cross-examiner may legitimately attempt to force the witness to concede the historical fact of the prior inconsistent statement. Now assume that the witness admits the statement. It would be impermissibly argumentative to ask, "How can you reconcile that statement with your testimony on direct examination?" The cross-examiner is not seeking any additional facts; rather, the cross-examiner is challenging the witness about an inference from the facts. Questions such as "How can you expect the jury to believe that?" are similarly argumentative and objectionable. The attorney may argue the inferences during summation or closing argument, but the attorney must ordinarily restrict his or her questions to those calculated to elicit facts.

2. PRACTICAL RULES

Negatively, the cross-examiner should scrupulously avoid argumentative questions. If a hostile witness is intelligent, the witness usually will not easily concede the favorable inference you want to draw. An argumentative question often prompts a heated exchange between the cross-examiner and the witness. The lay jurors sympathize with the lay witness, and you can antagonize the jurors by arguing with the witness. Unless the witness has a particularly abrasive personality, arguments between the attorney and witness are usually "no-win" situations for the attorney. If the attorney appears to dominate the exchange, the jurors may infer that the attorney does not want the witness to tell the whole truth; but if the witness appears to dominate, the jurors may conclude that the attorney is diffident — perhaps because the attorney lacks faith in his or her case. Elicit the historical facts you are morally certain the witness will concede, and draw your inferences during closing argument.

Affirmatively, as a general proposition, you should consistently use leading questions on cross-examination. You ordinarily do not want to give a hostile witness any opening. Do not give that witness an opportunity to explain by asking "Why?" If you want to impeach a witness with a conviction, ask, "Isn't it true that in 1978, a New York court convicted you of perjury?" If you want to prove a prior inconsistent statement, ask, "Isn't it a fact that right after the fight, you told the officer that the hallway was so dark that you couldn't identify your attacker?" You can preface your questions with "Isn't it true ...?", "Isn't it correct ...?" or "Isn't it a fact ...?" to maintain control over the witness; or you can make a declarative statement and add a tag sentence such as "Isn't that true?" at the very end of your question.

I have attempted to begin every question in the sample foundations for cross-examination with such prefatory language. The preface is in capital letters. My purpose is to help the reader develop the habit of consistently using leading questions on cross-examination. Again, I do not advocate beginning every question with blatantly leading introductory language. Sometimes you will want to use non-leading questions. For instance, you may suspect that an adverse child witness has a memorized story. As the cross-examiner, you might want to pose an open-ended, non-leading question to the witness to give the child another opportunity to repeat the story verbatim. In other cases, if the topic is safe, you can use gently leading questions, beginning with such words as "Is," "Was," and "Did." However, the primary failing of neophyte cross-examiners is that they do not lead enough. I have deliberately exaggerated and begun every cross-examination question with blatantly leading language to underscore the importance of maintaining witness control. Albert Krieger, the former president of the National Association of Criminal Defense Lawyers, has remarked that under the guise of asking questions, a good cross-examiner actually makes factual assertions and forces the witness to express assent on the record.

Finally, remember that your demeanor and tone should ordinarily be friendly even when you are using narrowly-phrased, leading questions. You want the opposing witness to cooperate. You will not get that cooperation if your demeanor is combative or offensive. Quite to the contrary, if your demeanor is aggressive, the witness will put up his or her defenses, and you will have a very difficult time eliciting favorable information. You will sometimes want to make a show of righteous indignation at an opposing witness caught in an obvious lie; but when you are using the opposing witness to lay a foundation, the wisest tactic is to be friendly and low-key.

Chapter 2

RELATED PROCEDURES

A. INTRODUCTION

Most law students realize the importance of learning the procedures the proponent uses to present evidence. The subsequent chapters outline those procedures. However, there are two other sets of procedural rules a trial attorney must master: (1) the procedures the opponent uses to object to the admission of the proponent's evidence; and (2) the procedures the proponent uses if the trial judge sustains the opponent's objection. The purpose of this chapter is to familiarize the student with these two sets of procedural rules. Sections B through E describe the procedures the opponent must invoke to exclude evidence. Section F illustrates the procedures the proponent resorts to if the judge sustains an objection by the opponent.

B. PRETRIAL MOTION *IN LIMINE* BY THE OPPONENT

1. THE DOCTRINE

If the opponent anticipates an evidentiary issue arising at trial, the opponent need not wait until trial to voice the objection. The opponent may raise the objection by a pretrial motion *in limine*. The proponent may make a motion *in limine* to obtain an advance ruling of the evidence's admissibility, but such motions are more frequently used by the opponent to suppress evidence before the trial begins. The opponent may use the motion for such purposes as preventing any mention of a wrongful death plaintiff's re-marriage, a civil defendant's liability insurance or a criminal defendant's prior convictions.

There are several tactical reasons why the opponent may employ a motion *in limine*. The most obvious reason is that the objectionable evidence might be highly prejudicial. If the opponent delays objecting until trial, during trial the jurors may at least hear some mention of the evidence. It would be preferable to litigate the issue before trial and preclude the proponent from even mentioning the evidence during trial. If the jurors hear any mention of the evidence, they may conclude that the opponent is hiding the truth from them. Further, the opponent may need an advance ruling to make strategy decisions for trial. Should the criminal defense attorney put his or her client on the stand? The defense attorney must consider the risk that if the client testifies, the judge may permit the prosecutor to impeach the client with prior

convictions. If the judge grants a pretrial motion *in limine* to exclude
the convictions, the defense attorney can confidently place the client on
the stand. Without the benefit of the pretrial ruling, the defense attorney must gamble that the judge will exclude the convictions on objection.

How does the opponent make a motion *in limine*? Some jurisdictions
require that the opponent give the proponent advance notice of the
motion. In any case, as a matter of fairness, the opponent should give
advance notice. Some jurisdictions also require or strongly prefer that
the opponent reduce the motion to writing. However, perhaps the majority still permits oral motions. The opponent actually makes the motion at the in-chambers conference before the trial begins; the attorneys and the judge meet in the judge's chambers before they walk into
open court and meet the jurors. The trial judge has discretion whether
to entertain the motion; the judge may prefer to rule on the issue
during trial. If the judge entertains the motion and hears it on its
merits, there are several possible rulings: (1) The judge may overrule
the objection; (2) the judge may enter an absolute order prohibiting the
proponent from mentioning the evidence during the trial; or (3) the
judge may enter a preliminary order. On the one hand, a preliminary
order prohibits the proponent from mentioning the evidence to the jury
without the judge's consent. The order can be worded to apply not only
to witnesses' testimony but also to any reference to the evidence by the
attorney during voir dire examination and opening statement. On the
other hand, a preliminary order permits the proponent to request a
hearing out of the jury's presence during the trial. At the hearing, the
proponent may attempt to persuade the judge to admit the evidence. A
preliminary order is appropriate when the judge finds that the evidence is prejudicial but does not want to rule finally until he or she
knows the final state of the evidence at trial.

If the judge denies the motion, there is a split of authority over the
question of whether the moving party must renew the objection at trial
to preserve the issue for appeal. Most federal courts require the party
to renew the objection. There is an additional requirement to preserve
the objection when the objection challenges convictions offered as impeachment evidence under Federal Rule 609. The requirement was
announced in *Luce v. United States*, 469 U.S. 38 (1984). In that case,
the defense moved *in limine* to exclude the defendant's conviction on
the ground that the prejudicial character of the evidence outweighed
its probative value. The defense argued that the prospect of the admission of the conviction would deter the defendant from even testifying
and thereby deprive the jury of the defendant's valuable testimony.
The trial judge denied the motion, and the defendant elected not to
testify. On appeal, the defense challenged the denial of the motion. The
Court held that the alleged error will not be reviewed unless the defen-

dant actually testifies at trial. Writing for the majority, former Chief Justice Burger asserted that without the benefit of the defendant's trial testimony, "[a]ny possible harm flowing from a district court's *in limine* ruling permitting impeachment by a prior conviction is wholly speculative."

2. ELEMENTS OF A MOTION *IN LIMINE*

The following are the elements of a motion *in limine* to exclude evidence:

1. The opponent states his or her intent to move *in limine* to exclude certain evidence.
2. The opponent has reason to believe that the proponent possesses the evidence and will offer the evidence at trial.
3. The opponent briefly states the ground on which the evidence is inadmissible. The opponent must state the ground with the same specificity with which he or she would make a trial objection. *See* Section C, *infra*.
4. The opponent explains why an ordinary trial objection would be inadequate protection for the opponent.
5. The opponent presents the legal argument in favor of the motion. After the proponent's response, the judge rules.

3. SAMPLE MOTION *IN LIMINE*

The fact situation is a criminal prosecution in the hypothetical State of El Dorado. The defendant is charged with armed robbery. The defendant has a prior, 1986 conviction for armed robbery in Alabama. The judge has already begun the in-chambers conference before trial. The opponent is the defense counsel.

J   Are there any other matters either of you think we should take up before trial begins?

O   Yes, Your Honor. I would like to make a motion *in limine* to absolutely preclude the prosecutor from mentioning my client's 1986 armed robbery conviction. (1) When the prosecutor gave me the discovery file, the file contained a certified copy of the judgment of conviction. I assume that if my client takes the stand, the prosecutor will attempt to use the conviction to impeach my client. (2) I have given the prosecutor a week's advance notice of my intention to make this motion. I have given her a copy of the memorandum of law, citing the cases I'm relying on as authority.

J   (To the prosecutor) Did you receive the advance notice?

P   Yes.

J   And is it your intention to use the conviction?

P   Yes, Your Honor. It is well-settled in El Dorado that you can use a felony conviction to impeach a witness, even a criminal defendant. In Alabama, this type of armed robbery is a felony.

O   Your Honor, I'm aware of the usual rule in El Dorado. However, our position is that since the 1986 conviction is for the same type of crime my client is now charged with, the conviction is too prejudicial; there's too great a risk that the jurors will misuse this impeachment evidence and treat it as evidence of the defendant's bad character.

J   I normally defer ruling on this type of issue until trial.

O   I'm aware of that, your Honor. However, I think that you should dispose of this issue before trial begins; a trial objection won't adequately protect my client. In this case, the charged crime and the crime my client was previously convicted of are absolutely identical. If there's any mention of this conviction at trial, the jurors simply won't be able to follow any curative instruction you give to disregard the evidence. Moreover, I'm trying to decide whether to put my client on the stand. Your ruling is going to be a major factor in my decision. (4)

J   Do you have any authority to support your motion?

O   I've cited the most important cases in my memorandum of law. *Luck,*[1] on page two of my memo, is authority that as trial judge, you have discretion to balance a conviction's probative value against its prejudicial character; if the prejudicial character outweighs the probative value, you may exclude an otherwise admissible conviction. *Rist,*[2] on page four, emphasizes the extreme potential prejudice when the charged crime is identical to the crime of which the defendant was previously convicted. *Rist* establishes a norm that identical offenses are inadmissible. This case falls within *Rist.* (5)

P   Your Honor, all you have to do is give the jurors a limiting instruction. Tell them affirmatively that they are to consider the conviction solely as impeachment evidence. Tell them negatively that they're not to use the conviction as evidence of the defendant's bad character; they're not to infer that he committed the charged robbery because he committed a previous robbery or because he is a bad person.

O   As the cases point out, we can't trust a limiting instruction here. The crimes are identical, and we consequently can't naively assume that the jurors will follow the limiting instruction. (5)

P   My last point, your Honor, is that we have a substantial need for this evidence. There's only one eyewitness, the victim. This trial is going to be a classic swearing contest. The outcome is going to turn on whom the jury believes. We need all the impeaching evidence at our disposal.

J   I think that this is an appropriate case for a preliminary rather than an absolute order. I agree that since the crimes are identical, the conviction has tremendous potential for prejudice. Yet I don't want to absolutely preclude any use of the conviction; if the trial becomes the swearing contest the prosecutor predicts, the prosecution's need for the impeaching evidence may outweigh its prejudicial character. Hence, I'm going to enter a preliminary order. I don't want any mention of the conviction in the jury's hearing without my prior permission. Ms. Prosecutor, if at any point during the trial you think that the record establishes your need for the evidence, I want you to request a hearing out of the jurors' presence. You can make an offer of proof at the hearing, and then I'll finally rule whether you can use the conviction.

---

1. Luck v. United States, 348 F.2d 763 (D.C. Cir. 1965).
2. People v. Rist, 16 Cal. 3d 211, 127 Cal. Rptr. 457, 545 P.2d 833 (1976).

C. OBJECTIONS AT THE TRIAL BY THE OPPONENT

1. THE DOCTRINE

If the opponent does not move *in limine* or the judge refuses to entertain the pretrial motion, the opponent must object at trial. When the opponent objects, the opponent in effect asserts that it is improper to admit the proponent's evidence. The American litigation system is patterned after an adversary model: the burden of presenting evidence is on the proponent, and the onus of excluding evidence is on the opponent. In rare cases, an error can be so plain and prejudicial that the judge will exclude the evidence on his or her own motion. However, given our adversary model, the opponent must ordinarily assume the responsibility for excluding evidence by objecting.

An objection must be courteous, timely, and specific. The opponent owes a duty of courtesy to the trial judge. The opponent should stand to state any objection and preface the objection with "Your Honor ...." An objection must also be timely. The objection must be neither too early nor too late. Suppose that the objection relates to a foundational issue such as authentication, best evidence, or hearsay. Foundational objections are premature until the questioning attorney attempts to elicit the objectionable testimony. Thus, if the opposing attorney believes that there is an inadequate authentication foundation for a letter, the attorney must reserve the objection until the questioning attorney offers the letter into evidence. Similarly, when the opposing attorney believes that there is an inadequate hearsay foundation for an out-of-court statement, the attorney must reserve the objection until the questioning attorney asks the witness to state the contents of the out-of-court statement. In contrast, if the objection relates to a form problem such as leading or argumentative questioning, the opponent should state the objection immediately after the improper question and before the witness begins the answer. If the opponent delays the objection, the opponent has waived the objection.

Finally, to be effective, an objection must be specific; the opponent must specify both what he or she is objecting to and why they are objecting. The opponent should identify the word, phrase, or question he or she is objecting to. In addition, he or she must state the legal ground for the objection. Federal Rule of Evidence 103(a)(1) requires that the opponent state "the specific ground of objection, if the specific ground (is) not apparent from the context ...." The overwhelming majority view is that it is sufficient to cite the generic evidentiary doctrine the opponent claims the proponent is violating; the opponent names the violated rule by stating "not the best evidence" or "incompetent hearsay." In the presence of the jury, the opponent should slightly vary the objection's wording to ensure that the jury does not gain the impression that the opponent is invoking technical rules to suppress or hide the truth. For example, the opponent should state that the proponent is "unfairly" leading the witness or attempting to introduce "unreliable" hearsay. While tailoring the objection's phrasing for the jury, the opponent must not make a "speaking objection." That expression refers to long-winded objections; the opponent makes a speech rather than briefly stating the legal ground for the objection. Trial judges will not tolerate speaking objections.

2. ELEMENTS OF AN OBJECTION

A proper objection includes the following elements:
1. The opponent addresses the judge.
2. The opponent indicates that he or she is raising an objection.
3. The opponent specifies what he or she is objecting to, *e.g.*, the particular word, phrase, or question.
4. The opponent specifies the legal ground for the objection, that is, the generic evidentiary doctrine the proponent is violating.

3. SAMPLE OBJECTIONS

Some of the opponent's objections will claim violations of substantive evidentiary doctrines. These objections are illustrative.

Your Honor (1), I object (2) to any testimony by this proposed witness (3) on the ground that this person is incompetent to be a witness. (4) *(See* Chapter 3, *infra.)*

Your Honor (1), I object (2) to the admission of that exhibit (3) on the ground that there has been insufficient authentication. (4) *(See* Chapter 4, *infra.)*

Your Honor (1), I object (2) to the admission of that copy (3) on the ground that it is not the best evidence. (4) *(See* Chapter 8, *infra.)*

Your Honor (1), I object (2) to that question (3) on the ground that it calls for improper opinion. (4) *(See* Chapter 9, *infra.)*

Your Honor (1), I object (2) to that question (3) on the ground that it calls for incompetent hearsay. (4) *(See* Chapter 10, *infra.)*

Your Honor (1), I object (2) to that question (3) on the ground that it calls for a privileged communication. (4) *(See* Chapter 7, *infra.)*

Most of the objections made during the typical trial relate to matters of form rather than substance. The following are examples of form objections:

Your Honor (1), I object (2) to that question (3) on the ground that it is vague and ambiguous. (4)

Your Honor (1), I object (2) to that question (3) on the ground that it is leading. (4)

Your Honor (1), I object (2) to that question (3) on the ground that it is compound. (4)

Your Honor (1), I object (2) to that question (3) on the ground that it has already been asked and answered. (4)

Your Honor (1), I object (2) to that question (3) on the ground that it is argumentative. (4)

Your Honor (1), I object (2) to that question (3) on the ground that it calls for a narrative answer. (4)

Your Honor (1), I object (2) to that question (3) on the ground that it assumes facts not in evidence. (4)

D. MOTIONS TO STRIKE AT TRIAL BY THE OPPONENT

1. THE DOCTRINE

In most cases, when the opponent desires to exclude the proponent's evidence, the opponent uses the procedural device of an objection. However, in three situations, the opponent must use the procedural device of a motion to strike. The first situation is the case in which the question is proper, but the witness' answer is improper. Second, the witness answers so rapidly that the opponent did not have a fair opportunity to interpose an objection. Finally, after the witness has given apparently proper testimony, it develops that the testimony was improper. For example, on direct examination, the lay witness purports to testify from personal knowledge; and on cross-examination, the witness makes the surprise concession that he was actually relating what he was told by third parties. In all three instances, the opponent should "move to strike" rather than "object."

Like an objection, a motion to strike must be courteous, timely, and specific. The general requirements for objections apply to motions to strike. If the witness' answer is improper, the opponent should move to strike immediately after the answer and before the next question. If the judge grants the motion, the opponent should then request a curative instruction to disregard; the judge informs the jury that the answer was improper and orders the jurors to disregard the answer.

2. ELEMENTS OF A MOTION TO STRIKE

The elements of a motion to strike are roughly the same as those of an objection:

1. The opponent addresses the judge.
2. The opponent indicates that he or she is moving to strike.
3. The opponent specifies what he or she is moving to strike.
4. The opponent specifies the legal ground for the motion.
5. If the judge grants the motion, the opponent requests a curative instruction to disregard.

If the improper remark was highly inflammatory, the opponent should seriously consider moving for a mistrial.

3. SAMPLE MOTION TO STRIKE

The fact situation is a burglary prosecution. The defendant has a number of previous burglary arrests. The prosecution witness is the arresting officer. The officer is testifying that he observed the burglary in progress. The proponent is the prosecutor.

P   Officer Jordan, WHERE were you when the defendant left the building?

W   I was standing across the street — maybe 50 feet away.

P   WHAT did you observe the defendant do?

W   I saw him place a bag in the truck, look all around, and then enter the car to start the engine. Knowing the defendant's long arrest record for burglaries, I immediately concluded that he had just completed a burglary.

O   Your Honor (1), I move to strike (2) that last sentence (3) on two grounds. First, the answer is non-responsive. Second, the answer is clearly improper character evidence. (4)

J   Motion granted. Officer, I want to caution you very strongly just to answer the questions asked.

O   Your Honor, would you please instruct the jury to disregard the answer? (5)

J   Certainly. Ladies and gentlemen of the jury, the officer just made a reference to the defendant's arrest record. I have stricken that statement from the record, and I instruct you to disregard it. The only testimony you may consider is the officer's testimony about what he personally saw the defendant do.

E. REQUEST BY THE OPPONENT TO TAKE A WITNESS ON VOIR DIRE

1. THE DOCTRINE

There are two types of preliminary facts which condition the admissibility of evidence. One type of fact conditions only the logical relevance of the evidence. For example, if the item of evidence is a letter, one preliminary fact conditioning its admissibility is its authenticity; the letter is inadmissible unless it is authentic. If the letter is not genuine, it has no logical relevance or probative value in the case. If the fact falls within this category, the judge uses the following procedure. The judge listens to only the proponent's evidence and decides the question of law whether that evidence has sufficient probative value to support a rational jury finding of the fact's existence. Federal Rule of Evidence 104(b) states that "(w)hen the relevancy of evidence depends upon the fulfillment of a condition of fact, the court shall admit it upon, or subject to, the introduction of evidence sufficient to support a finding of the fulfillment of the condition." Is there enough evidence to support a rational finding that the letter is authentic? If there is enough evidence, the judge submits the letter to the jury. The opponent submits any controverting evidence to the jury, and the jury finally decides whether the letter is genuine. Rule 104(b) applies to such foundational facts as whether a letter is genuine, whether a lay witness has personal knowledge of the facts she intends to testify about, and whether the defendant is the person who committed an act offered as uncharged misconduct under Rule 404(b). *Huddleston v. United States*, 485 U.S. —, 108 S. Ct. 1496 (1988). These facts condition the logical relevance of the evidence. We entrust these decisions to the jury because we are confident that if the jury decides that the letter is a fake or that the witness lacks firsthand knowledge or that another person committed the act, common sense will lead the jury to disregard the testimony during deliberations.

The other type of preliminary fact conditions the application of doctrines which exclude logically relevant evidence: the best evidence, hearsay, opinion, and privilege rules. These rules exclude relevant evidence either because the evidence presumably is unreliable, such as hearsay, or to promote social policies, such as the protection of confidential relations. If the fact falls within this category, the judge listens to the evidence on both sides and finally decides whether the fact exists. Federal Rule of Evidence 104(a) provides that when the fact falls within this category, the trial judge makes the final decision. Thus, the judge finally decides whether the original document was destroyed, whether a witness qualifies as an expert, whether a communication was intended to be confidential, whether an out-of-court declarant was excited when he made a hearsay statement, or whether at the time of the statement the declarant was the member of the same criminal conspiracy which the defendant belonged to. *Bourjaily v. United States*, 483 U.S. 171 (1987).

When the fact falls within the second category, the opponent has the right to take the witness on voir dire examination before the judge rules on the evidence's admissibility. As previously stated, the judge must listen to both sides' evidence before ruling. How does the opponent interrupt the proponent's direct examination to present the contrary evidence? The opponent interrupts by requesting the judge's permission to take the witness on voir dire. In one respect, the voir dire is functionally a cross-examination during the proponent's direct examination: the opponent conducting the voir dire may ordinarily use leading questions. However, the opponent must remember that the voir dire's limited purpose is to test the competency of the witness or evidence. The voir dire has a limited scope, and the opponent may not conduct a general cross-examination on the case's merits under the guise of voir dire.

2. SAMPLE REQUEST TO TAKE A WITNESS ON VOIR DIRE

The fact situation is a homicide prosecution. The prosecution witness is an ambulance attendant. The prosecutor hopes to elicit the ambulance attendant's testimony that he heard the decedent identify the defendant as the assailant. The prosecutor's theory is that the decedent's statement falls within the dying declaration exception to the hearsay rule. The proponent is the prosecutor.

P   WHAT is your occupation?
W   I am an ambulance attendant employed by the emergency ward of General Hospital.
P   WHAT were you doing on the evening of January 19, 1989?
W   I was on duty when we received a call about a shooting at the Senator Hotel downtown.
P   WHAT did you do then?
W   We responded to the call.
P   WHAT did you find when you arrived at the scene?
W   We found Mr. Jones there.
P   WHAT was his condition?
W   He had a very serious gunshot wound. He'd lost a lot of blood. You could hardly make out what he was talking about.
P   WHAT, if anything, did he talk about?
W   He talked about the fight in which he received the wound.
P   WHO did he say had shot him?
O   Your Honor, I object to that question on the ground that it calls for incompetent hearsay. I request permission to take the witness on voir dire before you rule on my objection.
J   Very well.
O   ISN'T IT TRUE THAT before he died, Mr. Jones said he was going to get the person who had shot him?
W   Yes.
O   ISN'T IT ALSO A FACT THAT he wanted to be rushed into surgery as soon as possible?
W   Right.
O   Your Honor, I renew my objection. The witness' testimony shows that the decedent did not believe that imminent death was certain. The declarant had not abandoned all hope of recovery. For that reason, the dying declaration exception is inapplicable.
J   Objection sustained.

F. OFFER OF PROOF BY THE PROPONENT

1. THE DOCTRINE

Assume that the judge grants the opponent's pretrial motion *in limine* or sustains an objection at trial. The trial judge thus precludes the proponent from pursuing the line of inquiry. What should the proponent do at this point? The rule is that the proponent should make an offer of proof. There are two senses of the expression, "offer of proof." The first is the broad, nontechnical meaning; the proponent "offers" proof whenever he or she presents evidence. However, we are now using the expression in the second, technical sense; for the record, the proponent states what the witness would have testified to and why the proponent wanted to elicit that testimony. Federal Rule of Evidence

103(a)(2) requires that the proponent ensure that "the substance of the evidence was made known to the court by offer ...."

Why should the proponent make an offer of proof? There are several reasons. When the proponent makes the offer of proof, the judge may reconsider and change the ruling. Until the offer of proof, the judge may not have realized where the line of questioning was leading. The offer of proof is also important if there is an appeal. If there is no offer of proof, the appellate court will have a difficult time evaluating the propriety and effect of the judge's ruling. With an offer of proof in the record of trial, the appellate court can make much more intelligent decisions whether there was error, whether the error was prejudicial, and whether the appropriate disposition of the case is to simply remand or enter judgment for a party.

The proponent should make the offer of proof out of the jury's hearing. If the proponent anticipated the unfavorable ruling, the proponent can prepare a written offer of proof for insertion in the record. Otherwise, the proponent usually makes an oral statement at a sidebar conference. If the expected testimony is complex, the proponent may make the offer in question-and-answer form; the proponent actually elicits the testimony out of the jury's hearing. The judge may insist that the proponent do so if the judge doubts that the witness' testimony will match the proponent's description of the expected testimony in the offer of proof.

2. ELEMENTS OF AN OFFER OF PROOF

An offer of proof contains the following elements:
1. The proponent asks for permission to approach the bench or for an out-of-court hearing.
2. The proponent states that he or she intends to make an offer of proof.
3. The proponent states what the witness would have testified to if the judge had permitted the proponent to pursue the line of inquiry.
4. The proponent states the purpose for which he or she wanted to offer the testimony. The proponent explains the testimony's logical relevance.
5. If the judge sustained the objection on the ground of a competence doctrine such as hearsay, the proponent explains why the evidence is admissible.

When you move to sidebar, make certain that the court reporter is in a position to hear the conference. Unless the court reporter records the conference, the appellate court will never learn the tenor of the offer of proof at trial.

3. SAMPLE OFFER OF PROOF[3]

The fact situation is a rape prosecution. The defendant denies the rape. The defendant denies any intercourse with the alleged victim. The defendant calls Ms. Gerhard as his next witness.

P   WHAT is your name?

W   Jane Gerhard.

P   WHAT is your address?

W   I live at 4502 New Hampshire Street in Morena, El Dorado.

P   WHAT is your occupation?

W   I am a physician.

P   WHERE did you attend medical school?

W   I attended Washington University Medical School in Missouri.

P   WHERE are you licensed?

W   In California, New York, Missouri, and here in El Dorado.

P   WHAT, if anything, is your specialty?

W   I specialize in the treatment of venereal disease.

P   HOW many cases of venereal disease have you treated in your practice?

O   Your Honor, I object to this line of questioning on the ground that it is irrelevant.

J   I'm inclined to agree. Objection sustained.

P   Your Honor, may we approach the bench? (1)

J   Yes.

P   I would like to make an offer of proof for the record. (2)

J   Very well.

P   If Dr. Gerhard is permitted to testify, she will state that: She examined the alleged victim last week; the victim is now suffering from an advanced stage of syphilis chancroids, a venereal disease; at the time of the alleged rape, the disease would undoubtedly have been in a highly infectious and communicable stage; anyone who had intercourse with the alleged victim at that time would probably contract the disease; and the doctor examined the defendant yesterday and found no evidence of the disease. (3) This testimony would be logically relevant to support my client's denial that he had intercourse with the alleged victim. (4)

J   Now I can see what you're driving at. I'm going to change my ruling and permit you to pursue this line of inquiry. Now I can see its logical relevance.

P   Dr. Gerhard, let me repeat the question. HOW many cases of venereal disease have you treated in your practice?

---

3. This hypothetical is based on DEPARTMENT OF THE ARMY PAMPHLET 27-10: MILITARY JUSTICE HANDBOOK 205 (1969).

Chapter 3

THE COMPETENCY OF WITNESSES

A. INTRODUCTION

Some evidentiary doctrines can keep a prospective witness off the stand altogether; the doctrines can prevent the person from giving any testimony at all in the case. These doctrines govern the competency of the person to be a witness in the case. For example, in some jurisdictions, one spouse is incompetent to testify against the other spouse in a criminal prosecution if the other spouse is the defendant and objects. The defendant spouse can preclude the witness spouse from testifying at all. Even if the witness is competent, other evidentiary doctrines may prevent the witness from testifying to certain facts. Thus, even if the witness spouse is competent to testify, he or she may not be able to testify to privileged, confidential communications with the other spouse. In this chapter, we are concerned with competency doctrines that have the more drastic effect of keeping the witness off the stand.

Federal Rule of Evidence 601 abolishes most of the traditional requirements for competency. The witness must have personal or first-hand knowledge under Rule 602, but the proponent need not demonstrate that the prospective witness satisfies the other common-law requirements. (Some commentators believe that even in federal practice, a judge can sometimes bar a witness from the stand. These commentators argue that the judge has the power to do so under Rule 403 when it is clear as a matter of law that the prospective witness lacks one of the testimonial abilities required at common law. Chapter 5 discusses Rule 403.)

However, in some jurisdictions, the common-law requirements are still in effect. At common law, to prove that the prospective witness is competent, the proponent must show that the person possesses the following abilities: (1) to observe — the testimonial quality of perception; (2) to remember — the testimonial quality of memory; (3) to relate — the testimonial quality of narration; and (4) to recognize a duty to tell the truth — the testimonial quality of sincerity. These abilities ensure that the witness' testimony will have at least some reliability. If the person lacks one or more of these capacities, the person is incompetent to be a witness.

Even if the person is competent in the sense that he or she possesses these four capacities, the law may render the person incompetent as a witness. The law may do so to promote some social policy such as protecting the stability of marriages. Hence, even if a witness spouse has all four capacities, the witness may be disqualified from testifying against his or her spouse.

How does the opponent challenge the prospective witness' competency? In most jurisdictions, the opponent must raise the objection as soon as the person is called to the stand. The opponent objects before the person is even sworn as a witness. The opponent both objects and requests a voir dire of the person concerning his or her qualifications to be a witness. In some jurisdictions, the person then takes a special oath to answer the voir dire questions about his or her competency. The bailiff or reporter might administer this oath: "Do you swear the answers you will give to these questions about your competency to be a witness shall be the truth, the whole truth, and nothing but the truth? So help you God." In other jurisdictions, the voir dire examination is unsworn.

In most jurisdictions, the judge has discretion to determine who shall examine the person and the order of the examinations. Competency doctrines do not simply condition the testimony's logical relevance; rather, they fall within the category of doctrines designed to ensure the reliability of concededly relevant evidence. For that reason, the trial judge finally decides the question of the witness' competency and may permit the opponent to present extrinsic evidence such as a psychiatrist's testimony. If at the end of the presentation of the evidence the judge decides that the person is incompetent, the judge sustains the objection and directs the person to leave the witness stand. If the judge finds that the person is competent, the judge overrules the objection, and the person then takes the normal oath in the case.

B. THE VOIR DIRE OF A CHILD BY THE WITNESS' PROPONENT

1. THE DOCTRINE

In some jurisdictions, there are presumptions concerning children's competency to serve as witnesses. For example, the dividing line might be 7, 10, or 12 years of age; if the child is 12, the child is presumed competent, but if the child is younger, the child is presumed incompetent. The presumption is usually rebuttable; even if the child is presumed incompetent, the proponent may attempt to show that in fact, the child possesses the four requisite abilities.

Most jurisdictions have no presumptions. In these jurisdictions, it is a question of fact whether the person has the requisite capacities. The trial judge finally decides the question.

2. ELEMENTS OF THE FOUNDATION

When the opponent challenges the proponent's witness' competency, the proponent must lay a foundation showing that the person possesses the four capacities. The proponent must demonstrate that:

1. The child has the capacity to observe.
2. The child has the capacity to remember.
3. The child has the capacity to relate.
4. The child recognizes a duty to tell the truth.

3. SAMPLE FOUNDATION

The fact situation is a personal injury action arising from a traffic accident at an intersection. The plaintiff, the proponent, calls a child as a witness. The child witnessed the collision.

P   As his next witness, the plaintiff calls Master James Giannelli.
O   Your Honor, we object to any testimony by this child on the ground that the child is incompetent to be a witness. We request a voir dire examination of the child concerning his competency.
J   Request granted.
P   Your Honor, may I conduct the initial voir dire of Master Giannelli?
J   You may.
P   Master Giannelli, do you swear that the answers you will now give concerning your competency to be a witness will be the truth, the whole truth, and nothing but the truth? So help you God. *(Please remember that in many jurisdictions, the voir dire examination is unsworn, especially when the prospective witness is a child. In those jurisdictions, this oath would not be administered.)*
W   I do.
P   WHAT is your name and address?
W   My name is Jim Giannelli. I live at 12 Frontage Road in town with my parents.
P   James, HOW well do you see? (1)
W   I have no problems. I can see real well.
P   HOW well do you hear? (1)
W   Just great.
P   HOW old are you? (2)
W   I'm six. I had my birthday last month.
P   WHAT day is your birthday? (2)
W   It's September 28, just after my mommy's birthday.
P   WHERE do you live? (2)
W   Like I said, on Frontage Road with my folks.
P   HOW long have you lived there? (2)
W   Gee. I guess as long as I can remember.
P   HOW many brothers and sisters do you have? (2)
W   I have one sister.
P   WHAT is her name? (2)
W   Amy.
P   HOW old is Amy? (2)
W   She's older than me. She's almost 15.
P   WHAT school do you go to? (2)
W   Horace Mann.
P   WHERE is that school located? (2)
W   On Fourth Street.
P   WHAT grade are you in? (2)
W   I'm in the first grade.

P   WHO is your teacher? (2)

W   Her name is Mrs. Lederer. She's real nice.

P   WHAT courses do you take? (3)

W   We take arithmetic and English.

P   WHAT do you learn in English? (3)

W   We learn about words and sentences and stuff.

P   WHAT grades do you get in English? (3)

W   I do real well. I got an A on the last paper.

P   WHAT does "car" mean? (3)

W   My dad has one. You drive around in them. They take you places.

P   WHAT does "fast" mean? (3)

W   Well, when you drive, you should go slow. You can get hurt if you don't go slow, if you go too fast.

P   James, WHAT is an "intersection"? (3)

W   That's where two streets meet. They sort of come together.

P   WHAT is the truth? (4)

W   The truth is what really happens — not a story you come up with.

P   WHAT is a lie? (4)

W   That's when you don't tell the truth.

P   WHAT happens when you don't tell the truth? (4)

W   Your parents can get real mad at you, and God won't love you.

P   HOW do you know that? (4)

W   I learned that at Sunday School.

P   WHERE do you go to Sunday School? (4)

W   At our church.

P   WHICH church is that? (4)

W   Holy Comforter on 12th Avenue.

P   WHAT do you learn at Sunday School? (4)

W   We learn that you have to be good. You gotta obey your parents and tell the truth and stuff like that.

P   WHAT is an oath? (4)

W   I promise to tell the truth to the judge.

P   WHAT happens if you don't tell the judge the truth? (4)

W   He can punish you.

P   I have no further questions of Master Giannelli about his competency. Your witness.

O   I have no questions. I renew my objection on the ground that the child is too young to be a witness.

P   Your Honor, I think the child's answers demonstrate the capacities to observe, remember, and relate, and his recognition of a duty to tell the truth.

J   I agree. The objection will be overruled. Please administer the oath to Master Giannelli.

C. THE QUESTIONING OF A LAY WITNESS BY THE PROPONENT TO DEMONSTRATE PERSONAL KNOWLEDGE

1. THE DOCTRINE

All courts agree that a lay witness must have personal or firsthand knowledge of facts or events to testify about them at trial. Personal knowledge is a common-law requirement. Although the Federal Rules generally abolish the traditional competency requirements, Rule 602 still insists upon personal knowledge. Before questioning a lay witness about an event, the proponent should show that the witness has personal knowledge of the event.

2. ELEMENTS OF THE FOUNDATION

The proponent should show that:
1. The witness was in a physical position to perceive the event. The witness normally observes the event by the sense of sight, but the witness may use any sense to perceive the event.
2. The witness actually perceived the event.

3. SAMPLE FOUNDATION

We can continue the hypothetical in Section B, *supra*. Assume that the judge rules that the child is a competent witness. The child takes the oath and begins testifying. Now the plaintiff wants to elicit the testimony about the accident. The accident occurred at the intersection of Fourth and Main Streets.

P   James, WHERE did you go on Monday, January 21, 1989? (1)
W   I went to school.
P   WHERE is your school located? (1)
W   It's on Fourth Street.
P   WHERE on Fourth Street? (1)
W   Right at Main Street. There's a big intersection there. There's lots of cars.
P   WHAT happened at the intersection that day at about noon? (1)
W   There was this big crash.
P   WHERE were you at the time of the crash? (1)
W   I was standing at that corner.
P   WHAT crashed? (2)
W   Two cars.
P   WHO was driving the cars? (2)
W   The man over there in green and that lady over there in yellow.
P   Please let the record reflect that the witness has pointed to the plaintiff and defendant.
J   It will so reflect.
P   HOW do you know they were driving the cars? (2)
W   I ran up right after the big noise, and I saw them get out of their cars.
P   HOW well could you see the cars? (2)
W   I got a good look. They were real close to me when they crashed. I was real scared.
P   HOW well could you see the drivers? (2)
W   Gee. I got right up close to them. I ran up right after the big noise, and I saw them get out of their cars.
P   HOW much time passed between the crash and the time when you ran up to see the drivers? (2)
W   Only a couple of seconds.

P   James, now I want to ask some questions about how the crash occurred
      ....

D. THE OPPONENT'S PRESENTATION OF PSYCHIATRIC TESTIMONY ATTACKING A PROSPECTIVE WITNESS' COMPETENCY

1. THE DOCTRINE

Trial judges rarely sustain objections to prospective witnesses' competency; a judge will sustain an objection in only an extreme case. The opponent may prove recent adjudications of incompetency such as civil commitments. These adjudications are relevant to prove incompetency; but, as a practical matter, the opponent must present expert, psychiatric testimony attacking the witness' competency. The psychiatrist will have to testify that the person is suffering from a full-fledged psychosis and that the psychosis grossly interferes with one of the testimonial qualities such as perception or memory.

2. ELEMENTS OF THE FOUNDATION

The opponent should demonstrate that:
1. The witness is a qualified psychiatrist.
2. The psychiatrist has examined the prospective witness.
3. The prospective witness has certain symptoms.
4. The symptoms lead to the conclusion that the prospective witness is suffering from a psychosis.
5. The psychosis grossly interferes with one or more of the prospective witness' testimonial qualities such as perception or memory.

3. SAMPLE FOUNDATION

The fact situation is a rape prosecution. The prosecution calls Ms. Janet Lincoln as a witness. Ms. Lincoln has told the police that she witnessed the rape; her window overlooks the park, and she saw the defendant attack the alleged victim. The defense counsel objects to any testimony by Ms. Lincoln; the counsel contends that she is incompetent to be a witness. The defense counsel has already taken Ms. Lincoln on voir dire and questioned her.

J   Do you have anything further you'd like to present on the issue of Ms. Lincoln's competency?
O   Yes, Your Honor. At this point, I would like to call Dr. Kenneth Rogers.
J   Proceed.
B   Do you swear that the evidence you will give in the case now in hearing will be the truth, the whole truth, and nothing but the truth? So help you God.
W   I do.

O   WHAT is your name?
W   Kenneth Rogers.
O   WHERE do you live?
W   I reside at 1774 Club Drive.
O   WHAT is your occupation? (1)
W   I am a physician.
O   WHERE are you licensed to practice medicine? (1)
W   Here in El Dorado and in California and New York as well.
O   WHEN did you obtain your license in El Dorado? (1)
W   Approximately 10 years ago.
O   WHAT medical school did you attend? (1)
W   Washington University in Missouri. I received my M.D. degree in
     1980.
O   WHERE did you intern? (1)
W   I interned at U.S.C. Medical Center in California.
O   HOW long did you intern there? (1)
W   Approximately one year.
O   WHAT field of medicine, if any, is your specialty? (1)
W   Psychiatry.
O   WHAT is the subject matter of that specialty? (1)
W   A psychiatrist studies the diseases and disorders of the mind.
O   WHAT special training have you had in psychiatry? (1)
W   I spent three years as a resident in psychiatry.
O   WHERE did you take this residence? (1)
W   At Bellevue in New York City.
O   WHAT other special training have you had in psychiatry? (1)
W   I'm a diplomate with the American Board of Psychiatry. I passed the
     oral and written examinations for the diploma. I've taught psychiatry
     at two medical schools, and I've written thirteen articles for psychiat-
     ric journals.
O   WHO is Janet Lincoln? (2)
W   She's a woman I've had occasion to interview several times.
O   WHY have you interviewed her? (2)
W   One of the local judges, Judge Lopardo, asked me to do so. It was a
     court appointment.
O   HOW many times did you interview her? (2)
W   Three times.
O   WHEN was the first interview? (2)
W   Approximately three months ago.
O   HOW long did this interview last? (2)
W   Roughly two and a half hours.
O   WHAT was her appearance at the time of the interview? (3)
W   It was rather unkempt. She was rather dirty.
O   WHAT was her general attitude? (3)
W   At first, she seemed rather detached and distant. She became excited
     and angry whenever I tried to question her about sexual subjects.
O   WHAT, if anything, did she say during the interview? (3)
W   At first she just told me to keep my distance.
O   WHAT did she say then? (3)
W   She said that all men were sex fiends and could not be trusted. She
     said that as long as she could remember, at least once a day a man had
     attempted to assault her.
O   HOW would you characterize her statements? (3)

W   They were delusional. A delusion is a belief that a rational person would not entertain under the same circumstances. The person persists in the belief although all the evidence is to the contrary.

O   WHY did she have this belief? (3)

W   She said that voices told her to distrust all men.

O   WHO were the voices? (3)

W   She didn't know.

O   HOW would you characterize those statements? (3)

W   They are hallucinations; she has auditory experiences when in fact there is no voice or sound.

O   WHAT did you do after you interviewed Ms. Lincoln? (3)

W   I tried to gather her history.

O   WHAT is a history? (3)

W   The background of an illness. You trace it through the years and its various stages.

O   HOW did you gather Ms. Lincoln's history? (3)

W   I spoke with her brother, Vance Lincoln.

O   WHO is he? (3)

W   He's a certified public accountant in town.

O   WHAT was her background or history? (3)

W   Evidently she had made numerous rape complaints to the police. In each case, the police or medical investigation had shown the complaint was groundless. She had spent almost a year in a hospital in the East for mental illness.

O   WHAT did you do then? (3)

W   I conducted further interviews with Ms. Lincoln.

O   WHAT happened during those interviews? (3)

W   She repeated her beliefs. She told me about some incidents in her life — sometimes giving me conflicting stories about the same incident. On several occasions she accused me of making advances towards her. She again became quite restless.

O   WHAT, if anything, did you do to lead her to believe that you were making an advance against her? (3)

W   Nothing, as far as I could tell. My mere physical presence seemed to trigger that belief.

O   WHAT, if any, diagnosis have you reached of Ms. Lincoln's psychiatric condition? (4)

W   I would diagnose her condition as a schizophrenic reaction of the paranoid type.

O   WHAT does that mean? (4)

W   A schizophrenic person has a sort of split personality. They live in two worlds — one the world of fantasy, the other the world of reality. They have lost contact with reality to a severe extent. Her disorder manifests itself in paranoid beliefs that men are persecuting and constantly attacking her.

O   WHAT leads you to this diagnosis? (4)

W   The irrational content of her statements for one thing. I also consider her appearance and attitude. Finally, I attach particular importance to her delusions and hallucinations. Her history confirms the diagnosis.

O   Doctor Rogers, in this case Ms. Lincoln wants to testify about a sexual assault she allegedly observed. WHAT effect, if any, would her psychosis have on her ability to accurately observe an encounter between a man and a woman? (5)

W   The psychosis grossly interferes with that capacity. She's going to see things that didn't really happen — just as she hears voices when they're not there. Every male-female encounter tends to become an assault in her mind.

O   WHAT effect, if any, would her psychosis have on her ability to accurately remember a male-female encounter she had observed? (5)

W   It's going to severely distort the memory process. A psychosis of this magnitude is going to attack her abilities to perceive and remember. Her purported recollections will be untrustworthy. In the process of remembering, she'll add assaultive aspects to the encounter.

O   Thank you, doctor. Your witness.

E. THE WITNESS SPOUSE

1. THE DOCTRINE

Modernly, there are four views of the competency of one spouse to testify against another. The first view, followed in approximately ten jurisdictions, is that the spouse is as competent as any other witness. Even if the defendant and witness spouses object, the witness spouse may be called as a witness against the defendant spouse. Although in these 10 states the witness spouse is fully competent, most jurisdictions recognize a disqualification in criminal cases. However, even the majority jurisdictions differ over the scope of the disqualification. The second view is that if the marriage exists when the witness spouse is called, the defendant spouse can object and keep the witness spouse off the stand altogether. Under this view, the privilege belongs to the defendant spouse. The third view is that the witness spouse is the holder of the privilege. The witness spouse may testify if he or she desires. The defendant spouse may not prevent the witness spouse from testifying. The United States Supreme Court opted for this view in *United States v. Trammel*, 445 U.S. 40 (1980). The fourth and final view is that both the defendant and witness spouses have privileges. They each have a privilege and may exercise their privileges independently.

There are two important exceptions to the scope of the privilege. The first exception is the so-called injured spouse doctrine: The privilege is inapplicable if the charged offense is a crime against the other spouse. For example, if the criminal defendant is charged with a battery against his wife, he cannot invoke the privilege to bar her from testifying. Some jurisdictions recognize a second exception; they do not apply the privilege if the witness spouse's testimony relates to an event that occurred before the marriage. These jurisdictions sometimes refer to the disqualification as the anti-marital facts privilege.

2. ELEMENTS OF THE FOUNDATION

The party attempting to invoke the privilege must show that:

1. The witness spouse married the party spouse.

2. The marriage is still in existence.

The party attempting to invoke the exceptions to the privilege must show that:

   3. The witness spouse was the victim of the charged crime; or

   4. The witness spouse's expected testimony relates to an event occurring before the marriage.

3. SAMPLE FOUNDATION

The fact situation is a criminal prosecution. George Nerney, the defendant, is charged with two batteries. The indictment first alleges that on January 1, 1989, the defendant committed a battery against Grenda Kuhns. The second count of the indictment alleges that on July 1, 1989, the defendant committed a battery against Susan Grace. The proponent of the witness is the prosecutor.

P   As its next witness, the State calls Ms. Susan Grace.

O   Your Honor, I object to any testimony by this witness on the ground that she is incompetent. The witness is married to my client, and my client invokes his privilege to keep her off the witness stand. May I voir dire the witness?

J   You may.

O   Ms. Grace, ISN'T IT TRUE THAT on March 1, 1989, you married a George Nerney? (1)

W   Yes.

O   ISN'T IT A FACT THAT George Nerney is the defendant in this case, seated at this table? (1)

W   Yes.

O   ISN'T IT CORRECT THAT there has been no divorce proceeding since the marriage? (2)

W   Yes.

O   ISN'T IT TRUE THAT there hasn't been any annulment proceeding since the marriage? (2)

W   Yes.

O   Your Honor, I have no further questions. We renew our objection.

P   Your Honor, may I voir dire Ms. Grace?

J   Yes. Proceed.

P   WHEN did you marry the defendant? (4)

W   I think it was March 1, 1989.

P   WHO is Grenda Kuhns? (4)

W   She's a desk clerk at a hotel in a town which the defendant and I once visited.

P   WHEN did you visit that hotel? (4)

W   In early January of 1989.

P   WHAT, if anything, happened between the defendant and Ms. Kuhns? (4)

W   Unfortunately, they got into an argument, and the defendant punched Ms. Kuhns.

P   WHICH came first — the defendant's argument with Ms. Kuhns or your marriage to the defendant? (4)

W   The argument with Ms. Kuhns. It came first by several months.
P   WHAT, if anything, happened on July 1, 1989? (3)
W   That's when George and I had an argument.
P   WHAT happened during the argument? (3)
W   HE slashed me with a knife.
P   WHOM did he slash? (3)
W   Me.
P   WHO else was involved in this argument? (3)
W   No one else. I was the only other person there, and I was the only one George attacked.
P   Thank you, Ms. Grace. Your Honor, this voir dire examination demonstrates that Ms. Grace is competent to testify about both counts in the indictment. The first count alleges a battery that occurred before her marriage to the defendant. In the second count, she is the victim, and the injured spouse exception obviously applies. The marital privilege shouldn't preclude Ms. Grace from testifying about either count.
J   I concur. Objection overruled. You may administer the oath to the witness.

F. DEAD PERSONS STATUTES OR SURVIVORS EVIDENCE ACTS

1. THE DOCTRINE

Suppose that two parties enter into a contract. One dies, and the other files suit for breach of contract against the decedent's estate. The decedent can no longer testify to rebut any false claims. Is it fair to permit the survivor to testify against the estate? Roughly half the state legislatures have enacted dead persons or survivors evidence statutes. These statutes represent a judgment that it is unfair to permit the survivors to testify in these circumstances. The survivor possesses the four capacities requisite at common law, but fairness dictates the exclusion of the witness' testimony. The statute's coverage varies from state to state, and there is no such thing as a "typical" statute. However, many provide that in actions defended by the decedent's personal representative, the survivor or any interested person may not testify adversely to the estate about a transaction with a decedent.

The coverage of a particular statute is a problem of statutory construction. Most statutes address four questions: (1) To what types of actions does the statute apply? As previously stated, the statutes usually apply at least to actions filed or defended by the decedent's personal representative. The statute might also apply to wrongful death actions brought by the decedent's heirs. (2) Whom does the statute disqualify from testifying? The survivor is ordinarily disqualified. "Interested persons" are also frequently disqualified. In some jurisdictions, a person is deemed interested only if the judgment in the case will have a direct legal operation against that person. Other jurisdictions use a broader definition of interest and consider a person interested if the person has a direct economic stake in the case's outcome.

(3) What type of incompetence does the statute impose? The dead persons statutes impose a peculiar type of incompetence. The statutes usually do not keep the witness off the stand altogether. Rather, they have the limited effect of precluding the witness from testifying against the estate about certain topics. (4) What topics is the witness precluded from testifying about? The statute usually uses the expression, "transactions with the decedent." A contract with the decedent is obviously a transaction with the decedent. Moreover, many courts use this broad definition of transaction: A witness' testimony is testimony about a transaction with the decedent if the decedent might have contradicted the testimony from personal or firsthand knowledge.

These same four questions indicate how the proponent of the witness can defeat a dead persons statute objection: The opponent need show only that one element of the statute is missing. The proponent can argue that the statute does not apply to this type of action, *or* the witness is neither a survivor nor an interested person, *or* the statute does not impose this type of incompetence, *or* the witness is not testifying about a transaction with the decedent.

2. ELEMENTS OF THE FOUNDATION

To invoke a dead persons or survivors evidence statute, the opponent of the evidence must show that:
1. The statute applies to this type of action.
2. The witness is a survivor or an interested person.
3. The witness is testifying about a forbidden topic, *e.g.*, a transaction with the decedent.

The first element presents a question of law; the judge construes the statute and compares the statute's coverage to the pleadings on file in the case. However, the opponent may have to voir dire the witness to develop factual support for the second and third elements of the foundation.

3. SAMPLE FOUNDATIONS

The first hypothetical is a contract action against the decedent's estate. The decedent is John Grant. The plaintiff is Miles Dalton. Dalton alleges that the decedent breached a contract with Dalton. Dalton calls his brother, William, as a witness. William will testify about the conversation in which Dalton and Grant formed the contract. The plaintiff is the proponent of the witness.

P   WHAT did the two men say during this conversation?
O   Your Honor, I object to the last question on the ground that under the dead persons statute, this witness is incompetent to testify on that topic.
P   Your Honor, may I be heard?
J   Yes.

P   It's true that the statute applies to contract actions against the decedent's estate (1) and that a conversation with the decedent is a transaction. (3) However, this witness isn't the plaintiff. Moreover, although
he's the plaintiff's brother, he doesn't have any direct economic stake
in the case. He's not an interested person. (2)

O   May I voir dire the witness?

J   Yes. Proceed.

O   ISN'T IT TRUE THAT on January 1, 1989, you gave your brother,
Miles, $50,000 as an investment in his business? (2)

W   Yes.

O   ISN'T IT A FACT THAT in exchange for that $50,000, Miles gave you
a quarter share in the business? (2)

W   Yes.

O   ISN'T IT CORRECT THAT you are Miles' silent partner? (2)

W   Yes.

O   ISN'T IT TRUE THAT you expect to receive a share of whatever
money your brother recovers in this suit? (2)

W   Yes.

O   Your Honor, the witness' answers demonstrate that he has a direct
economic stake in the case's outcome. I renew my objection.

J   Objection sustained.

The second hypothetical is a wrongful death action brought by the
decedent's heirs. They allege that the defendant, Steven Pollet, negligently caused the death of the decedent, Kathryn Manning, in a traffic
accident. The defense attorney calls the defendant as a witness. The
defense attorney is the proponent. The defendant has already testified
about what happened earlier in the day. The defendant has just testified that he reached a narrow curve in the road. The collision occurred
as he rounded the curve.

P   WHAT happened when you rounded the curve?

W   I saw this other car coming.

P   HOW did you maneuver your car after you saw this other car coming?

O   Your Honor, I object to that question on the ground that under the
dead persons statute, the witness is incompetent to testify about that
topic.

P   Your Honor, may I be heard?

J   Yes.

P   It's true that in this jurisdiction, the statute applies to actions filed by
the heirs (1) and that the witness is the surviving party. (2) However,
the witness isn't testifying about any transaction with the decedent;
he's testifying about how he maneuvered his own car. (3)

O   May I voir dire the witness?

J   Yes. Proceed.

O   ISN'T IT TRUE THAT when you rounded the curve, you had an unob-
structed view of the decedent's car? (3)

W   Yes.

O   ISN'T IT A FACT THAT it was a clear day? (3)

W   Yes.

O   ISN'T IT CORRECT THAT the stretch of road just past the curve was
straight and level? (3)

W   Yes.

O   ISN'T IT TRUE THAT from the time you rounded the curve until the time of the collision, you had a clear view of the decedent's car? (3)

W   Yes.

O   Your Honor, the witness' testimony shows that the decedent must have had a clear view of the manner in which the defendant's car maneuvered. If she had survived, the decedent might have contradicted the defendant's testimony from personal knowledge. Thus, this testimony is testimony about a "transaction" with the decedent. I renew my objection.

J   Objection sustained.

Chapter 4

AUTHENTICATION

A. INTRODUCTION

This chapter deals with the authentication of evidence. The common law generally requires that the proponent of evidence prove the evidence's authenticity as a condition to the admission of the evidence. To authenticate an item of evidence, the proponent must present proof that the article is what the proponent claims that it is. Federal Rule 901(a) states: "The requirement of authentication or identification as a condition precedent to admissibility is satisfied by evidence sufficient to support a finding that the matter in question is what its proponent claims." Thus, if the proponent claims that the decedent signed a letter, the proponent must prove that the document is a genuine letter signed by the decedent. If the proponent offers a photograph of an intersection, the proponent must show that the photograph accurately depicts the intersection. Or if the prosecutor alleges that a pistol is the defendant's pistol, the prosecutor must present evidence tracing the pistol to the defendant's possession.

In addition to stating the requirement for authentication, Federal Rule 901(a) outlines the procedure for determining the evidence's authenticity. Rule 901(a) prescribes the same procedure as Rule 104(b). The test is whether the proponent has presented sufficient evidence to support a rational jury finding that the letter is genuine or the photograph is accurate. The trial judge looks to only the proponent's evidence and asks that question of law. Of course, the opponent may have controverting evidence. For example, although the proponent has a lay witness prepared to identify a friend's handwriting on a letter, the opponent may have an expert questioned document examiner ready to testify that the letter is a forgery. In this circumstance, the trial judge would admit the letter, and the opponent would present his or her controverting evidence to the jury. The trial judge would instruct the jurors that they must finally decide whether the letter is genuine.

What are the mechanics of presenting physical or documentary evidence? Until the proponent is ready to use the evidence, the proponent should keep the evidence out of the sight of the jury. When the proponent wants to use the evidence, the proponent should first request that the item be marked for identification. Many jurisdictions insist that the proponent ask only that "this" be marked for identification. To make the record of trial clearer to the appellate court, some trial judges permit the proponent to use a short description of the exhibit. For example, these judges would permit the proponent to request that "this letter" or "this knife" be marked for identification. The court reporter or bailiff handles the marking of the exhibits. In many jurisdictions, plaintiffs and prosecutors use numbers to identify their exhibits ("plaintiff's exhibit number two for identification") while defense attorneys use letters ("defense exhibit C for identification"). After marking the exhibit for identification, the proponent hands the exhibit to the opposing attorney for inspection. In some jurisdictions, it is customary at this point for the proponent to ask that the record reflect that the opposing attorney is examining the exhibit.

The proponent then hands the exhibit to the witness. The proponent should describe the exhibit as an exhibit for identification: "I now hand you prosecution exhibit number seven for identification." In most jurisdictions, it is improper to state, "I now hand you a letter purportedly signed by the defendant"; the proponent's attorney is not a witness, and that description would amount to unsworn testimony. Once the exhibit is in the witness's hands, the proponent asks the witness to identify the article. The proponent now lays the foundation for the exhibit's admission. At the very least the foundation usually includes proof of the item's authenticity. When the foundation has been laid, the proponent formally offers the exhibit into evidence. The proponent can "move" the item's admission or "offer defense exhibit G for identification into evidence as defense exhibit G." Some judges prefer a simpler style; rather than insisting that the proponent "offer defense exhibit G for identification into evidence as defense exhibit G," these judges permit the proponent to simply "offer defense exhibit G for identification into evidence."

If there is no objection or the trial judge overrules the objection, the item is received in evidence. In the case of a letter, the proponent should then request the judge's permission to read all or part of the document to the jury. When the proponent makes this request, the opposing attorney occasionally objects on best evidence grounds and states that "the document speaks for itself." This objection is bogus. W. Brockett & J. Keker, *Effective Direct and Cross-Examination* § 11.11 (1986). The judge has discretion to permit the witness or the attorney to quote from a document which has already been admitted into evidence. In the case of any documentary or physical evidence, the proponent may request the judge's permission to hand the item to the jurors for their inspection. In some courts, it is customary to request permission to "publish" the exhibit to the jury. When the proponent has completed using the exhibit, the proponent should hand the exhibit back to the court reporter or bailiff.

B. THE AUTHENTICATION OF PRIVATE WRITINGS

There are several, well-settled techniques for authenticating private writings. These techniques are alternative methods of establishing the writing's authenticity.

The reader should develop the habit of automatically thinking of authentication, best evidence, and hearsay whenever a document is used in the courtroom. Whenever a document is used, the proponent will have to authenticate it. If the document's terms are in issue, the proponent will have to comply with the best evidence rule. Finally, if the proponent wants to use the document's contents as substantive evidence, the proponent will probably have to show that the document falls within a hearsay exception. In short, the proponent offering a document will often have to lay three separate foundations — authenticity, best evidence, and hearsay. The proponent should thus consult Chapters 8 and 10 as well as this chapter.

1. TESTIMONY OF A WITNESS WHO OBSERVED THE DOCUMENT'S EXECUTION

The proponent can use direct evidence. If a witness observed the writing's execution and recognizes the document executed, the witness' testimony is sufficient authentication. Federal Rule 901 (b) (1) sanctions authentication by "[t]estimony that a matter is what it is claimed to be."

The following are the elements of the foundation:
1. Where the witness observed the document's execution.
2. When the witness observed the execution.
3. Who was present.
4. What happened — the writing's execution.
5. The witness recognized the exhibit as the document previously executed.
6. How the witness recognizes the document.

Assume that one issue in a commercial case is whether the defendant signed a certain check. The defendant's acquaintance, Mr. Bucher, observed the defendant sign the check. The plaintiff is the proponent.

P WHERE were you on the afternoon of February 4, 1989? (1), (2)
W I was at the defendant's house.
P WHO was there? (3)
W It was just me, the defendant, and his wife, Ruth.
P WHAT, if anything, happened while you were there? (4)
W The defendant was writing out some checks to pay his month's bills.
P Your Honor, I request that this be marked plaintiff's exhibit number seven for identification.
J It will be so marked.

P Please let the record reflect that I am showing the exhibit to the opposing counsel.

J It will so reflect.

P I request permission to approach the witness.

J Permission granted.

P Mr. Bucher, I now hand you plaintiff's exhibit number seven for identification. WHAT is it? (5)

W It's one of the checks the defendant signed that afternoon.

P HOW do you recognize it? (6)

W Well, the defendant handed it to me and asked me to take a look at it. I recognize the signature and other writing on it.

P HOW long did you have to examine it? (6)

W About a minute or so.

P HOW carefully did you examine it? (6)

W Closely enough to recognize it now.

P WHAT characteristics of the exhibit are you relying on as the basis for your identification? (6)

W I remember the amount of the check, the payee, the defendant's rather peculiar signature, and the color of the check.

P Your Honor, I now offer plaintiff's exhibit number seven for identification into evidence as plaintiff's exhibit number seven.

J It will be received.

P I request permission to hand the exhibit to the jurors for their inspection.

J Permission granted.

2. TESTIMONY OF A WITNESS FAMILIAR WITH THE AUTHOR'S HANDWRITING STYLE

Even if the proponent cannot locate a person who observed the writing's execution, the proponent may be able to find someone familiar with the author's handwriting style. It is true that courts usually prohibit opinion testimony by lay witnesses, but the admissibility of lay opinion testimony on handwriting style is a recognized exception to the general prohibition. The primary problem of proof for the proponent is establishing that the witness is sufficiently familiar with the author's handwriting style to recognize that style. Ideally, the witness will have observed the author sign his or her name on several previous occasions. It is sufficient if the witness has seen the author's signature under reliable circumstances. For example, one corporate executive's secretary may have seen documents bearing the signature of another executive of the same corporation on hundreds of prior occasions. Even if the witness has never seen that second corporate executive sign a document, the witness is sufficiently familiar with the executive's handwriting style. Federal Evidence Rule 901(b) (2) recognizes this authentication technique. The Rule permits "[n]onexpert opinion as to the genuineness of handwriting, based upon familiarity not acquired for purposes of the litigation."

The foundation is very simple; the elements are:

1. The witness recognized the author's handwriting on the document.
2. The witness is familiar with the author's handwriting style.
3. The witness has a sufficient basis for familiarity.

Now vary the original hypothetical. Assume that the witness, Mr. Bucher, did not observe the check's execution but is familiar with the author's handwriting style:

P   Your Honor, I request that this be marked plaintiff's exhibit number seven for identification.
J   It will be so marked.
P   Please let the record reflect that I am showing the exhibit to the opposing counsel.
J   It will so reflect.
P   I request permission to approach the witness.
J   Request granted.
P   Mr. Bucher, I now hand you plaintiff's exhibit number seven for identification. WHAT is it?
W   It seems to be a check.
P   WHO signed the check? (1)
W   I'd say that the defendant signed it.
P   WHY do you say that? (2)
W   I recognize the defendant's handwriting style on the check.
P   HOW well do you know the defendant's handwriting style? (3)
W   Very well.
P   HOW did you become familiar with his handwriting style? (3)
W   We've been friends for years.
P   HOW many years? (3)
W   About ten.
P   HOW often have you seen the defendant sign his name? (3)
W   Tens, maybe hundreds.
P   Your Honor, I now offer plaintiff's exhibit number seven for identification into evidence as plaintiff's exhibit number seven.
J   It will be received.
P   I request permission to hand the exhibit to the jurors for their inspection.
J   Permission granted.

3. THE REPLY LETTER DOCTRINE

The courts assume that the mails are reliable. Given that assumption, the courts have developed the so-called reply letter doctrine. Suppose that the witness sent a letter to a certain person. In the due course of mail, the witness receives a letter. The letter purports to be signed by the person to whom the witness sent the first letter, and the second letter refers to or at least purports to respond to the first letter. The courts generally hold that this fact pattern creates a sufficient circumstantial inference that the second letter is authentic.

This foundation contains several elements:

1.   The witness prepared the first letter.

2. The witness placed the letter in an envelope and properly stamped the envelope.
3. The witness addressed the letter to the author.
4. The witness mailed the letter to the author.
5. The witness received a letter.
6. The letter arrived in the due course of mail.
7. The second letter referred to the first letter or was responsive to it.
8. The second letter bore the name of the author.
9. The witness recognizes the exhibit as the second letter.
10. The witness specifies the basis on which he recognizes the exhibit.

Our fact situation is a contract case. The plaintiff wants to prove that the defendant sent a letter containing an express warranty of the goods' condition. The plaintiff had not had previous dealings with the defendant, and, hence, cannot recognize the defendant's handwriting style. The witness is the plaintiff. The plaintiff has just testified that he had a telephone conversation with the defendant. The plaintiff's attorney is the proponent.

P   WHAT did you do after this telephone conversation? (1)
W   I decided to send the defendant a letter requesting some specific assurances and warranties about the goods.
P   HOW did you do that? (1)
W   I typed it up and then signed it.
P   WHAT did you do with it after you signed it? (2), (3), (4)
W   I stuck it in an envelope. I stamped the envelope, addressed it, and stuck it in the mail.
P   WHERE did you get the defendant's address? (3)
W   Out of the telephone book.
P   WHEN did you mail the letter? (4)
W   I think it was that afternoon. Yes, it was Monday afternoon.
P   WHAT happened then? (5)
W   I got a reply letter.
P   WHEN did the letter arrive? (6)
W   The following Monday.
P   HOW often have you exchanged letters with people in Atlantic City? (6)
W   I've done it hundreds of times in the course of business.
P   HOW long does it usually take to get a reply from Atlantic City? (6)
W   About a week.
P   HOW much time passed between the time you mailed your letter and the time when you received this second letter? (6)
W   About a week. It was right on time.
P   WHY did you refer to the letter as a reply letter? (8)
W   Well, it referred to my letter. It said it was going to answer my questions.
P   WHOSE name appeared on this second letter? (8)
W   The defendant's.

P   Your Honor, I request that this be marked plaintiff's exhibit number eight for identification.

J   It will be so marked.

P   Please let the record reflect that I am showing the exhibit to the opposing counsel.

J   It will so reflect.

P   I request permission to approach the witness.

J   Permission granted.

P   I now hand you plaintiff's exhibit number eight for identification. WHAT is it? (9)

W   It's the letter I just referred to.

P   HOW can you recognize it? (10)

W   I remember the contents, and the signature on the bottom is rather unique.

P   Your Honor, I now offer plaintiff's exhibit eight for identification into evidence as plaintiff's exhibit eight.

J   It will be received.

P   I request permission to have the witness read the last paragraph and signature block.

J   Permission granted.

P   (To the witness) Please read this passage to the jurors.

W   It reads: "I guarantee that it's a first-rate product. Nobody makes a better shingle. They'll last at least 15 years. Sincerely yours, John Bettencourt."

P   Your Honor, I now request permission to hand the exhibit to the jurors for their inspection.

J   Permission granted.

4. A COMPARISON BY AN EXPERT QUESTIONED DOCUMENT EXAMINER

Subsection 2 analyzed nonexpert lay opinion testimony about the author's handwriting style. The proponent may use expert testimony rather than lay testimony. Federal Evidence Rule 901(b)(3) allows a "[c]omparison by ... expert witnesses with specimens which have been authenticated." Before presenting the expert questioned document examiner, the proponent must authenticate the other specimens or exemplars. The proponent may use any authentication technique other than expert comparison to establish the exemplars' genuineness. The traditional practice is that the trial judge rules finally on the authenticity of the exemplars. However, in federal practice the authenticity of the exemplars is considered a Rule 104(b) issue. The judge admits the exemplars so long as there is sufficient evidence to support a permissive inference of their genuineness, and the jury finally decides whether the exemplars are authentic. The expert will compare the questioned document with these exemplars. The proponent then calls the expert to the stand. After qualifying as an expert, the witness compares the exemplars with the questioned document. On the basis of this comparison, the expert may testify whether in his or her opinion, the same person who wrote the exemplars authored the questioned document. In most cases, the expert has viewed the documents before trial; pretrial comparison makes the in-court testimony more reliable and credible.

The elements of the foundation are:

1. The proponent authenticates the exemplars.
2. The witness qualifies as an expert questioned document examiner.
3. The witness compares the exemplars and the questioned document.
4. After the comparison, the witness concludes that the same person who wrote the exemplars authored the questioned document.
5. The witness specifies the basis for his or her opinion, namely, the similarities between the exemplars and the questioned document.

Assume that the proponent has already authenticated the exemplars. Someone who saw the defendant sign two letters authenticated the letters. The letters are marked plaintiff's exhibits three and four. The plaintiff will mark the disputed check as plaintiff's exhibit number five for identification. The plaintiff is the proponent. The next witness is the questioned document examiner. The witness has already identified himself as John Glenn and stated his address.

P   WHAT is your occupation? (2)
W   I am a technician with Richard Whaley and Associates.
P   WHAT line of business is that firm in? (2)
W   It is a private forensic laboratory. We do all sorts of scientific work for legal cases.
P   HOW long have you worked there? (2)
W   For about 12 years.
P   WHAT are your duties there? (2)
W   I do mainly questioned document examination.
P   WHAT does a questioned document examiner do? (2)
W   Among other things, we attempt to determine who signed writings.
P   WHAT is your formal education? (2)
W   I have a Bachelor of Science degree from Pennsylvania State University.
P   WHAT other training, if any, have you had? (2)
W   I attended several two-week courses on questioned document examination at Northwestern University. I've also attended many seminars on the subject sponsored by the Law Enforcement Assistance Administration.
P   HOW long have you been a questioned document examiner? (2)
W   The whole time I've had my present position — roughly seven years.
P   WHAT part of your working time do you devote to questioned document examination? (2)
W   All of it. It's my specialty.
P   HOW often have you testified as an expert questioned document examiner? (2)
W   At least one hundred times.
P   WHERE have you testified? (2)
W   Mainly in the courts in this state.

P WHEN was the last time you testified as a questioned document examiner? (2)

W Last month.

P WHERE was that? (2)

W In another courtroom in this same building.

P Your Honor, permission to approach the witness?

J Granted.

P Mr. Glenn, I now hand you plaintiff's exhibits number three and four and plaintiff's exhibit number five for identification. WHAT are they?

W They're handwriting specimens.

P HOW many times have you seen these documents? (3)

W Once before.

P WHEN was that? (3)

W An investigator brought them to my office.

P WHAT happened when the investigator came to your office? (3)

W Well, I examined them. I studied them under an optical microscope to determine whether they had a common authorship.

P HOW long did you study them? (3)

W I spent the better part of the afternoon, maybe three hours, working on the comparison.

P HOW did you make the comparison? (3)

W I studied the documents. I had some blown up into enlarged photographs and studied the enlargements as well.

P HOW can you recognize these documents as the ones you previously examined? (3)

W I noted the peculiarities of the handwriting style. They were uniform throughout each document. They're quite distinctive.

P Do you have an opinion on the question whether the author of exhibits three and four also wrote plaintiff's exhibit five for identification?

W Yes.

P WHAT is that opinion? (4)

W I'm convinced that it was the same author.

P WHAT is the basis for your opinion? (5)

W In all, I detected five unique writing characteristics common to all three documents. There was a common misspelling, a spacing peculiarity, the tail on each *y*, the pronounced loop on each *o*, and the rather unique way in which they are written. These characteristics all point to common authorship.

P Your Honor, I now offer plaintiff's exhibit number five for identification into evidence as plaintiff's exhibit number five.

J It will be received.

P I now request permission to hand exhibits three, four and five to the jurors for their inspection.

J Permission granted.

C. THE AUTHENTICATION OF BUSINESS WRITINGS

1. CONVENTIONAL BUSINESS WRITINGS

Authenticating an ordinary business record is a very simple matter. The cases teach that proper custody is sufficient authentication for business records. It is sufficient if the witness is familiar with the business' filing system, took the record from the right file, and recognizes the exhibit as the record removed from the files.

The foundation is brief; the elements are:

1. The witness has personal knowledge of the business' filing system.
2. The witness removed a record from a certain file.
3. It was the right file.
4. The witness recognizes the exhibit as the record he or she removed from the files.
5. The witness specifies the basis on which he or she recognizes the exhibit.

In a contract action, the plaintiff's business, Collegiate Clothing Manufacturers, wants to authenticate a bill it prepared in December 1988. The plaintiff calls Ms. Peters as its witness.

P   WHAT is your occupation? (1)
W   I am a chief bookkeeper.
P   WHERE do you work? (1)
W   I work at the main office of the plaintiff.
P   HOW long have you worked there? (1)
W   About seven years.
P   WHAT are your duties? (1)
W   As chief bookkeeper, I ensure that we have proper records of all the money and goods flowing into and out of the company. I supervise the records' preparation, maintenance, and eventual destruction.
P   HOW well do you know the plaintiff's filing system? (1)
W   I know it backwards and forwards. In fact, I helped design the system.
P   Ms. Peters, WHERE were you this morning? (3)
W   I was picking up the records I thought we would need for the trial today.
P   WHERE did you go to get the files? (4)
W   I went to the file cabinet for our 1988 records. I was particularly interested in the records for December of that year.
P   WHAT did you find in the file? (3)
W   I located all the bills and invoices we needed.
P   Your Honor, I request that this be marked as plaintiff's exhibit number three for identification.
J   It will be so marked.
P   I request permission to approach the witness.
J   Permission granted.
P   Ms. Peters, I now hand you plaintiff's exhibit number three for identification. WHAT is it? (4)
W   It's one of the bills I removed from the file for December 1988.
P   HOW can you recognize it? (5)
W   I recognize the handwriting of the clerk, John Winters; I've known him for years. In addition, I can generally recall the contents of each of the bills I took out of the file cabinet.
P   Your Honor, I now offer plaintiff's exhibit number three for identification into evidence as plaintiff's exhibit number three.
J   It will be received.

P   I now request permission to hand the exhibit to the jurors for their
     inspection.
J   Permission granted.

2. COMPUTER RECORDS

Computer-generated evidence is a species of scientific evidence. The
process of generating data by computer is beyond the knowledge of
most laypersons. As Section J of this chapter explains, the presentation
of scientific evidence usually requires proof of the validity of the underlying theory and the reliability of the instrument. However, computers
are so widely accepted and used that the proponent of computer evidence need not prove those two elements of the foundation; the trial
judge will judicially notice the validity of the theory underlying computers and the general reliability of computers.

In the past, many courts have been lax in applying the authentication requirement to computer records; they have been content with
evidence that the business has successfully used the computer system
in question and that the witness recognizes the record as output from
the computer. Peritz, *Computer Data and Reliability: A Call for Authentication Under the Federal Rules of Evidence,* 80 Nw. U.L. Rev.
956 (1986). However, following the recommendations of the Federal
Judicial Center's *Manual for Complex Litigation,* some courts now
require a more extensive foundation. *Id.* These courts require the proponent to authenticate a computer record by proving the reliability of
the particular computer used, the dependability of the business' input
procedures for the computer, the use of proper procedures to obtain the
document offered in court, and the witness' recognition of that document as the readout from the computer.

It is important to remember that the readout may not be readable by
a layperson. The readout may use symbols and terminology only an
expert may understand. If that is the case, after introducing the record,
the proponent will have to have the expert explain the record to the
trier of fact.

The elements of the foundation are these:
1.   The business uses a computer.
2.   The computer is reliable.
3.   The business has developed a procedure for inserting data into
     the computer.
4.   The procedure has built-in safeguards to ensure accuracy and
     identify errors.
5.   The business keeps the computer in a good state of repair.
6.   The witness had the computer readout certain data.
7.   The witness used the proper procedures to obtain the readout.
8.   The computer was in working order at the time the witness
     obtained the readout.

9. The witness recognizes the exhibit as the readout.

10. The witness explains how he or she recognizes the readout.

11. If the readout contains strange symbols or terms, the witness explains the symbols or terms for the trier of fact.

Suppose that Acme Corporation brings an anti-trust suit against Bechtor, Inc. To prove its damages, Acme wants to show that its gross sales declined from 1982 to 1988. Acme wants to use a computer print-out to show its gross sales in those two years. As its witness, Acme calls Mr. Schons. Acme is the proponent.

P   Mr. Schons, WHAT is your occupation?
W   I am one of the accountants from Acme Corporation.
P   HOW long have you worked for Acme Corporation?
W   Roughly ten years.
P   HOW long have you worked for Acme Corporation as an accountant?
W   Again, roughly ten years.
P   WHAT are your duties with Acme Corporation?
W   My specialty is the maintenance of our computer records.
P   HOW does Acme maintain its business records? (1)
W   We maintain the overwhelming majority of our data in our computer.
P   WHICH computer do you use? (1)
W   We use an IBM 720.
P   HOW long have you used that computer? (2)
W   For the last three years.
P   HOW widely used is that model computer? (2)
W   There are hundreds in use throughout the country. When it was first marketed, it was the top of the line. There's a somewhat more sophisticated model available now, but the 720 is regarded as one of the most dependable models on the market.
P   WHAT procedure does Acme have for using the computer to maintain its records? (3)
W   When an order comes in from a customer, we ship it straight to the sales department. They check it to ensure that the order has the correct spelling of the product name.
P   WHAT does the sales department do with the order then? (3)
W   They send it to the computer center. The center personnel punch the information onto cards. We use the cards to feed the data into the computer. The computer tries to make certain that the merchandise is available and that the purchaser's credit is good. If the order passes those tests, the computer then makes entries on the customer's account and stores data for statistical and management reports.
P   HOW do you know that that is the procedure? (3)
W   I helped design the procedure. As I said, computer record maintenance is my specialty.
P   WHAT safeguards, if any, do you use to ensure that your records are accurate? (4)
W   There are double checks at several points. For example, one computer center employee prepares the card, and another checks the card against the data on the order slip. Perhaps the most important safeguard is the customers' review of the bills we printout and send them. If anything's wrong, they let us know right away.
P   HOW is the computer maintained? (5)

W It's checked nightly for any obvious problems. Whenever an operator encounters a mechanical problem, they call maintenance immediately. In addition, IBM personnel visit the center every two weeks and check the system thoroughly.

P WHERE were you yesterday afternoon? (6)

W I was at my office.

P WHAT were you doing there? (6)

W I was trying to get the data I thought we'd need today in court.

P WHAT data was that? (6)

W I knew we'd need the total sales figures for 1982 and 1988.

P HOW did you obtain the data? (6)

W I had the computer print it out.

P HOW did you obtain the printout? (7)

W I went to the terminal, set it in the printout mode, and then requested the sales figures.

P HOW many times did you request the data from the computer? (7)

W Twice.

P WHY did you do it twice? (7)

W I wanted to make certain I had the right figures.

P WHAT was the result of your doublecheck? (7)

W The computer read out the same data both times.

P WHAT condition was the computer in at the time? (8)

W It seemed to be O.K. There were certainly no obvious problems. It had been checked the night before, and we'd used it several times already that day without any difficulty.

P Your Honor, may this be marked plaintiff's exhibit number ten for identification?

J It will be so marked.

P May the record reflect that I am showing exhibit number ten to the opposing attorney?

J It will so reflect.

P Request permission to approach the witness.

J Permission granted.

P Mr. Schons, I now hand you plaintiff's exhibit number ten for identification. WHAT is it? (9)

W It's the second printout I just referred to.

P HOW can you recognize it? (10)

W I put my initials and the date in that corner. I can easily recognize them.

P Your Honor, I now offer plaintiff's exhibit number ten for identification into evidence as plaintiff's exhibit number ten.

J It will be received.

P Now, Mr. Schons, directing your attention to this notation on the exhibit, WHAT does it say there? (11)

W It reads "MER S."

P WHAT does that mean? (11)

W It means sales of merchandise.

P HOW do you know that? (11)

W I helped select the symbols and terminology the computer would use in printouts.

P WHAT are these figures? (11)

W They're the dollar amounts of sales for the years indicated, for example, $2,675,334 in 1982.

P Your Honor, may exhibit ten be handed to the jurors for their inspection?

J Yes.

D. THE AUTHENTICATION OF OFFICIAL WRITINGS

1. THE DOCTRINE

The government often possesses information relevant to the outcome of civil and criminal actions. Thus, it often becomes necessary for one of the parties to introduce an official record. It would obviously be inconvenient to require public officials to appear in court to authenticate official records; their appearance would not only divert them from their official duties but also create the risk of the record's loss.

To remedy this problem, almost every jurisdiction has adopted the rule that a properly attested copy of an official record is self-authenticating. The party obtains a copy of the official record from the official custodian, and the custodian attaches an attesting certificate. The certificate reads along these lines: "I, Robert Dondero, certify that I am the County Clerk of San Francisco, California and that the attached document is a true and accurate copy of an original, official record in my custody." The certificate is signed and often bears the seal of the official's office. The courts have developed the doctrine that the purported signature or seal of an official is presumed to be authentic. Federal Evidence Rule 902 treats domestic public documents under seal as self-authenticating.

2. ELEMENTS OF THE FOUNDATION

The mechanics of introducing a properly attested copy of an official record are simple; the elements of the foundation include:

1. The document purports to be a copy of an official record.
2. A certificate is attached to the copy.
3. The certificate states that the signatory is a public custodian of official records.
4. The certificate states that the document is a true and accurate copy of an original, official record.
5. The certificate bears a presumptively authentic signature and/or seal.

3. SAMPLE FOUNDATION

The fact situation is a probate contest. At one point in the trial, the contestant must prove that a Jean Simmons was born in San Francisco, California in 1956. The contestant is the proponent. The contestant is attempting to introduce a copy of a birth certificate in the custody of the San Francisco County Clerk. The hearing is a bench trial without a jury.

P Your Honor, I request that this be marked contestant's exhibit number four for identification.

J It will be so marked.

P Please let the record reflect that I am showing the exhibit to the opposing counsel.

J The record will so reflect.

P I now offer contestant's exhibit number four for identification into evidence as contestant's exhibit number four.

O I object on the ground that there has been insufficient authentication. No sponsoring witness has come forward to verify the authenticity of this document.

J (To the contestant) What is your response to the objection?

P Your Honor, live testimony is unnecessary. In this jurisdiction, the purported signatures and seals of public officials are presumed genuine. This document bears both a purported official signature and seal. The signature and seal authenticate the certificate itself. The certificate states that the attached document is a true and accurate copy of an official record in Mr. Dondero's custody. Thus, the certificate serves to authenticate the attached copy.

J Objection overruled.

P Your Honor, at this point I would like to invite the court's attention to the body of exhibit four.

J Yes.

P I would like to point out that it states that a Jean Simmons was born in San Francisco, California on September 19, 1956.

J I have noted that.

This hypothetical example is so short because the proponent needed only an attesting certificate to make the document self-authenticating. In an attesting certificate, the signatory writes that he or she is the custodian or deputy custodian of a set of official records and that the attached document is an original official record or a copy of an original official record in their custody. If the court can presume the authenticity of the signature or seal on the attesting certificate, that presumption authenticates the certificate; and in turn, the attesting certificate authenticates the attached document. Suppose, however, that the document originates in a foreign country. The presumption of authenticity may not attach to a foreign official's signature, and consequently, a foreign official's attesting certificate will probably not suffice to authenticate the attached document. In that event, the proponent will need a chain of certificates, usually culminating in an authenticating certificate executed by an American official. In an authenticating certificate, one official writes that he or she is familiar with the position and handwriting of another official and that the signature attached to another certificate in the chain is the signature of that other official. The chain used to authenticate a foreign record might include an attesting certificate by a local foreign official, an authenticating certificate by a national foreign official, and finally an authenticating certificate by an American consular officer.

E. THE AUTHENTICATION OF ORAL STATEMENTS

Like written statements, oral statements must be authenticated. In the case of a written statement, authentication consists in identifying the author. In the case of an oral statement, authentication consists in identifying the speaker. To do so, the proponent may use several techniques.

1. LAY OPINION TESTIMONY OF A WITNESS FAMILIAR WITH THE SPEAKER'S VOICE

The proponent may use lay opinion testimony to authenticate an oral statement just as the proponent may use lay opinion testimony to authenticate a writing. In the case of a writing, the witness must testify that he or she is familiar with the author's handwriting style. Now the witness must testify that he or she is familiar with the person's voice. Federal Evidence Rule 901 (b) (5) recognizes this method of voice identification.

The foundation contains these elements:

1. At a specific time and place, the witness heard a voice.
2. The witness recognized the voice as that of a certain person.
3. The witness is familiar with that person's voice.
4. The witness explains the basis for his or her familiarity with that person's voice.
5. The person made a statement during the conversation.

The fact situation is a tort action for slander. The plaintiff, Brown, sues the defendant, Nolan. The plaintiff alleges that Nolan slandered the plaintiff during a telephone conversation with Parish. The plaintiff calls Parish to the stand.

P   Mr. Parish, WHERE were you on the evening of April 6th of this year? (1)
W   I was at home.
P   WHAT, if anything, happened while you were home? (1)
W   I received a phone call.
P   WHO was the caller? (2)
W   It was the defendant, Ms. Nolan.
P   HOW do you know that it was Ms. Nolan? (3)
W   I recognized her voice, and she said it was Ms. Nolan.
P   HOW did you become familiar with her voice? (4)
W   We've known each other for years.
P   HOW many years? (4)
W   Easily fifteen.
P   HOW often have you spoken with her? (4)
W   I can't answer; we've spoken thousands of times, I guess. We're neighbors. I see her at least a couple of times a week.
P   WHAT condition was your telephone in when you received this call?
W   It was in good working condition. There was no static or anything.
P   HOW much noise was there in the background?

W None that I could tell. I didn't have the stereo on or anything like that, and I couldn't hear any noise at the other end other than Ms. Nolan talking.

P WHAT did Ms. Nolan say during this telephone conversation? (5)

W She said that she had a hot item of news for me.

P WHAT was that? (5)

W She said that the plaintiff, Mr. Brown, had paid $6,000 to bribe one of the City Councilmen to get favorable zoning on some commercial property Brown owns.

2. THE TELEPHONE DIRECTORY DOCTRINE

The telephone directory doctrine parallels the reply letter doctrine. Under the reply letter doctrine, the courts trust the reliability of the Post Office. Under this doctrine, the courts place their faith in the accuracy of telephone directories. Federal Evidence Rule 901(b) (6) describes the doctrine: The proponent may authenticate a "(t)elephone conversation, by evidence that a call was made to the number assigned at the time by the telephone company to a particular person or business, if ... in the case of a person, circumstances, including self-identification, show the person answering to be the one called ...." This fact pattern creates a circumstantial inference that the person answering was the person the telephone number is assigned to.

The foundation includes these elements:

1. The telephone directory assigns a certain number to the person.
2. The witness called that number.
3. The witness asked for the person to whom the number is assigned.
4. The person answering identified himself or herself as the person to whom the number is assigned.
5. Any other circumstances indicating that the person answering was the person to whom the number was assigned.

The fact situation is a tort action arising from a crash. The expert testimony indicates that the failure of the defendant's brakes caused the crash. One issue is whether the defendant knew his brakes were defective. The plaintiff wants to elicit Mr. Martinez' testimony that he worked on the defendant's car, found the brakes defective, and notified the defendant by telephone. The telephone conversation was Mr. Martinez' only contact with the defendant, Mr. Jackson. The plaintiff is the proponent.

W After examining the brakes, I concluded that they were in dangerous condition.

P WHAT did you do then?

W I decided to notify the owner, this fellow Jackson.

P HOW did you notify him?

W I wanted to phone him and let him know.

P HOW did you do that? (1)

W First I checked the telephone directory to get his number.

P WHAT did you do then? (2)

W   I called the number.

P   WHERE was the directory when you were dialing? (2)

W   It was right in front of me. I was looking at it as I dialed.

P   WHAT happened next? (3)

W   It rang, and a man answered.

P   WHAT did you say? (3)

W   I asked to speak to Mr. Jackson, the owner of the purple Corvette.

P   HOW did the person answering the phone identify himself? (4)

W   He just said he was Jackson, the person I wanted to talk to.

P   WHAT, if anything, did he say about the Corvette? (5)

W   He told me that he realized that it had some problems.

P   WHAT problems? (5)

W   He mentioned a problem with the exhaust and the windshield wipers.

P   HOW accurate were those statements? (5)

W   The guy was right. I'd looked at the car, and I'd seen those problems, among others. The guy I was talking with was obviously familiar with the car.

P   WHAT did you say then?

W   I told him about the brakes.

P   Specifically, WHAT did you tell him?

W   I said that they were defective and dangerous. I told him that they could fail anytime and that he should have them repaired immediately.

3. TESTIMONY BY A VOICEPRINT OR SOUND SPECTROGRAPHY EXPERT

The sound spectrography expert is to the identification of speakers what the questioned document examiner is to the identification of writers. The voiceprint witness is the supposed expert. There are two theoretical premises underlying sound spectrography. The first premise is that interspeaker variability exceeds intraspeaker variability; even though a person's voice pattern changes from time to time, the voice pattern differences among speakers are greater than the variations in a single speaker's voice pattern. The second premise is intraspeaker invariant speech: Each voice has certain unique characteristics that it will invariably display under spectrographic analysis. Most speech scientists accept the first premise, but there is still a good deal of controversy in scientific circles over the second premise. Many critics of sound spectrography argue that there has been insufficient experimental verification of the theory of invariant speech. A report of a committee of the National Academy of Sciences found insufficient verification.

The spectrograph instrument itself includes: (1) a magnetic recording device; (2) a variable electronic filter; (3) a paper-carrying drum coupled to the magnetic recording device; and (4) an electronic stylus that marks the paper as the drum rotates. The spectrograph operates in this fashion. The operator starts with a tape of certain, commonly used English cue words such as "the," "and," "me," "on," "is," "it," "I," "a," and "you." The cue words are static-state words; the words preceding and following them have little effect on their pronunciation and, hence, on the spectrograms they produce. The operator prepares the tape by having the suspect read the words into the tape or excerpting the words from a tape of the known suspect's speech. The operator plays the tape repeatedly on the magnetic recording device. The device is attached to the electronic filter; and each time the operator replays the tape, the filter lets another frequency pass through. The frequencies pass through to an electronic stylus; and as the frequencies pass through, the stylus marks the paper-carrying drum. The stylus thus produces a spectrogram, a graphic depiction of the voice pattern. The usual spectrogram is a bar spectrogram. The vertical axis is frequency, the horizontal axis is time, and the darkness is the voice's amplitude.

BAR SPECTROGRAPH

frequency

time

The operator then takes the unknown voice, for example, the tape of a bomb threat or obscene telephone call. The operator excerpts the same words from the tape of that voice and prepares another spectrogram in the same fashion. The operator then compares the two spectrograms and forms an opinion whether the same voice produced the two spectrograms. Experts vary on the number of points of similarity required for a match; some will accept as few as 16 while others insist upon as many as 33.

Given the division in the scientific community over sound spectrography, it is understandable that the courts are also split. Some courts reject the evidence. In *People v. Kelly,* 17 Cal. 3d 24, 130 Cal. Rptr. 144, 549 P.2d 1240 (1976), the California Supreme Court excluded the evidence. Courts in the District of Columbia, Louisiana, Maryland, Michigan, New Jersey, and Pennsylvania have followed *Kelly.* Other courts continue to accept the evidence. For example, the federal Court of Appeals for the Second Circuit, the Maine Supreme Judicial Court, and the Rhode Island Supreme Court have sustained the admission of sound spectrography evidence. One thing is clear: If the proponent is going to offer sound spectrography evidence, the proponent must lay a complete foundation. Since sound spectrography is a scientific technique, the proponent must lay the foundation outlined in Section J of this chapter.

The elements of a foundation for sound spectrography evidence include:

1. The tape recordings used to produce the spectrograms are authentic. *See* Section F of this chapter.
2. The witness has the qualifications to explain sound spectrography's underlying premises and to conduct the test.
3. The underlying premises of sound spectrography are interspeaker variability and invariant speech.
4. Those premises are generally accepted as valid in the relevant scientific circles.
5. The instrument is the sound spectrograph.
6. The instrument is generally accepted as reliable in the relevant scientific circles.
7. At a particular time and place, the witness conducted a voiceprint examination.
8. The witness used the tape recordings mentioned in element #1.
9. The witness excerpted the cue words from both tapes.
10. The witness used a spectrograph to analyze the tapes of the cue words.
11. The spectrograph was in good working condition at the time.
12. The witness used the proper procedures.
13. The analysis produced two spectrograms.
14. The witness identifies the spectrograms.
15. There are several points of similarity between the two spectrograms.
16. In the witness' opinion, the same voice produced the two spectrograms.

The following is a sample foundation. The fact situation is a bomb threat prosecution. A police officer recorded the threat and authenticated the tape recording as prosecution exhibit number one. Another officer obtained a voice exemplar recording from the defendant; the officer has authenticated that tape recording as prosecution exhibit number two. Thus, the two officers have laid the first element of the foundation. The prosecution now calls Mr. James Cottrell, a sound spectrography expert. The prosecution is the proponent. Mr. Cottrell has already identified himself and stated his address.

P   WHAT is your occupation? (2)
W   I am a member of the staff of the Pittsburgh Police Department Police Laboratory.
P   HOW long have you worked there? (2)
W   For the past six years — ever since I graduated from college.
P   WHERE did you attend college? (2)
W   I attended University of California, Berkeley.

P WHAT was your undergraduate major? (2)

W I was a Science major, specializing in speech science and acoustics.

P WHAT are your present duties? (2)

W I do all the sound spectrography or voiceprint analysis for the Pittsburgh Police Department.

P WHAT is sound spectrography? (3)

W It's a scientific technique for identifying a speaker.

P WHAT is the basis of this technique? (3)

W It has two premises. One is interspeaker variability.

P WHAT does that mean? (3)

W It means simply that the difference between your and my voice is greater than the fluctuations in my voice. Depending on whether I'm alert or sleepy, my voice pattern changes; but the differences between our two voices are still greater than the changes in my voice pattern from time to time. That's one of the two major premises of sound spectrography.

P WHAT is the other premise? (3)

W Invariant speech.

P WHAT does that mean? (3)

W Each person's voice has some unique characteristics, and you'll always be able to detect those characteristics with the instrument we use, the spectrograph.

P WHAT experiments have been conducted to verify these theories? (3)

W There has been extensive experimentation at Stanford, Michigan State, and a number of industrial laboratories.

P WHAT has been the outcome of these experiments? (3)

W They show that if you have a trained examiner, the examiner will ordinarily be able to determine whether the same voice produced two spectrograms, the charts of the voice patterns.

P HOW high has the error rate been? (3)

W It depends on the type of error you're talking about. If you're talking about false identifications, erroneously identifying a suspect as the person who produced the unknown spectrogram, it's pretty low. If you give the examiner the right to say that a particular test is too close to call, the error rate is likely to be only one or two percent.

P HOW widely are these theories accepted? (4)

W There's still some controversy. However, I think that the people who are knowledgeable, who have read the available data, accept both premises.

P HOW do you apply these theories to a particular case? (5)

W As I said, you use a spectrograph. In our laboratory, we use a Series 700 Sound Spectrograph manufactured by Voiceprint Laboratories in New Jersey.

P WHAT is a sound spectrograph? (5)

W It has four basic components. First, there's a magnetic recording device. Then there's an electronic filter. Third, the machine has a stylus. Finally, it has a paper-carrying drum.

P HOW does the spectrograph operate? (5)

W You put a tape on the recording device. You play it again and again. Every time you play it, the filter lets a different frequency of the voice through. The frequencies activate the stylus, and the stylus marks the paper. The end result is a sort of chart that we call a spectrogram. In effect, it's a visual display of a voice pattern. You compare two charts;

and if there are enough points of similarity, you conclude that the same voice produced the two spectrograms and, hence, the two tape recordings.

P   WHAT experiments have been conducted to verify the spectrograph's reliability? (5)

W   Basically the same ones I mentioned before. The researchers have tested both the theory and the instrument. The test results I mentioned before tend to validate the instrument as well.

P   HOW widely is the spectrograph accepted? (6)

W   I'd say that its reliability is accepted to the same extent as the underlying theories — generally accepted by the really knowledgeable people in the field.

P   Mr. Cottrell, WHERE were you on the morning of July 17 of this year? (7)

W   I was at my office at the lab.

P   WHAT happened while you were there? (7)

W   A police officer dropped by some tape recordings for spectrographic analysis.

P   I now hand you prosecution exhibits numbers one and two. WHAT are they? (8)

W   They're the tape recordings I was given.

P   HOW can you recognize them? (8)

W   I remember the notations on the containers, and I made these small marks, my initials on the label, on the reels themselves.

P   WHAT did you do with the tapes? (7)

W   I proceeded to conduct the analysis.

P   HOW did you do that? (9)

W   First I had to excerpt common words from both tapes. That took a little while.

P   Then WHAT did you do? (10)

W   One at a time, I put the new tapes of the excerpts on the spectrograph.

P   WHAT condition was your spectrograph in at the time? (11)

W   It was in good working condition.

P   HOW do you know that? (11)

W   I ran through the manufacturer's maintenance checklist before I used the spectrograph. The instrument checked out fine.

P   HOW are you supposed to operate the machine? (12)

W   You let it warm up a bit, mount the tape you're analyzing, activate the machine, and then let it run until the spectrogram is complete.

P   WHAT procedure did you use on this occasion? (12)

W   I followed the proper procedure exactly. I did just what I outlined for you.

P   WHAT was the result of the test? (13)

W   At the end, I had two spectrograms, two visual displays of voice patterns.

P   Your Honor, I request that these be marked prosecution exhibits numbers three and four for identification.

J   They will be so marked.

P   Please let the record reflect that I am showing these exhibits to the opposing attorney.

J   It will so reflect.

P   Mr. Cottrell, I now hand you prosecution exhibit three for identification. WHAT is it? (14)

W   It's the spectrogram of that tape, prosecution exhibit number one.
P   HOW can you recognize the spectrogram? (14)
W   As you can see, on the other side, I marked my initials, the date, and the number of the tape it corresponded to.
P   I now hand you prosecution exhibit number four for identification. WHAT is it? (l4)
W   It's the spectrogram produced by analyzing the other tape, prosecution exhibit number two.
P   HOW can you recognize it? (14)
W   I made the same sort of notations on the back here.
P   Your Honor, I now offer prosecution exhibits three and four for identification into evidence as prosecution exhibits three and four.
J   They will be received.
P   Mr. Cottrell, WHAT did you do with the spectrograms? (15)
W   I compared them.
P   WHAT was the result of your comparison? (15)
W   I found a large number of points of similarity between the two spectrograms.
P   HOW many points of similarity? (15)
W   32 in all.
P   Do you have an opinion on the question whether the same voice produced the two spectrograms? (16)
W   Yes.
P   WHAT is that opinion? (16)
W   In my judgment, it was the same voice.
P   WHAT is the basis of that opinion? (15)
W   Not just the number of points of similarity, but some of them were really unique. I'm confident that the same person who phoned in this bomb threat made this other voice exemplar.
P   Request permission to hand exhibits three and four to the jurors for their inspection.
J   Permission granted.

F. TAPE RECORDINGS

1. THE DOCTRINE

Like computers, tape recorders present scientific evidence issues. However, the validity of the underlying theory and the reliability of recorders in general are so well accepted that the judge will judicially notice those elements of the foundation. However, notwithstanding the courts' willingness to notice those foundational elements, the courts have traditionally taken a strict attitude towards tape recordings. The courts realize that tapes can be tampered with. For that reason, the courts generally insisted on a very complete foundation: the operator's qualifications, the equipment's working condition, custody of the tape, an identification of the speakers on the tape, and finally testimony of someone who heard the conversation that the tape is an accurate reproduction of the conversation.

However, the courts have begun to liberalize the standards for the admission of tape recordings. There are two reasons for the liberalization. First, there are now electronic techniques for determining whether a tape has been altered. If the opponent seriously contests a tape's accuracy, the opponent can use an expert to detect the tampering. Secondly and more importantly, the courts have gone back to fundamentals and begun to treat the question of a tape recording's authenticity as a simple question of authentication under Rule 104(b). As Section A of this chapter emphasizes, the test for authentication is lax: Has the proponent presented sufficient evidence to support a rational finding of fact that the tape recording is authentic? Given that test, many modern courts are no longer insisting on the traditional, strict foundation. In truth, the last element of the traditional foundation, standing alone, has sufficient probative value to authenticate the tape. If a witness testifies that he or she heard a conversation and that the tape accurately reproduces the conversation, there is a permissive inference of the tape's genuineness. Similarly, proof of the other elements of the traditional foundation is sufficient authentication without the last element. Proof of the operator's qualifications, the equipment's working condition, and the tape's custody shows that the tape is an accurate reproduction of some conversation; and in principle, testimony identifying the speakers (by any person familiar with their voices) is sufficient to complete the foundation to authenticate the tape.

2. ELEMENTS OF THE FOUNDATION

The strict, traditional foundation includes the following elements:
1. The operator of the equipment was qualified.
2. The operator recorded a conversation at a certain time and place.
3. The operator used certain equipment to record the conversation.
4. The equipment was in good working order.
5. The operator used proper procedures to record the conversation.
6. The tape was a good reproduction of the conversation.
7. The operator accounts for the tape's custody between the time of taping and the time of trial.
8. The operator recognizes the exhibit as the tape.
9. The tape is still a good reproduction of the conversation.

3. SAMPLE FOUNDATIONS

The first foundation is an example of a strict, traditional foundation. The fact situation is a contract action. The contracting parties were rather suspicious of each other, and they had a private investigator tape a key negotiating session.

P   WHAT is your occupation? (1)
W   I'm a private investigator.
P   WHO is your employer? (1)

W   I work for the Stead Detective Agency downtown.
P   HOW long have you worked there? (1)
W   For about ten years now.
P   WHAT are your duties for your employer? (1)
W   My real specialty is electronic surveillance and tape recording.
P   HOW long have you worked in that field? (1)
W   About fifteen years.
P   WHEN did you begin working in that field? (1)
W   When I was in the military service.
P   WHICH military service were you in? (1)
W   I was in the Army.
P   WHAT did you do while you were in the service? (1)
W   I specialized in radar.
P   WHAT training did you receive in that specialty? (1)
W   I took a four month course and was even able to get a first class license from the Federal Communications Commission.
P   WHAT additional training have you had in the field? (1)
W   Since leaving the service, I've taken ten college level courses in electronics. I've also attended a number of seminars on tape recording and electronic surveillance techniques.
P   WHERE were you on the morning of January 17, 1989? (2)
W   I went to the offices of Atco Corporation.
P   WHY did you do that? (2)
W   The president of the corporation, Mr. Semegen, had asked me to come and record a negotiating session between him and a Mr. Heiser, the head of another corporation.
P   WHAT did you do while you were at the offices of Atco Corporation? (3)
W   I did what I'd been asked to do; I recorded this conversation.
P   WHAT equipment did you use to record the conversation? (4)
W   I used a Uher recorder, microphones, and a seven inch reel of Ampex audio tape.
P   WHAT do "Uher" and "Ampex" mean? (3)
W   They're tradenames. They are two of the most dependable manufacturers in the field.
P   HOW often had you used that equipment in the past? (3)
W   Hundreds of times. I really trust their equipment; it's very reliable.
P   WHAT condition was the equipment in that morning? (4)
W   It was in good condition.
P   HOW do you know that? (4)
W   Well, I checked out the recorder and microphones. I test recorded some conversation and replayed it; it was a good quality reproduction. I took the tape out of the original wrapper; it was fresh and had never been used before.
P   HOW did you use the equipment? (5)
W   I followed my standard procedure. First, I plugged the recorder into a wall outlet. Then I attached the mikes. After I'd test recorded some sound on one track — that is, half of the width of the tape, I turned the reel over, threaded the tape again, and set up to record on the second track.
P   WHAT did you do then? (5)
W   Before I started recording the conversation, I asked the parties, Messrs. Semegen and Heiser, to speak into the microphones. I got the right voice level, and then I was all set to record.

P WHAT happened then? (5)

W They spoke continuously for about half an hour. I then read my name, the date, and the address into the tape. After doing that, I turned off the recorder.

P HOW well did the recorder work during the conversation? (6)

W Very well.

P HOW do you know that? (6)

W In the first place, I didn't experience any technical or mechanical difficulties during the recording session. Secondly, right after the session, I rewound the tape onto the feeder reel and replayed it.

P WHAT happened when you replayed the tape? (6)

W I could hear the recording of the conversation.

P WHAT was the quality of the recording? (6)

W Excellent. As far as I could tell, the recorder picked up everything; and the recording was loud and clear.

P WHAT did you do with the tape after you replayed it? (7)

W I put it in an envelope and wrote my name, the parties' names, the date, and address on it.

P WHAT did you do with the envelope? (7)

W I took it back to my office.

P WHERE did you put it in your office? (7)

W In my evidence locker.

P HOW many people have access to the locker? (7)

W Only me. I have a combination lock on it, and I'm the only one who knows the combination.

P WHAT happened to the tape after you placed it in your evidence locker? (7)

W With one exception until today, it's been in the locker the whole time.

P WHAT was that exception? (7)

W You and I took it out several months ago and listened to it.

P WHO was present during that playing of the tape? (7)

W You and I were the only two persons present.

P WHERE were you while the tape was out of the evidence locker? (7)

W I was present the whole time. I took it out, played it for you, and then immediately put it back.

P WHERE has the tape been since then? (7)

W In the locker the whole time.

P Your Honor, I request that this tape be marked plaintiff's exhibit ten for identification.

J It will be so marked.

P May the record reflect that I am showing plaintiff's exhibit number ten for identification to the opposing counsel?

J It will so reflect.

P I request permission to approach the witness.

J Permission granted.

P I now hand you plaintiff's exhibit number ten for identification. WHAT is it? (8)

W It's the tape I've been talking about.

P HOW can you recognize it? (8)

W I recognize my handwriting. I made those markings on the label on the reel.

P WHAT condition is the tape recording in? (9)

W It's in excellent condition.

P   HOW do you know that? (9)
W   When I removed it from the locker this morning, I replayed it.
P   WHAT was the quality of the recording? (9)
W   It hasn't changed at all. It was and is an excellent reproduction of the conversation.
P   Your Honor, I now offer plaintiff's exhibit number ten for identification into evidence as plaintiff's exhibit ten.
J   It will be received.
P   I request permission to have the bailiff play the exhibit for the jury.
J   Permission granted.

The second foundation is a simple, modern foundation. Here the witness overheard the conversation. Suppose that Mr. Semegen's secretary, Ms. Grant, was present during the negotiating session.

P   WHAT is your occupation?
W   I'm a secretary at Atco Corporation.
P   WHO do you work for?
W   I work directly for the president, Mr. Jason Semegen.
P   HOW long have you worked for him?
W   Easily three years.
P   WHERE were you on the morning of January 17, 1989?
W   I was at the office at work.
P   WHAT happened that morning?
W   Mr. Semegen had a bargaining session with a Mr. Heiser.
P   WHERE were you when this session occurred?
W   I was in the room.
P   HOW close were you to them?
W   I was sitting right next to them to take notes.
P   HOW well could you hear the conversation?
W   Just fine.
P   Your Honor, I request that this be marked plaintiff's exhibit number ten for identification.
J   It will be so marked.
P   Please let the record reflect that I am showing plaintiff's exhibit number ten for identification to the opposing counsel.
J   It will so reflect.
P   I request permission to approach the witness.
J   Permission granted.
P   I now hand you plaintiff's exhibit number ten for identification. WHAT is it?
W   It's a tape of the conversation between Mr. Semegen and Mr. Heiser.
P   HOW do you know that?
W   I listened to the tape in the judge's chambers just a few hours ago.
P   WHAT is the quality of the tape recording?
W   It's an excellent reproduction of the conversation as far as I can tell.
P   HOW can you recognize this tape recording as the one you listened to in the judge's chambers?
W   I recognize the marking on the reel, and I've kept it in my possession ever since I listened to it.
P   WHERE have you kept it?
W   I've kept it on my person while I was sitting listening to this trial.
P   HOW long did you have it in your possession?

W   About two hours. I kept it until I put it on your counsel table as I
    walked to the witness stand just a few minutes ago.
P   Your Honor, I now offer plaintiff's exhibit number ten for identifica-
    tion into evidence as plaintiff's exhibit number ten.
J   It will be received.
P   I request permission to have the bailiff play the tape recording for the
    jury.
J   Permission granted.

G. DEMONSTRATIVE EVIDENCE

The types of articles we have discussed to date are real or original
evidence; the articles have an historical connection with the transaction giving rise to the suit. For example, the document is a will the
decedent signed before death, or the item is the very pistol the defendant used during the assault. Sometimes the proponent may use an
item even if the item has no connection with the case. Suppose, for
example, that the police never found the pistol used in the assault. The
trial judge might permit an eyewitness to the assault to use another,
similar pistol to illustrate his or her testimony. The courts often refer
to this latter type of evidence as demonstrative; the article helps the
witness to demonstrate or illustrate oral testimony. The only limits on
the use of demonstrative evidence are the trial judge's discretion and
the trial attorney's imagination.

1. VERIFICATION OF A DIAGRAM

The verification of a diagram is very similar to the verification of a
photograph. The diagram need not be to scale. However, the sponsoring witness must testify that the diagram is generally a "true," "accurate," "good," or "fair" depiction of the scene or object shown. If the
diagram is not to scale, the opposing counsel is entitled to a limiting
instruction.

The elements of the foundation are:

1. The diagram depicts a certain area or object.
2. The witness is familiar with that area or object.
3. The witness explains the basis for his or her familiarity with the
   area or object.
4. In the witness' opinion, the diagram is an accurate depiction of
   that area or object.

The fact situation is an assault prosecution. The indictment alleges
that the defendant attacked the victim, Mr. Williams, in a bathroom in
the Senator Hotel in San Diego. The prosecutor wants to use a chart to
illustrate the victim's testimony. The witness is the victim. The prosecutor is the proponent. The victim has just testified that he was attacked.

P   WHERE did this attack occur?
W   As I said, it occurred in the bathroom on the second floor of the hotel.

P   Your Honor, I request that this be marked prosecution exhibit number three for identification.

J   It will be so marked.

P   Please let the record reflect that I am showing the exhibit to the defense attorney.

J   It will so reflect.

P   Request permission to approach the witness.

J   Permission granted.

P   Mr. Williams, I hand you prosecution exhibit number three for identification. WHAT is it? (1)

W   It's a chart of the bathroom I was just referring to.

P   HOW do you recognize it? (2)

W   I know that hotel very well.

P   HOW did you become familiar with the hotel? (3)

W   I've lived in it for two years. It's a boarding hotel.

P   HOW many times have you been in that bathroom? (3)

W   Lots of times. I couldn't give you a specific figure.

P   HOW accurate is the diagram? (4)

W   Well, it's not to scale. That's for sure.

P   Otherwise, HOW accurate is the diagram? (4)

W   It's correct. It shows everything in roughly the right place.

P   Your Honor, I now offer prosecution exhibit number three for identification into evidence as prosecution exhibit three.

O   Your Honor, may a limiting instruction be given that the diagram is not to scale?

J   Yes. The exhibit will be received. (To the jurors) Ladies and gentlemen of the jury, the prosecutor is now going to show you a diagram of the bathroom in the Senator Hotel. The witness has testified that the diagram is basically accurate, but the witness also stated that the diagram is not to scale. In deciding what weight to attach to the diagram, you should consider the fact that the diagram is not to scale.

P   I now request permission to hand the diagram to the jurors for their inspection.

J   Permission granted.

2. MARKING A DIAGRAM

To effectively use a chart, the proponent will sometimes have to have the witness mark on the chart. The marking will help the jury visualize the testimony. Moreover, the marking will help the appellate court understand the record of trial. Unless the diagram is marked, the record of trial may be positively confusing to the appellate court; the court will not know where "here" or "there" was on the map. The proponent should give the witness specific instructions as to how to mark the chart. Moreover, in some jurisdictions, it is customary to have the record reflect that the witness complied with the proponent's instructions.

To illustrate these techniques, we shall use the original hypothetical:

P   Mr. Williams, using the chart, WHERE were you when the defendant first walked into the bathroom?

W   I was standing over here.
P   Please take this pen, place a circle where you were standing, and write the letter W in the circle.
W   *(The witness complied.)*
P   Please let the record reflect that the witness complied with my instruction.
J   The record will so reflect.
P   Now, Mr. Williams, WHAT direction was the defendant Dugan walking in when he first entered the room?
W   He was going that way.
P   Please use the pen again, draw an arrow showing that direction, and write the letter D at the tip of the arrow.
W   *(The witness complied.)*
P   Please let the record reflect that the witness complied with my direction.
J   The record will so reflect.

The reader should bear in mind two important caveats. Many trial judges prefer that the chart be completely marked before it is formally offered into evidence. These judges will not permit any further marking after the exhibit has been received into evidence. If you contemplate using a chart during a trial, you should inquire about the judge's preference during the chambers conference before the trial begins. The second caveat is that if you ultimately want the judge to send the chart to the jury during deliberation, you may want to add a legend at the bottom of the chart. Of course, the jurors may remember that "W" represents Williams and "D" the defendant Dugan. However, to ensure that the jury correctly interprets the markings on the chart, you can instruct the witness to indicate on the bottom of the chart the significance of each mark. For example, you might add, "Mr. Williams, would you please indicate on the bottom of the chart that the letter 'D' represents or equals the defendant?"

3. MODELS

The use of models is becoming increasingly common in courtrooms. The proponent may use a skeletal model or a model of a house or machine. Models present more logistical problems for trial courts than simple diagrams. For that reason, some judges are more reluctant to permit the use of models. Indeed, in some jurisdictions, before resorting to a model, the proponent must affirmatively show that the witness needs the model to adequately explain his or her testimony.

The foundation for the use of a model should include the following elements:

1. The witness needs the visual aid to explain his or her testimony.
2. The aid depicts a certain scene or object.
3. The witness is familiar with the scene or object.

4. The witness explains the basis for his or her familiarity with the scene or object.
5. In the witness' opinion, the aid is a "true," "accurate," "good," or "fair" model of the scene or object.

The fact situation is a tort action for injuries. The plaintiff, Ms. Graham, suffered extensive bone damage. The next witness is Dr. Miller, a bone specialist. In general terms, Dr. Miller has already described the extensive nature of the bone damage.

P   Now, Doctor, in detail, WHAT are the injuries to Ms. Graham's bones? (1)

W   That question is really difficult to answer orally.

P   WHY? (1)

W   Well, in the first place, a large number of bones have been damaged. Secondly, it's sometimes difficult for me to explain the precise location of the bone. Finally, some of the damage is really to the way bones work and fit together. It's hard to put all that into words.

P   HOW could you explain the detailed injuries more effectively? (1)

W   It would be much better if I were permitted to use a skeletal model.

P   Your Honor, I request that this be marked plaintiff's exhibit number seven for identification.

J   It will be so marked.

P   Doctor, I now show you plaintiff's exhibit number seven for identification. WHAT is it? (2)

W   It's the sort of skeletal model I just mentioned.

P   HOW do you know that? (3), (4)

W   I'm not only a medical doctor; I'm a bone specialist. I've studied and used models such as this one for years. In fact, I've consulted with some of the art companies that manufacture these models.

P   HOW accurate is this skeletal model? (5)

W   It's quite good. It depicts the bone structure of a female of the approximate height and build of the plaintiff, Ms. Graham.

P   HOW helpful would this be to illustrate your testimony about the specific bone injuries? (1)

W   Very. I can point to the location of the bones, show you what they look like, and demonstrate how they're supposed to fit together with adjacent bones.

In some jurisdictions, models such as the one in the hypothetical are used without even marking them for identification. That practice makes it difficult for the appellate court to understand the record of trial. Perhaps the prevailing practice modernly is at least to mark the model as an exhibit for identification. However, in many jurisdictions, if an exhibit is merely marked for identification, it cannot be sent to the jury for use during deliberation. A few jurisdictions require the proponent to formally offer the model into evidence. In such a jurisdiction, the sample foundation would continue:

P   Your Honor, I now offer plaintiff's exhibit number seven for identification into evidence as plaintiff's exhibit number seven.

J   It will be received.
P   I now request permission to use the model to illustrate Dr. Miller's
     testimony.
J   Permission granted.

One final point is that the proponent does not always have to leave
the model in the court's possession after trial. In most jurisdictions, the
trial judge has discretion to permit the proponent to later substitute a
photograph or written description for insertion in the record of trial. If
the proponent wishes to do so, after the judge receives the exhibit into
evidence, the proponent should state: "I request permission to later
substitute a photograph of this model into the record of trial."

H. THE IDENTIFICATION OF REAL OR ORIGINAL PHYSICAL EVIDENCE

1. THE DOCTRINE

Section G of this chapter discussed demonstrative physical evidence.
Demonstrative evidence has two characteristics. On the one hand, it
illustrates or demonstrates the witness' testimony. On the other hand,
the object itself has no historical connection with the facts of the case;
it is not the actual pistol or knife used in the crime.

In contrast, real or original physical evidence has a connection with
the case. For example, the prosecutor may contend that it is the very
pistol or knife used. If the prosecutor makes that claim, the prosecutor
must authenticate the evidence by proving the claim. The prosecutor
must demonstrate the object's connection with the case. The process of
demonstrating this historical connection is usually termed the identification of the physical evidence. There are two recognized methods of
identifying physical evidence.

The first method is ready identifiability. If the article has a unique,
one-of-a-kind characteristic, the characteristic makes the article readily identifiable. The foundation is complete so long as the witness testifies that he or she previously observed the characteristic and presently
recalls the characteristic. An identification resting on that characteristic is sufficient. The foundation is sufficient to establish the exhibit's
identity as the object the witness previously observed. Federal Rule of
Evidence 901(b)(4) expressly permits identification of an object by its
"distinctive characteristics."

Suppose, however, that one of the elements of the foundation for
ready identifiability is missing; the object lacks a unique characteristic, the witness did not observe the characteristic on the previous occasion, or the witness cannot presently recall the characteristic. Or suppose that the proponent is interested in the object's condition rather
than its simple identity; the proponent might want a laboratory techni-

cian to testify about a chemical analysis of the object. In these circumstances, the proponent must establish a chain of custody. Chain of custody is the second method of identifying physical evidence.

Who are the links in the chain? The links are people who actually handle the object. Other persons who merely have access to the object are not considered links. Thus, even if two other laboratory technicians know the combination to the safe where the witness kept the object, the other technicians are not deemed links. The only link would be the technician who physically handled the object. The proponent would have to account for that technician's handling of the object.

How does the proponent account for handling? The proponent must show the link's initial receipt of the object, ultimate disposition of the object (retention, destruction, or transfer), and safekeeping of the object between receipt and disposition. The witness can keep the object in a locked safe, a secure evidence container, or any other place where substitution and tampering are unlikely.

Ideally, the proponent should call each link to the stand in the sequence in which they handled the object. The proponent would mark the object for identification and hand it to the first link for identification. The proponent would also hand it to every intermediate link for identification. However, the proponent does not formally tender the exhibit into evidence until the last link's testimony; at that point, the foundation is complete.

2. ELEMENTS OF THE FOUNDATION

The foundation for ready identifiability is very short:
1. The object has a unique characteristic.
2. The witness observed the characteristic on a previous occasion.
3. The witness identifies the exhibit as the object.
4. The witness rests the identification on his or her present recognition of the characteristic.
5. As best he or she can tell, the exhibit is in the same condition as it was when he or she initially received the object.

The foundation for chain of custody must be laid during the testimony of each link in the chain:
1. The witness initially received the object at a certain time and place.
2. The witness safeguarded the object; the witness testifies to circumstances making it unlikely that substitution or tampering occurred.
3. The witness ultimately disposed of the object (retention, destruction, or transfer to another person).
4. As best he or she can tell, the exhibit is the object he or she previously handled.

5. As best he or she can tell, the exhibit is in the same condition as it was when he or she initially received the object.

3. SAMPLE FOUNDATIONS

The fact situation for the ready identifiability foundation is a civil tort case. The complaint alleges that the defendant assaulted the plaintiff with a knife. The witness is a police officer who investigated the complaint. The proponent is the plaintiff. The officer has just testified that he reported to the scene and began inspecting the scene.

P   WHAT did you do during this inspection?
W   I was looking for any evidence.
P   WHAT, if anything, did you find?
W   I found a knife answering the description the plaintiff, Ms. Brown, gave me.
P   WHERE did you find it?
W   Right at the corner of the building where the alleged assault occurred.
P   WHAT did you do with the knife? (1)
W   I followed standing operating procedure.
P   WHAT is that procedure? (1)
W   I marked it for identification.
P   HOW did you do that? (1)
W   In the case of a relatively inexpensive item such as this one, I tagged it and scratched my initials and the date onto the wooden handle.
P   WHEN did you do this? (2)
W   As soon as I found it.
P   HOW much time passed between your discovery of this knife and your marking it? (2)
W   No more than a couple of minutes.
P   Your Honor, I request that this be marked plaintiff's exhibit number two for identification.
J   It will be so marked.
P   Please let the record reflect that I am showing the exhibit to the opposing counsel.
J   It will so reflect.
P   I request permission to approach the witness.
J   Permission granted.
P   I now hand you plaintiff's exhibit number two for identification. WHAT is it? (3)
W   It's the knife I found.
P   HOW can you recognize it? (4)
W   As I testified, I marked my initials and the date on the handle. They're right there.
P   WHAT condition is the exhibit in? (5)
W   It's in good condition.
P   HOW has it changed since you found it at the scene? (5)
W   It doesn't appear to have changed at all. It seems to be in the same condition.
P   Your Honor, I now offer plaintiff's exhibit number two for identification into evidence as plaintiff's exhibit number two.
J   It will be received.

P I request permission to hand the exhibit to the jurors for their inspection.

J Permission granted.

The fact situation for the chain of custody foundation is a criminal assault prosecution. The government alleges that the defendant, Mr. Morris, used his feet to kick and beat the victim, Mr. Navin. The government wants to show that the blood grouping of stains on the defendant's shoes matches the victim's blood grouping. As a predicate for that scientific analysis, the government must establish a chain of custody for the shoes; the government must demonstrate that the shoes were in the same condition at the time of analysis as they were when they were seized from the defendant. The seizing police officer, Officer Stevens, has already testified. He testified that he seized the shoes from Morris, kept them safe, and then delivered them to the laboratory technician, Ms. Quinn. Ms. Quinn is the next witness. The prosecutor is the proponent. The shoes have been marked prosecution exhibit four for identification.

P WHAT is your occupation?

W I am a laboratory technician with the Baltimore Police Department.

P HOW long have you worked for the Baltimore Police Department?

W About six years.

P WHAT are your duties?

W I specialize in blood and stain analysis.

P HOW long have you done that sort of work?

W About six years — ever since I graduated.

P WHAT school did you graduate from?

W Oregon State.

P WHAT was your major area of study?

W Chemistry, especially organic chemistry.

P Ms. Quinn, WHERE were you on the afternoon of November 12, 1988? (1)

W I was on duty at work at the laboratory.

P WHAT, if anything, happened that afternoon? (1)

W Officer Stevens delivered some shoes to me for analysis.

P WHO is Officer Stevens? (1)

W He was the last witness on this case.

P HOW do you know that? (1)

W I was sitting in the spectators' section over there when he testified.

P WHAT did you do with the shoes when he delivered them to you? (2)

W I followed standard practice. The very first thing I did was initial the evidence slip that's attached.

P WHAT is an evidence slip? (2)

W It's a chain of custody receipt. You sign off on it when you receive the attached object.

P WHAT did you do with the shoes after you initialed the evidence slip? (2)

W I immediately conducted an analysis of some stains on the soles of the shoes.

P   HOW much time passed between his delivery of the shoes and your analysis? (2)

W   Only about five minutes. I wasn't very busy when he walked in.

P   WHAT did you do after you conducted the analysis? (2)

W   I put the shoes in my evidence locker.

P   WHERE is this locker? (2)

W   It's in my work area in the lab.

P   HOW secure is this locker? (2)

W   Well, I have a combination lock on it.

P   WHO knows the combination? (2)

W   Just me and the head of the Fluids section of the lab, Mr. Guinn.

P   WHAT happened to the shoes after you put them in the locker? (3)

W   They've just been sitting there until today.

P   HOW often have you opened the locker between the time you placed the shoes there and today? (2)

W   Probably hundreds of times.

P   WHAT procedure do you use to open the locker? (2)

W   I use the combination to open it, remove what I want, and immediately close and lock it.

P   HOW have the shoes changed since you placed them in the locker? (2)

W   They're certainly a little dustier than before, but otherwise they haven't changed.

P   Your Honor, I request permission to approach the witness.

J   Permission granted.

P   I now hand you prosecution exhibit four for identification. WHAT is it? (4)

W   They seem to be the shoes I analyzed.

P   HOW can you recognize them? (4)

W   I notice my handwriting on the attached slip, and I recognize their general appearance, including the scrapes and the stains on the soles.

P   HOW did the shoes get out of the evidence locker? (4)

W   I removed them just before coming here to testify.

P   WHO has had possession of them since you removed them from the locker? (4)

W   I had possession until I got here.

P   WHAT did you do then? (4)

W   I placed them on your counsel table so you could use them.

P   WHAT did you do then? (4)

W   I sat in the spectators' area and observed the trial and kept an eye on the shoes.

P   HOW often did you leave the room? (4)

W   I didn't. I've been here this entire morning, watching the trial and the shoes.

P   WHAT condition are the shoes in? (5)

W   They seem to be in the same condition as when Officer Stevens delivered them to me.

P   WHAT condition are the stains in? (5)

W   They're a bit changed because I had to scrape some off to analyze the stains. Otherwise they're in the same condition.

P   Your Honor, I now offer prosecution exhibit number four for identification into evidence as prosecution exhibit number four.

J   They will be received.

P   I request permission to hand the exhibit to the jurors for their inspection.
J   Request granted. *(The jurors inspect the shoes.)*
P   Now, Ms. Quinn, I'd like to ask you a few questions about your analysis of the shoes.

I. THE VERIFICATION OF PHOTOGRAPHS

1. STILL PHOTOGRAPHS

Like other articles, still photographs must be authenticated or verified. In the past, some courts insisted that the photographer appear as the sponsoring witness. Modernly, the prevailing view is that any person familiar with the scene or object depicted may verify the photograph.

The foundational elements are as follows:
1. The witness is familiar with the object or scene.
2. The witness explains the basis for his or her familiarity with the object or scene.
3. The witness recognizes the object or scene in the photograph.
4. The photograph is a "fair," "accurate," "true," or "good" depiction of the object or scene at the relevant time.

Our fact situation is a civil tort action arising from a collision. The collision occurred at the intersection of A and Third Streets. The plaintiff calls a witness to verify a photograph of the intersection. The witness has already identified himself as Mr. Donald Adams. The accident occurred in 1988.

P   WHERE do you work? (2)
W   Downtown.
P   WHERE downtown? (2)
W   I'm a teller at the First National Bank on Third Street.
P   WHERE is the bank located on Third Street? (2)
W   I think it's the 400 block. The bank is between A and B Streets.
P   HOW long have you worked there? (2)
W   A good seven years.
P   Your Honor, I request that this be marked plaintiff's exhibit number three for identification.
J   The record will so reflect.
P   I request permission to approach the witness.
J   Permission granted.
P   I now hand you plaintiff's exhibit number three for identification. WHAT is it? (3)
W   It's a photograph of the intersection of A and Third Streets.
P   HOW can you recognize it? (2)
W   As I said, I've worked in that area for years.
P   HOW often have you passed that intersection? (2)
W   I couldn't give you a figure. I've been there hundreds of times.
P   WHAT perspective or viewpoint does this photograph show? (3)
W   Let's see. Third Street runs north-south. A Street runs east-west.

P   WHICH corner are you on? (3)
W   You're on the southwest corner.
P   In WHICH direction are you facing? (3)
W   You're facing north; you're looking up Third Street.
P   HOW accurate is this photograph? (4)
W   Very. It's a good, true depiction as far as I can tell.
P   HOW accurately does it show the intersection as it was in 1988? (4)
W   Well. It's a good photograph for that purpose. I worked downtown then,
     and I think it shows roughly how the intersection looked then.
P   HOW has the intersection changed since 1988? (4)
W   Some of the signs have changed; businesses come and go. However, the
     intersection itself really hasn't changed. As best I can recall, it's the
     same size, the street markings are the same, and traffic flows the same
     way.
P   Your Honor, I now offer plaintiff's exhibit number three for identifica-
     tion into evidence as plaintiff's exhibit number three.
J   It will be received.
P   I request permission to hand the exhibit to the jurors for their inspec-
     tion.
J   Permission granted.

2. MOTION PICTURES AND VIDEOTAPES

Like computers and tape recorders, motion pictures raise scientific
evidence issues. Again, the validity of the underlying theory and the
general reliability of motion picture and videotape cameras are now so
well accepted that the judge will judicially notice those two elements of
the foundation. The Evidence law governing motion pictures parallels
the law governing tape recorders in another respect; as in the case of
tape recorders, the courts were initially very conservative in their
treatment of motion pictures. The traditional view was that because of
the possibility of distortion, the proponent had to lay a very strict
foundation: the operator's qualifications, the good working condition of
the equipment, the custody of the film, identification of the persons or
objects depicted in the film, and testimony by someone present that the
film accurately depicts the activity filmed. The law governing the admission of motion pictures has been liberalized in recent years. The
testimony of any person present when the activity occurred is sufficient to authenticate the film; and even without the testimony of such
a person, the remaining foundation elements have sufficient probative
value to verify the film.

A complete, traditional foundation includes these elements:
1. The operator was qualified to take a motion picture film.
2. The operator filmed a certain activity.
3. The operator used certain equipment to film the activity. Some
   trial attorneys prefer to present very detailed testimony about the
   equipment, especially the lens used. As the sample foundation
   indicates, a general description of the equipment is sufficient.
4. The equipment was in good working order.

5. The operator used proper procedures to film the activity. Here again some attorneys like to offer detailed testimony. Their foundation covers such technical matters as the speed of the film and the lens aperture. General testimony is satisfactory.
6. The operator accounts for the custody of the film and the developed movie.
7. The developed movie was a good reproduction of the activity.
8. The operator recognizes the exhibit as the film he or she took.
9. The film is still a good depiction of the activity.

The fact situation is a civil tort action. The plaintiff's theory is that the defendant, Polecat Motors, defectively designed the 1986 Sport Sprint. The plaintiff wants to introduce films depicting impact experiments with a 1986 Sport Sprint. The plaintiff calls the photographer who filmed the experiment. The photographer has already identified himself as Mr. Blair McIntosh.

P   WHAT is your occupation? (1)
W   I am a professional photographer.
P   WHERE do you work? (1)
W   I have my own studio at 1333 Front Street downtown.
P   HOW long have you been a professional photographer? (1)
W   For over 12 years now.
P   HOW did you become a professional photographer? (1)
W   I started working for another professional photographer in Denver right after graduation from high school.
P   WHAT training have you had as a photographer? (1)
W   I've taken ten college level courses in photography and attended numerous seminars and training conferences.
P   HOW long have you had your own professional photography business? (1)
W   The last seven years.
P   Mr. McIntosh, WHERE were you on the morning of August 17th of this year? (2)
W   I was at Abbott Laboratories on C Street here in Fort Collins.
P   WHY did you go there? (2)
W   You asked me to go there to film some experiments.
P   WHAT experiments? (2)
W   It was an impact experiment with a 1986 Polecat Sport Sprint.
P   WHAT did you do when you arrived at Abbott Laboratories? (2)
W   I carried out my assignment. I introduced myself to the personnel conducting the experiment and proceeded to film their experiment.
P   WHAT equipment did you use? (3)
W   I used a Kodak, ten millimeter motion picture camera and Kodak film and a standard Kodak lens.
P   HOW widely is this equipment used? (3)
W   Lots of professional photographers, especially television news photographers, use the very same set of equipment. It's a very reliable set.
P   WHAT condition was the equipment in when you filmed the experiment? (4)
W   Good, operating condition.
P   HOW do you know that? (4)

W   I didn't have any mechanical difficulty with the camera or lens during the filming, and I had just given my equipment complete maintenance a week before.

P   HOW did you learn to maintain this equipment? (4)

W   I attended a maintenance seminar sponsored by Kodak.

P   WHAT condition was the film in? (4)

W   It was brand new. I had to break the wrapper to take it out of the box.

P   HOW did you film the experiment? (5)

W   I checked my light meter to make certain that I had the right opening on the lens. Then I set the camera upon the tripod and focused until I had a clear image in my viewer.

P   HOW long did it take you to film the experiment? (6)

W   Only about twenty minutes.

P   WHAT did you do after you filmed the experiment? (6)

W   I disassembled my equipment and went back to my studio.

P   WHAT did you do after you arrived there? (6)

W   It was still early in the day, and I didn't have much else to do so I developed the film immediately.

P   WHERE did you do that? (6)

W   In my own dark room.

P   HOW did you learn to develop film? (6)

W   My old boss taught me, and I studied developing techniques in many of my college photography courses.

P   WHAT did you do after you developed the film? (7)

W   I set up a projector and screen to view the film. I then viewed the entire film.

P   WHAT was the quality of the film? (7)

W   It was excellent. As far as I could tell, it was a fine depiction of the experiment.

P   WHAT did you do after you viewed the film? (6)

W   I put it in my files.

P   WHERE did you keep the film after that? (6)

W   With one exception, it's been in my files the whole time.

P   WHAT was that exception? (6)

W   You and I viewed the film two weeks ago.

P   WHO was present during the viewing? (6)

W   Just the two of us. And the other attorney over there.

P   WHERE were you during the viewing? (6)

W   I was present during this viewing.

P   WHAT did you do with the film after the viewing? (6)

W   I put it back in my files.

P   Your Honor, I request that this be marked plaintiff's exhibit number five for identification.

J   It will be so marked.

P   Please let the record reflect that I am showing the exhibit to the opposing counsel.

J   The record will so reflect.

P   I request permission to approach the witness.

J   Permission granted.

P   Mr. McIntosh, I now hand you plaintiff's exhibit number five for identification. WHAT is it? (8)

W   It's the motion picture of the experiment.

P   HOW do you recognize it? (8)

W   I recognize my handwriting on the label on the reel.

P   HOW did the film get from your files to the courtroom today? (6)

W   I took it out of my files this morning and brought it here myself.

P   WHAT did you do with it after you arrived here? (9)

W   You, the other attorney, the judge, and I viewed the film in the judge's chambers.

P   WHAT condition was the film in? (9)

W   Fine. It's in the same excellent condition it was in after I developed it.

P   WHAT happened to the film after we viewed it in the judge's chambers? (6)

W   I kept it in my possession.

P   WHEN did you surrender possession of it? (6)

W   I put it on your counsel table as I walked up to the witness stand.

P   Your Honor, I now offer plaintiff's exhibit number five for identification into evidence as plaintiff's exhibit number five.

J   It will be received.

P   I request permission to have the bailiff show the motion picture to the jurors.

J   Permission granted.

When the proponent offers a videotape, the proponent must not only lay the normal foundation for a motion picture, he or she must also authenticate the noises, especially voices, heard on the videotape. If the proponent's sponsoring witness was present at the activity shown on the videotape, that witness can ordinarily identify the noises heard on the tape. If for some reason that witness cannot identify the voices heard on the tape, the proponent could call another witness familiar with those voices to lay that element of the foundation.

3. X-RAYS

X-rays are also photographs. In most cases, the counsel stipulate to the authenticity of X-rays in the case. However, occasionally, the proponent will have to authenticate the X-ray. The authentication of an X-ray is a rather peculiar process. No one can testify that he or she saw what the X-ray depicts and verify the X-ray on that theory.

Because of that peculiarity, the proponent must resort to some other authentication technique. Some judges treat X-rays as business records of the hospital; they accept authentication by the testimony of the hospital's X-ray librarian that he or she removed the X-ray from the right file. Other judges view X-ray evidence as presenting both scientific and physical evidence problems; the proponent must show the operator's qualifications, the working order of the X-ray, and a chain of custody for the X-ray cassette. In many hospitals, however, the X-ray technician uses an identification assembly during the X-ray; the assembly is composed of lead letters and numbers and casts a shadow of the letters and numbers on the cassette. In effect, the letters and numbers make the cassette a readily identifiable article.

If the hospital follows the customary practice of using an identification assembly, the complete foundation for the X-ray would include the following elements:

1. The operator was a qualified X-ray technician.
2. The operator filmed a certain part of a person's body at a certain time and place.
3. The operator used certain equipment.
4. The equipment was in good working condition.
5. The operator used the correct procedures.
6. The operator used an identification assembly on the cassette.
7. The operator accounts for the cassette's custody between filming and trial; the chain of custody includes proof of the proper development of the cassette.
8. The witness recognizes the exhibit as the cassette.

The fact situation is a civil action. The plaintiff contends that as a result of the tort, she suffered severe personal injuries, including bone fractures. The plaintiff wishes to introduce an X-ray to depict some of the fractures. The plaintiff calls Mr. Paul Nesbitt. Mr. Nesbitt has already identified himself.

P   WHAT is your occupation? (1)
W   I am an X-ray technician at Sharp Hospital downtown.
P   HOW long have you worked as an X-ray technician? (1)
W   For seven years.
P   WHAT is your formal education? (1)
W   I have a degree from Cornell.
P   WHAT was your major field of study? (1)
W   Science.
P   WHAT other training have you had as an X-ray technician? (1)
W   I attended a three month course at U.C.L.A. Medical School, and I've also attended numerous seminars on the subject.
P   WHERE were you on the afternoon of July 7th, 1988? (2)
W   As I recall, I was on duty at the X-ray lab.
P   WHAT, if anything, happened that afternoon? (2)
W   Doctor Bertrand asked me to take the plaintiff's X-ray, and the plaintiff stopped by for the X-ray.
P   WHO is the plaintiff? (2)
W   The woman at the table to the right over there.
P   WHAT is she wearing? (2)
W   The green dress and yellow scarf.
P   Your Honor, please let the record reflect that the witness has identified the plaintiff, Ms. Wohlmuth. (2)
J   It will so reflect.
P   WHAT did you do when Ms. Wohlmuth arrived at the lab? (3)
W   I showed her how to position herself on the table to enable me to get a good X-ray of her right leg.
P   WHAT happened then? (3)
W   Then I set up the equipment.
P   WHAT equipment? (3)
W   The X-ray machine and the cassette with identification assembly.

P   WHAT is the X-ray machine? (3)
W   It's the camera that you use to take an X-ray.
P   WHAT is the cassette? (3)
W   It's the film. The X-rays make the impression on the cassette.
P   WHAT is the identification assembly? (6)
W   It consists of lead numbers and letters. The lead casts shadows on the cassette; you sort of outline the letters and numbers.
P   WHAT are these letters and numbers? (6)
W   The practice varies from hospital to hospital. Some hospitals use the numbers for the patient's file number; each patient has a different file number. We usually spell out the patient's name if it's short and then list the date of the X-ray in numbers.
P   WHAT condition was the equipment in? (4)
W   It was in fine condition.
P   HOW do you know that? (4)
W   I had checked it myself the day before. I always check it Monday morning. I took this X-ray on a Tuesday.
P   HOW did you learn to check the equipment? (4)
W   That was one of the subjects we studied at U.C.L.A.
P   HOW did you take the plaintiff's X-ray? (5)
W   After I set up the equipment, I told the plaintiff to position her leg. Then I stepped behind the lead and leaded glass. I viewed the plaintiff during the X-ray. I adjusted the amperage and voltage settings, and then I turned the machine on to make the exposure.
P   WHAT did you do then? (5)
W   I re-entered the room and removed the cassette.
P   WHAT did you do with the cassette? (7)
W   I put it in a corner in the room and developed it that afternoon.
P   WHAT happened to the cassette between the filming and development? (7)
W   As far as I know, nothing. It was just there in the room.
P   WHO handled the cassette between the filming and development? (7)
W   As far as I can tell, I was the only one.
P   HOW did you develop the X-ray? (7)
W   I went into the dark room, removed the film from the cassette, and then put it through the developing process.
P   HOW did you learn to develop X-rays? (7)
W   That was another subject we studied in detail at U.C.L.A.
P   WHAT did you do with the film after you developed it? (7)
W   I brought it down to our X-ray records library on the second floor.
P   WHAT happened then? (7)
W   I gave it to the clerk and asked her to file it under the plaintiff's name.
P   Your Honor, I request that this be marked plaintiff's exhibit number four for identification.
J   It will be so marked.
P   Please let the record reflect that I am showing the exhibit to the opposing counsel.
J   It will so reflect.
P   I request permission to approach the witness.
J   Permission granted.
P   Mr. Nesbitt, I now hand you plaintiff's exhibit number four for identification. WHAT is it? (8)
W   It's the X-ray I took of the plaintiff's leg.

P   HOW can you recognize it? (8)

W   I recognize this type of film, and I see the plaintiff's name and the date just as I set them up in the identification assembly. I also recognize the general appearance of the bones depicted.

P   HOW did the film get to court today? (7)

W   I went to the file for that month and looked for the X-ray with the plaintiff's name and the date.

P   HOW many were there? (7)

W   Only the one I took.

P   HOW many times have you used that filing system in the past? (7)

W   Hundreds.

P   WHO taught you how to use the system? (7)

W   The X-ray records librarian herself, Doctor Riley.

P   Your Honor, I now offer plaintiff's exhibit number four for identification into evidence as plaintiff's exhibit number four.

J   It will be received.

The proponent will use the X-ray later during a doctor's testimony. The doctor will testify about the extent of injury and use the X-ray to illustrate the injuries.

J. THE VALIDATION OF SCIENTIFIC EVIDENCE

1. THE DOCTRINE

At first glance, the validation of scientific evidence appears to be a simple problem of authentication: The proponent need only present sufficient evidence to support a rational jury finding that the underlying theory is valid and the instrument is reliable. However, the courts have long been suspicious of scientific evidence. In the first place, the courts have sometimes been skeptical of scientists' claims of the virtual infallibility of scientific techniques. Secondly, the courts fear that scientific evidence will overwhelm the jury; the jurors will be so impressed by the scientific evidence that the scientist witness will effectively usurp the jurors' fact-finding duties. The jurors will uncritically accept the scientist's testimony.

For these reasons, most courts require an extraordinary foundation for scientific evidence. *Frye v. United States,* 293 F. 1013 (D.C. Cir. 1923), holds that the proponent must show that the theory and instrument have been generally accepted within the relevant scientific circles. Absent that showing, the scientific evidence is inadmissible. Roughly a third of the state and federal courts have rejected *Frye* and require only that the proponent present an expert vouching for the experimental verification of the theory and instrument. However, notwithstanding those jurisdictions, the prevailing view is still that the proponent must demonstrate general acceptance.

The foundation will often require two witnesses. If the theory and instrument are very generally accepted, the judge will judicially notice those elements of the foundation upon a proper timely request by counsel. However, when judicial notice is inapplicable, the proponent will probably have to call an expert with heavy academic credentials to lay those elements of the foundation. The proponent will then call a technician as the second witness to lay the balance of the foundation.

2. ELEMENTS OF THE FOUNDATION

1. Witness #1 is qualified to establish the theory's validity and the instrument's reliability.
2. The underlying theory is valid.
3. The underlying theory is generally accepted as valid.
4. The instrument is reliable.
5. The instrument is generally accepted as reliable.
6. Witness #2 is qualified to conduct and interpret the test results.
7. The instrument witness #2 used was in good working condition.
8. The witness used the instrument in the test.
9. The witness used the proper procedures.
10. The witness states the test results.

3. SAMPLE FOUNDATION

The fact situation is a speeding prosecution. The government charges that the defendant, Mr. Berton, was going 45 miles an hour on a street posted for 30 miles an hour. Officer Jones used a radar speedmeter to clock the defendant. Most jurisdictions would judicially notice the validity of the underlying theory and the reliability of speedmeters; but for illustrative purposes, the prosecutor will call a witness to lay those elements of the foundation.

The prosecutor first calls Professor Jerold Harter. The professor first identified himself.

P   WHAT is your occupation? (1)
W   I teach at Ohio State University.
P   WHAT do you teach? (1)
W   I teach physics and electronics.
P   WHAT is your formal education? (1)
W   I have a B.S. from Ohio State and both a Master's and a Doctorate from University of California, Davis.
P   WHAT was your major area of study? (1)
W   My specialty has been radar and electronics.
P   HOW long have you been teaching? (1)
W   For approximately 10 years.
P   WHAT, if anything, have you published? (1)
W   I've published roughly twenty articles, most of them dealing with radar and electronics.
P   Professor, WHAT is the Doppler Shift principle? (2)
W   It's a theory about beams of microwaves. If a beam bounces off an approaching object, the frequency of the beam changes; the change is

an increase, and it is proportional to the speed of the approaching object.

P   WHAT would be a simple example of the operation of this principle? (2)

W   Well, suppose that you're standing at a train station. A train is coming, and it's blowing its whistle. When the train is approaching you, the pitch of the whistle sounds higher. As soon as the train passes you and begins receding, the pitch sounds lower. The whistle, of course, hasn't changed. It's the Doppler Shift principle which explains why it sounds as if the whistle is changing.

P   WHAT experiments, if any, have been conducted to verify this theory? (2)

W   You couldn't count the number. The theory is one of the most fundamental principles in the field.

P   HOW widely is the principle accepted? (3)

W   It's regarded as a truism, a basic principle. Everyone in the field knows about and accepts the principle.

P   Now, professor, WHAT is a radar speedmeter? (4)

W   It's a device for measuring the speed of cars.

P   WHAT are the components of a radar speedmeter? (4)

W   It has a component for transmitting a beam of microwaves and another component for receiving.

P   HOW does the speedmeter work? (4)

W   For example, the transmitter sends a beam toward an approaching vehicle. The beam strikes the vehicle, shifts, and then bounces back to the receiver. The receiver measures the change in frequency, and the speedmeter then reads out the speed of the approaching vehicle.

P   WHAT experiments, if any, have been conducted to test the reliability of the speedmeter? (4)

W   There have been numerous experiments, particularly some at Northwestern and the University of North Carolina.

P   WHAT has been the outcome of these experiments? (4)

W   If the instrument is in good condition and the operator is qualified, the instrument will give you a very reliable speed estimate.

P   HOW widely is the radar speedmeter accepted? (5)

W   It's used extensively, and its reliability is almost universally accepted.

The second witness will be the officer who used a radar speedmeter to clock the defendant. The officer has already testified that he arrived at the scene and set up his equipment.

P   WHAT equipment were you using? (8)

W   A General Electric radar speedmeter.

P   WHAT training, if any, have you had in using a speedmeter? (6)

W   I spent a week studying the speedmeter at the Police Academy.

P   HOW did you study the speedmeter? (6)

W   First, we had several lectures on the speedmeter and its operation. Then we saw demonstrations of its use. Finally, we participated in exercises where we used the speedmeter and more experienced officers doublechecked us.

P   HOW many times have you used the speedmeter? (6)

W   Hundreds of times.

P   HOW long have you used a speedmeter? (6)

W I've been assigned to Traffic for three years, and you use the speedmeter almost daily in Traffic detail.

P WHAT did you do after you arrived at the scene? (8)

W I checked to ensure that the speedmeter was in working order.

P WHAT condition was the speedmeter in? (7)

W Good, operational condition.

P HOW do you know that? (7)

W I used a tuning fork test.

P WHAT is the tuning fork test? (7)

W The manufacturer supplies you with several tuning forks. I have 30, 45 and 60 mile an hour forks. You set them off, and the speedmeter is supposed to register those speeds.

P HOW did you conduct the test on this occasion? (7)

W I used all three forks, and the machine checked out all three times; it registered the right speed.

P WHAT did you do then? (9)

W I let the machine warm up and then aimed the transmitter down the road.

P WHAT happened after you aimed the transmitter? (8)

W I saw the defendant's car approaching.

P WHO is the defendant? (8)

W He's the fellow sitting at the table over there.

P HOW is he dressed? (8)

W He's wearing a blue suit and red tie.

P HOW long did you have to observe the defendant at the scene? (8)

W About three minutes. I saw him as he passed by, and then later, after we stopped him, I talked to him for several minutes.

P Your Honor, please let the record reflect that the witness has identified the defendant. (8)

J It will so reflect.

P WHAT did you do when you saw the defendant's car approaching? (8)

W I checked to ensure that the speedmeter was on, and then I clocked his car.

P WHAT does "clocked" mean? (10)

W It means that I measured his speed.

P WHAT was the clocking? (10)

W The speedmeter flashed a signal that his car was going 45 miles an hour.

Chapter 5

RULE 403 AND LEGAL RELEVANCE LIMITATIONS ON CREDIBILITY EVIDENCE

A. INTRODUCTION

The last chapter focuses on the probative value of evidence. To be admissible, evidence must have probative value in two senses. First, on its face, the evidence must be material; the evidence must have some logical connection with the material facts of consequence in the case. In the words of Federal Evidence Rule 401, the evidence must have some "tendency to make the existence of any fact that is of consequence to the determination of the action more probable or less probable than it would be without the evidence." Secondly, as we have seen, the evidence must have underlying probative value; the common law will not accept evidence at face value and stubbornly insists that the proponent authenticate his or her evidence. Rules 104(b) and 901-02 set out the authentication rules.

Even if the evidence is logically relevant in both senses, the trial judge may exclude the evidence on the ground that the evidence is "legally irrelevant." The expression, "legal relevance," is a rubric for excluding evidence on the theory that the probative dangers attending the evidence outweigh the evidence's probative value. Federal Evidence Rule 403 states the doctrine: "Although (logically) relevant, evidence may be excluded if its probative value is substantially outweighed by the danger of unfair prejudice, confusion of the issues, or misleading the jury, or by considerations of undue delay, waste of time, or needless presentation of cumulative evidence."

Underlying Rule 403 is a model of optimal jury behavior. Ideally, we want the jury to: use admitted items of evidence as proof of only the factual propositions the judge admits them to prove, ascribe the proper probative weight to each item of evidence, and concentrate on the historical issues in dispute in the case. Rule 403 empowers the judge to exclude technically relevant evidence which realistically poses a danger to this model. This model not only explains the general discretionary power conferred on the judge under Rule 403; the model also helps explicate many of the more specific doctrines set out in Articles IV and VI of the Federal Rules of Evidence.

To begin with, if the judge admits an item of evidence to legitimately prove one factual proposition, we do not want the jury to misuse the item as proof of another factual proposition in the case. This probative danger helps to explain the doctrine stated in Rule 411. Rule 411 limits the admissibility of evidence of a defendant's liability insurance. Evidence of liability insurance creates a grave danger of jury misuse of the testimony; once the jury learns of the existence of the insurance, they may be tempted to find the defendant liable even though the evidence of fault is weak. Evidence which realistically tempts the jury to decide the case on an improper basis is "prejudicial" within the meaning of that term in Rule 403.

Moreover, there may be a risk that the jury will overestimate the probative value of the evidence. Psychology studies tell us that on the one hand, laypersons tend to attach a great deal of weight to evidence of specific instances of a litigant's bad behavior. For instance, after learning of a defendant's criminal record, the jurors may form a simplistic notion of the defendant's character and reason that "if he did it once, he probably did it again." On the other hand, the studies tell us that a person's general character is a poor predictor of the person's conduct in a specific situation. In short, lay jurors could easily overvalue evidence of a party's bad character. That risk in part accounts for the restrictions on character evidence in Rule 404-05.

Finally, we want the jurors to concentrate on the historical facts and events in dispute under the pleadings. It is true that the jurors must also resolve incidental disputes over the witnesses' credibility. However, to the extent that the jurors become bogged down in resolving credibility contests, they may lose sight of their primary task, the resolution of the historical merits of the case. This risk accounts for many of the limitations on credibility evidence in Article VI.

As previously stated, these probative dangers both help to explain the specific rules in Articles IV and VI and factor into the general balancing test stated in Rule 403. Even when an item of evidence passes muster under the specific rules in Articles IV and VI, in most instances the judge has discretion to exclude the item if the judge concludes that the probative dangers substantially outweigh the probative value of the item. Note two features of Rule 403. To begin with, the rule is cast in the passive voice, suggesting that the opponent of the admission of the evidence has the burden of persuading the judge that the probative dangers outstrip the probative value. Moreover, the rule includes the adverb "substantially." The opponent must not only convince the judge that the dangers outweigh the probative value; the opponent must convince the judge that the dangers do so by a wide margin. Rule 403 thus reflects a marked bias in favor of the admission of logically relevant evidence.

B. THE STAGES OF CREDIBILITY ANALYSIS

If the trial judge rules that the prospective witness is competent, the bailiff or court reporter administers the oath to the witness. The witness' proponent immediately begins direct examination. As soon as the witness answers one question on direct examination, his or her credibility becomes an issue in the case.

The proponent naturally wants to build up the witness' believability or credibility in the jury's eyes. Conversely, the opponent wants to tear down that credibility. The opponent's attacks on the witness' credibility are termed impeachment. If the proponent attempts to build up the witness' credibility before any attempted impeachment, the proponent is said to be bolstering the witness' credibility. For example, the proponent might attempt to increase the witness' credibility during the direct examination before the opponent has had any opportunity to cross-examine the witness. If the proponent attempts to repair the witness' credibility after attempted impeachment, the proponent is said to be rehabilitating the witness' credibility. If the opponent attempted to impeach during cross-examination, the proponent could attempt to rehabilitate the witness during redirect.

Most of the Evidence law dealing with credibility focuses on impeachment. For that reason, most of the sections in this chapter deal with the various impeachment techniques. Some of the impeachment techniques may be used only during cross-examination of the witness to be impeached — intrinsic impeachment: the opponent may use the technique then, but the opponent must accept the witness' answer in the sense that the opponent may not present other evidence to contradict the witness' answer. Section E of this chapter deals with such a technique, proof that the witness has committed bad acts which have not resulted in a conviction.

Other impeachment techniques necessarily entail extrinsic evidence and cannot be used during cross-examination. Sections F, G, and H of this chapter are illustrative. Section F deals with proof that witness #1 has a character trait of untruthfulness. Use of this technique requires that the opponent present witness #2, a character witness, to testify to the bad character of witness #1. Section G deals with polygraph examination. Use of this technique requires that the opponent call a polygraph examiner to testify that a prior witness flunked an examination. Section H discusses specific contradiction. In this technique, the opposing attorney calls witness #2 to contradict facts asserted in witness #1's testimony.

The remaining impeachment techniques permit both cross-examination and extrinsic evidence. Sections I-L analyze these techniques: convictions, prior inconsistent statements, bias, and attacks on the witness' mental capacity.

As you review the credibility doctrines in this chapter, remember that the doctrines are largely explicable in terms of the model of jury behavior underlying Rule 403. All of the evidence in question is logically relevant to the witness' credibility, but the doctrines discussed in this chapter restrict the admissibility of credibility evidence in the hope that the jury will focus primarily on the historical merits of the case.

Part 1. Bolstering Witnesses Before Impeachment

C. PRIOR IDENTIFICATION

1. THE DOCTRINE

The general common-law rule is that the proponent may not bolster the witness' credibility before any attempted impeachment. The jurors' principal focus should be on the historical issues in the case rather than the witness' credibility. To ensure that the jurors maintain that focus, the common law excludes evidence of the witness' believability until the opponent has attacked the witness.

There are special exceptions to the rule. One exception is the prior identification doctrine. In many jurisdictions, if the witness has already made an in-court identification of a person such as the criminal defendant, the witness' proponent may prove that the witness made a pretrial identification of the same person. The prior identification is not admitted as substantive evidence that the prior identification was correct; rather, the proof is admitted for the limited purpose of increasing the witness' credibility. The fact that the witness identified the same person on a prior occasion tends to strengthen the inference of the witness' credibility; at least the witness is consistent. When the judge admits prior identification evidence on this theory, the opponent is entitled to a limiting instruction under Federal Rule 105. Upon the opponent's request, the judge must instruct the jury that the proof is not admitted as substantive evidence but only on a bolstering theory.

Some jurisdictions have taken a step beyond this view; they now permit the proponent to use the prior identification as substantive evidence that the person identified was the perpetrator or actor. Federal Rule of Evidence 801(d)(1)(C) now exempts prior identification evidence from the definition of hearsay. The effect of the exemption is to enable the proponent to use the evidence as substantive proof. On this theory, the opponent has no right to a limiting instruction. Some courts have construed 801(d)(1)(C) as applying even when the witness cannot make an in-court identification. The Supreme Court has held that a prior identification may be admitted as substantive evidence even when at trial the witness cannot explain the basis for the pretrial identification. *United States v. Owens*, 108 S. Ct. 838 (1988).

2. ELEMENTS OF THE FOUNDATION

The proponent must show that:
1. The witness has already made an in-court identification of the person.

2. The witness had a pretrial opportunity to observe the person.
3. The witness had an adequate opportunity to observe the person.
4. The pretrial encounter was conducted in a fair manner.
5. At the pretrial encounter, the witness identified the same person.

3. SAMPLE FOUNDATION

The fact situation is a tort action arising from a hit-and-run accident. The plaintiff calls a witness, Jane Morris. The witness is prepared to testify that the defendant was the driver of the hit-and-run car. She is also ready to testify that she identified the defendant at a lineup at the local police station shortly after the accident. The witness has already described the accident which occurred at noontime. The proponent is the plaintiff.

P   WHAT did the car do after it struck the plaintiff?
W   It sped away from the scene.
P   WHO was driving that car? (1)
W   The defendant.
P   WHERE is he sitting? (1)
W   At the end of the table over there to the right.
P   HOW is he dressed? (1)
W   He's wearing a blue suit, white shirt, and striped tie.
P   Your Honor, may the record reflect that the witness has identified the defendant, John Ursin? (1)
J   It will so reflect.
P   Ms. Morris, HOW many times have you seen the defendant? (2)
W   Three times.
P   WHAT were those occasions? (2)
W   Well, I saw him at the scene of the accident, today in court, and one other time.
P   WHAT was that other time? (2)
W   It was at a lineup at the police station on Delaware Street.
P   WHEN did this lineup occur? (2)
W   It was about 5:00 p.m. the afternoon of the accident.
P   WHERE did the police hold this lineup? (2)
W   It was on a stage in the big room off the entrance.
P   HOW was the lighting in the room? (3)
W   It was fine.
P   HOW close were you to the stage? (3)
W   I was only ten feet away.
P   HOW were you facing? (3)
W   I was facing straight ahead and looking at all the men in the lineup.
P   HOW long did the police permit you to observe the lineup? (3)
W   They gave me as much time as I wanted. I didn't need long.
P   HOW many men were in the lineup? (4)
W   There were six.
P   HOW were they dressed? (4)
W   They all were wearing dark clothes.
P   HOW tall were they? (4)
W   They were roughly the same height, five ten to six feet.
P   WHAT, if anything, did the police say about the men in the lineup? (4)

W   They didn't say anything. They just ushered me into the room and asked me if I recognized anyone.

P   WHAT did the men in the lineup do while they were on the stage? (4)

W   Nothing. They just stood there.

P   WHAT happened after the lineup? (5)

W   The police asked me if I recognized the driver of the car in the lineup.

P   WHAT did you say? (5)

W   I told them that I did.

P   WHOM did you identify at that lineup? (5)

W   The defendant, the same person I just pointed out in court.

O   Your Honor, at this time, I would request a limiting instruction under Rule 105.

J   Very well. Ladies and gentlemen of the jury, you've just heard the witness testify about her identification of the defendant at a pretrial lineup. You may not consider her testimony as proof that the identification was correct. You may consider the testimony only for the light it sheds on the witness' credibility. The witness has identified the same person on a previous occasion, and you should decide for yourselves whether that consistency affects credibility.

D. FRESH COMPLAINT

1. THE DOCTRINE

Another exception to the norm against bolstering is the fresh complaint doctrine. Most jurisdictions restrict the doctrine to sex offense cases; a few jurisdictions also recognize the doctrine in burglary and robbery cases. The underlying assumption is that the victim of this type of offense is likely to make an immediate report or complaint about the offense. The fact of a fresh complaint tends to strengthen the inference of the truthfulness of the complainant. Moreover, especially in sex offense cases, there is a crying need for credibility evidence; there are rarely eyewitnesses, and the trial usually becomes a swearing contest.

Under this theory, the courts usually restrict the evidence to proof that the victim made a complaint about a certain type of offense and identified a certain person as the perpetrator. The other details of the offense are inadmissible. As in the case of prior identification evidence, the opponent is entitled to a limiting instruction. The judge is admitting the proof as credibility evidence rather than as substantive proof that a certain person committed the offense. On the other hand, the fresh complaint may also qualify as an excited utterance. As Chapter 10 notes, excited utterances fall within an exception to the hearsay rule. If the fresh complaint qualifies as an excited utterance, all the details about the offense are admissible; and more importantly, the details are admissible as substantive evidence.

2. ELEMENTS OF THE FOUNDATION

The proponent must show that:

1. The victim made a complaint.

2. The victim made the complaint shortly after the offense.
3. The victim made the complaint to the authorities or the first person he or she encountered after the offense.
4. The report stated that the complainant was the victim of an offense.
5. The report identified the perpetrator of the offense.

3. SAMPLE FOUNDATION

The fact situation is a criminal prosecution for kidnapping and rape. The victim, Ms. McDonald, is on the stand on direct examination. She has already testified that the defendant abducted her, drove her to a remote cabin, raped her, and then left her tied in the cabin. The proponent is the prosecutor.

P   WHAT did you do after the defendant left?
W   I struggled to get free from the ropes. Fortunately, the knot was so loose that I got free.
P   WHAT did you do next?
W   I got out of the cabin and started running down the dirt road. I wanted to escape and get back to safety.
P   WHAT, if anything, happened while you were running down the road?
W   I ran into a fellow driving a jeep.
P   WHO was this person? (3)
W   He told me that his name was Jeff Seltzer.
P   Between the time you escaped from the cabin and the time you met Mr. Seltzer, HOW many people had you met? (3)
W   None. He was the very first person I met after escaping.
P   HOW much time elapsed between the rape and the time you met Mr. Seltzer? (2)
W   About an hour.
P   HOW much time elapsed between your escape from the cabin and the time you met Mr. Seltzer? (2)
W   Only about five minutes. I hadn't run very far before I met him.
P   WHAT, if anything, happened after you met Mr. Seltzer? (1)
W   I told him everything that had happened. Then he gave me a ride back to town and took me to the hospital.
P   Precisely WHAT did you tell him? (4)
W   I said I had just been raped at a cabin just up the road.
P   WHO did you say had raped you? (5)
W   I said it was the defendant, Henry Miles.
O   Your Honor, at this time I request a limiting instruction under Rule 105.
J   Very well. Ladies and gentlemen of the jury, you have just heard Ms. McDonald testify that she made a complaint to Mr. Seltzer shortly after the alleged offense. In this complaint, she said she had been raped and that the defendant was the rapist. You may not consider her testimony as proof that, in fact, a rape occurred or that the defendant was the rapist. I'm admitting the testimony only for whatever light it

sheds on Ms. McDonald's credibility. You must decide whether the fact that she made this complaint affects her credibility.

Part 2. Impeachment of Witnesses

E. BAD ACTS THAT HAVE NOT RESULTED IN A CONVICTION

1. THE DOCTRINE

Modernly, most jurisdictions permit the opponent to impeach the witness with proof that the witness has committed untruthful acts. The opponent may do so even if the acts have not resulted in the witness' conviction. Federal Rule of Evidence 608(b) (b) (1) states the prevailing view: "Specific instances of the conduct of a witness, for the purpose of attacking ... the witness' credibility, other than conviction of crime as provided in Rule 609, may not be proved by extrinsic evidence. They may, however, in the discretion of the court, if probative of ... untruthfulness, be inquired into on cross-examination of the witness ... concerning the witness' character for ... untruthfulness ...." The theory of logical relevance is simple: If the witness has been willing to commit untruthful and deceitful acts in the past, the witness may be willing to lie on the witness stand. Of course, the doctrine is limited to acts which reflect adversely on the witness' truthfulness.

As the Federal Rule indicates, the opponent is ordinarily restricted to cross-examination. On cross-examination the opponent may inquire whether the witness committed the act. However, the opponent must "accept" or "take" the answer. The opponent must take the answer in the sense that the opponent cannot use extrinsic evidence to contradict the answer. Thus, if witness #1, the witness to be impeached, denies committing the deceitful act, the opponent cannot call witness #2 to testify that he or she was an eyewitness to witness #1's act.

This restriction is a remnant of the broader, common-law collateral fact rule. The collateral fact rule announced that the impeaching attorney is limited to intrinsic impeachment when the impeaching fact relates only to the witness' credibility. An untruthful act may reflect adversely on the witness' credibility; but the argument runs that when the act has no relevance to the merits of the case, it would be an undue expenditure of time to allow the impeaching attorney to present extrinsic evidence. By banning the use of "extrinsic evidence," the first sentence of Rule 608(b) codifies this application of the collateral fact rule.

2. ELEMENTS OF THE FOUNDATION

The opponent must show:
1. When the witness committed the act.
2. Where the witness committed the act.

3. The nature of the act reflects adversely on the witness' credibility.

3. SAMPLE FOUNDATION

The fact situation is a contract action. The plaintiff alleges that the defendant corporation breached its contract to deliver a generator to the plaintiff. The plaintiff alleges that he entered into the contract with the defendant's president during a conversation in the president's office. The plaintiff calls Mr. Giles as a witness. Giles testifies that he is a friend of the plaintiff and accompanied the plaintiff to the defendant's president's office. Giles testifies that he overheard the conversation in which the parties formed the contract. Now the defendant has Giles on cross-examination. The defendant is the opponent.

O   Mr. Giles, ISN'T IT A FACT THAT on June 1st of this year, you applied for work with Acme Corporation downtown? (1)
W   Yes.
O   ISN'T IT TRUE THAT on that date, you had a job interview with Ms. Grant, the corporation's president at her office? (2)
W   Yes.
O   ISN'T IT CORRECT THAT during that interview, you told her that you had a Master's degree from Harvard Business School? (3)
W   Yes.
O   ISN'T IT A FACT THAT you don't have a Master's degree from that school? (3)
W   Yes. I have only an undergraduate degree from that school.

Suppose that Giles denied making the false statement about his credentials. Under this impeachment technique, the cross-examiner could not call Ms. Grant to prove the misrepresentation. Her testimony is a textbook illustration of the type of "extrinsic evidence" barred by Rule 608(b).

F. PROOF OF THE CHARACTER TRAIT OF UNTRUTHFULNESS

1. THE DOCTRINE

To impeach the witness, the opponent may prove that the witness has a character trait of untruthfulness. The opponent uses the proof of the character trait as circumstantial proof of conduct. The opponent reasons that if the witness has that character trait, the character trait increases the probability that the witness is lying — acting in conformity with the character trait.

Unlike the last impeachment technique, the technique is not limited to the cross-examination of the witness to be impeached. Quite to the contrary, the opponent usually resorts to extrinsic evidence. To impeach witness #1, the opponent calls witness #2 who testifies that witness #1 has a character trait of untruthfulness. The courts usually term witness #2 a character witness. In some jurisdictions, the character witness must restrict his or her testimony to reputation evidence; the character witness describes the witness' reputation for untruthfulness in the community. The majority view, however, is that opinion evidence is also admissible; the character witness may express his or her opinion of witness #1's truthfulness. Federal Rule of Evidence 405(a) commits the federal courts to the latter view.

2. ELEMENTS OF THE FOUNDATION

The foundation varies, depending upon whether the evidence is reputation or opinion. The reputation foundation includes these elements:
1. Witness #2 is a member of the same community (residential or social) as witness #1. Modernly, any large social group can qualify as a community. For instance, a church congregation or the student body of a school can constitute a community.
2. Witness #2 has resided there a substantial period of time.
3. Witness #1 has a reputation for untruthfulness in the community.
4. Witness #2 knows witness #1's reputation for untruthfulness.
5. Some jurisdictions permit witness #2 to add that given witness #1's reputation, witness #2 would not believe him or her under oath.

The opinion foundation includes the following elements:
1. Witness #2 is personally acquainted with witness #1.
2. Witness #2 knows witness #1 well enough to have formed an opinion of witness #1's truthfulness.
3. Witness #2 has an opinion of witness #1's untruthfulness.
4. Witness #2 has the opinion that witness #1 is an untruthful person.

Again, some courts permit witness #2 to opine whether, given that opinion, he or she would believe witness #1 under oath.

3. SAMPLE FOUNDATIONS

The following is a reputation foundation. The witness to be impeached is Mr. Harding:

P   WHO is Mr. Harding?
W   He's an acquaintance of mine.
P   WHEN is the last time you saw him?
W   Here in the courtroom. He testified for the other side a couple of hours ago.
P   WHERE does he live? (1)
W   Here in Atlanta.
P   HOW long has Mr. Harding lived in Atlanta? (2)
W   All his life, I think. I can remember him twenty years back.
P   HOW long have you lived here in Atlanta? (2)

W   All my life.
P   HOW many years have you lived here? (2)
W   Thirty-seven years.
P   Does Mr. Harding have a reputation for truthfulness or untruthfulness in Atlanta? (3)
W   Yes.
P   WHAT is that reputation? (4)
W   It's bad. He's known as an untruthful person.
P   Given Mr. Harding's reputation, would you believe him under oath? (5)
W   No.

The following is an opinion foundation:

P   WHO is Mr. Harding? (1)
W   He's an acquaintance of mine.
P   WHEN is the last time you saw him?
W   Here in the courtroom. He testified for the other side a few hours ago.
P   HOW did you come to know him? (2)
W   We've lived in the same neighborhood for a long time. I've had a lot of contact with him.
P   HOW many years have you known him? (2)
W   I'd say easily nine years.
P   In WHAT contexts have you known him? (2)
W   As I said, we've lived in the same neighborhood for a long time. I see him around the neighborhood a lot. In addition, we've worked at the same plant together for the last five years.
P   HOW often do you talk with him? (2)
W   Usually several times a week. We're always bumping into each other.
P   Do you have an opinion of his truthfulness? (3)
W   Yes.
P   WHAT is that opinion? (4)
W   In my opinion, he's an untruthful person.
P   Given that opinion, would you believe Mr. Harding under oath? (5)
W   No.

G. PROOF THAT THE WITNESS HAS FAILED A POLYGRAPH EXAMINATION

1. THE DOCTRINE

Like proof of the character trait of untruthfulness, this impeachment technique requires extrinsic evidence. The opponent calls a polygraph examiner, witness #2, to impeach witness #1. Many people believe that when used by an experienced, competent examiner, the polygraph can be an effective tool for detecting deception. The examiner's diagnosis of deception is logically relevant to show that when the witness gave a certain answer, the witness was lying.

The prevailing view today is still that polygraph evidence is inadmissible. However, in a minority of jurisdictions, the courts have gained faith in polygraphy. In these jurisdictions, polygraph evidence is admissible at least when the parties stipulate to the admissibility of the evidence.

Even in the jurisdictions permitting polygraph evidence without a stipulation, the proponent must lay a good foundation. Most jurisdictions hold that scientific evidence is admissible only if the underlying principle and the instrument are generally accepted in the relevant scientific circles. The general acceptance requirement is the famous *Frye* test. The very first reported polygraph case, *Frye v. United States,* 293 F. 1013 (D.C. Cir. 1923), held that the proponent of scientific evidence must not only present expert testimony vouching for the principle and instrument; the proponent must also show that as a matter of historical fact, the principle and instrument have gained general acceptance in the pertinent scientific circles. Section J of Chapter 4 discusses the *Frye* test.

2. ELEMENTS OF THE FOUNDATION

1. The witness has the qualifications to establish the underlying principle's validity and the instrument's reliability.
2. The witness has the qualifications to administer a polygraph examination.
3. The witness has the qualifications to interpret a polygraph test result.
4. The underlying principle of polygraphy is valid.
5. The underlying principle is generally accepted as valid.
6. The polygraph instrument is reliable.
7. The instrument is generally accepted as reliable.
8. The examiner tested the subject.
9. When the examiner tested the subject, the witness to be impeached, the instrument was in working order.
10. At the time, the examiner used certain procedures to conduct the test.
11. The procedures used were proper.
12. The subject had a certain result on the test.
13. The results of the test indicate that the subject was lying when he or she made a certain statement.

3. SAMPLE FOUNDATION

The fact situation is a paternity action. Ms. Gust sued Mr. Martin for child support. The witness is Mr. Bechtel, a polygraph examiner. Mr. Bechtel is prepared to testify that he examined Mr. Martin. Mr. Bechtel will testify that in his opinion, Mr. Martin was telling the truth when he denied having intercourse with Ms. Gust. The proponent is the defendant.

P   WHAT is your name?

W   Cleve Bechtel.
P   WHAT is your address?
W   1554 Skinker Boulevard in St. Louis.
P   WHAT is your occupation? (1), (2), (3)
W   I am a polygraph examiner. I have my own business.
P   WHAT is your educational background? (1)
W   I have a bachelor's degree in Psychology from Stanford.
P   WHAT formal training, if any, have you had in polygraphy? (2), (3)
W   I attended the Keeler Polygraph Institute in Chicago.
P   WHAT is that Institute? (2), (3)
W   It's one of the best known and best established polygraph schools in the world.
P   WHAT sort of training did you receive there? (2), (3)
W   First we had classroom instruction on the underlying principles of polygraph and the instrument, the polygraph. Then we had training in conducting and interpreting polygraph tests. We were given an opportunity to conduct and evaluate tests during the course.
P   WHAT experience have you had in the polygraph field? (2), (3)
W   After completing my training at Keeler, I worked as an apprentice for a year. I worked for a very experienced examiner. Then I started my own business. I've owned that business for the past twelve years.
P   During your career, HOW many polygraph examinations have you conducted? (2), (3)
W   Several thousand. Too many to keep count of.
P   HOW many times, if any, have you qualified as a polygraph expert in court? (2), (3)
W   About fifty times.
P   HOW many times in this state? (2), (3)
W   Ten times.
P   WHEN was the last time? (2), (3)
W   About six months ago.
P   WHAT is the underlying principle of polygraphy? (4)
W   The theory is that conscious deception causes certain physiological changes that the subject has little or no control over — blood pressure, pulse rate, breath, and galvanic skin response.
P   WHAT experiments, if any, have been conducted to verify the theory? (5)
W   Actually, scientists have been working in this area for decades. Almost all the studies document the theory.
P   HOW widely accepted is the theory? (5)
W   Most people familiar with the area — examiners, psychologists and psychiatrists — accept the theory.
P   WHAT is the polygraph itself? (6)
W   It's the instrument the examiner uses. It measures the psychological responses I mentioned. It records them on a graph called the polygram.
P   WHAT experiments, if any, have been conducted to test the reliability of the instrument? (7)
W   Again, there have been a large number of reported tests. Under typical laboratory conditions, the examiners reach accurate diagnoses in roughly 85% of the cases. In field conditions, the accuracy level often reaches the high ninety percents; in field conditions, there is real motivation to deceive, and diagnosing deception is easier.
P   HOW widely accepted is the instrument? (7)

W   There's been a lot of controversy over the years, but today I think that most experts in the field accept the polygraph. Most knowledgeable people would say that in the hands of a competent, experienced examiner, the polygraph is a reliable instrument for diagnosing deception.

P   WHO is George Martin? (8)

W   He's the defendant in this case.

P   HOW do you know him? (8)

W   I had occasion to conduct a polygraph examination of Mr. Martin several weeks ago.

P   WHEN and WHERE did you do that? (8)

W   I did that at my office on February 13th. It was about ten in the morning. I used my polygraph to test him.

P   WHAT condition was the polygraph in when you tested Mr. Martin? (9)

W   It was in proper working order.

P   HOW did you know that? (9)

W   I use a Lafayette polygraph, and the company provides purchasers with a checklist for ensuring the instrument's operational condition. I went through the checklist before the test, and the instrument checked out perfectly.

P   HOW did you conduct Mr. Martin's examination? (10)

W   I followed the standard operating procedure and took all the steps you're supposed to use.

P   HOW are you supposed to conduct an examination? (11)

W   First you conduct the pretest interview.

P   WHAT is that? (11)

W   Before you actually conduct a polygraph examination, you interview the subject. You show the subject the machine, explain its operation, and try to convince the subject that the instrument is effective. You also begin forming your relevant and control questions.

P   WHAT are relevant and control questions? (11)

W   Relevant questions are the questions about the incident being investigated.

P   WHAT would be an example? (11)

W   Here the most relevant question is "Mr. Martin, did you have intercourse with Ms. Gust?"

P   WHAT is a control question? (11)

W   It's a probable lie question. The subject will probably lie in response.

P   WHAT is an example? (11)

W   "In your first 25 years of life, did you ever steal anything?" The subject is likely to lie and deny stealing.

P   HOW do you use the relevant and control questions? (11)

W   You compare the responses on the chart to the relevant and control questions. Simply stated, if the subject reacts more to the relevant questions than to the control questions, the person's probably lying. On the other hand, if the subject reacts more to the control questions, the subject is probably telling the truth in his or her responses to the relevant questions.

P   HOW did you conduct the test of Mr. Martin? (11)

W   I followed the procedure I just described. I conducted a pretest interview and formed my relevant and control questions, including the ones I've already mentioned. Then I ran the test. I spaced the questions about 30 seconds apart to permit the reactions to register fully on the polygram. The test consisted of ten questions, and I ran the test three times during the space of an hour.

P   Your Honor, I request that this be marked defense exhibit C for identification.

J   It will be so marked.

P   Your Honor, please let the record reflect that I am showing the exhibit to the opposing counsel.

J   It will so reflect.

P   Your Honor, may I have permission to approach the witness?

J   Yes.

P   Mr. Bechtel, I now hand you defense exhibit C for identification. WHAT is it? (12)

W   It's the chart of Mr. Martin's test.

P   HOW can you recognize it? (12)

W   I recognize my handwriting on it.

P   WHAT condition is it in? (12)

W   It's in roughly the same condition it was in when I ran the test.

P   WHERE has it been since that time? (12)

W   In my files. I personally removed it from my files before coming to court.

P   Your Honor, I now offer defense exhibit C for identification into evidence as defense exhibit C.

J   It will be received.

P   Mr. Bechtel, WHAT are the circled areas on exhibit C? (13)

W   They're the responses to the control questions, such as the one I mentioned about stealing.

P   WHAT are the areas in the squares? (13)

W   They're the responses to the relevant questions including the one about intercourse.

P   WHAT is your diagnosis of that response? (13)

W   In my opinion, Mr. Martin was telling the truth when he denied having intercourse with Ms. Gust.

P   WHAT is the basis for that opinion? (13)

W   The responses to the control questions were fairly mild. There were also mild reactions to the relevant questions. That indicates to me that Mr. Martin was not engaging in conscious deception when he denied intercourse.

P   Your Honor, I request permission to hand exhibit C to the jurors for their personal inspection.

J   Yes.

If the witness' opinion had been that Martin had been lying, the opinion would have been impeaching.

H. PROOF THAT ANOTHER WITNESS SPECIFICALLY CONTRADICTS THE TESTIMONY OF THE WITNESS TO BE IMPEACHED

California Evidence Code § 780(i) states that the opposing attorney may impeach a witness by showing "[t]he ... nonexistence of any fact testified to by him." This impeachment technique is usually termed contradiction. Witness #1 testifies to A, and the opposing attorney calls witness #2 to testify to non-*A*. The impeaching effect of witness #2's testimony is indirect and inferential: If witness #2 is correct, witness #1 must be mistaken or lying. Just as Article VI of the Federal Rules is silent on bias impeachment, the Rules make no mention of specific contradiction. Nevertheless, as in the case of bias impeachment, the courts continue to permit attorneys to employ specific contradiction impeachment.

Suppose, for example, that plaintiff's witness #1 testifies that the traffic light facing the defendant's car was red. The defense calls witness #2 who testifies that the light facing the defendant's car was green. Since witness #2's testimony is logically relevant to the historical merits, it is admissible both to prove that the light was green and to impeach witness #1 by contradiction.

The problem arises when witness #2's testimony is logically relevant only to witness #1's credibility. Suppose a traffic accident occurred in a rural area near Philadelphia. During his direct examination, witness #1 testified that he was walking near the intersection where the collision occurred. Witness #1 adds that in the adjacent field, there were "about 20 cows grazing." During the defense case-in-chief, the defense calls the farmer who owns the field. The farmer is prepared to testify that there were only 10 cows grazing at the time. The farmer's testimony would specifically contradict witness #1's testimony. The farmer's testimony is logically relevant to impeach witness #1; if the farmer is correct, witness #1 erred in perception or memory. However, the farmer's testimony has no logical relevance to the historical merits; the number of cows in the field has no impact on the facts relating to the traffic accident. Before the adoption of the Federal Rules, the common-law collateral fact rule would have mandated the exclusion of the farmer's testimony. *People v. Dice,* 120 Cal. 189, 52 P. 477 (1898).

However, the Federal Rules probably abolish the collateral fact rule. The admission of extrinsic evidence to contradict witness #1 is now governed by Rule 403. The judge weighs the importance of the witness and the strength of the inference that the witness is wrong about the historical merits if the witness is wrong about the detail in question. When the witness is the star witness for one side and the inference is strong, the judge can admit the extrinsic evidence. As the McCormick hornbook explains:

Suppose a witness has told a story of a transaction crucial to the controversy. To prove him wrong in some trivial detail of time, place or circumstance is "collateral." But to prove untrue some fact recited by the witness that if he were really there and saw what he claims to have seen, he could not have been mistaken about, is a convincing kind of impeachment that the courts must make place for .... To disprove such a fact is to pull out the linchpin of the story. [W]e must recognize this ... type of allowable contradiction ... of any part of the witness' account of the background of a material transaction, which as a matter of human experience he would not have been mistaken about if his story were true.

C. McCormick, *Evidence* § 47, at 111-12 (3d ed. 1984).

Suppose, for example, that in the hypothetical, witness #1 testified that there is a large, red cowbarn at the intersection. The farmer will testify that the fields near the intersection are vacant and that the nearest red barn is two miles away at another intersection. If witness #1 is mistaken about the barn, he may be testifying about another collision at another intersection. Under Rule 403, the trial judge would probably be justified in admitting the farmer's testimony to contradict witness #1.

If the extrinsic evidence in question passes muster under Rule 403, the proponent must simply ensure that he or she lays all of the other foundations normally required for that type of evidence. In the case of the farmer's testimony, the only required foundation would be first-hand knowledge of the vicinity. Assume, for instance, that all the intersections in question are located within Meridian Township. The proponent might establish the farmer's personal familiarity:

P   WHERE do you live?
W   I live in Meridian Township.
P   HOW long have you lived there?
W   All my life. I was raised right here.
P   HOW many years have you lived here in Meridian?
W   Fifty-two years, give or take a couple of months.
P   HOW familiar are you with the roads in the township?
W   Real familiar. At one time or another, I've probably driven every one of them a time or two.
P   HOW well do you know the intersection of Rural Routes 31 and 99?
W   Real well. I live only about three miles from there. In fact, it's on the route I take to town almost every weekday.
P   HOW well do you know the intersection of Rural Routes 31 and 102?
W   Just about as well. That's right on the way we take to church on Sundays.

At this point, the proponent would elicit the farmer's testimony contradicting the testimony of the earlier witness. A common technique for highlighting the contradiction is to preface the questions to the farmer with references to the contradictory testimony by the earlier witness:

P   Earlier today a plaintiff's witness, Mr. Greenfield, testified that there's a large red barn at the intersection of Rural Routes 31 and 99. WHAT buildings, if any, are there at that intersection?

Some judges permit such references. However, the proponent certainly has no right to make such cross-references. The cross-references are declarative statements about witness #1's testimony, and the only thing the proponent has the right to do during the examination of witness #2 is to put questions to witness #2.

I. PROOF THAT THE WITNESS MADE A PRIOR INCONSISTENT STATEMENT

Section E of this chapter discusses bad acts impeachment. As previously stated, that technique is ordinarily limited to intrinsic impeachment, that is, the cross-examination of the witness to be impeached. At the opposite extreme are the impeachment techniques discussed in Sections F-H: Proof of witness #1's character trait of untruthfulness, evidence that witness #1 failed a polygraph examination, and witness #2's testimony specifically contradicting witness #1's testimony. Those three techniques require extrinsic evidence. This section begins our discussion of a series of impeachment techniques which can be developed by either cross-examination or extrinsic evidence. The first such technique is proof that the witness made a prior statement inconsistent with his or her trial testimony.

On the morning of January 15, 1989, at the intersection of University and Felton Streets, Mr. Miller's car collided with Ms. Dolan's van. Mr. Miller's car is red, and Ms. Dolan's van is blue. Mr. Williams happened to be standing at a corner of the intersection when the collision occurred. Later that day he had a conversation with his neighbor, Mr. Jensen. During the conversation, he told Mr. Jensen that he witnessed the collision and that the collision occurred because the red car (Mr. Miller's car) ran a red light. Mr. Miller files a personal injury action against Ms. Dolan. At the trial, Mr. Miller calls Mr. Williams as a witness. On direct examination, Mr. Williams testifies that he witnessed the collision and that Ms. Dolan's van caused the accident by running a red light. On cross-examination, may the defense attorney call Mr. Jensen as a defense witness to testify to Mr. Williams' earlier statement? In the last section, we saw that we may call witness #2 to specifically contradict witness #1's testimony. May we similarly prove that witness #1 has contradicted himself or herself by making an inconsistent statement?

1. CROSS-EXAMINATION TO ELICIT A WITNESS' CONCESSION THAT THE WITNESS EARLIER MADE AN INCONSISTENT STATEMENT

As soon as Mr. Williams testifies at the trial, his credibility becomes one of the facts in issue in the case. Common sense suggests that the jury is entitled to know that Mr. Williams made an earlier, inconsistent statement. The fact that he has made inconsistent statements about the same fact calls into question his memory and sincerity. In everyday life, if a person tells us differing stories about the same event, we pause before deciding to believe either story. For that reason, the Federal Rules permit the defense attorney to cross-examine Mr. Williams about his statement to Mr. Jensen. Rule 613(a) makes it clear that the cross-examination of Williams about the earlier statement is a proper method of impeachment.

At common law, if Ms. Dolan's attorney forced Williams to concede the earlier statement to Jensen, Mr. Miller's attorney would be entitled to a limiting instruction. In the instruction, the judge would tell the jurors that they could not use Mr. Williams' earlier statement to Jensen as evidence that in fact, Mr. Miller ran a red light; the judge would instruct the jurors that they could consider the evidence only for the limited purpose of deciding whether they want to believe the testimony that it was green. So limited, the evidence would not be subject to a hearsay objection. Quite apart from its truth or falsity, the statement to Jensen is logically relevant; Mr. Williams' credibility is an issue, and the fact that he said one thing at one time and another thing another time about the same subject lowers his credibility. On that reasoning, the common law courts treated prior inconsistent statements as nonhearsay.

However, in federal practice the impeaching attorney need not be content to offer the prior inconsistent statement for the limited purpose of attacking Williams' credibility. As we shall see in Chapter 10, Rule 801(d)(1)(A) provides that if a statement qualifies as a prior-inconsistent statement of an in-court witness, in some circumstances the statement is admissible as substantive evidence. Under Rule 801, Williams' out-of-court statement could be used as evidence that the light was red if he had made the prior statement under oath in a formal proceeding. The person is available for questioning, and the cross-examiner can ask the witness about both the witness' direct testimony and the witness' earlier statements. Furthermore, the drafters of Rule 801 doubted that many jurors can follow a judge's limiting instruction admitting a prior inconsistent statement merely as credibility evidence.

The opponent seeking to cross-examine a witness about a prior inconsistent statement should lay the following foundation:

1. The opponent should get the witness committed to the testimony he gave on direct examination. Unless the opponent does so, the witness may later attempt to explain away the inconsistency by testifying that he or she innocently misspoke. The opponent might attempt to commit the witness by asking directly, "ISN'T IT TRUE THAT on direct examination you testified that ...?" Many experienced trial attorneys counsel against such direct questions because they alert the proponent, often the witness, that the opponent is going to use a prior inconsistent statement. Moreover, on various theories, many trial judges believe that the question is objectionable. In the interests of completeness, we

have included the question in the sample foundations, but be aware that this tactic can be dangerous.

2. The witness made an earlier statement at a certain place. (For a written prior inconsistent statement, the place where the witness wrote the document is usually not essential.)
3. The witness made a statement at a certain time.
4. Certain persons were present.
5. The statement was of a certain tenor.
6. The prior statement is more likely to be reliable than the present testimony. In the sample foundations, the opponent attempts to force the witness to concede that the witness' memory was fresher at the time of the inconsistent statement, than the memory is at trial. Many experienced counsel prefer not to attempt to force that concession; these counsel elicit the facts about the statement's timing and then argue the relative reliability of the statements during closing argument. These attorneys forego attempting to force the concession in part because they realize that some judges regard such questions as objectionably argumentative. We have included the question in the sample foundations in the interests of completeness. But, as with element #1, be aware that this tactic can be dangerous.

If the witness made the prior statement at a deposition hearing, the opponent should elicit the following facts: The witness' attorney was present at the deposition; a court reporter was also there; the reporter administered an oath to the witness; at the beginning of the deposition, the opposing attorney told the witness that if any question was unclear, the witness should request clarification; the opposing attorney asked whether the witness was experiencing any mental or physical problem that would interfere with testifying at the deposition; the witness assured the attorney that there was none; the reporter later prepared a transcript of the questions and answers at the deposition; the reporter gave the witness a copy of the transcript to review; and the witness signed the transcript without making any changes.

If the statement is written, there is an additional element:

7. If the opponent proposes to hand the writing to the witness, the opponent should first show the writing to the other counsel. Under Federal Rule 613(a), the opponent need not show the writing to the witness.

We shall now set out two sample foundations. The first foundation is based on the original version of our hypothetical involving Mr. Williams. In this version, the inconsistent statement is oral. In the second version, the inconsistent statement will be a writing. In both cases, the opponent is the defense counsel cross-examining Mr. Williams.

O   Mr. Williams, if I correctly understood your testimony on direct exami-
     nation, my client's car was the car that ran a red light. IS THAT
     CORRECT? (1)
W   Yes.
O   ISN'T IT A FACT THAT on the afternoon of the accident, you had a
     conversation with a Mr. Walter Jensen at your house? (2), (3), (4)
W   Yes.
O   ISN'T IT CORRECT THAT during that conversation, you discussed
     the collision between my client's car and the plaintiff's car? (5)
W   Right.
O   ISN'T IT ALSO TRUE THAT during the conversation, you told Mr.
     Jensen that it was the defendant's car that had run a red light? (5)
W   Yes.
O   ISN'T IT A FACT that, in point of time, that conversation was closer to
     the accident than your testimony today? (6)
W   Yes.
O   ISN'T IT CORRECT that your memory was fresher then? (6)
W   Yes.
P   Your Honor, may I please have a limiting instruction that the jurors
     may use this evidence only in evaluating Mr. Williams' credibility?
     Mr. Williams wasn't under oath at the time of the statement, and Rule
     801(d)(1)(A) is therefore inapplicable.
J   Correct. For that reason, I am going to grant the request for a limiting
     instruction.

Now suppose that Williams made the inconsistent statement in a
letter that he mailed to Jensen.

O   Mr. Williams, if I correctly understood your testimony on direct exami-
     nation, my client's car was the car that ran a red light. IS THAT
     CORRECT? (1)
W   Yes.
O   Your Honor, may this be marked defense exhibit F for identification?
J   It will be so marked.
O   Please let the record reflect that I am showing the exhibit to the oppos-
     ing counsel. (7)
J   It will so reflect.
O   Mr. Williams, I now hand you defense exhibit F for identification.
     WHAT is it? *(If the exhibit were a deposition transcript, the opponent
     would show the witness the title page with the witness' name and the
     signature page with the notary's and the witness' signatures.)*
W   It's a letter.
O   ISN'T IT TRUE THAT the letter is in your handwriting?
W   Yes.
O   ISN'T IT A FACT THAT you wrote that letter?
W   Yes.
O   ISN'T IT CORRECT THAT on the day of the collision between my
     client's car and the plaintiff's car, you wrote that letter at your house?
     (2), (3)
W   Right.
O   ISN'T IT A FACT THAT you then sent the letter to your friend, Mr.
     William Jensen? (4)
W   Yes.

O   Let me direct your attention to the third paragraph on page one of the exhibit. *(If the exhibit were a deposition transcript, the opponent would specify the page and line numbers: "Let me direct your attention to page 13, lines 11 through 20.")* Please read that paragraph silently to yourself. ISN'T IT TRUE THAT in that paragraph, you wrote that it was the red car — the plaintiff's car — that ran a red light? (5)

W   Yes.

O   Your Honor, I now offer paragraph three of the exhibit into evidence.

P   Your Honor, this is merely a prior inconsistent statement by a non-party witness. It can't be admitted as substantive evidence, and for that reason the exhibit shouldn't be formally received as evidence. Mr. Williams wasn't under oath at the time of the statement, and Rule 801(d)(1)(A) is therefore inapplicable.

J   I agree. The exhibit will not be received.

O   Mr. Williams, ISN'T IT CORRECT THAT, in point of time, the date of the letter was closer to the accident than your testimony today? (6)

W   Yes.

O   ISN'T IT ALSO A FACT THAT your memory was fresher then? (6)

W   Yes.

2. EXTRINSIC EVIDENCE OF A PRIOR INCONSISTENT STATEMENT

In both variations of the hypothetical in the last subsection, the witness obligingly admitted that he made the prior inconsistent statement. When the witness makes that concession, the impeachment is complete. However, if the witness denies the statement, the opponent has a choice. If the statement is in writing and the opponent has not yet shown the writing to the witness, the opponent can immediately confront the witness with the writing and attempt to refresh the witness' memory. Section F of Chapter 10 contains a sample foundation for present recollection refreshed. Alternatively, the opponent may attempt to introduce "extrinsic evidence" of the inconsistent statement after the witness leaves the stand. "Extrinsic evidence" refers to any other evidence of the inconsistent statement that Ms. Dolan's attorney might offer after Williams leaves the witness stand. For example, if the defense attorney called Mr. Jensen to testify to Williams' oral inconsistent statement, Jensen's testimony would be extrinsic evidence. Or suppose that the defense attorney called another of Mr. Williams' acquaintances, Ms. Bigelow, to identify Williams' handwriting on a written inconsistent statement. Again, the writing would be extrinsic impeachment of Williams.

At common law, there were two restrictions on the admissibility of extrinsic evidence of a prior inconsistent statement.

One restriction was the rule that the opponent could present such evidence only if the opponent laid a foundation while cross-examining the witness to be impeached. The theory is that fairness dictates giving the witness an opportunity to explain or deny the impeaching evidence. The Federal Rules relax the common-law requirement. If the opponent is attacking an in-court witness' credibility, the Rules recognize alternatives to a traditional foundation on cross-examination. Rule 613(b) requires only that the witness be "afforded an opportunity to explain or deny" the statement. The opponent attacking the witness' credibility can afford the witness that opportunity by having the witness excused subject to recall. If the judge excuses the witness subject to recall, the witness' proponent can later recall the witness to deny the statement or explain away the apparent inconsistency. Even when there is no foundation on cross and the witness has been permanently excused, the judge retains discretion to admit extrinsic evidence in "the interests of justice" under Rule 613(b). Despite the exercise of due diligence, the party seeking to introduce the statement may not have learned of its existence until after the witness has left the witness stand.

The common law imposed a further restriction on the admissibility of extrinsic evidence of a prior inconsistent statement. The collateral fact rule decreed that if the statement related to a purely collateral fact, with no relevance to the historical merits, extrinsic evidence was automatically inadmissible. As previously stated, the Federal Rules do not codify the collateral fact rule. Only Rule 403 remains. If the trial judge believes that the issue is important enough to an assessment of the witness' credibility, the judge may permit the introduction of extrinsic evidence of the prior statement.

The following three foundations illustrate the presentation of extrinsic evidence of a prior inconsistent statement. For purposes of each foundation, assume that the defense attorney satisfied Rule 613(b). Initially suppose that the defense calls Mr. Jensen to testify to Williams' oral prior inconsistent statement.

O   WHERE were you on the afternoon of January 15, 1989? (2), (3)
W   At Mr. Williams' house.
O   WHO was there? (4)
W   Just Mr. Williams and myself.
O   WHAT happened while you were there?
W   We just talked.
O   WHAT did you talk about? (5)
W   A lot of things, including the accident he evidently witnessed that morning.
O   WHAT did Mr. Williams say about the accident? (5)
W   He said that the guy in the red car had clearly caused the accident by running a red light.

In the next variation of the hypothetical, Jensen will authenticate a letter, containing the inconsistent statement, that Williams sent to Jensen.

O   Your Honor, may this be marked defense exhibit F for identification?

J It will be so marked.

O Let the record reflect that I am showing the exhibit to the opposing counsel.

J It will so reflect.

P Mr. Jensen, I now hand you defense exhibit F for identification. WHAT is it? (4)

W It's a letter I received.

O WHEN did you receive it? (3)

W It was in January of this year. It arrived in the mail at my apartment. (2)

O WHOSE handwriting is the letter in?

W Mr. Williams'.

O HOW do you know that?

W We've worked together for years in different offices of the same company.

O HOW many times have you seen Mr. Williams' handwriting?

W Hundreds of times. We exchange business memos. Sometimes we'll be at each other's office, and I'll be present when he signs documents.

O HOW familiar are you with his handwriting style?

W Very.

O WHOSE handwriting appears on this letter?

W Mr. Williams'. I'm certain of that.

O Your Honor, I now offer the third paragraph of defense exhibit F for identification into evidence as defense exhibit F.

J It will be received.

O Mr. Jensen, permit me to direct your attention to the second sentence in paragraph three of the exhibit. WHAT does that sentence say? (5)

W It reads: "The guy in the red car ran right through a red light."

O Your Honor, I now request permission to submit the exhibit to the jurors for their inspection.

J Permission granted.

In the final version of the hypothetical, the written statement is in the form of a deposition transcript. The notary public's certificate at the end of the transcript makes the transcript self-authenticating under Rule 902. After the witness to be impeached leaves the stand, the opponent may request the judge's permission to read the inconsistent passage to the jurors. When the opponent makes the request, the opponent should specify the page and lines to be read. If the transcript has already been filed with the court, there is no need to mark the transcript even for identification. However, in some cases, the transcript has not been filed with the court. In that event, the opponent should have the transcript marked for identification:

O Your Honor, I request that this be marked defense exhibit F for identification.

J It will be so marked.

O Please let the record reflect that I am showing the exhibit to the opposing counsel.

J It will so reflect.

O   I now offer page 8, lines 17 through 23, into evidence and request permission to read those lines to the jurors.

J   The passage will be admitted, and you may read the passage to the jury.

J. PROOF THAT THE WITNESS HAS SUFFERED A CONVICTION

1. THE DOCTRINE

If the witness has suffered a conviction, the conviction tends to impeach the witness' credibility. Proof of the conviction creates a general inference that the witness is sometimes willing to disobey social norms; the conviction thus strengthens the inference that the witness is violating another norm and lying now. Of course, the conviction has much more probative value if the underlying offense is a crime such as perjury or embezzlement involving an element of deceit or fraud. All jurisdictions recognize this method of impeachment, but they differ on the types of convictions usable to impeach. Most courts allow the opponent to use any felony conviction. Other courts restrict the technique to crimes involving an element of deceit or fraud. The Federal Rule 609(a) reads: "For the purpose of attacking the credibility of a witness, evidence that the witness has been convicted of a crime shall be admitted if elicited from the witness or established by public record during cross-examination but only if the crime (1) was punishable by death or imprisonment in excess of one year under the law under which the witness was convicted, and the court determines that the probative value of admitting this evidence outweighs its prejudicial effect to the defendant, or (2) involved dishonesty or false statement, regardless of the punishment." Convictions for offenses such as perjury and fraud certainly qualify as crimes of "false statement" under Rule 609(a)(2). However, the legislative history of the rule supports a strong argument that the expression "'dishonesty' [in Rule 609(a)(2)] was devoid of significant meaning ...." Cleary, *Preliminary Notes on Reading the Rules of Evidence,* 57 Neb. L. Rev. 908, 919 (1978). The courts are currently divided over the question of whether theft offenses such as larceny fall within 609(a)(2).

As in the case of prior inconsistent statement impeachment, this technique permits the opponent to both cross-examine the witness to be impeached and use extrinsic evidence. In most jurisdictions, the opponent may choose between cross-examination and extrinsic evidence. There is no requirement that the opponent lay a foundation on cross as a condition to introducing extrinsic evidence. However, if the opponent does cross-examine the witness and the witness admits all the facts about the conviction, most courts then prohibit the introduction of extrinsic evidence. The rationale is simply that it would be cumulative and a waste of time to introduce the extrinsic evidence after the witness has conceded all the facts.

When the opponent resorts to extrinsic evidence, the evidence usually takes the form of an attested copy of the judgment of conviction. The properly attested copy is self-authenticating; the opponent does not need a live, sponsoring witness to authenticate the copy. In rare cases, the opponent will present live testimony such as the testimony of someone who was present in the courtroom when the witness was convicted.

The courts differ on the number of details the opponent may prove about the conviction. Some courts limit the opponent's proof to evidence that in a certain jurisdiction in a certain year, the witness suffered "a felony conviction." However, most courts permit the opponent to identify the crime of which the witness was convicted. Some courts also allow the opponent to prove the sentence the witness suffered. The consensus is that the opponent may not inquire about other details, especially any aggravating facts about the particular manner in which the witness committed the crime.

2. ELEMENTS OF THE FOUNDATION

The opponent must establish the following foundation:
1. The witness is the person who suffered the prior conviction.
2. The conviction is for one of the crimes this jurisdiction holds to be impeaching.
3. The conviction was entered in a certain jurisdiction.
4. The conviction was entered in a certain year.
5. The witness received a certain sentence.

If the opponent is using a copy of the judgment of conviction, there is another element of the foundation:
6. The copy of the judgment of conviction is authentic.

3. SAMPLE FOUNDATIONS

The first sample foundation illustrates cross-examination about a conviction. Assume that this jurisdiction limits conviction impeachment to felonies but permits the opponent to inquire about the sentence. The opponent is the attorney attempting to impeach the witness.

O   ISN'T IT TRUE THAT you are the same Steven Giles who once was convicted of a felony? (1), (2)
W   Yes.
O   ISN'T IT A FACT THAT the felony was a robbery? (2)
W   Yes.
O   ISN'T IT CORRECT THAT you were convicted of that crime in 1988 in New York? (3), (4)
W   Yes.

O   ISN'T IT ALSO A FACT THAT you were sentenced to 15 years in state prison for that robbery? (5)
W   Yes.

The next foundation illustrates the use of an attested copy of a judgment of conviction to impeach. Assume that the witness, Mr. Giles, has already left the stand.

O   Your Honor, may this be marked defense exhibit D for identification?
J   It will be so marked.
O   Please let the record reflect that I am showing the exhibit to the opposing counsel.
J   It will so reflect.
O   I now offer defense exhibit D for identification into evidence as defense exhibit D.
P   Your Honor, I object on the grounds that there's insufficient authentication of this document.
O   Your Honor, the exhibit includes a properly executed attesting certificate. The certificate makes the exhibit self-authenticating under Rule 902. (6)
J   The objection will be overruled. The exhibit will be received.
O   Your Honor, may I read these two sentences to the jury?
J   Permission granted. Ladies and gentlemen of the jury, I have just accepted into evidence defense exhibit D. This exhibit is a properly authenticated copy of a judgment of a conviction of a crime. You will please bear in mind that the last prosecution witness was Mr. Steven Judson Giles, Jr. You may proceed.
O   Ladies and gentlemen, the exhibit reads: "On this day, July 13th, 1988, the Supreme Court of the State of New York, Hudson County, the Honorable Paul Lederer presiding, duly found the defendant, Steven Judson Giles, Jr., guilty of the crime of robbery. (1), (2), (3), (4) For this crime, the defendant is hereby sentenced to 15 years' confinement in the prisons of the State of New York." (5)

K. PROOF THAT THE WITNESS IS BIASED

1. THE DOCTRINE

Like a conviction, the witness' bias is logically relevant to impeach the witness. Although Article VI of the Federal Rules does not expressly mention bias impeachment, the Supreme Court has held that as at common law, under the Federal Rules a witness may be impeached on the ground of bias. *United States v. Abel,* 469 U.S. 45 (1984). Bias may affect the witness consciously or subconsciously. The courts grant the opponent great latitude in proving bias. In fact, the courts often allow the opponent to use bias impeachment as a method of circumventing other evidentiary rules. For example, there is a general rule that in a civil action, the plaintiff may not prove that the defendant has settled any other claims arising from the same accident. The justification for the rule is that the admission of such evidence would discourage desirable, out-of-court settlements. Suppose, though, that the defendant calls a witness who has settled his or her claim with the defendant. The fact of the settlement is logically relevant and admissible to show the witness' bias in the defendant's favor. Another illustration is the rule that the plaintiff ordinarily may not prove that the defendant has liability insurance. The admission of such evidence would tempt the jury to decide the case on an improper basis; they might find in the plaintiff's favor because in reality, the insurance company will pay the judgment. Assume, however, that the defendant calls one of the insurance company's investigators as a witness. In many jurisdictions, the plaintiff may now prove the defendant's liability insurance. The fact that the witness works for the defendant's liability carrier is logically relevant to show the witness' bias in favor of the defendant.

This impeachment technique is similar to conviction impeachment in another respect: The opponent may both cross-examine the witness to be impeached and use extrinsic evidence. On cross-examination, the courts grant the opponent a very wide scope of inquiry. Jurisdictions following the traditional view require that the opponent lay a foundation on cross-examination as a predicate for extrinsic evidence. These courts reason that as a matter of fairness, the opponent should give the witness an opportunity to explain or deny the impeaching facts. If the witness fully admits all the facts, the judge may exercise discretion to limit or exclude extrinsic evidence. However, when the witness denies any of the relevant impeaching facts, the opponent may introduce extrinsic evidence. The Federal Rules do not require a foundation on cross-examination.

2. ELEMENTS OF THE FOUNDATION

There are no special foundational requirements for bias evidence; the opponent may prove any fact or event logically relevant to show bias. If the impeaching evidence is an event, the foundation usually includes the following elements:

1. Where the event occurred.
2. When the event occurred.
3. Who was present.
4. What occurred.

Some counsel attempt to lay an additional element; namely, they seek the witness' concession that:

5. The fact or event will tend to bias the witness.

Most experienced counsel avoid such attempts. The witness will often not make that concession; and in the attempt to force the concession, the counsel might become argumentative. Experienced counsel prefer to invite the jury to draw the inference of bias during closing argument.

3. SAMPLE FOUNDATIONS

The fact situation is a civil suit between a Mr. Martinez and a Mr. Saltzman. Mr. Martinez calls Mr. Fargo as a witness. After the direct examination, Mr. Saltzman's attorney begins cross-examination. Mr. Saltzman's attorney is the opponent.

O   ISN'T IT TRUE THAT on July 4, 1988, you attended a party at Jane Fleming's house? (1), (2)

W   Yes.

O   ISN'T IT A FACT THAT Ms. Fleming and Mr. Saltzman, the defendant in this case, were also at the party? (3)

W   Yes.

O   ISN'T IT CORRECT THAT during the party, you punched Mr. Saltzman? (4)

W   Yes.

O   ISN'T IT ALSO TRUE THAT before you left the party, you told Ms. Fleming that you had a strong, personal dislike for Mr. Saltzman? (4)

W   Yes.

Assume that the witness had denied the impeaching facts. Then the opponent could present extrinsic evidence such as Ms. Fleming's testimony.

O   WHERE were you on the evening of July 4, 1988? (1), (2)

W   At my house. I was throwing a party for some friends.

O   WHO attended the party? (3)

W   There were a lot of people. Mr. Fargo, the last witness, was there. The defendant, Mr. Saltzman, was also in attendance.

O   WHAT, if anything, unusual happened during the evening? (4)

W   I couldn't believe it, but Mr. Fargo actually punched Mr. Saltzman. They were just standing talking, and all of a sudden Fargo slugged him.

O   WHAT happened then? (4)

W   I asked Fargo to get out.

O   WHAT, if anything, did Mr. Fargo say? (4)

W   He said he'd be glad to. He said that he had a strong, personal dislike for Mr. Saltzman and that he, Fargo, wouldn't stay under the same roof as Saltzman. Fargo said that if he'd known Saltzman was going to be at the party, he never would have accepted my invitation.

L. PROOF THAT THE WITNESS IS DEFICIENT IN AN ELEMENT OF COMPETENCY

1. THE DOCTRINE

Section A of Chapter 3 listed the elements of competency. At common law, to be a competent witness, a person must possess the testimonial qualities of perception, memory, narration and sincerity. If the opponent can negative one or more of those elements, the person is incompetent; the person cannot testify at all during the trial. However, even if the opponent's evidence does not completely negative one of the elements, the evidence may be logically relevant on an impeachment theory. For example, a color-blind person is a competent witness; but the color blindness is a deficiency which can tend to reduce the value of the witness' testimony.

The courts liberally admit evidence of deficiencies in elements of competency. The courts have admitted evidence that: The witness was intoxicated when he or she observed the event they testified about; the witness has a psychiatric disorder affecting his or her testimonial qualities; the witness has subnormal intelligence; and, in some jurisdictions, the witness is a drug addict or user.

As a general proposition, the opponent may use either cross-examination or extrinsic evidence. For example, on cross-examination, the opponent may attempt to force a witness to concede that he or she was intoxicated at the time of event. Or the opponent may rely on extrinsic evidence and call a psychiatrist to testify that the psychiatrist examined the subject witness and discovered a disorder that calls into question the witness' credibility. Thus, in some jurisdictions, the opponent may cross-examine the witness to expose the witness' subnormal intelligence. The opponent may use the "hop, skip and jump" method of cross-examination to do so; the opponent cross-examines the witness about a number of events out of chronological sequence. The opponent's hope is that the witness will flounder and the jury will conclude that the witness has a deficient memory. However, in these jurisdictions, the courts feel that subnormal intelligence has relatively little probative value and bar extrinsic evidence.

2. ELEMENTS OF THE FOUNDATION

This impeachment technique often requires proof of a particular historical event such as an occasion when the witness was drunk. The normal foundation will include:

1. Where the event occurred.
2. When the event occurred.
3. Who was present.
4. What happened.
5. What happened may have affected the accuracy of his testimony.

In addition, the technique often necessitates lay or expert opinion testimony. Chapter 9 illustrates the foundations for lay and expert testimony. When such testimony is necessary, the opponents will also have to establish:

6. The qualifications of the expert, if expert testimony is necessary.
7. The basis for the opinion.
8. The opinion itself.

3. SAMPLE FOUNDATIONS

We shall first illustrate cross-examination to attack a deficiency in the witness' competency. The fact situation is a tort case arising from a traffic collision. The plaintiff, Ms. Schmitt, sues the defendant, Mr. Jackson. The plaintiff calls a witness, Mr. Oser. On direct examination, Mr. Oser testifies that he observed the accident from 150 feet away; he testifies that the defendant swerved into the plaintiff. The defendant is the opponent.

O   ISN'T IT TRUE THAT on direct examination, you testified that on January 4th, you observed a collision between the plaintiff's and defendant's cars just outside the Sports Arena? (1), (2), (3)
W   Yes.
O   Mr. Oser, ISN'T IT CORRECT THAT you are nearsighted? (4)
W   Yes.
O   ISN'T IT A FACT THAT as a nearsighted person, you have difficulty seeing anything at a distance? (4)
W   Yes.
O   ISN'T IT CORRECT THAT your doctor has prescribed glasses for you to correct your nearsightedness? (4)
W   Yes.
O   ISN'T IT ALSO TRUE that when you supposedly saw the collision, you weren't wearing your glasses? (4)
W   Yes.
O   Finally, ISN'T IT A FACT THAT you were at least 150 feet away from the collision when you supposedly saw it? (5)
W   Yes.

Next we turn to an example of extrinsic testimony impeaching a prior witness. Mr. Oser has left the witness stand. The defendant calls Mr. Thelan. The defendant is still designated the opponent. The defendant is conducting the direct examination of Mr. Thelan.

O   WHERE were you on the evening of January 4th of this year? (1), (2)
W   I was downtown with Mr. Oser.
O   WHO is Mr. Oser? (3)
W   He's Ed Oser, the last witness in this case.
O   WHAT were you and Mr. Oser doing? (4)
W   We had a bite and some drinks at a bar. Then we were going home to our respective wives.
O   WHEN did you and Mr. Oser start drinking? (7)
W   At about 5:30 in the early evening.
O   HOW many drinks did Mr. Oser have? (7)
W   He was really putting them away. I'd say he had five before we left.
O   WHAT was he drinking? (7)
W   He was having screwdrivers, orange juice and vodka.
O   WHEN did you leave the bar? (7)
W   At about 7. Maybe a little later.
O   WHAT was Mr. Oser's appearance when you left?
W   His face was a little red.
O   HOW was he acting? (7)
W   Pretty silly. He was stumbling and acting giddy.
O   HOW did his breath smell? (7)
W   He had a strong odor of alcohol on his breath.

O   WHAT was his speech like? (7)

W   It was slurred. He was having trouble pronouncing words.

O   WHAT, if anything, happened after you left the bar?

W   Just down the street a collision occurred.

O   WHAT collision? (7)

W   The collision Ed testified about, the one between the plaintiff and the defendant.

O   WHEN did you see this collision? (5)

W   Maybe five minutes after we left the bar.

O   In your opinion, WHAT was Mr. Oser's condition when the collision occurred? (5), (8)

W   I hate to say it, but I think he was drunk.

The preceding foundation illustrates lay opinion testimony attacking the witness' credibility. The opponent may also use expert opinion testimony. Section D of Chapter 3 contained a sample foundation for a psychiatrist's testimony. In Chapter 3, the opponent used the testimony to attack the prospective witness' competency. The opponent could use the very same foundation to show a deficiency in the witness' competency.

Part 3. Rehabilitation of Witnesses After Impeachment

M. PRIOR CONSISTENT STATEMENT

1. THE DOCTRINE

After the opponent attempts to impeach the witness' credibility, the witness' proponent may attempt to repair the damage. These attempts are called rehabilitation. One of the most common rehabilitation techniques is proof of a prior consistent statement. The proponent shows that the witness testified to the fact at the time of trial and that witness made a pretrial statement to the same effect. Just as inconsistency has an impeaching effect, consistency has a rehabilitating effect.

However, the courts do not want trials to be bogged down with proof of all of the witness' pretrial statements. For that reason, most jurisdictions impose timing requirements on prior consistent statements. For example, assume that the opponent impeached the witness with a prior inconsistent statement. Many jurisdictions take the position that the proponent may rehabilitate with a prior consistent statement only if the consistent statement preceded the allegedly inconsistent statement. Or assume that the opponent charged that the witness recently fabricated his or her testimony. Many jurisdictions permit the proponent to rehabilitate by prior consistent statement only if the witness made the statement before he or she had any motive to lie.

2. ELEMENTS OF THE FOUNDATION

The statement itself is an event. For that reason, the foundation includes the four normal foundational elements for proof of any event:

1. Where the statement was made.
2. When the statement was made.
3. Who was present.
4. The tenor of the statement.

In addition, if the proponent must comply with a timing requirement, the proponent must show that:

5. The statement preceded (a) the prior inconsistent statement or (b) any motive on the part of the witness to fabricate.

3. SAMPLE FOUNDATION

The fact situation is a tort action arising from a collision on December 14th. The plaintiff, Mr. Gillis, alleges that the defendant, Ms. Bollack, negligently caused the accident by crossing over into his lane. On direct examination, Mr. Gillis testifies to that effect. On cross-examination, the defense attorney charges that Mr. Gillis fabricated his story. Specifically, the defense attorney asked this question, "ISN'T IT TRUE THAT you never thought of that story until you consulted your attorney, Mr. Clark?" The plaintiff now begins redirect examination. The plaintiff is the proponent.

P Mr. Gillis, WHAT happened after the accident?
W The police arrived, and I went down to the nearest station with them.
P WHERE is the station located? (1)
W I think it's at the intersection of Elm and Maryland.
P WHEN did you arrive there? (2)
W About two hours after the accident. It might have been three in the afternoon.
P WHO was there? (3)
W A lot of police officers, myself, and Ms. Bollack.
P WHO were the officers? (3)
W There was one named Jorgenson, and then there was Desk Sergeant Allen.
P WHAT, if anything, did Desk Sergeant Allen do?
W He questioned me about the accident.
P Again, on WHAT day did you have this conversation with Desk Sergeant Allen? (2)
W December 14th.
P WHEN was the first time you ever consulted me about this case? (5)
W I guess it was three weeks later.
P So WHICH came first — your conversation with Desk Sergeant Allen or your conversation with me? (5) *(Many experienced trial attorneys omit this question. They feel that the timing is obvious and that the question will offend intelligent judges or jurors by insulting their intelligence.)*
W As I just said, my conversation with Allen.
P WHAT, if anything, did you tell Allen? (4)
W I told him about the accident. I said that the other driver caused it by coming into my lane. I was minding my own business, and then this car is coming across the lane right at me.

Now assume that in the same fact situation, the defendant attempted a different impeachment technique. On cross-examination, the defendant asked this question, "ISN'T IT TRUE THAT on Christmas Day that year, you told your brother that the accident occurred because your brakes failed?" This question amounts to attempted impeachment by prior inconsistent statement. The foundation would be exactly the same until the last three questions. Now the foundation on redirect would read:

P   WHEN did you have the conversation with your brother the defense attorney mentioned? (5)
W   I'm pretty sure it was on Christmas Day, December 25th.
P   So WHICH came first — your conversation with Desk Sergeant Allen or your conversation with your brother? (5)
W   My conversation with Allen — it was about a week and a half before I saw my brother over the holidays.
P   WHAT, if anything, did you tell Allen? (4)
W   I told him about the accident. I said that the other driver caused it by coming into my lane. I was minding my own business, and then this car is coming across the lane right at me.

N. PROOF OF THE CHARACTER TRAIT OF TRUTHFULNESS

1. THE DOCTRINE

Many of the impeachment techniques available to the opponent are express or implied attacks on the witness' character. If the opponent calls a character witness to testify to witness #1's character trait of untruthfulness, the testimony is an express attack. If the opponent proves specific bad acts or convictions, there is an implied attack on the witness' character. Even bias impeachment sometimes involves an attack on the witness' credibility; for instance, the proof of bias may be evidence of a corrupt financial motive. In all these cases, the judge will permit the proponent to rehabilitate by proving a character trait of truthfulness. The sequence would be the following. The proponent, perhaps the plaintiff, calls witness #1 to testify about the historical merits of the case. The opponent then calls witness #2, a character witness; witness #2 testifies that witness #1 has a reputation for untruthfulness. To rehabilitate witness #1, the proponent calls witness #3, another character witness. Witness #3 contradicts witness #2; witness #3 testifies that witness #1 has a good reputation for truthfulness.

In general, the rules governing the opponent's character evidence also apply to the proponent's character evidence. Section F of this chapter outlines those rules. There is only one other rule the proponent should bear in mind: The trial judge is likely to limit the proponent's character evidence to the same type, time, and community as the opponent's evidence. If the opponent used reputation evidence, the judge may not permit the proponent to use opinion evidence. The judge may limit the proponent's character evidence to roughly the same time period and community as the opponent's evidence. If the opponent presented character evidence about the witness' reputation in Detroit within the past five years, the judge might exclude the proponent's character evidence relating to the witness' reputation in Las Vegas ten years before. The courts do not want trials to bog down in collateral disputes over witnesses' credibility. The proponent should respond in kind to the opponent's attacks on the witness' credibility.

2. ELEMENTS OF THE FOUNDATION

The foundational elements are the same as in Section F of this chapter.

3. SAMPLE FOUNDATION

With one exception, the foundations are the same as in Section F of this chapter. The exception is that the final answers will be favorable to witness #1 rather than unfavorable. Thus, the reputation foundation would end in this fashion:

P   WHAT is that reputation? (4)
W   It's good. He's known as a truthful person.
P   Given Mr. Harding's reputation, would you believe him under oath? (5)
W   Yes.

The opinion foundation would conclude in this fashion:

P   WHAT is that opinion? (4)
W   In my opinion, he's a truthful person.
P   Given that opinion, would you believe Mr. Harding under oath? (5)
W   Yes.

Chapter 6

LEGAL RELEVANCE LIMITATIONS ON EVIDENCE THAT IS RELEVANT TO THE HISTORICAL MERITS OF THE CASE

A. INTRODUCTION

In the last chapter, we saw that the dangers listed in Rule 403 can lead to the exclusion of evidence that is logically relevant to the witness' credibility. The "legal relevance" doctrine codified in Rule 403 is not limited to credibility evidence; the doctrine can also apply to evidence that is logically relevant to the historical merits.

The premier danger noted in Rule 403 is "prejudice." In this context, "prejudice" means the evidence's tendency to tempt the jury to decide the case on an improper, usually emotional, basis. For instance, in a homicide prosecution, gruesome photographs of the victim could be excluded if, after viewing them, the jurors could no longer dispassionately evaluate the evidence of guilt or innocence. Most of the types of evidence analyzed in this chapter present the danger of prejudice. Several sections discuss evidence of other misdeeds by a criminal defendant. Such evidence creates a risk that the jurors will convict, not because they are convinced beyond a reasonable doubt of the defendant's commission of the charged crime, but rather because they conclude that the defendant is a bad person who should be behind bars. Evidence of a civil defendant's liability insurance raises a similar danger. Although the evidence of liability may be weak, the jurors may return a plaintiff's verdict because they assume the insurer — the "deep pocket" — will absorb the economic loss.

Simply stated, Rule 403 embodies the doctrine that the trial judge may exclude logically relevant evidence if, in his or her judgment, the evidence's dangers outweigh its probative value. The judge's application of the doctrine involves several steps. At the outset, the trial judge must determine the probative value of the evidence. How clear is the evidence? How strong is the logical link between the evidence and the fact it is offered to prove? How positive is the witness? These are just some of the questions the judge asks in evaluating probative value. Then the judge identifies the countervailing dangers and finally balances the probative value against the dangers. For some types of evidence, such as inflammatory photographs, the doctrine remains highly discretionary. Trial judges resolve the questions case-by-case. For other types of evidence, including most of those examined in this chapter, relatively rigid rules have evolved.

B. CHARACTER EVIDENCE

Section F of Chapter 4 discussed evidence of a witness' character trait of truthfulness. Under that theory of admissibility, the opponent of the witness uses the witness' character trait of untruthfulness as circumstantial proof of the witness' conduct. The opponent reasons that since the witness has a character trait of untruthfulness, the witness' present testimony is probably untruthful. We now turn to character evidence on the historical merits of the case. Much of what we said about character on a credibility theory applies here as well. Once again, we are using character as circumstantial evidence of conduct. For example, a criminal defendant may introduce testimony that he or she is a moral, law-abiding person. The defendant reasons that if he or she is that type of person, they would probably not commit the crime that they are charged with. Or, in a prosecution for a violent crime, the defendant may introduce evidence that the alleged victim is an aggressive person. The defendant is inviting the jury to infer that the alleged victim was in reality the aggressor on the occasion in question.

The rules governing character evidence on the merits resemble the rules for character evidence of untruthfulness in another respect: the methods of proof. We previously noted that the opponent presenting evidence of the witness' character trait of untruthfulness is ordinarily restricted to reputation and opinion evidence. The same restriction generally applies to character evidence on the historical merits. Thus, the criminal defendant is usually limited to reputation or opinion evidence of moral, law-abiding character. The major difference in methods of proof is that when the defendant places in issue the character of the alleged victim of a violent or sex offense, some jurisdictions permit the defendant to prove specific instances of the alleged victim's violent or promiscuous conduct.

There are several other differences between the credibility theory for character evidence and the use of character evidence on the historical merits. The following questions highlight those differences.

Whose character is in issue? On a credibility theory, the character of any witness in any type of case is in issue. Once the person takes the witness stand and gives any testimony in the case, his or her credibility becomes one of the material facts of consequence. On a character theory on the merits, the rules are quite different. The following statements are over-simplifications; but it is generally true that: (1) The parties may not use character evidence as circumstantial proof of conduct on the merits in civil cases; and (2) in criminal cases, we may use character evidence as circumstantial proof of the conduct of only the defendant and the alleged victim.

What part of the person's character is in issue? On a credibility theory, we focus squarely on the witness' character trait of truthfulness; that is the only part of the witness' character that is in issue. In contrast, on a character theory on the merits, we are interested in a different part of the person's character. If the person is the criminal defendant, we may be interested in the defendant's general, moral, law-abiding character. Or we may focus on a specific character trait relevant to the nature of the offense such as peacefulness in an assault prosecution or honesty in a theft prosecution.

Finally, when does the person's character come into issue? On a credibility theory, the witness' character trait of truthfulness comes into issue as soon as the witness gives any testimony in the case. In most jurisdictions, the defendant's character on the merits does not come into issue until the defendant affirmatively presents character evidence. It is not enough that the defendant has taken the witness stand. The defendant has the choice whether to place his or her character in issue on the merits. The prosecution ordinarily may present evidence of the defendant's immoral, law-breaking character only in rebuttal to defense character evidence.

1. REPUTATION CHARACTER EVIDENCE

The foundation for reputation character evidence on the historical merits is strikingly similar to the foundation for reputation character evidence on credibility:

1. The witness is a member of the same community (residential, business, or social) as the defendant.
2. The witness has resided there a substantial period of time.
3. The defendant has a reputation for: (a) general, moral, law-abiding character; or (b) a specific, relevant character trait. Federal Rule 404(a)(1) seems to confine the defendant to a relevant specific trait.
4. The witness knows the reputation.
5. The witness states the reputation.

Our fact situation is an assault prosecution. The government has charged Mr. Lowe with a violent assault. During its case-in-chief, the defense calls Mr. Nieman as a character witness. Mr. Nieman has already identified himself. The defense is the proponent.

P   WHO is Mr. Lowe?
W   He's a neighbor of mine.
P   WHEN is the last time you saw him?
W   He's in the courtroom right now.
P   WHERE is he sitting?
W   He's sitting there at the table with you.
P   HOW is he dressed?
W   He's wearing a brown suit and yellow tie.
P   Your Honor, may the record reflect that the witness has identified my client, Mr. Lowe?
J   The record will so reflect.
P   Mr. Nieman, WHERE does Mr. Lowe live? (1)

W   Here in Scotsdale.
P   WHERE do you live? (1)
W   I also reside in Scotsdale.
P   HOW close do you live to Mr. Lowe? (1)
W   No more than half a mile away.
P   HOW long has Mr. Lowe lived in Scotsdale? (2)
W   I'd say easily seven years.
P   HOW long have you lived in Scotsdale? (2)
W   For the past ten years.
P   Does Mr. Lowe have a reputation for violence or peacefulness in Scotsdale? *(Or "Does Mr. Lowe have a reputation as a law-breaking or law-abiding person in Scotsdale?")* (3)
W   Yes.
P   Do you know that reputation? (4)
W   Yes.
P   WHAT is that reputation? (5)
W   He's known as a peaceful person. *(Or "He's known as a moral, law-abiding person.")*

2. OPINION CHARACTER EVIDENCE

This foundation is very similar to the foundation for opinion character evidence on credibility:
1. The witness is personally acquainted with the defendant.
2. The witness knows the defendant well enough to have formed a reliable opinion of the defendant's character.
3. The witness has an opinion of the defendant's character.
4. The witness states his or her opinion.
Assume the same, hypothetical assault prosecution.

P   WHO is Mr. Lowe? (1)
W   He's a neighbor of mine.
P   WHEN is the last time you saw him? (1)
W   He's in the courtroom right now.
P   WHERE is he sitting? (1)
W   He's sitting right there at the table with you.
P   HOW is he dressed? (1)
W   He's wearing a brown suit and yellow tie.
P   Your Honor, please let the record reflect that the witness has identified my client, Mr. Lowe.
J   It will so reflect.
P   Mr. Nieman, WHERE does Mr. Lowe live? (2)
W   Here in Scotsdale.
P   HOW long has he lived here? (2)
W   I'd say easily seven years.
P   WHERE do you live? (2)
W   I also reside in Scotsdale.
P   HOW close do you live to Mr. Lowe? (2)
W   No more than half a mile away.
P   HOW long have you lived in Scotsdale? (2)
W   Over ten years.
P   HOW long have you known Mr. Lowe? (2)

W   I guess seven years — ever since he moved here.
P   HOW did you come to know Mr. Lowe? (2)
W   We have several mutual acquaintances, and we both are members of some local clubs, including the Optimists.
P   HOW often do you see Mr. Lowe? (2)
W   At least once or twice each week.
P   HOW well do you know him? (2)
W   I consider him a good, close friend.
P   Do you have an opinion whether he is a violent or peaceful person? *(Or "Do you have an opinion whether he is a law-breaking or law-abiding person?")* (3)
W   Yes.
P   WHAT is your opinion? (4)
W   In my opinion, he is a peaceful person. *(Or, "In my opinion, he is a moral, law-abiding person.")*

At least a significant minority of jurisdictions permit the proponent to use expert opinion testimony as well as lay opinion. Suppose, for example, that a psychiatrist diagnoses the defendant as a passive personality with an aversion to violence. That expert opinion would certainly be relevant evidence to reduce the probability that the defendant initiated a violent, unprovoked attack. If the proponent wanted to present such testimony, the proponent would have to comply with the foundational requirements for an expert opinion, described in Chapter 9.

3. PROOF OF CHARACTER BY SPECIFIC INSTANCES OF CONDUCT

In some jurisdictions, a defendant charged with a violent crime may attempt to prove the violent character of the alleged victim. The logical relevance is that if the alleged victim has a violent personality, that personality increases the probability that the alleged victim threw the first punch and was the aggressor. The Federal Rules limit the defendant to the use of reputation and opinion testimony as methods of proving the victim's violent character. However, many jurisdictions permit the defendant to prove the alleged victim's violent character by specific instances of conduct.

The elements of the foundation are:

1. Where the event occurred.
2. When the event occurred.
3. Who was involved.
4. What happened — namely, a violent act by the alleged victim.
5. The circumstances indicating that on the prior occasion, the alleged victim was the aggressor.

Assume that the government charges Mr. Lowe with assaulting Mr. Gilligan on December 1, 1988. During the defense case-in-chief, the

defense calls Mr. Nieman as a witness. Mr. Nieman has already identified himself. The defense is the proponent.

P   WHERE were you on the evening of November 1, 1988? (1), (2)
W   I was at Tarantino's restaurant in downtown Topeka.
P   WHY were you there?
W   I was attending a party.
P   WHO else was there? (3)
W   A number of people, including Mr. Gilligan.
P   WHO is Mr. Gilligan? (3)
W   He's the complaining witness in this case.
P   WHEN did you last see him? (3)
W   About an hour ago.
P   WHERE was he? (3)
W   He was in this courtroom.
P   WHAT was he doing? (3)
W   He was testifying for the prosecution.
P   WHAT, if anything, happened at this party at the restaurant? (4)
W   Mostly we just had a good time. There was one unfortunate incident.
P   WHAT was that? (4)
W   There was a fight.
P   WHO was involved in the fight? (4)
W   Mr. Gilligan and a Mr. Jones.
P   WHERE were you when the fight started? (5)
W   I was standing only a few feet away.
P   HOW well could you see what happened? (5)
W   Very well. I was standing right next to both of them when the fight
      started.
P   HOW did the fight start? (5)
W   They were just talking, and then Mr. Gilligan started screaming at Mr.
      Jones.
P   HOW loudly was he screaming? (5)
W   At the top of his voice.
P   WHAT happened then? (5)
W   Mr. Gilligan punched Mr. Jones.
P   WHO threw the first punch? (5)
W   Mr. Gilligan.
P   HOW many punches did he throw? (5)
W   He threw five or six.
P   WHAT happened then? (5)
W   I grabbed Jones, someone else grabbed Gilligan, and we separated
      them.
P   WHAT happened when the other person grabbed Mr. Gilligan? (5)
W   He struggled to get free and started calling everyone names.

Several jurisdictions also permit a criminal defendant to attack the
chaste character of the alleged victim in a sex offense prosecution.
Many courts and legislatures now restrict this type of evidence; but in
some jurisdictions, the defendant may still prove specific instances of
promiscuous conduct by the alleged victim. The line of reasoning is
that if the alleged victim consented to intercourse on prior occasions,

her prior consent increases the probability that she consented to intercourse with the defendant.

Roughly the same foundation would apply if the defendant were trying to prove the promiscuous character of the alleged victim of a sex offense:

1. Where the act occurred.
2. When the act occurred.
3. Who was present.
4. What happened.
5. The circumstances indicating that the alleged victim was acting promiscuously on the prior occasion.

Assume that the government charges Mr. Lowe with raping Ms. Younger on December 1, 1988. During the defense case-in-chief, the defense calls Mr. Norton as a witness. Mr. Norton has already identified himself. The defense is the proponent.

P   WHERE were you on the evening of November 1, 1988? (1), (2)
W   I was at Gino's bar in downtown Peoria.
P   WHAT were you doing there?
W   I was hanging out and looking for some women to pick up.
P   WHAT do you mean by "pick up"?
W   I was trying to find someone to have some fun with that night.
P   WHAT happened after you arrived at the bar? (3)
W   I bumped into a woman.
P   WHO was the woman? (3)
W   Ms. Nancy Younger.
P   WHEN did you last see her? (3)
W   Today.
P   WHERE was she? (3)
W   She was testifying for the prosecution a couple of hours ago in this courtroom.
P   WHAT happened after you met Ms. Younger? (4)
W   We spent a couple of hours at the bar and had some drinks.
P   WHAT happened next? (4)
W   We went to my apartment.
P   WHAT happened then? (4)
W   We had a couple of more drinks there, and she spent the night.
P   WHAT, if anything, happened that night? (5)
W   We had sex.
P   WHAT do you mean by "we had sex"? (5)
W   We had intercourse.
P   WHAT was your legal relation to Ms. Younger at that time? (5)
W   We didn't have any legal relation. We weren't married or engaged or anything like that.
P   HOW long had you known her before she had intercourse with you? (5)
W   A couple of hours.
P   WHAT force did you use to get her to consent to intercourse? (5)
W   None.
P   WHAT threats did you make against her? (5)
W   None. She did it of her own free will.
P   WHAT happened the next morning? (5)

W   She just left. I didn't see her again until today when I walked into the courtroom.

In federal practice, Rule 412 governs defense attacks on the character of the alleged victim in sex offense prosecutions. Rule 412(a) announces a categorical rule that the defense may not offer reputation or opinion testimony of the alleged victim's character. However, Rule 412(b)(2)(B) states that the defense may offer evidence of the alleged victim's "past sexual behavior with the accused ... upon the issue of whether the alleged victim consented to the sexual behavior with respect to which" the crime is alleged.

4. CROSS-EXAMINATION OF A CHARACTER WITNESS

After the defense conducts the direct examination of a character witness, the prosecution has a right to cross-examine the witness.

Suppose that on direct examination, the witness testified that the defendant had a reputation for peacefulness. Further assume that the prosecutor knows that the defendant was arrested for a violent battery only two months before the alleged battery. The traditional view is that during the cross-examination, the prosecutor may ask, "Have you heard a report that the defendant was arrested for battery in October 1988?" If the witness denies hearing the report, the denial impeaches the witness; the denial indicates that the witness really is not familiar with the defendant's reputation. If the witness admits hearing the report, the admission impeaches the witness; the admission indicates that the witness has a rather strange standard for evaluating good reputation. The prosecutor may inquire about reports that the defendant committed or was arrested for, indicted for, or convicted of a crime. Of course, the crime must be logically relevant to the character trait the witness testified to on direct examination. Thus, if on direct examination the witness testified to the defendant's character trait of peacefulness, the prosecutor may not inquire about an arrest for mere drunkenness.

If the jurisdiction permits opinion character evidence and on direct examination the witness expresses his or her opinion, the wording of the question on cross-examination is slightly different. The prosecutor no longer uses the "Have you heard ...?" formula. Rather, the prosecutor may ask, "Do you know that the defendant was arrested for battery in October 1988?" If the witness denies knowing about the arrest, the denial indicates that the witness may not know the defendant well. If the witness admits knowing about the arrest, the admission indicates that the witness has a strange personal standard for evaluating good character. Again, the crime inquired about must be logically relevant to the character trait the witness testified to on direct examination.

Federal Rule of Evidence 405 governs character evidence in federal trials, and the Advisory Committee's Note to the Rule states that the Committee intended to abolish the old, formal distinctions in the phrasing of the questions on cross-examination. The Note asserts that the Committee intended to "eliminate them [the distinctions] as a factor in formulating questions." Thus, under the Federal Rules, it would be permissible to use normal, cross-examination phrasing: "HAVEN'T YOU HEARD A REPORT THAT the defendant was arrested for battery in October 1988?"

Of course, in any jurisdiction, the prosecutor must have a good faith basis in fact for inquiring about the incident. The prosecutor cannot smear the defendant's character by inventing derogatory reports about the defendant. Hence, the prosecutor must have a basis in fact for believing that the defendant committed, was arrested for, was indicted for, or was convicted of the crime. The basis in fact need not be admissible evidence. For example, the prosecutor could use an eyewitness' written statement or a police report as the basis in fact. The statement and report would normally be inadmissible hearsay, but they are sufficient to give the prosecutor a good faith belief that the incident occurred. When the defense attorney challenges the prosecutor to show the basis in fact for the belief that the incident occurred, the prosecutor usually makes a statement for the record outside the jurors' hearing. In some jurisdictions, it is customary for the prosecutor to insert any documentary material into the record; the material is not admitted as a formal exhibit to be submitted to the jury, but it is sometimes marked for identification or marked as an appellate exhibit.

Assume that during cross-examination of a character witness, the prosecutor inquired about an arrest of the defendant for battery. The prosecutor might have used the classic language, "Have you heard a report that the defendant was arrested for battery in October 1988?" As opponent, the defense counsel objects:

O   Your Honor, may we approach the bench?

J   Yes.

O   Your Honor, I want to object to the last question on the ground that the prosecutor hasn't shown a good faith basis in fact for believing that this arrest occurred.

P   Your Honor, I would like to mark this document as prosecution appellate exhibit number one.

O   What is that document?

P   It is an arrest report from the Salt Lake City Police Department. The report names the defendant George Larson as the arrestee and states that he was arrested for battery on a Mr. George Langdale.

O   That report is inadmissible hearsay.

P   That would normally be true, but the material creating the basis in fact for believing the incident occurred need not qualify as admissible evidence.

J   I agree with the prosecutor. I will receive the appellate exhibit, and the objection to the question will be overruled.

P   Mr. Stacey, let me repeat the question. Have you heard a report that the defendant was arrested for battery in October 1988?

W   No.

C. HABIT EVIDENCE

1. THE DOCTRINE

The proponent may use habit evidence as well as character evidence as circumstantial proof of conduct. Federal Evidence Rule 406 states the habit evidence doctrine: "Evidence of the habit of a person or of the routine practice of an organization, whether corroborated or not and regardless of the presence of eyewitnesses, is relevant to prove that the conduct of the person or organization on a particular occasion was in conformity with the habit or routine practice."

Although both character and habit evidence serve as circumstantial proof of conduct, there are major differences between the two theories of admissibility.

The first difference is that although character evidence is usually admissible only after the criminal defendant opens the issue, under the modern view either party in a civil or criminal case may introduce habit evidence. It is true that some jurisdictions admit habit evidence only if there are no eyewitnesses to the conduct in question or only if there is corroboration of the conduct. However, Rule 406 embodies the emerging view that habit evidence is always admissible to prove the conduct of a person or business organization.

The second difference is that while character evidence permits the proponent to prove general character or character traits, habit evidence requires proof of a very specific, frequently repeated behavioral pattern. For instance, the proponent may prove the precise manner in which a decedent routinely executed right-hand turns or the specific mailing procedure a business customarily used.

Finally, the habit and character evidence theories differ in the method of proof. The proponent of character evidence ordinarily presents reputation or opinion evidence. In contrast, the proponent of habit evidence may not use reputation evidence. However, most jurisdictions sanction opinion character evidence, and opinion is the most common method of proving habit. To be qualified to express an opinion on the existence of a habit, the witness must have been familiar with the person or business for a substantial time and observed numerous instances of the person's or business' conduct. Opinion habit evidence is typically presented by a single witness who is familiar with a large number of instances of the conduct of the person or business in question. Other jurisdictions permit habit to be proven by the testimony of several witnesses. Each witness testifies to the instances of conduct he or she knows of; if the behavioral pattern is specific enough and the instances numerous enough, the judge allows the jury to infer the existence of the habit. When the proponent opts for this method of proving the existence of a habit, each witness' testimony must comply with the foundational requirements set out in Section B.3 of this chapter.

2. ELEMENTS OF THE FOUNDATION

The foundation for opinion habit evidence includes these elements:
1. The witness is familiar with the person or business.
2. The witness has been familiar with the person or business for a substantial period of time.
3. In the witness' opinion, the person or business has a habit, a specific behavioral pattern.
4. The witness has observed the person or business act in conformity with the habit on numerous occasions.

In some jurisdictions, in addition to establishing these elements of the foundation, the proponent must show that:
5. The record indicates that there were no eyewitnesses to the person's or business' conduct on the occasion involved in the case; or
6. The record contains corroboration that the person or business acted in conformity with the habit on the occasion involved in the case, *e.g.,* an eyewitness who described the person's conduct as consistent with the habit.

3. SAMPLE FOUNDATION

The fact situation is a tort action. The plaintiff sues the decedent's estate on the theory that the decedent negligently caused the traffic accident. The decedent is Mr. Myles. The collision occurred as the decedent was making a right-hand turn at a stop sign. The estate's personal representative contends that the decedent drove carefully. To support that contention, the representative desires to offer evidence of the decedent's driving habits. To do so, the representative calls Ms. Vincent, an acquaintance of the decedent. The decedent's personal representative is the proponent. Ms. Vincent has already identified herself.

P   WHO was Joshua Myles? (1)
W   He was a friend of mine. I know that he died in an accident about a year and a half ago.
P   HOW long did you know him? (2)
W   For about seven years.
P   HOW did you come to know him? (2)
W   We worked at the same bank. In fact, we were in the same car pool.
P   HOW many people were in this car pool? (2)
W   Three of us, Joshua, Kathy Jacobs, a teller, and I.

P   HOW often did you see the decedent drive a car? (2)
W   Hundreds of times. I couldn't give you a precise number.
P   WHEN did you see him drive a car? (2)
W   He did a lot of the driving in our car pool; he took me to work.
P   HOW many times a week did the decedent drive you to work? (2)
W   Usually twice.
P   HOW many weeks during the year did he drive you to work? (2)
W   About 50 per year. You have to exclude our vacation times.
P   HOW many years were you in this car pool? (2)
W   Roughly five years.
P   HOW many years was the decedent in this car pool? (2)
W   The same — five years.
P   WHAT did the decedent do when he came to a stop sign? (3)
W   He came to a complete stop.
P   HOW regularly did he do that? (4)
W   Always.
P   HOW often did you see him do that? (4)
W   Hundreds of times.
P   HOW did the decedent make right-hand turns after coming to a stop? (3)
W   He'd look both ways and start up only after he could see that it was safe.
P   HOW fast did he go immediately after starting up? (3)
W   Usually quite slowly and cautiously.
P   HOW often did you see him make a right-hand turn in that manner? (4)
W   All sorts of times.

D. OTHER CRIMES OR UNCHARGED MISCONDUCT EVIDENCE

1. THE DOCTRINE

Even in rebuttal to defense character evidence, the prosecution may not prove other crimes by the defendant simply to prove that the defendant is a law-breaking, immoral person. However, the prosecution may introduce such evidence for other purposes. As Federal Evidence Rule 404(b) announces, "Evidence of other crimes, wrongs, or acts is not admissible to prove the character of a person in order to show that he acted in conformity therewith. It may, however, be admissible for other purposes, such as proof of motive, opportunity, intent, preparation, plan, knowledge, identity, or absence of mistake or accident." Thus, if the evidence is logically relevant to a fact in issue other than character, and the prosecution's need for the evidence outweighs its prejudicial character, the prosecution may introduce the proof of the uncharged act. The federal courts follow the inclusionary approach to the uncharged misconduct doctrine: The prosecution may offer the evidence on any theory of logical relevance other than the theory explicitly forbidden by Rule 404(b).

The prosecutor offering uncharged misconduct evidence faces two primary problems. First, the prosecutor must demonstrate that the evidence is logically relevant to a material fact in issue other than character. If the defendant is charged with a specific intent crime, the defendant's commission of similar, deliberate acts may be logically relevant to prove the specific intent. If the defendant claims entrapment, proof of the defendant's voluntary commission of similar crimes is relevant to rebut the entrapment defense.

Second, the prosecutor must convince the judge that the prosecution's need for the evidence outweighs its prejudicial character. To be sure, such evidence is highly prejudicial, and there is a grave danger that the jurors will misuse it as evidence of the defendant's bad, law-breaking disposition. However, if the element of the crime the prosecution wants to offer the uncharged misconduct evidence to prove is disputed, the judge will probably admit the evidence. Hence, if the prosecution wants to offer the evidence to prove identity and the defendant denied committing the crime, the judge would probably rule in the prosecution's favor.

2. ELEMENTS OF THE FOUNDATION

The foundation includes these elements:
1. Where the other act occurred.
2. When the act occurred.
3. What the nature of the act was.
4. The defendant committed the other act. In *Huddleston v. United States,* 485 U.S. __, 108 S. Ct. 1496 (1988), the Court held that Rule 104(b) governs this foundational fact. The judge accepts the prosecution's foundational evidence at face value and asks only whether the evidence is sufficient to create a permissive inference that the defendant committed the act.
5. The surrounding circumstances making the uncharged act relevant to the charged crime. The prosecutor must convince the trial judge that the act is logically relevant to a material fact other than the defendant's criminal disposition or propensity.

Even after the prosecutor lays a proper foundation, the defense counsel will have a right to a limiting instruction. Under Rule 105, the judge must inform the jury that they may not use the evidence as general character evidence; rather, the jury must use the evidence only in deciding the existence of the fact the judge admitted the evidence to prove, *e.g.,* motive, intent, or identity.

3. SAMPLE FOUNDATION

Suppose that the government has charged the defendant, Mr. Standish, with armed robbery. During the prosecution case-in-chief, a single eyewitness identified the defendant as the robber. A police officer also testified on behalf of the prosecution. He testified that he searched the crime scene and found a .32 caliber pistol with the serial number, 789444. During the defense case-in-chief, the defendant testified and denied committing the robbery. During the prosecution rebuttal, the prosecution calls Mr. Usher. Mr. Usher has already identified himself. The prosecution is the proponent.

P WHAT is your occupation?
W I own a gun store.
P WHERE were you on March 15th of this year? (1), (2)
W I was at work at my store.
P WHAT, if anything, happened that day? (3)
W I was the victim of a theft that day.
P WHAT was stolen? (5)
W A pistol.
P WHAT pistol? (5)
W It was a .32 caliber pistol, serial number 789444.
P HOW do you know that? (5)
W I handle all my inventory personally, and I refreshed my memory by reviewing my records before trial.
P HOW was the pistol stolen? (4)
W A guy came in in broad daylight, pretended he was looking to buy, and then grabbed the pistol and ran out the door.
P HOW well did you see the thief? (4)
W Very well.
P HOW close were you to the thief? (4)
W When he was at the counter, he was only about five feet away.
P HOW much time did you have to observe the thief? (4)
W He was in the store for at least a couple of minutes.
P WHO was the thief? (4)
W I'm not sure of his name, but I see him in the courtroom right now.
P WHERE is he sitting? (4)
W At that table over there.
P HOW is he dressed? (4)
W He's wearing a blue suit and green tie.
P Your Honor, may the record reflect that the witness has identified the defendant?
J It will so reflect.
P Your Honor, at this point, I would request a limiting instruction.
J I will grant the request. Ladies and gentlemen of the jury, you have just heard testimony that the defendant stole a pistol, serial number 789444. You may not infer from that evidence that the defendant is generally a bad person and, for that reason, more likely to have committed the robbery. However, there is evidence that a pistol with that serial number was found at the robbery scene. You may use Mr. Usher's testimony in deciding whether the defendant had possession of that pistol before the robbery.

E. UNCHARGED MISCONDUCT EVIDENCE IN CIVIL ACTIONS

1. THE DOCTRINE

Rule 404(b) refers not only to evidence of other "crime[s]" but also to evidence of other "wrong[s] ... or other act[s]." Moreover, while statutes such as Rule 404(a)(1) are expressly limited to criminal actions, there is no such limitation in Rule 404(b). Therefore, 404(b) should apply to civil actions as well as prosecutions. In a prosecution, the government may not use evidence of a defendant's other crimes as circumstantial proof of conduct; the prosecution may not argue that the defendant has a bad character and that his bad character increases the probability that he committed the charged crime. Similarly, in a tort action, the plaintiff may not use evidence of a defendant's other torts as circumstantial proof of conduct; the plaintiff may not argue that the defendant is a careless driver and that his character trait of careless driving increases the likelihood that he ran the red light. To this extent, the criminal and civil cases are parallel.

However, in another respect, the civil cases differ from the criminal cases. As stated in the last section, in contemporary criminal cases most courts follow the inclusionary approach; they permit the prosecutor to rely on any noncharacter theory of logical relevance. They do so because 404(b) prefaces the list of acceptable theories of logical relevance with the words, "such as." In contrast, many civil cases still follow an exclusionary approach; they insist that the proponent of other misconduct in a civil case bring the evidence within a pigeonhole exception such as proof of a defendant's earlier notice of the existence of a dangerous condition. However, the use of an exclusionary approach seems to violate 404(b). As the preceding paragraph pointed out, 404(b) is not restricted to prosecutions; and 404(b) codifies an inclusionary approach. In the past, the courts have looked to Rule 403 as a source of authority to continue to enforce the rigid, common law restrictions on the admission of a defendant's other torts. However, rather than analyzing the admissibility of other torts under 403, the courts should test their admissibility under 404(b). As the more specific statute, 404(b) should control. Hence, like a criminal prosecutor, the proponent of uncharged misconduct in a civil case should be permitted to introduce the evidence on any noncharacter theory. The proponent should be able to rely on any theory of logical relevance other than the general inference that the person's other negligent or wrongful acts increase the likelihood of fault on the pleaded occasion. The federal cases now apply Rule 404(b) in civil cases. Annot., 64 A.L.R. Fed. 648 (1983).

2. ELEMENTS OF THE FOUNDATION

The list of foundational elements is the same as the list for uncharged misconduct evidence in criminal cases:

1. Where the other act occurred.
2. When the act occurred.
3. What the nature of the act was.
4. The defendant committed the other act.
5. The surrounding circumstances make the unpleaded act relevant to the pleaded act. The proponent must convince the trial judge that the act is logically relevant to a material fact other than the defendant's disposition or propensity.

3. SAMPLE FOUNDATION

The fact situation is a wrongful discharge action. The plaintiff, Morrison, contends that the defendant, Ziegler, fired him because the plaintiff is black. The complaint alleges that the defendant employed the plaintiff as a Shop Supervisor and that the defendant fired the plaintiff on May 12, 1989. The defendant purchased the company in 1988. As his next witness, the plaintiff calls Mr. Foote. Mr. Foote has already identified himself.

P   WHERE do you work?

W   At the moment I'm unemployed.

P   WHAT was your last job? (4), (5)

W   I worked for the defendant, Ron Ziegler.

P   WHERE is he now? (4)

W   In the courtroom. He's sitting at the table to my right. He's got on a brown suit.

P   Your Honor, please let the record reflect that the witness has identified the defendant.

J   It will so reflect.

P   WHAT type of work did you do for the defendant? (5)

W   I was a Shop Supervisor from 1985 to 1989. I worked on the assembly line from 1971 to 1985.

P   WHY did you stop working for him? (3)

W   He fired me.

P   WHEN did he do that? (2)

W   It was in late April 1989.

P   WHERE did it happen? (1)

W   One day over the public address system he just called me into his office. I reported there as soon as I heard the call.

P   WHAT happened after you reported to his office? (3)

W   He said he was firing me.

P   WHAT did you do then? (5)

W   I demanded an explanation. I'd put in a lot of good years at that company, and I wanted to know why he was letting me go.

P   WHAT, if anything, did the defendant say when you demanded an explanation? (5)

W   He said he was letting me go because I was black. He said he didn't
    like me; and since there were no witnesses to our conversation, he
    didn't mind telling me the real reason he was giving me my walking
    papers.

O   Your Honor, may we approach the bench?

J   Certainly.

O   Your Honor, I move to strike this entire line of questioning on the
    ground that it's irrelevant and that it amounts to bad character evi-
    dence.

P   May I be heard?

J   Yes.

P   Your Honor, I'm not going to offer this evidence to support a general
    inference that the defendant is a bad person. I know that it would
    violate Rule 404(b). Rather, I'm offering this evidence on a
    noncharacter theory of logical relevance. The defendant fired Mr.
    Foote a few days before he fired the plaintiff. Like the plaintiff, Mr.
    Foote is a black man. Given the surrounding circumstances, including
    the defendant's statements to Mr. Foote, the firing of Mr. Foote shows
    that the defendant had a racial prejudice that motivated him to fire
    black employees. In this case, we have to show that the defendant fired
    the plaintiff because he was black, and this April incident tends to
    show the defendant's later intent.

J   I agree. Motion to strike denied.

O   If you're going to overrule my motion, will you at least give the jury a
    limiting instruction?

J   Of course. I'll tell them that they can't use it as proof that your client is
    a bad person. I'll direct them to consider the evidence only in deciding
    why your client discharged the plaintiff.

F. SIMILAR HAPPENINGS EVIDENCE

1. THE DOCTRINE

In the last section, we saw that Rule 404(b) applies in a civil case
when a party offers evidence of a person's misdeeds that are not mentioned in the pleadings. The first sentence of Rule 404(b) bars the party
from using the misdeeds as circumstantial proof of the person's conduct, but the second sentence permits the party to use noncharacter
theories of logical relevance to introduce evidence of the misdeeds.
Whether the case is a prosecution or a civil action, under Rule 404(b)
the focus is on the conduct of some person.

In other cases, the focus is on the qualities or properties of a physical
object. Was a sidewalk cracked at the time the plaintiff slipped and
fell? Was a steering wheel's design dangerously defective? To prove the
quality of the object, the plaintiff may attempt to introduce evidence of
other accidents involving the same or similar objects. Article, *Similar
Facts Evidence: Balancing Probative Value Against the Probable Dangers of Admission*, 9 U.C. Davis L. Rev. 395 (1976). For example, the
plaintiff may offer evidence that the day before her mishap, another
bypasser slipped and fell at the same location on the sidewalk.

On the one hand, Rule 404(b) does not apply directly when a plaintiff offers evidence of such a similar happening. Rule 404(b) comes into play when the party offers evidence of another incident to prove a person's conduct. The focus is now on the property of an object rather than any conduct by a person. On the other hand, like evidence of a person's misdeeds used as circumstantial proof of the person's conduct, evidence of the other slip and fall poses probative dangers. The presentation of the testimony about the other accident may confuse the trier of fact, consume an undue amount of time, and sidetrack the trial. For that reason, although the evidence of the other slip and fall is relevant to prove the existence of the crack in the sidewalk, the judge might exclude the evidence under Rule 403.

In the past, most courts adopted an exclusionary approach to the admission of evidence of other accidents. The courts announced a general rule that such evidence is inadmissible. The courts recognized only a limited number of exceptions to the general rule; they permitted plaintiffs to introduce evidence of other torts to show that: A particular physical condition existed at the time of plaintiff's accident; the condition was dangerous or defective; the defendant had noticed that the condition existed; and the condition caused the accident. Further, even if the evidence otherwise fell within an exception to the general exclusionary rule, the plaintiff had to demonstrate that the conditions obtaining at the time of the pleaded accident were substantially similar to the circumstances surrounding the unpleaded tort.

The courts have begun to liberalize the standards for admitting evidence of other torts and accidents. In *Ault v. International Harvester Co.*, 13 Cal. 3d 113, 528 P.2d 1148, 117 Cal. Rptr. 812 (1974), the plaintiff claimed that he was injured when the gear box of the vehicle manufactured by the defendant failed. The plaintiff offered evidence of several other accidents involving the defendant's motor vehicle and seemingly caused by metal fatigue of the aluminum gear box. However, the plaintiff did not introduce any other evidence of the circumstances surrounding the other accidents. On appeal, the California Supreme Court held that the evidence of the other accidents was admissible. One commentator writes:

> *Ault* ... creates an exception to the general rule .... This exception permits evidence of a prior or subsequent accident in a defective-product-strict-liability case without a showing of similarity of circumstances ... if the defect claimed is that of the physical and mechanical characteristics of a product, and the evidence of the prior or subsequent accident establishes that the product involved in such accident and the product involved in the accident in question possessed inherent similarities in their physical and mechanical characteristics, and that the two products possessed similar defects because of the product's physical and mechanical characteristics that caused the two accidents. If these conditions are satisfied, it

is of no moment that the two accidents may have occurred under substantially different circumstances or conditions.

1 B. Jefferson, *California Evidence Benchbook* § 21.7, at 573 (3d ed. 1982).

2. ELEMENTS OF THE FOUNDATION

The foundation is similar to the foundation for evidence of an uncharged crime in a prosecution or tort offered under Rule 404(b):
1. Where the other accident occurred.
2. When the accident occurred.
3. What the nature of the accident was.
4. The defendant's responsibility for the accident.
5. The surrounding circumstances making the unpleaded happening relevant to show the property or quality of the object mentioned in the pleading.

3. SAMPLE FOUNDATION*

The fact situation is a products liability case arising from a traffic accident. The plaintiff, Ms. Ramachotti, alleges that she purchased a 1988 Polecat Centuria and that the car's steering mechanism had a design defect. Specifically, the plaintiff contends that the mechanism had a tendency to freeze in lengthy, uphill turns.

The plaintiff has already testified. During her testimony the plaintiff testified that she was driving north on a freeway and entered an off-ramp leading to the eastbound lane of a street near the freeway. She described the off-ramp as turning to the right, sloping slightly uphill, and being approximately 2,000 feet in length. The plaintiff stated that the steering wheel froze when her car was halfway through the off-ramp. The plaintiff used a chart to illustrate her testimony.

The plaintiff's attorney calls Mr. Dorsey to testify about an uncharged accident involving Dorsey's 1988 Polecat Centuria with a stick shift. The purpose of Dorsey's testimony is to show the existence of a defect in the Centuria's steering mechanism.

Assume that the witness has already identified himself. As in the criminal case, the next part of the direct examination establishes the witness' personal knowledge of the uncharged accident.

P   WHERE were you on the morning of September 19th?
W   I drove from my home in San Lorenzo to downtown Livermore. (1), (2)
P   WHO was driving the car?
W   I was.

---

*Adapted from E. Imwinkelried, *Uncharged Misconduct Evidence* § 9:26 (1984). Reprinted with permission.

(The next part of the direct examination is devoted to showing the similarity of circumstances between the uncharged accident and the accident alleged in the pleading. The plaintiff wants to demonstrate that the physical layout of the site of the uncharged accident is comparable to that of the pleaded accident.)

P   WHAT route did you take?

W   I drove Highway 580 most of the way. (1)

P   In WHAT direction were you driving on Highway 580? (1)

W   I was traveling east.

P   WHEN did you get off Highway 580? (2)

W   I tried to get off at the exit for traffic going south on Hanley Avenue.

P   HOW can you remember that exit?

W   I use it all the time when I go into Livermore.

P   Your Honor, I request that this be marked plaintiff's exhibit number four for identification.

J   It will be so marked.

P   Please let the record reflect that I am showing the exhibit to the opposing counsel.

J   The record will so reflect.

P   I request permission to approach the witness.

J   Permission granted.

P   Mr. Dorsey, I now hand you what has been marked plaintiff's exhibit number four for identification. WHAT is it? (1)

W   It's a map showing Highway 580 and the off-ramp for Hanley going south.

P   HOW can you recognize it? (1)

W   As I said, I've used that off-ramp lots of times.

P   WHEN you enter this off-ramp, in WHAT direction are you traveling?

W   At first, you're still going east.

P   Please use this blue marker and write "east" at the mouth of the off-ramp.

W   Yes.

P   Your Honor, please let the record reflect that the witness has complied with my request.

J   It will so reflect.

P   WHEN you finally reached Hanley, in WHAT direction were you traveling? (1)

W   South.

P   Please write "south" at the off-ramp's exit.

W   Done.

P   In WHAT direction were you turning on the off-ramp? (1)

W   I was turning to the right.

P   HOW long is the off-ramp? (5)

W   It's pretty long. It's a gradual thing. It's maybe 2000 feet.

P   HOW does the off-ramp slope? Does it go up to Hanley or down to Hanley? (5)

W   It slopes up. You're going up maybe 10 feet in all.

P   Please draw an arrow from the mouth of the off-ramp to the exit and write "up" next to the arrow.

W   O.K.

P   HOW steep is the slope? (5)

W   I'm no engineer, but it's pretty gradual.

P   In general, HOW accurate is this exhibit? (1)

W   I don't know if it's to scale, but on the whole it seems correct.

P   Your Honor, I now offer plaintiff's exhibit number four for identification into evidence as plaintiff's exhibit number four.

J   It will be received.

(The plaintiff now begins to invoke process-of-elimination reasoning. To single out the defect in the vehicle's steering as the cause of the accident, the plaintiff questions the witness to negate other possible causes of the accident such as lack of maintenance, speeding, intoxication, poor visibility, and the witness' inattention.)

P   Now, Mr. Dorsey, I'd like to ask you a few question about the car you were driving toward this off-ramp. WHERE did you purchase this car? (4)

W   From a Polecat dealer in Hayward.

P   Was the car new or used?

W   New. I was the first owner.

P   HOW long had you owned the car before the accident on September 19th? (4)

W   I'd had it for only two months before this occurred.

P   HOW often, if at all, had you had the car serviced before the accident? (4)

W   I took it in twice. The first time I took it in about two weeks after buying it, and then I took it in about a week before the accident for the 2,500-mile maintenance under the warranty.

P   WHERE did you take the car for service? (4)

W   I took it back to the same Polecat dealer that I initially bought it from.

P   Mr. Dorsey, to the best of your knowledge, WHAT was the condition of your car on the day of the accident?

W   As far as I knew, it was in good working order.

P   All right, now let's get back to the exhibit. Could you show us approximately WHERE your car was on the map when you were 1,000 feet from the entrance to the off-ramp? (1)

W   I'd say right here.

P   Please place a dot and "D-1" at that point.

W   Here it is.

P   At that point, HOW fast were you doing? (5)

W   I was doing about 55, but this is the point where I began to slow down.

P   WHAT is the posted speed limit along this portion of Highway 580? (5)

W   55.

P   Now please indicate with a dot and "D-2" WHERE you would be when you were 100 feet from the entrance to the off-ramp. (1)

W   Right.

P   HOW fast were you going then? (5)

W   I had slowed to 30.

P   WHAT is the posted speed limit at the entrance to the off-ramp? (5)

W   I'm pretty sure it's 30.

P   WHAT was the condition of the pavement? (5)

W   It was dry.

P   WHEN was the last rain? (5)

W   Not in weeks.
P   HOW well could you see when you reached the mouth of the off-ramp? (5)
W   Perfectly.
P   WHAT were the lighting conditions at that time? (5)
W   It was mid-morning, and it was a beautiful, clear day.
P   WHAT, if anything, obstructed your view of the off-ramp? (5)
W   Nothing. The only shrubbery in the area is grass. There are no big trees or anything.
P   HOW closely were you paying attention to your driving? (5)
W   I was watching it close.
P   WHY? (5)
W   Hanley is a pretty busy street, and I wanted to have good control of my car before I got on a busy thoroughfare like Hanley.
P   HOW good was your vision that morning? (5)
W   Fine. I have 20-20 vision, and I've never worn glasses.
P   WHAT was your physical condition? (5)
W   Excellent.
P   HOW many drinks, if any, had you had that morning? (5)
W   None. None at all.

(At this point, the plaintiff elicits the description of the accident itself. The plaintiff wants to make the uncharged accident sound as similar as possible to the pleaded accident.)

P   WHAT happened after you entered the off-ramp? (3)
W   At first, everything was going smoothly.
P   WHAT happened next?
W   About halfway into the turn, the steering wheel just plain froze.
P   WHAT do you mean by "froze"? (5)
W   I couldn't move it at all.
P   Please indicate by placing "D-3" WHERE you were when the steering first froze. (1)
W   Right there.
P   HOW fast were you going then? (5)
W   Probably only 20 or 25.
P   WHAT did you do then? (5)
W   I hit the brakes and tried to move the wheel.
P   HOW quickly did you hit the brakes? (5)
W   As soon as I realized I was in trouble — immediately.
P   HOW did the wheel respond? (5)
W   Not at all.
P   WHAT happened after you hit the brakes? (5)
W   I slowed a bit, but it was just too late.
P   WHERE did the car go? (5)
W   It plowed through the railing, flew off the off-ramp, and finally stopped over here.
P   Please mark the resting point of your car with "D-4."
W   Right here.

(At this point, the plaintiff elicits the witness' testimony that his automobile contained the same design feature as the plaintiff's.)

P   Now the car that you were driving that morning, the car that eventually came to rest at D-4, WHAT was the make of that car? (4), (5)
W   It was a Polecat.
P   WHAT was the model of Polecat? (5)
W   It was the Centuria.
P   WHAT was the year of that model? (5)
W   1988.
P   Was the car automatic or stick shift? (5)
W   Stick shift.
P   WHAT, if any, accessories did you have on the car? (5)
W   Other than air-conditioning and radio, there were none. It was a basic 1988 Polecat Centuria right off the showroom floor.
P   Thank you, Mr. Dorsey. (To the defense counsel) Your witness.

G. IN-COURT EXHIBITIONS

The proponent will sometimes want to display something other than a normal, inanimate physical exhibit to the jurors. For example, in a personal injury case, the plaintiff's attorney may want the plaintiff to display the injured part of the body to the jurors. Such an exhibition can be helpful to the jury in determining the damages in the case. The probative danger is that the exhibition will inflame the jurors; after viewing a badly mangled limb, the jurors may not be able to dispassionately weigh the evidence on liability or damages.

Under Rule 403, the trial judge has wide discretion in deciding whether to permit an exhibition. The judge ordinarily considers three factors: (1) whether the object to be exhibited is relevant to the case; (2) whether the jurors need to see the object to understand the oral testimony about the object; and (3) the risk that viewing the object will inflame the jurors' emotions.

The fact situation is a products liability action. The plaintiff, Mr. Jansen, brought the action against Kenway, Inc., which manufactures electrical saws. The plaintiff alleges that the defendant defectively designed the saw and that the design defect caused the blade to come loose and slice the plaintiff's arms. The plaintiff takes the witness stand; when he does so, the plaintiff is wearing a jacket. The plaintiff has testified about his injuries in general terms. The proponent, the plaintiff's attorney, now wants to exhibit the injuries to the jurors.

P   WHAT were your injuries?
W   The blade sliced both of my arms very badly.
P   Mr. Jansen, would you please take off your jacket and show your arms to the jurors?
O   Your Honor, may we approach the bench?
J   Certainly.
O   Your Honor, I strenuously object to this exhibition.
P   Your Honor, the plaintiff's arms were injured in this accident, and it's certainly logically relevant to show the jurors what the arms look like now.

O   I admit that the exhibition would be relevant, but I object on the ground that the sight of the plaintiff's badly cut arms will arouse the jurors' emotions and prejudice my client.

P   The jurors simply won't understand the extent of the plaintiff's injuries unless they actually see the arms.

J   I tend to agree. The objection is overruled. You may proceed with the exhibition.

H. IN-COURT DEMONSTRATIONS

A demonstration is a step beyond an exhibition. In an exhibition, the proponent merely displays something for the jurors' view. In a demonstration, the proponent demonstrates some physical or mechanical process in action. The proponent may want to demonstrate how poorly the plaintiff can move his limbs or how a particular machine operates. Once again, under Rule 403, the trial judge has wide discretion in deciding whether to permit the demonstration. In exercising his or her discretion, the judge looks to the factors relevant to exhibitions plus an additional factor. The fourth factor is the risk that the party demonstrating a physical process may be feigning. A plaintiff can easily feign the extent of his or her disability, and it will be very difficult to expose the feigning plaintiff during cross-examination.

We shall continue the hypothetical in Section G. Suppose that the plaintiff claims that as a result of the saw accident, he can no longer straighten his arms.

P   Mr. Jansen, let me repeat my request. Please show your arms to the jurors.

W   *(The witness does so.)*

P   HOW has the accident affected your arms?

W   I have a good deal of pain, and I can't straighten them all the way any more.

P   Please show us how far you can straighten your arms.

O   Your Honor, may we approach the bench again?

J   Yes.

O   I hate to object again, Your Honor, but I feel compelled to register my objection to this demonstration.

P   Your Honor, this demonstration is indisputably logically relevant. To show the plaintiff's disability, we have to show the extent to which he's lost the use of his arms.

O   Your Honor, how can I cross-examine a demonstration? There's too great a risk that the plaintiff will be able to feign the extent of his disability.

P   We need this demonstration to help the jury understand our medical testimony about the extent of disability, and the defendant can cross-examine the experts about whether the plaintiff is faking.

J   The objection will be overruled. The demonstration may proceed.

I. LIABILITY INSURANCE

A tort plaintiff ordinarily may not prove that the defendant has liability insurance. There is a weak argument that the defendant's liability coverage is logically relevant to show the defendant's negligence; knowing that he or she has liability insurance, the defendant might be less careful. However, there is a prominent probative danger that the evidence will tempt the jury to decide the case on an improper basis; the jurors may find for the plaintiff — not because they are convinced of the defendant's fault but rather because they feel the insurance company can better afford to absorb the economic loss. Federal Evidence Rule 411 states the norm: "Evidence that a person was or was not insured against liability is not admissible upon the issue whether the person acted negligently or otherwise wrongfully. This rule does not require the exclusion of evidence of insurance against liability when offered for another purpose, such as proof of agency, ownership, or control, or bias or prejudice of a witness."

On the one hand, the evidence of the defendant's liability insurance may not be used to support a generalized inference of the defendant's negligence. On the other hand, as Rule 411 makes clear, the plaintiff may use the evidence for other purposes. The following foundations illustrate both the rule and two of the more important exceptions to the rule.

The first fact situation is a tort case. The plaintiff, Ms. Greenwich, sues the defendant, Mr. Fenton. The plaintiff alleges that the defendant's negligent driving caused the collision in which she was injured. The defendant takes the stand and denies driving carelessly. The plaintiff then begins cross-examination. The plaintiff is the opponent.

O   Mr. Fenton, ISN'T IT TRUE THAT you carry liability insurance?
P   Your Honor, I object to that question on the ground that it calls for evidence of liability insurance.
J   Objection sustained.
P   Your Honor, I request a curative instruction.
J   Yes. Ladies and gentlemen of the jury, you have just heard a reference to possible liability insurance in this case. You are to disregard that reference. You may not speculate whether the defendant has insurance, and you may not consider the possible existence of insurance in your deliberations. You are to decide whether the defendant is liable solely on the basis of the evidence admitted in this case.
P   Now, Your Honor, I must move for a mistrial.
J   Well, I don't think that the reference is serious enough to warrant that. The motion will be denied.

The hypothetical continues. Assume that the defendant called Mr. Graham as a witness. Mr. Graham inspected the accident scene and measured the plaintiff's skidmarks. The skidmarks supported the defendant's theory that the plaintiff caused the accident by speeding. The plaintiff now takes Mr. Graham on cross-examination.

P   Mr. Graham, ISN'T IT TRUE THAT you work for Allied Insurance Company?

W   Yes.

P   AND ISN'T IT ALSO A FACT THAT your company insures the defendant, Mr. Fenton?

O   Your Honor, I object to that question on the ground that it calls for evidence of liability insurance.

P   Your Honor, may we approach the bench?

J   Yes.

P   Your Honor, we are not offering the evidence to support a general inference of negligence on Mr. Fenton's part. Rather, we would offer the evidence to impeach Mr. Graham; the evidence is logically relevant to show Mr. Graham's bias in the defendant's favor.

J   The objection is overruled.

P   Mr. Graham, let me repeat the question. ISN'T IT CORRECT THAT your company insures the defendant?

W   Yes.

O   Your Honor, I request a limiting instruction under Rule 105.

J   Very well. Ladies and gentlemen of the jury, you have just heard evidence that the defendant has liability insurance. You may not consider that evidence in deciding whether the defendant was at fault in the accident. You also should not consider whether the insurance company is in a better economic position to absorb any loss than the plaintiff. I am admitting the evidence for one, limited purpose — to shed light on Mr. Graham's credibility. You may consider the fact that Mr. Graham works for Mr. Fenton's insurance company in deciding how much weight to attach to Mr. Graham's testimony.

The hypothetical continues. Now assume that Jennings Trucking Company is the codefendant. The codefendant denies that Fenton is its employee. The codefendant calls Mr. Munster as a witness. Mr. Munster testifies that he is the codefendant's general manager. On direct examination, he testifies that although Fenton once worked for Jennings Trucking Company, he was not an employee at the time of the accident. Suppose that the plaintiff gave Jennings notice to produce its insurance policy and thereby satisfied the best evidence rule. The plaintiff now takes Mr. Munster on cross-examination.

P   Mr. Munster, ISN'T IT TRUE THAT your company carries liability insurance?

O   Your Honor, I object to that question on the ground that it calls for evidence of liability insurance.

P   Your Honor, may we approach the bench?

J   Yes.

P   I offer to prove that if the witness is permitted to answer, the witness will testify that the codefendant's insurance policy listed Mr. Fenton as an employee at the time of the accident. The codefendant denies that Mr. Fenton was its employee at that time, and I am offering the evidence for the limited purpose of showing Mr. Fenton's agency.

J   The objection will be overruled.

P   Mr. Munster, let me repeat the question. ISN'T IT TRUE THAT your company carries liability insurance?

W   Yes.

P   ISN'T IT CORRECT THAT you are the custodian of the insurance policy?

W   Yes.

P   AND ISN'T IT A FACT THAT appendix II to the policy lists the employees covered by the policy?

W   That's correct.

P   ISN'T IT TRUE THAT at the time of the accident, appendix II to your policy listed Mr. Fenton as one of your employees?

W   That's right.

O   Your Honor, I would like a limiting instruction.

J   Yes. Ladies and gentlemen of the jury, you have just heard a reference to the codefendant's liability insurance. You are not to consider that evidence in deciding whether either defendant acted negligently. You are also not to speculate as to whether the insurance company could absorb the loss resulting from the accident. You are to consider the evidence only for the purpose of deciding whether, at the time of the accident, Mr. Fenton was an employee of Jennings Trucking Company.

Chapter 7

PRIVILEGES AND SIMILAR DOCTRINES

A. INTRODUCTION

In the past two chapters, we examined rules based on the concerns listed in Federal Rule 403. The concerns are that the jury will misuse the item of evidence, overestimate the probative value of the evidence, or lose sight of the historical merits of the case. The concerns reflect policies governing the way in which we want jurors to behave. Ideally, we want the jury to use items of evidence properly, ascribe the proper weight to each item, and concentrate on the historical merits of the case. When we exclude evidence under Rule 403 or any of the more specific rules in Articles IV or VI, we are excluding logically relevant evidence for a policy reason — a policy related to the way in which trials should be conducted.

This chapter is devoted to another type of evidentiary doctrine which results in the exclusion of logically relevant evidence for policy reasons. This type of doctrine bars the evidence to promote an extrinsic social policy, that is, a policy related to conduct outside the courtroom. The privileges for confidential relations epitomize this type of rule. Suppose that a party makes damaging admissions in a letter to his or her attorney. The party had firsthand, personal knowledge of the facts admitted. The admissions are not only logically relevant; they are highly reliable, since the party had personal knowledge of the facts. However, the judge will routinely exclude the letter on the ground that the letter is a privileged communication. The courts want to give clients the assurance that they can disclose all the facts to their attorneys without fear that the facts will be divulged to strangers. With fuller disclosure from their clients, attorneys can render more effective service. The courts believe that the policy is important enough to warrant excluding even relevant, reliable evidence.

Similar reasoning underlies the government privileges. Modern government needs a vast amount of information to perform its tasks, especially its regulatory functions, and sometimes the government cannot obtain information from particular sources without assuring confidentiality. The government's interest is even more compelling if the government information qualifies as a military or state secret. The balance of interests favors creating a doctrine which the government may invoke to suppress the information. The information may be highly relevant and thoroughly trustworthy, but the public interest in maintaining the information's secrecy outweighs the parties' interest in disclosure.

B. PRIVILEGES FOR CONFIDENTIAL RELATIONS — IN GENERAL

We can summarize the law of privileges for confidential relations in this fashion: In certain types of proceedings, the holder has certain privileges with respect to privileged information unless (1) the holder has waived the privilege, or (2) there is an applicable exception to the privilege's scope. This summational sentence raises six issues.

The first issue is in what types of proceedings privileges apply. The general rule is that privileges apply in any proceeding in which testimony can be compelled. A few privileges have a peculiar, limited scope. For instance, in many jurisdictions, the statutory physician-patient privilege does not apply in criminal prosecutions. However, with such rare exceptions, privileges apply in all legal proceedings.

The second question is who is the holder of the privilege. The original holder is the intended beneficiary of the privacy. Thus, the client is the holder of the attorney-client privilege, the patient the holder of the physician-patient privilege, and the penitent the holder of the penitent-clergyman privilege. Most jurisdictions consider both spouses holders of the spousal privilege. If the original holder of the privilege becomes mentally incompetent, that person's guardian or conservator becomes the successor holder of the privilege. In some jurisdictions, if the original holder dies, the personal representative such as the executor or heir becomes a successor holder of the privilege. Finally, the holder's agent may sometimes assert the privilege on the holder's behalf. The client may authorize the attorney to claim the attorney-client privilege for the client at a particular hearing. In some jurisdictions, the agent has implied-in-law authority to do so.

The third question is what is the nature of the privilege. The privilege can encompass three rights. The first right is the personal right to refuse to disclose the privileged information. A judge may neither hold the holder in contempt nor impose discovery sanctions on the holder if the holder is properly invoking a privilege. The second right is the right to prevent third parties from making disclosure. The recipient of the communication, the attorney, physician, or clergyman, is clearly bound. The troublesome question is whether eavesdroppers and interceptors are bound. The traditional view has been that they are not bound and may testify to the privileged communications. However, in recent years the courts have attached more weight to the interest in privacy, and the trend in both the cases and statutes is to silence eavesdroppers and interceptors. The third and final right is the right to preclude the opposing counsel and the judge from commenting on the invocation of the privilege. In roughly half the jurisdictions, the opposing counsel may argue that since the holder invoked a privilege to suppress the information, the information probably would have been unfavorable. Roughly half the jurisdictions prohibit such comment; they reason that it is inconsistent, on the one hand, to grant the privilege and, on the other hand, to permit adverse inferences from the privilege's invocation.

However, there is one right which a common-law or statutory privilege does not encompass: the right to exclude evidence derived from a violation of the privilege. In this respect, common-law and statutory privileges differ from constitutional privileges like the fourth amendment exclusionary rule. Assume that the police conduct an illegal warrantless search of the defendant's apartment and discover a diary showing the location of evidence of the crime. The police immediately go to the location and dig up the evidence. The police deliver the evidence to the prosecutor. The defendant can move to suppress not only the diary but also the derived evidence; the derived evidence is also suppressible as the fruit of the poisonous tree. In contrast, suppose that one spouse reveals a confidential communication from the other spouse to the police. The police then use that revelation as an investigative lead and uncover other evidence that incriminates the other spouse. In this setting, the derivative evidence is admissible. The defendant spouse could preclude the other spouse from repeating the revelation on the witness stand, but the defendant cannot suppress the evidence the police derived from the violation of the defendant's confidence.

The fourth question is the most difficult: What is privileged information? Simply stated, privileged information is a confidential communication between properly related parties and incident to the relation. This question presents several subissues.

What is a "communication"? Oral and written statements fall within the definition of "communication." However, in the case of some privileges, many jurisdictions use extraordinarily broad definitions of "communication." In the case of the physician-patient privilege, many jurisdictions extend the privilege to any information the physician gains by examining the patient. The physician could not testify about the patient's physical condition even though the observation of the patient's physical condition is not a "communication" in the orthodox sense of the term. Moreover, several jurisdictions use a broad definition of communication in the spousal privilege. These jurisdictions sometimes privilege any information one spouse gains from the other spouse by virtue of the marital relation. In some cases, the courts have applied the spousal privilege when one spouse witnessed the other spouse bury incriminating evidence in the backyard. The second spouse is relying upon marital privacy when he or she performs the act in the other spouse's presence, and the courts reason that the marital privacy deserves legal protection.

When is a communication "confidential"? Confidentiality entails two elements: (1) physical privacy; and (2) an intent on the holder's part to maintain secrecy. If third parties are present to the holder's knowledge, the courts usually hold that the communication is not confidential. For practical business reasons, the courts have allowed clerks and secretaries to be present without destroying confidentiality; the courts realize that attorneys and physicians use assistants to conduct their professional work. Even if there was physical privacy at the time of the communication, the communication is unprivileged if the holder intended subsequent disclosure outside the circle of confidence. Suppose that the client gave the attorney information for the specific purpose of including the information in a press release about the case. The normal inference would be that the client never intended confidentiality.

Next, what are the protected relations? The answer varies from jurisdiction to jurisdiction. There are now statutes and decisions recognizing privileges for the following relations, among others: attorney-client, physician-patient, psychotherapist-patient, accountant-client, social worker-client, penitent-clergyman, parent-child, and spouses. The courts and legislatures believe that these are useful social relationships and that the nature of the relationship requires an element of confidentiality. This belief is the policy judgment underlying the very existence of the privileges.

In applying the relationship requirement, the courts have found two fact situations troublesome. One situation is the case in which a corporate employee communicates with corporate counsel. When is the communication deemed a communication between the corporate client and the corporate counsel? Some jurisdictions limit the corporate attorney-client privilege to communications between corporate counsel and the members of the corporate "control group," the narrow circle of directors, officers, and high-ranking employees needing direct access to corporate counsel. However, in *Upjohn Co. v. United States,* 449 U.S. 383 (1981), the Court made it clear that it favors a broader test. Under the *Upjohn* test, a communication between any employee and the corporate counsel constitutes a corporate attorney-client communication if the employee is divulging information which he or she gained in the course of performing employment duties.

The second situation is the case in which the client communicates with an expert hired by the attorney. Suppose, for example, that the defense attorney sends the defendant to a psychiatrist for an evaluation. The client possesses private information, namely, his or her mental condition. The attorney needs an evaluation of the information to prepare for trial. However, neither the client nor the attorney possesses the expertise to perform the evaluation. In this situation, the majority view is that the attorney-client privilege attaches. The privilege protects not only the client's revelations to the expert but also the expert's report to the attorney.

When does a communication occur "incident to the relationship"? It is not enough that the communication occur between an attorney and his or her client. The client must be consulting the attorney in his or her professional capacity, *qua* attorney. The incidence requirement necessitates that the court examine the purpose of the communication. Why did the client consult the attorney? If the client was seeking legal information or advice, the communication satisfies the incidence requirement.

The fifth issue is waiver. If a holder invokes the right type of privilege in the right type of proceeding to suppress privileged information, there is a prima facie case for privilege. However, the opposing counsel can defeat the privilege by showing that the holder has waived the privilege. The waiver can occur inside or outside court. On direct examination by his or her attorney, the holder may have referred to the privileged communication. The in-court reference waives the privilege. The court may also find a waiver if the holder voluntarily discloses the privileged information to a third party outside the courtroom. Not every out-of-court disclosure effects a waiver because the disclosure itself might be a privileged communication; a husband might tell his wife what he previously told his attorney.

The sixth and final question is whether there is any special exception to the privilege's scope. The opponent can defeat a privilege by showing either waiver or a special exception. It may not serve the purpose of the privilege to apply it in a particular situation, or there may be a countervailing interest that overrides the privilege. In section E of this chapter, we shall illustrate several special exceptions to the privileges' scope.

C. PRIVILEGES FOR CONFIDENTIAL INFORMATION — INVOKING A PRIVILEGE

1. ELEMENTS OF THE FOUNDATION

The claimant has the burden of proving the existence of the elements of the prima facie case for privilege. The prima facie case for privilege includes these elements:

1. The privilege applies to this type of proceeding. The judge makes this determination by examining the pleadings in the case.
2. The claimant of the privilege is asserting the right type of privilege. The judge makes this determination by insisting that the claimant specify the right he or she is claiming, that is, the right to personally refuse to disclose, the right to prevent a third party from disclosing, or the right to comment on the invocation of the privilege.

3. The claimant is a proper holder.
4. The information the claimant seeks to suppress is privileged information.
   a. It was a communication.
   b. It was confidential. Some jurisdictions presume that a communication between properly related parties is confidential.
   c. It occurred between properly related parties.
   d. It was incident to the relation.

Rule 104(a) governs the judge's determination of these preliminary facts.

2. SAMPLE FOUNDATION

Our fact situation is a tort action arising from a collision. The plaintiff, Ms. Campbell, alleges that the defendant, Mr. Harris, caused the accident by speeding. Mr. Harris takes the stand during the defense case-in-chief. On direct examination, he testifies that he was going only 20 miles an hour, five miles under the speed limit. On cross-examination, the following occurs. The plaintiff's attorney is the proponent:

P   Mr. Harris, ISN'T IT A FACT THAT you testified on direct examination that you were going only 20 miles an hour before the collision?

W   Yes.

P   ISN'T IT TRUE, Mr. Harris, THAT when you spoke with Mr. Riley, you told him that you were going 35 miles an hour?

O   Your Honor, I object to that question on the ground that it calls for information protected by the attorney-client privilege. (2) I request permission to take the witness on voir dire examination.

J   Permission granted.

O   Mr. Harris, WHO is this Mr. Riley? (4c)

W   He's a long-time friend of mine.

O   WHAT is his occupation? (4c)

W   He's an attorney.

O   HOW do you know he is an attorney? (4c)

W   His office door says attorney, he has degrees on his wall, and he's represented my family in court before.

O   WHERE and WHEN did you talk to Mr. Riley about his case?

W   I think the first time was January 12th or 13th of 1989, just after the accident occurred.

O   WHAT happened during that meeting? (4a)

W   I told him about the accident.

O   Precisely, HOW did you give him information about the accident? (4a)

W   I told him about it. I didn't put it in writing or anything like that.

O   HOW many people were present when you had this meeting with Mr. Riley? (4b)

W   Just the two of us.

O   HOW many doors are there to his office? (4b)

W   Just one.

O   WHAT position was the door in while you talked with him? (4b)

W   It was closed.

O After you told him about the accident, WHOM did you authorize him to give the information to? (4b)

W No one.

O WHAT did you want him to do with the information? (4b)

W Keep it secret, of course. He was my attorney.

O WHY did you talk to him that day? (4d)

W I thought I might need legal help. Even at the accident scene, the plaintiff said something about suing.

O In WHAT capacity did you consult Mr. Riley? (4d), (2)

W I was talking to him as an attorney, not just a family friend.

O Your Honor, I have no further questions on voir dire. I renew my objection and assert my client's privilege to refuse to disclose his communications with his attorney. (2)

J Objection sustained.

D. PRIVILEGES FOR CONFIDENTIAL RELATIONS — DEFEATING A PRIVILEGE BY PROVING WAIVER

1. IN-COURT WAIVER

If the party opposing the privilege claim is going to argue an in-court waiver, that party must be prepared to point to the witness' testimony that effected the waiver. The following is a continuation of the immediately preceding tort hypothetical. The plaintiff is the proponent.

P Mr. Harris, ISN'T IT A FACT THAT when you first spoke with your family attorney, Mr. Riley, you told him that you were going 35 miles an hour?

O Your Honor, I object to that question on the ground that it calls for information protected by the attorney-client privilege.

P Your Honor, may we approach the bench?

J Yes.

P Your Honor, I concede that this communication would ordinarily be privileged. However, I contend that the defendant has already waived the privilege. I would request that the court reporter read back the last question and answer on direct examination.

J Very well.

CR It'll take me just a second to find the passage. Yes, here it is. My notes show that the last question was: "What was your speed just before the collision?" The last answer was: "I was going at a safe rate of speed. That's what I told my attorney when I first discussed the accident with him, and it's the same story I'm telling today. That's the truth."

P This shows that on direct examination, the defendant expressly referred to his previous conversation with his attorney about the collision. That reference waives the privilege.

J I agree. The objection is overruled.

P Mr. Harris, let me repeat the question. ISN'T IT TRUE THAT you told your attorney that you were going 35 miles an hour?

W Yes.

2. OUT-OF-COURT WAIVER

If the party opposing the privilege relies on the theory of out-of-court waiver, the party must lay the following foundation:

1. Where the out-of-court statement was made.

2. When the statement was made.

3. To whom the statement was made.

4. The holder knew that the addressee was outside the circle of confidence.

5. The holder disclosed information to the addressee.

6. The disclosure was voluntary.

We continue the hypothetical. Now the proponent will attempt to show that the holder waived the privilege by an out-of-court disclosure.

P   Mr. Harris, ISN'T IT A FACT THAT when you first spoke with your family attorney, Mr. Riley, you told him that you were going 35 miles an hour?

O   Your Honor, I object to that question on the ground that it calls for privileged information protected by the attorney-client privilege.

P   Your Honor, I request permission to take the witness on voir dire examination before you rule on the objection.

J   Granted.

P   Mr. Harris, ISN'T IT TRUE THAT on January 19th of this year, you had dinner with your cousin, James Carol? (1), (2), (3)

W   Yes.

P   ISN'T IT CORRECT THAT during this dinner, you discussed the accident with your cousin? (3)

W   Yes.

P   ISN'T IT A FACT THAT at the time, you knew your cousin wasn't working for your attorney in this case? (5)

W   Right.

P   ISN'T IT TRUE THAT you told your cousin what you told your attorney about the accident? (5)

W   Yes.

P   And no one forced you to tell that to your cousin. DID THEY? (6)

W   No.

P   And no one made any threats to make you tell your cousin. ISN'T THAT TRUE? (6)

W   Yes.

P   Your Honor, I have no further questions on voir dire.

J   I see. The objection will be overruled.

P   Mr. Harris, let me repeat the question. ISN'T IT CORRECT THAT you told your attorney that your were going 35 miles an hour?

W   Yes.

E. PRIVILEGES FOR CONFIDENTIAL RELATIONS — DEFEATING A PRIVILEGE BY PROVING A SPECIAL EXCEPTION

As previously stated, there are numerous special exceptions to the various privileges. Some privileges are virtually riddled with exceptions. The party opposing the claim of privilege usually relies on voir dire examination to show the factual predicate for the exception. The following subsections illustrate some of the more important exceptions.

1. AT THE TIME OF THE COMMUNICATION, THE HOLDER SOUGHT THE INFORMATION TO FACILITATE A FUTURE CRIME OR FRAUD

The courts will not permit holders to abuse and pervert the privileges. For that reason, the courts usually reject a privilege claim if the party opposing the claim shows that at the time of the communication, the holder sought the information or advice to facilitate the commission of a future crime or fraud. The foundation for this exception usually requires proof that:

1. At the time of the communication, the holder knew that the contemplated course of conduct was illegal or fraudulent.
2. The purpose of the communication was to obtain information or advice to facilitate the commission of a future crime or fraud. Because of the difficulty of proving the holder's state of mind, many courts recognize the exception so long as there is a prima facie case or permissive inference of the existence of the improper intent in the holder's mind.

Our fact situation is a prosecution for wilful tax evasion. Suppose that El Dorado law requires that the purchaser of goods pay a 4% sales tax unless the goods are intended for interstate shipment. If the goods are intended for interstate shipment, the purchaser obtains a tax exemption form from the seller and submits the completed form to the Franchise Tax Board. The People allege that in August 1988, the defendant, Mr. Lloyd Marx, purchased goods for intrastate shipment and wilfully evaded the tax. The goods were 230 air conditioners. The defendant took the stand during his case-in-chief. On direct examination, the defendant admits that he purchased the air conditioners and neither paid the tax nor filed the exemption form. However, he also testifies that he did not understand the procedures for filing the form and claiming the exemption. The following occurs on cross-examination. The proponent is the prosecutor. The prosecutor is attempting to prove wilfulness.

P   Mr. Marx, ISN'T IT TRUE THAT in June 1988, you spoke with Mr. Felton of the local office of the Franchise Tax Board? (1)

W   Yes.

P   ISN'T IT A FACT THAT during this conversation, you asked him whether you had to pay a sales tax on purchases for intrastate shipments? (1)

W   Right.

P   AND DIDN'T HE tell you that you had to do so? (1)

W   Yes.

P   ISN'T IT CORRECT THAT on July 1, 1988, you entered into a contract for the sale of air conditioners to Johnson Construction Company? (2)

W   Yes.

P   ISN'T IT TRUE THAT Johnson has its office in this city and state — Morena, El Dorado? (2)

W   Yes.
P   ISN'T IT A FACT THAT you promised to deliver the air conditioners in September to their office in this state? (2)
W   Yes.
P   ISN'T IT CORRECT THAT the number of air conditioners you promised to sell them was 230? (2)
W   Yes.
P   AND ISN'T THAT the exact number of air conditioners you bought on August 1, 1988? (2)
W   Yes.

Later, during the prosecution rebuttal, the prosecutor calls Ms. Celia Waylan as a witness. The prosecutor is still the proponent. Ms. Waylan has already identified herself and stated that she is an attorney.

P   Ms. Waylan, WHERE were you on the morning of July 20, 1988?
W   I was in my office.
P   WHERE is your office?
W   Downtown on High Street.
P   WHAT happened that morning?
W   I had a visit from a client.
P   WHO was that client?
W   It was the defendant, Mr. Marx.
P   WHERE is Mr. Marx now?
W   In this courtroom.
P   Specifically, WHERE in the courtroom?
W   He's sitting right there.
P   HOW is he dressed?
W   In plaid slacks and a blue shirt.
P   Your Honor, please let the record reflect that the witness has identified the defendant.
J   It will so reflect.
P   WHAT happened when the defendant came to your office that morning?
W   He asked for some advice.
P   WHAT advice?
O   Your Honor, I object to that question on the ground that it calls for information protected by the attorney-client privilege.
P   Your Honor, may we approach the bench?
J   Yes.
P   Your Honor, I concede that Ms. Waylan is an attorney and that the defendant consulted her as such. However, I offer to prove that the witness will testify that the defendant asked how he could evade paying a tax or filing a form on a shipment. She will further testify that she advised him that there was no way to avoid paying or filing. This conversation occurred in July, well before the purchase of the air conditioners in August. She will finally testify that he said that she obviously misunderstood his question and that he wanted her advice as to the best way to evade the law without getting caught. Since the defendant had already talked with Mr. Felton and had already entered into an intrastate shipment contract, the inference is that the defendant sought Ms. Waylan's advice to facilitate a future crime.

J   I think there's a sufficient showing to invoke the exception. I shall overrule the objection.

P   Ms. Waylan, WHAT advice did the defendant ask for?

W   He asked how he could get around paying a tax or filing a form.

P   WHAT did you tell him?

W   I said that there wasn't; he had to do one or the other. If the goods were destined for intrastate sale, he had to pay the tax. If the goods were destined for interstate shipment, he had to file a form with the state. It was one or the other.

P   WHAT did the defendant say then?

W   He told me that I'd obviously misunderstood his question. He said that he'd already entered into a contract for an intrastate shipment and that he wanted my advice as to how to evade the law without getting caught.

2. THE JOINT CONSULTATION SITUATION

If two parties consult an attorney about a common problem, there is an attorney-client privilege. Either party may assert that privilege against a third party. What happens, though, if the parties have a falling out and sue each other? May one party claim the privilege against the other party? In this situation, the courts have generally denied the privilege. The courts reason that there was no confidentiality as between the two parties; they freely communicated with each other and the attorney. To establish the joint consultation exception to the privilege, the party opposing the claim must show that:

1. They both met with the attorney.
2. They met with the attorney at a certain time.
3. They met with the attorney at a certain place.
4. The party claiming the privilege knew that the other party was present.
5. The party claiming the privilege voluntarily participated in the joint consultation.
6. The purpose of the consultation was to seek legal advice.
7. The advice related to a common problem.

Our fact situation is a contract action. The plaintiff, Zikes, sues the defendant, Adams, on a contract. The contract provides that the defendant was to pay the plaintiff a percentage of the receipts of the defendant's business in exchange for the plaintiff's investment in the business. The central dispute in the case is over the meaning of the term, "receipts." The plaintiff contends that the term means gross receipts while the defendant asserts that the term means net receipts after deducting certain expenses. The plaintiff takes the stand during his case-in-chief. The following occurs on cross-examination. The proponent is the defendant.

P   Mr. Zikes, ISN'T IT TRUE THAT you entered this contract on February 14, 1989?

W   Yes.

P   ISN'T IT A FACT THAT before you entered this contract, you consulted an attorney?

W   Yes.

P   ISN'T IT TRUE THAT that attorney was Marcia Harris?

W   Yes.

P   ISN'T IT CORRECT THAT you met with Ms. Harris at her office on February 12, 1989? (1), (2), (3)

W   Yes.

P   ISN'T IT TRUE THAT the defendant, Mr. Adams, was also present? (1)

W   Yes.

P   And no one forced you to attend the meeting with Mr. Adams, DID THEY? (5)

W   No.

P   And no one threatened you if you didn't attend the meeting, DID THEY? (5)

W   No.

P   ISN'T IT TRUE THAT at this meeting, you both spoke with Ms. Harris about the contract? (6), (7)

W   Yes.

P   AND ISN'T IT A FACT THAT you both asked for her advice about drafting the contract? (6), (7)

W   Yes.

P   ISN'T IT CORRECT THAT during this meeting, you told her that the receipts should be computed by deducting salary expenses?

O   Your Honor, I object to that question on the ground that it calls for information protected by the attorney-client privilege.

P   Your Honor, may we approach the bench?

J   Yes.

P   Your Honor, the record shows that this meeting was a joint consultation with the attorney. The plaintiff and defendant jointly consulted Ms. Harris about a common problem and the plaintiff cannot assert the privilege against the defendant.

J   I concur. The objection will be overruled.

P   Mr. Zikes, let me repeat the question. ISN'T IT A FACT during your meeting with the attorney, you told her that the receipts should be computed by deducting salary expenses?

W   Yes.

3. THE PATIENT LITIGANT EXCEPTION

One of the most important exceptions to the physician-patient privilege is the patient litigant exception. If the patient sues and tenders the issue of his or her condition, the patient loses the privilege for communications relevant to that condition. The theory is that it would be unfair to permit the patient litigant to suppress such highly relevant information. In effect, by suing, the patient makes a limited waiver of the privilege. To decide whether this exception applies in a particular case, the judge must examine the complaint and determine whether the complaint tenders an issue of physical condition which the communication is logically relevant to.

Our fact situation is a tort action in which the plaintiff claims extensive personal injuries. In particular, the complaint prays for $30,000 in damages for pain and suffering. The defendant calls Dr. Metal as a witness. Dr. Metal identifies himself and states that he formerly treated the plaintiff. He testifies that he examined the plaintiff two days after the accident. The defendant is the proponent.

P   Dr. Metal, during this examination, WHAT, if anything, did the plaintiff say about his pain?
O   Your Honor, I object to that question on the ground that it calls for privileged information protected by the physician-patient privilege.
P   Your Honor, may we approach the bench?
J   Yes.
P   Your Honor, I offer to prove that the witness will testify that the plaintiff said his pain was not intense. On page nine of his complaint, the plaintiff prays for $30,000 in damages for pain and suffering. As a litigant, the plaintiff tendered the issue of the extent of his pain. The statement he made to his physician is logically relevant to his condition and pain.
J   The objection is overruled.
P   Dr. Metal, let me repeat the question. WHAT, if anything, did the plaintiff say about his pain?
W   He said it wasn't very intense. He felt it occasionally, but it bothered him only off and on.

F. THE WORK PRODUCT PROTECTION

1. THE CONDITIONAL WORK PRODUCT PROTECTION

In the three previous sections we examined the privileges for confidential relations. At this point we should remember the limitations of the attorney-client privilege. Because of the requirements discussed in the last three sections, the attorney-client privilege may not protect such material as a witness' statement, an expert's report, or a model prepared for trial.

However, ours is an adversary system of litigation; and given their adversary training, most attorneys find it highly distasteful to disclose their pretrial preparation materials to opposing counsel. In addition, many judges believe that pretrial preparation materials deserve some protection; it strikes them as unfair to permit the opposing counsel to reap the benefit of the other attorney's factual investigation and legal research. Since the attorney-client privilege does not protect these materials, attorneys and courts looked elsewhere for a new rationale to protect trial preparation materials.

In the leading case of *Hickman v. Taylor,* 329 U.S. 495 (1947), the Supreme Court purported to construe the Federal Rules of Civil Procedure, but the Court in effect created a new doctrine, work product, to protect pretrial preparation materials. The Court commented: "Proper preparation of a client's case demands that he (the lawyer) assemble information, sift what he considers to be the relevant from the irrelevant facts, prepare his legal theories and plan his strategy without undue and needless interference." The Court emphasized that it was not creating an absolute privilege: "We do not mean to say that all written materials obtained or prepared by an adversary's counsel with an eye toward litigation are necessarily free from discovery in all cases. Where relevant and non-privileged facts remain hidden in an attorney's file and where production of those facts is essential to the preparation of one's case, discovery may properly be had." At first, the doctrine was viewed simply as a limitation on pretrial discovery. However, the doctrine has evolved into an evidentiary privilege assertable at trial. *United States v. Nobles,* 422 U.S. 225, 239 (1975); Feldman, *The Work Product Rule in Criminal Practice and Procedure,* 50 Cin. L. Rev. 495, 547 (1981).

Ultimately, the Supreme Court adopted Federal Rule of Civil Procedure 26 (b), stating and refining the *Hickman* doctrine: "Subject to the provisions of subdivision (b)(4) of this rule, a party may obtain discovery of documents and tangible things otherwise discoverable under subdivision (b)(1) of this rule and prepared in anticipation of litigation or for trial by or for another party or by or for that other party's representative (including his attorney, consultant, surety, indemnitor, insurer, or agent) only upon a showing that the party seeking discovery has substantial need of the materials in the preparation of the party's case and that the party is unable without undue hardship to obtain the substantial equivalent of the materials by other means."

The party invoking the work product privilege must establish the following foundational elements:

1. The party is invoking the privilege in the right type of proceeding. Although the privilege originated in civil actions, the majority of jurisdictions now recognize the doctrine in criminal cases. Feldman, *supra.* Most of these jurisdictions have codified the doctrine in statute or court rule. *Id.* The trial judge examines the pleadings to determine whether the instant case is the right type of proceeding.

2. The party is asserting the right type of privilege. The work product privilege is the personal right to refuse to disclose the material during pretrial discovery or at trial.

3. The party claiming the privilege is a proper holder. In most of the decided cases, the attorney has asserted the privilege. However, a few cases have granted the client standing to assert the protection.

4. The information the party seeks to suppress is work product material. To qualify as work product material, the information must satisfy three requirements:

    a. The information is derivative rather than primary material. Primary material is material historically connected to the case such as the actual brake from the car involved in an accident. An example of derivative material would be a model of the brake. Primary material would be the witness' knowledge of the accident; a party cannot invoke the work product privilege to prevent the opposing counsel from deposing a witness. However, the witness' written statement would be derivative material. In short, the attorney's effort and imagination play a role in the very creation of derivative material.

b. The information is the work product of an attorney. A few jurisdictions still insist that the attorney personally prepare the material. However, that requirement interferes with the manner in which attorneys customarily conduct their business. They often use clerks, investigators, and the client to gather information and prepare reports. For that reason, most jurisdictions now extend the privilege to information collected by the attorney's agent.

c. The material must be prepared in anticipation of litigation. Suit need not be filed, but the client and attorney must anticipate litigation when the material is prepared.

Many of the statutes and court rules codifying the work product protection in criminal cases purport to create an absolute privilege. Feldman, *supra,* at 506. However, in civil cases the prevailing view is that the protection is conditional and that the opposing party can override the protection by a compelling showing of need. The opposing party can do so by showing that:

5. The information is logically relevant to the material facts of consequence in the case.

6. The information is highly relevant to the outcome of the case. The opponent should argue that the information relates to the central or one of the central issues in the case. More precisely, the attorney should show that the information is needed to effectively prepare for trial.

7. There is no reasonably available, alternative source for the information. Either there is no alternative source at all, or resort to the alternative source would involve prohibitive expense or inconvenience.

The work product protection issue ordinarily arises during pretrial discovery; one party seeks discovery of a document, and the opposing party resists discovery by claiming the privilege. Given the pretrial context, attorneys usually present their supporting facts in affidavits rather than eliciting live testimony. To illustrate the doctrine, we shall present first a claimant's affidavit, then a sample foundation for the claimant in the unlikely eventuality the claimant uses live testimony, and finally the opponent's affidavit. In our hypothetical, the party seeking discovery desires an accident reconstruction report. The party resisting discovery is the plaintiff, Ms. Leonard. The expert was Professor Suarez. When the plaintiff submitted this, the attorney would simultaneously submit a declaration memorandum of points and authorities. The memorandum would cite the statutes and cases granting the material work product privilege.

STATE OF EL DORADO   ⎱

                            AFFIDAVIT

COUNTY OF MORENA   ⎰

I, the undersigned, being duly sworn, depose and say that:

1. My name is Stephen Metzger. I reside at 452 Madison Street, Morena, El Dorado. I am an attorney with the firm of Luce, Gray, Forward, and Ames, 433 B Street, Morena, El Dorado.

2. I represent Ms. Adrienne Leonard, the plaintiff in Leonard v. Morton, civil action number 1778 now pending in Morena Superior Court (1).

3. The defendant has moved for the production of a report submitted to me by Professor Paul Suarez. My client and I hereby claim the work product privilege, (3) and on that ground we refuse to surrender Professor Suarez' report to the defendant. (2)

4. On February 14, 1988, I decided that I needed an expert evaluation of the physical evidence left at the scene of the collision between the defendant's van and my client's car on February 11, 1988. (4c) In her complaint, my client alleges that the defendant's car drifted into her lane and that the point of impact was in her lane. The defendant's answer denies these allegations, and I lack the expertise in physics and the laws of motion to evaluate the physical evidence left at the accident scene. Consequently, on February 15, 1988, I telephoned Professor Paul Suarez who teaches in the Physics Department at the University of El Dorado, Morena. I have used him in several prior cases as an accident reconstruction expert. I told Professor Suarez that I needed an expert evaluation of the accident scene as part of my pretrial preparation; I asked him for a confidential report on that subject. He agreed to prepare the report and submit it to me. (4b) On February 16, 1988, Professor Suarez and I visited the accident scene, and on February 20, 1988, he submitted his personal written report to me. (4a) The report recites his findings and conclusions as to the manner in which the collision occurred. I have maintained the report's confidentiality; the only persons who have viewed the report are Professor Suarez, my client, and myself. At the present time, I have not decided whether to call Professor Suarez as a witness at trial.

/s/ Stephen Metzger

On April 2, 1989, before the undersigned, a Notary Public for the State of El Dorado, personally appeared Stephen Metzger, known to me to be the person whose name is subscribed to the within instrument, and acknowledged that he executed the same.

/s/ Linda Draper
Notary Public
My license expires May 1, 1992

In some instances, the party asserting the work product protection might present live testimony in opposition to the motion for the production of the protected report. Or the party might offer live testimony if the other side subpoenas the report's author and the party moves pretrial to quash the subpoena or objects at trial. In the following example, the witness is Professor Suarez. He has already identified himself and stated his occupation. The plaintiff, the party resisting discovery, is the proponent.

P   Professor, WHERE were you on the morning of February 15, 1988?
W   I was in my office at the U.E.D. Campus in Morena.
P   WHAT happened that morning?
W   I received a telephone call from you.
P   WHAT was said during this telephone call? (4a)
W   You told me that you wanted an expert evaluation of the scene of the accident between your client and the defendant.
P   WHAT was the purpose of this evaluation? (4c)
W   At least your stated purpose was that you needed it as part of your pretrial preparation.
P   WHAT was your response when I asked you to conduct the evaluation? (4b)
W   I agreed to do so.
P   WHAT happened then?
W   I met you and visited the accident scene on February 16.
P   Please be specific. WHERE did you go?
W   I went to the intersection of C and 5th Streets where this accident supposedly occurred.
P   WHAT did you do after you visited the accident scene? (4a)
W   I prepared a report.
P   WHAT form was the report in? (4a)
W   It was a typed, four-page document.
P   WHAT did you do with the report?
W   I gave the original and two copies to you.
P   HOW many copies were there?
W   Three.
P   WHAT did you do with the other copy?
W   I have it in my files.
P   WHO has access to your files?
W   Only myself.
P   WHOM have you shown the report to?

W   Only you.
P   WHY haven't you shown the report to other people?
W   You instructed me to keep it confidential, and I've carried out your instructions.
P   WHAT role will you have at the trial in this case?
W   I do not intend to testify in this case. You have not asked me to. For my part, I have not agreed to or indicated any willingness to do so.

Finally, the following is the format for an affidavit by the party seeking discovery:

STATE OF EL DORADO
                               }   AFFIDAVIT
COUNTY OF MORENA

I, the undersigned, being duly sworn, depose and say that:

1. My name is James Gamer. I reside at 7076 Vista Way, Del Mar, El Dorado. I am the attorney with the firm of Sullivan and Archer, 1234 1st Street, Morena, El Dorado.

2. I represent Mr. Philip Morton, the defendant in Leonard v. Morton, civil action number 1778 now pending in Morena Superior Court.

3. We have moved for the production of a report submitted by Professor Paul Suarez to the plaintiff's attorney, Mr. Stephen Metzger. The subject of the report is an expert evaluation of the physical evidence left at the scene of the collision between the plaintiff's car and my client's van at the intersection of C and 5th Streets in downtown Morena. The report is logically relevant to the material facts in this case. On page 12 of the plaintiff's complaint, she alleges that my client's van drifted into her traffic lane and the point of impact was in her lane. Page 4 of the defendant's answer denies those allegations. Thus, the point of impact is a material fact of consequence in this case, and Professor Suarez' accident reconstruction report undoubtedly discusses point of impact. (5)

4. The information contained in Professor Suarez' report is essential to the effective pretrial preparation of this case. If the jury finds as a matter of fact that my client's van drifted into the plaintiff's lane, that fact alone may persuade the jurors to conclude that my client was negligent. However, if the jury finds as a matter of fact that the point of impact was in my client's lane, again that fact alone may convince the jurors that the plaintiff's own carelessness caused the accident. (6)

5. There is no reasonably available, alternative source for this information. In the first place, Professor Suarez is widely regarded as the leading accident reconstruction expert in Morena County. During the past five years, our own law firm has used him more often than any other accident reconstruction witness in our cases. His report would be more authoritative than any other local expert's report. Secondly, Pro-

fessor Suarez' report may contain a more detailed description of the physical evidence at the accident than any other report. Page 4 of the February 12, 1988 Morena Police Department Accident Report filed in this case states that there was "a good deal of debris," but neither the report's narrative section nor the attached diagram indicates the nature or specific location of the debris. Mr. Morton did not employ this law firm until May 13, 1988. We immediately hired an accident reconstruction expert, but she was unable to visit the accident scene until March 16, 1988 — weeks after the accident. I accompanied her to the scene; but when we did so, we could not locate any skidmarks, gouge marks, or debris clearly attributable to the accident. In contrast, Professor Suarez visited the scene only a few days after the collision. Hence, Professor Suarez' report may be the only source for critical information about the accident scene.

/s/ James Gamer

On May 13, 1989, before the undersigned, a Notary Public for the State of El Dorado, personally appeared James Gamer, known to me to be the person whose name is subscribed to the within instrument, and acknowledged that he executed the same.

/s/ Susan Crosby
Notary Public
My license expires June 13, 1991

---

2. THE ABSOLUTE WORK PRODUCT PROTECTION

In most cases, work product protection is conditional; the party seeking discovery can overcome the privilege by showing a compelling need for the information. However, by statute, some jurisdictions recognize an absolute work product privilege for certain types of very sensitive trial preparation materials. Federal Rule of Civil Procedure 26(b) is illustrative. After stating the conditional work product privilege, the Rule continues: "In ordering discovery of such material when the required showing has been made, the court shall protect against disclosure of the mental impressions, conclusions, opinions, or legal theories of an attorney or other representative of a party concerning the litigation." Those materials are absolutely privileged; even if the party seeking discovery shows a compelling need for the material, the material cannot be discovered. The problem is definitional; if the material falls within one of the categories listed in the statute, the discovery motion must be denied. If a party seeks discovery of such material, the party claiming the absolute work product privilege usually responds by affidavit.

With one exception, the foundation for absolute work product privilege is roughly the same as the foundation for conditional work product privilege:

1. The party is invoking the privilege in the right type of proceeding. The judge examines the pleadings on file to determine whether the case is the right type of action. As previously stated, some jurisdictions recognize absolute protection in criminal cases. Feldman, *supra,* at 506.

2. The party is asserting the right type of privilege. The privilege is the personal right to refuse to disclose the material during pretrial discovery or at trial.

3. The party claiming the privilege is a proper holder. The courts treat the attorney as holder but sometimes grant clients standing to invoke the work product doctrine.

4. The information the party seeks to suppress is absolutely protected. In a civil action, to qualify for absolute protection, the material would ordinarily have to satisfy these requirements.

   a. The material reflects the attorney's creative thought process. A memorandum summarizing the attorney's impressions of a witness or outlining the attorney's legal theories would be absolutely protected.

   b. The material is the work product of an attorney. In the case of absolutely protected material, most courts require that the attorney personally prepare the material.

   c. The material was prepared in anticipation of litigation.

The following is an affidavit an attorney might file to assert absolute work product privilege:

STATE OF EL DORADO   ⎫

              ⎬   AFFIDAVIT

COUNTY OF MORENA   ⎭

I, the undersigned, being duly sworn, depose and say that:

1. My name is Peter Mehalick. I reside at 1333 Cape May Street, Morena, El Dorado. I am an attorney with the firm of Seltzer, Muns, and Mason, 2444 4th Street, Morena, El Dorado.

2. I represent Ms. Michelle Lucerne, the plaintiff in Lucerne v. Rodriguez, civil action number 1999 now pending in Morena Superior Court. (1)

3. The defendant has moved for the production of the witness statement of Mr. Giles Folsom, an eyewitness to the collision that gave rise to this suit. The defendant's motion specifically stated that the defendant desired Mr. Folsom's statement "and all attachments." My client

and I hereby claim the absolute work product privilege, (3) and on that ground we refuse to surrender one attachment, a memorandum that I personally prepared and that is dated February 17, 1989. (2)

4. On February 16, 1989, I interviewed Mr. Folsom at my office in downtown Morena. I interviewed Mr. Folsom because I realized that we might call him as a witness at trial. (4c) We had filed suit before I interviewed Mr. Folsom. (4c) After the interview, I had my secretary type a copy of his statement and submit it to him for his signature. My secretary did so before he left my office, and I have his signed statement dated February 16, 1989. We do not oppose the discovery of that witness statement. However, the next day, February 17, 1989, I dictated a memorandum for file. (4b) The memorandum outlines my impressions of Mr. Folsom as a potential witness. (4a) The memorandum also contains my conclusion as to how to conduct his direct examination and prepare him for cross-examination. (4a) Given the memorandum's contents, the memorandum is entitled to absolute work product protection. Although the memorandum is presently physically attached to Mr. Folsom's witness statement, the memorandum is not discoverable.

/s/ Peter Mehalick

On May 13, 1989, before the undersigned, a Notary Public for the State of El Dorado, personally appeared Peter Mehalick, known to me to be the person whose name is subscribed to the within instrument, and acknowledged that he executed the same.

/s/ Susan Crosby
Notary Public
My license expires June 13,
1993

As in the previous hypothetical, when the attorney submitted this affidavit, the attorney would also submit a memorandum of law. The memorandum should mention the statutes and cases conferring absolute work product privilege. At oral argument on the discovery motion, the attorney would use the memorandum as the source of law and the affidavit as the source of facts.

G. GOVERNMENT PRIVILEGES — MILITARY AND STATE SECRETS

1. THE DOCTRINE

Military and state secrets affect the vital interest of the country. The magnitude of the interest justifies creating an evidentiary privilege to cloak these secrets. Following the English precedents, the United States Supreme Court recognized a privilege for military and state secrets in *United States v. Reynolds,* 345 U.S. 1 (1953). The Court created an absolute privilege; if the material falls within the definition of military or state secret, the material is not discoverable even if the party seeking discovery can demonstrate a compelling need for the information.

The most troublesome problem has been defining military and state secret. Although no court has developed a simple definition of these terms, one commentator has offered a relatively comprehensive list of the types of materials falling within the definition: "The specific areas of sensitive information appear to be: (a) The plans and capabilities of specific combat operations; (b) the official estimates of the military plans and capabilities of potential enemy nations; (c) the existence, design, and production of new weapons or equipment or the existence and results of research programs specifically directed toward producing new weapons and equipment; (d) the existence and nature of special ways and means of organizing combat operations; (e) the identity and location of vulnerable areas such as production facilities, critical supply depots, or weapons installations; (f) the existence and nature of clandestine intelligence operations; (g) the keys to communication codes; and (h) the existence and nature of international agreements relative to military plans and capabilities and the exchange of intelligence." Zagel, *The State Secrets Privilege,* 50 Minn. L. Rev. 875, 884-85 (1966).

2. ELEMENTS OF THE FOUNDATION

The government can assert this privilege in any type of proceeding. Hence, the type of proceeding is not a required element of the foundation. The foundation includes these elements:

1. The government is asserting the right type of privilege. The government may refuse to disclose the information and prevent a third party from making unauthorized disclosure.
2. The party asserting the privilege is a holder. The holder is ordinarily the official in charge of the government department with jurisdiction over the information. The head of the department should make a formal, written claim of privilege.
3. The information the holder seeks to suppress is a military or state secret. The written claim should indicate the general nature of the privileged information and assert that the government department has maintained the confidentiality of the information.

3. SAMPLE FOUNDATION

The fact situation is a suit arising from a plane crash. Advanced Aircraft Company was testing a plane with a new guidance system for air-to-air missiles. The plane crashed during the test, and the test pilot was killed. The pilot's widow brings a wrongful death action against the company and the United States Government. If the government attorney anticipated claiming the military secret privilege, the attorney should contact the appropriate government official before trial and have that official prepare a formal, written claim of privilege.

CITY OF WASHINGTON		

CITY OF WASHINGTON

DISTRICT OF COLUMBIA ⎫⎬⎭ AFFIDAVIT

I, the undersigned, being duly sworn, depose and say that:

1. My name is John R. Overholt. I reside at 230 Fellmeth Drive, Arlington, Virginia. I am the Secretary of Defense of the United States. (2) My offices are in the White House at the nation's capital.

2. The United States is a party to Jennings v. Advanced Aircraft Co. and the United States, civil action C1477 now pending in Federal District Court in Washington, D.C.

3. It is my understanding that the plaintiff may seek to discover information about the guidance system for air-to-air missiles installed in the airplane involved in the crash which gave rise to this suit. That information is within the jurisdiction of my government, and I hereby claim the military secret privilege for such information. (2) On that ground, I refuse to disclose the information and request that the court preclude any third party from disclosing the information. (1)

4. This new guidance system has been in development for the past seven years. The system incorporates new features which, to the best of my knowledge, foreign countries neither use nor have knowledge of. (3) If perfected, the system would give our planes a decided advantage in aerial combat. (3) The disclosure of this information would significantly harm our national defense interests. (3) To date, our department has maintained the secrecy of this information. (3) The information has been classified COSMIC TOP SECRET, and only persons with both a proper security clearance and a proven need to know have had access to this information. (3)

/s/ John R. Overholt

On September 19, 1989, before the undersigned, a Notary Public for the District of Columbia, personally appeared John R. Overholt, known to me to be the person whose name is subscribed to the within instrument, and acknowledged that he executed the same.

/s/ Marcia Gallagher
Notary Public
My license expires October 19, 1991

At trial, the plaintiff's attorney calls Mr. Garrett Winslow as a witness. Winslow identifies himself and states that he is Advanced Aircraft's chief engineer in charge of the development of the new guidance system. The plaintiff is the proponent. The plaintiff is examining Mr. Winslow as a hostile witness. Since the written claim of privilege will not be tendered to the jury, it will be inserted in the record of trial, but it will not be offered as a formal exhibit.

P   Mr. Winslow, ISN'T IT TRUE THAT before this crash, the model of plane involved had a perfect safety record?
W   Yes.
P   ISN'T IT ALSO TRUE THAT you installed a new guidance system for missiles on this plane just before the test?
W   Yes.
P   IN FACT, WASN'T the very purpose of the flight to test the new guidance system?
W   Yes.
P   Please describe this guidance system for us.
O   Your Honor, I object to that question on the ground that it calls for privileged information. May we approach the bench?
J   Yes.
O   Your Honor, I request that this be marked defense exhibit C for identification.
J   It will be so marked.
O   Your Honor, please let the record reflect that I am showing the exhibit to the opposing counsel.
J   It will so reflect.
O   Your Honor, since this document is properly notarized and bears the purported signature of a public official, it is self-authenticating. The exhibit is a formal claim of the military secret privilege for the information about the guidance system.
J   Give me a minute to read the exhibit. *(Pause.)* The claim seems to be in proper order.
P   Your Honor, my client has a compelling need for that information. We contend that that guidance system caused this accident.
O   The military secret privilege is absolute. So long as the information falls within the definition of military secret, the information is undiscoverable. Secretary Overholt's affidavit clearly shows that this information falls within the definition.
J   I think you're right. The objection will be sustained.

H. GOVERNMENT PRIVILEGES — MINOR GOVERNMENT SECRETS

1. THE DOCTRINE

Military and state secrets are such major government secrets that the courts have granted them an absolute evidentiary privilege. There are other, lesser government secrets that also warrant a measure of protection. Minor government secrets are usually subject to a conditional privilege; the secret is ordinarily privileged, but the party seeking discovery can defeat the privilege by demonstrating a compelling need for the information.

The definition of a minor government secret varies from jurisdiction to jurisdiction. The federal courts have adopted a relatively narrow definition. In *Ackerly v. Ley,* 420 F.2d 1336, 1340 (D.C. Cir. 1969), the court referred to "the familiar doctrine that the Executive branch is privileged not to disclose intra-governmental documents reflecting advisory opinions, recommendations, and deliberations comprising part of a process by which governmental decisions are formulated." This doctrine is sometimes called the predecisional, deliberate process privilege. The federal courts have attempted to protect the secrecy of the decision-making process. The courts reason that the ultimate government decision will be of higher quality if public officials are candid in their policy discussions and they are more likely to be candid if they know that the decision-making process is confidential. The federal courts consequently limit their minor government secret privilege to documents which are an integral part of a government decision-making process. In most cases, this privilege does not protect raw factual data submitted to the government.

Many of the states use a much broader definition. Although the federal privilege is designed to promote candor within government, these states have created a more expansive privilege to facilitate the flow of information to government. In these states, a minor government secret privilege attaches if the government shows that: (1) It has a legitimate need for a certain type of information; and (2) it cannot be assured of a free flow of that type of information unless it assures confidentiality to the sources of information. A good example is a parole board. A parole board needs background information about prisoners applying for parole. The board cannot expect candid evaluation from citizens unless it assures those citizens that their letters and interviews will remain confidential.

Even if the government makes out a prima facie case for the application of the minor government secret privilege, the party seeking discovery can defeat the privilege. The party can overcome the privilege by showing an overriding need for the information. The party shows need in the same fashion as a party seeking to defeat a conditional work product privilege.

2. ELEMENTS OF THE FOUNDATION

To establish a prima facie case for invoking the minor government secret privilege, the party opposing discovery must show these foundational elements:

1. The party asserting the privilege is a holder. The government agency receiving the information is the holder. The judge will usually permit any government agent, including the prosecutor, to invoke the privilege.

2. The party is asserting the right type of privilege. The government may refuse to disclose the information and prevent a third party from making disclosure.
3. The information is privileged. In federal court, the party must show that:
   a. The document reflects part of the decision-making process; and
   b. The government has maintained the confidentiality of the document. In many state courts, the party must show that:
   c. The government has a legitimate need for this type of information; and
   d. The government cannot obtain a free flow of this type of information unless it assures its sources confidentiality.

To defeat the privilege, the party seeking discovery must show that:
4. The information is logically relevant to the material facts of consequence in the case.
5. The information is highly relevant to the outcome of the case. The party should argue that the information relates to the central or one of the central issues in the case.
6. There is no reasonably available, alternative source for the information.

3. SAMPLE FOUNDATIONS

This issue can arise during pretrial discovery or at trial. For that reason, we shall illustrate both an affidavit and a foundation at trial.

The first illustration is an affidavit claiming the privilege in federal court. The fact situation is a product liability suit. The suit is in federal court because of diversity of citizenship. The plaintiff, Mr. Michael Lindsey, sues Maitland Company. The plaintiff alleges that the defendant negligently manufactured a bottle of medicine and that when he consumed some of the medicine, he sustained serious internal injuries. The plaintiff has served a subpoena duces tecum on the Federal Trade Commission. Three years ago the F.T.C. conducted a national survey of drug stores to determine the number of complaints about certain medicines. One of the medicines was the product the plaintiff purchased. The plaintiff seeks the F.T.C.'s final report evaluating the survey. The F.T.C. moves to quash the subpoena. The following is the affidavit supporting the F.T.C.'s motion.

CITY OF WASHINGTON

} AFFIDAVIT

DISTRICT OF COLUMBIA

I, the undersigned, being duly sworn, depose and say that:
1. My name is Mrs. Jane Garson. I reside at 1440 Gilder Drive,

Silver Springs, Maryland. I am the Chairperson of the Federal Trade Commission. (1) My offices are in the White House at the nation's capital.

2. The plaintiff in Lindsey v. Maitland Company, civil action C2001, now pending in Federal District Court in Washington, D.C., has served a subpoena duces tecum upon me. The subpoena directs me to produce for inspection and copying our 1987 survey entitled "Complaints to Druggists About Medicines." That information is within the jurisdiction of my Commission. (1) I hereby claim the government information privilege for this report. (2) On that ground, I refuse to surrender the report and respectfully request that the court quash the subpoena served upon me. (2)

3. We began this survey in 1985 to decide whether we should remove any of the studied drugs and medicines from the market. (3a) The report was finished in 1987. The report summarizes the survey and discusses medical problems possibly caused by the various medicines. The report states conclusions and recommendations with respect to each medicine studied. (3a) In my judgment, it would be contrary to the public interest to release this report for public inspection. We assured the druggists responding to the survey that we would maintain the confidentiality of their responses; many expressed fear of reprisal from the manufacturers which were their suppliers. In addition, this sort of decision-making process requires candor among public officials, and we can achieve that candor only if the decision-making process is confidential. The report has never been released to any private person. (3b) Indeed, the report has been released only to government agencies directly concerned with medicine and health care. (3b)

/s/ Jane Garson

On December 22, 1989, before the undersigned, a Notary Public for the District of Columbia, personally appeared Jane S. Garson, known to me to be the person whose name is subscribed to the within instrument, and acknowledged that she executed the same.

/s/ Thomas Barton
Notary Public
My license expires January 22, 1991

We shall now illustrate a foundation at trial for a state minor government secret privilege.

The fact situation is a wrongful death action. The plaintiffs are the surviving relatives of the decedent, Andrew Kaye. The defendant is Gary Shelton. The complaint alleges that the defendant and a Mr. Michaels fatally shot Andrew Keye during a civil rights rally in early 1985. The defendant's answer denied all involvement in the shooting. Michaels was tried, convicted, and sentenced in late 1985. The plaintiff's civil action against Shelton comes to trial today. During their case-in-chief, the plaintiffs called Ms. Martha McGill. She testified that she witnessed the shooting. She identified the defendant as one of the assailants. During the defense case-in-chief, the defendant calls Mr. Daniel Riley as a witness. Mr. Riley identifies himself and states that he is an employee of the El Dorado Board of Prison Terms. Riley testifies that he prepared a parole report on Michaels when the Board was considering Michaels' parole application. The defendant hopes to prove that Riley interviewed Ms. McGill and that during the interview, Ms. McGill said that although she could recognize Michaels as one killer, she could not identify the other assailant. The defendant is the proponent. The opponent is a Deputy Attorney General. When Riley was subpoenaed, he notified the Office of the Attorney General; and the State entered an appearance for the purpose of asserting the minor government secret privilege.

P   When you prepared this report, WHOM did you interview?
W   Several people.
P   Specifically WHOM?
W   A Genevieve Morton, Brian Michaels, and a Ms. McGill, who witnessed the shooting itself.
P   WHAT is Ms. McGill's full name?
W   Martha McGill.
P   WHAT was her occupation?
W   She was the cashier at a store near the killing.
P   WHAT did she say during her interview?
O   Your Honor, I object to that question on the ground that it calls for privileged government information. I request permission to take the witness on voir dire.
J   Permission granted.
O   Mr. Riley, WHY did you interview Ms. McGill? (3c)
W   I wanted to get some information about the robbery.
O   WHY did you need that information? (3c)
W   Actually it's the Board who needs it. The Board wants to know as much as they can about the gravity of the crime to determine an appropriate release date.
O   HOW do you get the information? (3c)
W   I interview the witnesses to the crime.
O   WHERE and WHEN did you interview Ms. McGill? (3d)
W   In my office three months ago.
O   WHO else was there? (3d)

W   Only the two of us.

O   HOW many doors does your office have? (3d)

W   Two.

O   WHAT position were they in at the time of the interview? (3d)

W   They were both closed.

O   WHAT, if anything, did you tell Ms. McGill at the beginning of the interview? (3d)

W   I thanked her for taking the time to stop by. I told her that her information would be very helpful to the Board, and I assured her that we would keep the interview confidential to the extent possible.

O   WHY did you give her that assurance? (3d)

W   People are often reluctant to talk to the parole officials.

O   WHY? (3d)

W   Most obvious reason is that they're afraid of reprisals from the criminal. We always tell interviewees that we'll keep the information confidential as far as possible.

O   WHAT did you do after you interviewed Ms. McGill? (3d)

W   I summarized her statements and included them in the report.

O   WHOM did you give the report to? (3d)

W   The Board.

O   HOW did you deliver it to them? (3d)

W   I hand delivered it to them in a sealed envelope.

O   WHO else have you shown the report to? (3d)

W   No one.

O   WHY haven't you shown it to anyone? (3d)

W   I want to keep my promise to the interviewees that the information will be confidential. Once word gets out that you don't keep that promise, the sources of information dry up.

O   Your Honor, I have no further questions of this witness on voir dire. May we approach the bench?

J   Yes.

O   Your Honor, it's clear at this point that the witness was gathering information that the government has a legitimate need for. It's also the type of information that the government can't gather unless it assures its sources confidentiality. For that reason, the privilege applies here.

J   I agree. The objection will be sustained.

If the party seeking discovery wants to overcome the conditional privilege, the party should file an affidavit. The affidavit should detail the logical relevance of the information, the party's need for the information, and the unavailability of alternative proof. The party should use the same format as James Gamer's affidavit in Section F of this chapter. Paragraph 3 of that affidavit explains the logical relevance of the information sought. Paragraph 4 shows that the information relates to a pivotal issue in the case. Finally, paragraph 5 shows that it would be difficult or impossible for the party to obtain substitute evidence.

I. GOVERNMENT PRIVILEGES — AN INFORMANT'S IDENTITY

1. THE DOCTRINE

The last section discussed the rules for the qualified privilege for minor government secrets. This section deals with a particular application of those rules: the government privilege for an informer's identity. In many cases, an informant would not report a law violation unless the government assured him or her confidentiality; the informant sometimes fears reprisals from the criminal, and in other cases the informant does not want to expose his or her own involvement in the crime to public scrutiny. To encourage informants to report violations of the law, the courts have created a conditional privilege for the informant's identity. The privilege does not protect the informant's report; given its narrow purpose, the privilege protects only the identity of a person who confidentially reports a law violation to law enforcement authorities.

Like other conditional privileges, this privilege can be defeated if the defendant shows a compelling need for the informant's testimony. In most cases, the court will find a compelling need when the defendant demonstrates that the informant has personal knowledge of the facts determining the defendant's guilt or innocence. If the informer merely supplied an investigative lead and pointed a finger of suspicion at the defendant but did not observe the crime, the informer is only a "tipster"; and the court will not order the disclosure of the informer's identity. However, when the informer personally observed the facts relevant to the crime's elements or an affirmative defense, the informer is a "percipient witness"; and the court will usually order disclosure. In *Roviaro v. United States,* 353 U.S. 53 (1957), the Supreme Court stated that the defendant has a due process right to discover the identity of a percipient witness. The defense does not have to make a preliminary showing that the percipient witness's testimony will be favorable. The defense need show only that the witness has personal knowledge of facts material to the theory of the defense.

2. ELEMENTS OF THE FOUNDATION

The foundation for the privilege itself includes these elements:
1. The privilege applies in this type of proceeding. Most of the cases recognizing the privilege are criminal prosecutions. However, the issue can arise in civil actions such as civil rights cases and actions for libel or malicious prosecution.
2. The party claiming the privilege is a proper holder. The government is the formal holder. The courts usually permit the government's agents, including prosecutors, to invoke the privilege on the government's behalf.

3. The holder is asserting the right type of privilege. The government can refuse to disclose the informer's identity. Further, the government can prevent another person from disclosing the informer's identity. However, the government cannot silence the informer himself or herself; if the informer is brave or foolhardy enough to admit his or her identity, the government loses the privilege.
4. The information is privileged.
   a. A person made a confidential report.
   b. The subject of the report was a violation of law.
   c. The person made the report to a law enforcement agency such as the police, a prosecutor's office, an administrative agency charged with enforcing the law, or a legislative committee investigating law enforcement.

The foundation for the percipient witness exception is quite simple. The defendant shows that the informer was in a physical position — the proper time and place — to observe the facts determining guilt or innocence. In some jurisdictions, the practice now is to have the informer testify in chambers after the defendant makes the preliminary showing. If, in the judge's mind, the informer's testimony is favorable to the defense, the judge then orders disclosure of the informer's identity to the defense. If the judge concludes that the informer's testimony would not be helpful to the defense, the judge denies the discovery motion. The record of the testimony in chambers is sealed and filed with the regular record of trial; if there is an appeal, the appellate court opens the sealed transcript to review the trial judge's determination.

3. SAMPLE FOUNDATION

Our fact situation is a drug prosecution. The government alleges that the defendant, Ms. Jane Moreland, wrongfully sold heroin to a Mr. Vincent Styles. The prosecution calls Officer Bernard Lopardo as a witness. Officer Lopardo testifies that he was hiding in the house where the alleged sale occurred and observed the sale. Then cross-examination begins. The defense attorney is the proponent.

P   Officer Lopardo, ISN'T IT TRUE THAT someone else was with you when you observed the alleged heroin sale?

W   Yes.

P   WHO was that other person?

O   Your Honor, I object to that question on the ground that it calls for privileged information. May we approach the bench?

J   Yes.

O   Your Honor, on behalf of the government, I claim the privilege for the identity of an informer. (2), (3) I request permission to take the witness on voir dire examination.

J   Permission granted.

O   WHEN did you first meet the person who was with you in the house?
W   About two months before.
O   WHAT happened when you met this person? (4b)
W   He told me that he thought a drug sale was going to occur in the neighborhood within the next few months.
O   WHERE did he make this report? (4c)
W   At the local police station.
O   WHOM did he report it to? (4c)
W   To me.
O   HOW were you dressed at the time? (4c)
W   I was wearing my regular police uniform.
O   WHO else was present when he made this report? (4a)
W   No one else. Just the two of us.
O   WHERE did this conversation occur? (4a)
W   In a room in the station.
O   HOW many doors did the room have? (4a)
W   Only one.
O   WHAT position was the door in when you met this person? (4a)
W   It was closed.
O   WHAT, if any, assurances did you give the informant when he made this report to you? (4a)
W   I told him that I wouldn't disclose his identity to anyone.
O   To WHOM have you revealed his identity? (4a)
W   No one. I've worked with him directly. I haven't even revealed his identity to the desk sergeant. I'm the informer's only contact.
O   Your Honor, I have no further questions on voir dire. I renew my claim of the privilege for an informer's identity.

(Now the defense counsel will attempt to lay the foundation for the percipient witness exception.)

P   Your Honor, may I also voir dire the witness?
J   Very well.
P   Officer Lopardo, ISN'T IT TRUE THAT this person accompanied you to the house where the alleged sale occurred?
W   Yes.
P   ISN'T IT A FACT THAT the informer was standing next to you when you observed the alleged sale?
W   Yes.
P   ISN'T IT CORRECT THAT most of the time the informer was facing in the same direction as you?
W   Yes.
P   Your Honor, I have no further questions on voir dire examination. Although the privilege for the informer's identity applies in this case, the percipient witness viewed the very transaction that the defendant's guilt or innocence depends on.
J   I concur. I am going to order the prosecutor to produce the informer in my chambers tomorrow morning. At that time, I shall question the informer and determine whether his testimony would be helpful to the defense. If his testimony would be favorable, I'll order that the prosecution disclose his identity. Court will be recessed. The prosecutor, the informer, and I will meet in my chambers at 9:00 a.m. tomorrow morning. Open court will convene at 10:30 a.m.

J. SUBSEQUENT REPAIRS

1. THE DOCTRINE

The next two sections analyze evidentiary doctrines similar to the privileges for confidential relations; they are doctrines excluding logically relevant evidence to promote extrinsic social policies. The subsequent repair doctrine bans evidence of subsequent precautionary measures by tort defendants; the primary rationale for the doctrine is that admitting the evidence would discourage desirable safety improvements. The second doctrine, excluding statements made during civil settlement and criminal plea negotiations, has a similar justification; the doctrine's underlying theory is that the admission of such statements would discourage negotiated settlements and pleas. The adherents of the doctrine argue that settlements and pleas serve the critical function of easing the trial courts' burden. Since, like privileges, these doctrines exclude logically relevant evidence to promote extrinsic policies, some commentators refer to these doctrines as quasi-privileges.

Federal Evidence Rule 407 states the exclusionary rule for subsequent repairs: "When, after an event, measures are taken which, if taken previously would have made the event less likely to occur, evidence of the subsequent measures is not admissible to prove negligence or culpable conduct in connection with the event." The courts have stated two justifications for this doctrine. One is that the evidence is logically irrelevant; the defendant's subsequent conduct has no bearing on the question whether the defendant was guilty of antecedent negligence. This justification is flawed. The subsequent repair has some, slight probative value on the question of negligence; at the very least, the evidence suggests that the defendant could have taken steps to eliminate or reduce the danger. Increasingly, however, the courts are relying on a second justification for the doctrine: Admitting the evidence would create a disincentive for repairs, and the public interest in safety will not tolerate such a disincentive.

This doctrine bans the evidence only when the evidence is offered for a particular, forbidden purpose; in the words of the Federal Rule, the evidence is inadmissible when the proponent offers the evidence "to prove negligence or culpable conduct in connection with the event." The exclusionary rule bans the evidence when the only theory of logical relevance the proponent articulates is the general inference that the defendant was negligent or culpable. If the proponent can articulate a different theory of logical relevance, the rule is inapplicable. Federal Rule 407 declares: "This rule does not require the exclusion of evidence of subsequent measures when offered for another purpose, such as proving ownership, control, or feasibility of precautionary measures, if controverted, or impeachment." When the proponent identifies a theory of logical relevance other than a general inference of negligence or fault, the opponent is entitled to a limiting instruction; the trial judge informs the jury of the permissible and impermissible uses of the evidence.

2. ELEMENTS OF THE FOUNDATION

The party attempting to exclude the repair evidence should lay the following foundation:

1. The defendant took certain action.
2. The defendant took the action as a safety measure.
3. The defendant took the action after the accident that gave rise to the suit. Some jurisdictions have applied Rule 407 in product liability cases in which the defendant made the design change after the sale to the plaintiff but before the accident involving the plaintiff.

The party can assert this doctrine pretrial by a motion *in limine*. If the issue arises at trial, the party can conduct voir dire examination to lay the foundation.

If the party seeking to introduce the evidence is going to invoke an alternative theory of logical relevance, the party must make a proper offer of proof. The offer of proof should include these elements:

4. What the witness will testify to if the judge permits the proponent to pursue the line of inquiry.
5. The evidence is logically relevant to some issue other than the general question of negligence or fault. In *Ault v. International Harvester Co.*, 13 Cal. 3d 113, 528 P.2d 1148, 117 Cal. Rptr. 812 (1974), the California Supreme Court held that its statutory version of the subsequent repair doctrine does not apply to strict product liability actions. The court reasoned that strict product liability is not "culpable conduct" within the meaning of the statute. Most jurisdictions, however, have rejected the *Ault* view.
6. The issue the evidence relates to is disputed in the case. Many judges insist upon this showing as a separate element of the foundation. The Federal Rules explicitly impose this requirement. The evidence will always be relevant to show the feasibility of repairs; if the courts did not require that the issue be disputed, the feasibility theory of logical relevance would swallow the exclusionary rule. The proponent of the evidence should point to specific testimony by the opposing witnesses which disputes the issue.

As previously stated, if the proponent of the evidence successfully invokes an alternative theory of logical relevance, the opponent has the right to insist that the judge give the jurors a limiting instruction under Rule 105.

3. SAMPLE FOUNDATIONS

Our first fact situation illustrates the general rule. The fact situation is a tort action arising from a slip and fall on the entrance to a department store. The plaintiff, Mr. Jarvis, alleges that the defendant, Merrill Department Store, had a dangerous and unsafe slope on its entrance. During the defense case-in-chief, the defense calls Ms. Fenton as a witness. Ms. Fenton identifies herself and states that she was the store manager the day of the accident. She describes the day, including her conversation with the plaintiff after the slip and fall. On cross-examination, the following occurs. The proponent is the plaintiff.

P   Ms. Fenton, ISN'T IT TRUE THAT one week after the plaintiff's accident, you hired a contractor to reduce the slope on the entrance?

O   Your Honor, I object to that question on the ground that it calls for evidence of a subsequent repair.

J   Objection sustained.

O   Your Honor, will you please give the jury a curative instruction?

J   Yes. Ladies and gentlemen of the jury, the plaintiff's attorney just referred to a change made in the entrance to the defendant's store. I am instructing you to disregard that reference. You may not even speculate whether there were any subsequent changes. The only issue before you is whether the defendant was negligent at the time the alleged accident occurred.

(If the defendant thought that the reference would taint the rest of the case, the defendant would next move for a mistrial. Many trial judges feel very strongly about this matter. They will rebuke the questioner — often even before an objection. These same judges frequently grant the mistrial motion.)

O   Your Honor, I now move for a mistrial.

If there is any doubt about the soundness of the objection, the opponent should request permission to take the witness on voir dire to lay a complete foundation for the objection.

P   Ms. Fenton, ISN'T IT TRUE THAT one week after the plaintiff's accident, you hired a contractor to reduce the slope on the entrance?

O   Your Honor, I object to that question. May we approach the bench?

J   Yes.

O   Your Honor, I object to that question on the ground that it calls for evidence of a subsequent repair. I request that you excuse the jurors and permit me to voir dire the witness before you rule on my objection.

J   Very well. Ladies and gentlemen of the jury, I am going to excuse you from the courtroom for a few moments. The bailiff will escort you to the jury room.

(The jurors leave.)

O   Ms. Fenton, WHAT did you hire this contractor to do? (1)

W   I hired a Mr. Darby to reduce the angle of the slope on the entrance.

O   WHY did you do that? (2)

W　We did it as a safety measure. We wanted to ensure that there wouldn't be a recurrence of the accident. We're concerned about the safety of our customers.

O　WHEN did you hire Mr. Darby? (3)

W　In late February of 1989.

O　WHEN did the plaintiff's accident occur? (3)

W　In early February. I think it was February 2.

O　Your Honor, I have no further voir dire questions of this witness. I renew my objection.

J　The objection will be sustained.

The second fact situation is a suit against a railroad company. The plaintiff, Hughes Corporation, sues West Central Railroad. The plaintiff alleges that the defendant's train derailed near the plaintiff's plant and caused extensive property damage. The defendant's answer alleges that the cause of the derailment was the defective condition of the track and that under the railroad's contract with the adjacent landowner, the landowner was responsible for maintaining the track. The plaintiff calls Mr. Karl as a witness. Mr. Karl identifies himself and states that he is one of the plaintiff's employees. He is prepared to testify that on December 3, 1988, the day after the accident, one of the defendant's work crews repaired the track. The proponent is the plaintiff.

P　Mr. Karl, WHERE were you on December 3, 1988?

W　I was at work at our main plant in Cheyenne.

P　WHAT happened that day?

W　I was working outside, trying to repair some of the damage caused by the derailment the day before.

P　WHAT, if anything, did you see while you were outside?

W　I saw some of the defendant's employees arrive.

P　HOW do you know that they were the defendant's employees?

W　They all had coveralls on, and the coveralls had the defendant's name on them. They drove to the site in a truck with the defendant's name on the side.

P　WHAT were the defendant's employees doing?

O　Your Honor, I object to that question. May we approach the bench?

J　Yes.

O　Your Honor, I suspect that the plaintiff is attempting to elicit inadmissible evidence of subsequent repairs to the track.

J　(To the plaintiff's attorney) Is that your intention?

P　Your Honor, I do intend to try to prove a subsequent repair. However, I contend that the evidence is admissible. I offer to prove that the witness will testify that he saw the defendant's employees repair the track. (4) The evidence is logically relevant to prove that the defendant had control of the track and thus a duty to keep the track in a state of good repair. (5) The defendant's answer specifically denied that it had control of the track or a duty to repair. (6) The defendant's general manager testified to that effect yesterday afternoon. (6) The evidence should be admitted for the limited purpose of proving the defendant's control of the track.

J   I agree. The objection is overruled.
P   Mr. Karl, let me repeat the question. WHAT were the defendant's
     employees doing?
W   They were repairing the track.
O   Your Honor, I request a limiting instruction.
J   Granted. Ladies and gentlemen of the jury, you have just heard evi-
     dence that the day after the accident, the defendant's employees were
     repairing the track. You are not to use that evidence as proof that the
     defendant was careless at the time of the accident. You may use the
     evidence only in deciding whether the defendant had control of the
     track and a duty to repair it.

The third fact situation is a product liability suit. The plaintiff, Mr.
James Barry, sues the defendant, Enright Corporation. The plaintiff
alleges that in January 1989, the defendant sold plaintiff a defectively
designed microwave oven and that in February 1989, the oven ex-
ploded, injuring the plaintiff. During the defense case-in-chief, the defendant calls Dr. Verna Gunther. Dr. Gunther identifies herself and
states that she is the defendant's chief safety engineer. On direct examination, she testifies that in her opinion, the oven was properly designed. She adds that the oven was the safest oven on the market and
represented the state of the art; it was as safely designed as the state of
the art permitted. The following occurs on cross-examination. The
plaintiff is the proponent.

P   Dr. Gunther, ISN'T IT TRUE THAT in March 1989 you redesigned the
     oven?
O   Your Honor, may we approach the bench?
J   Yes.
O   Your Honor, I object to that question on the ground that it calls for
     evidence of a subsequent repair.
J   (To the plaintiff) Is that what you're attempting to prove?
P   Yes, Your Honor. However, I think the evidence is admissible. I offer
     to prove that the witness will testify that the oven's safety features
     were redesigned only a month after the plaintiff's accident. (4) Since
     there is such a short time lapse between the accident and the redesign,
     the evidence is logically relevant to show that the defendant could
     have marketed a safer product. (5) On direct examination, this witness
     claimed that the oven was as safe as possible; the state of the art
     wouldn't permit a safer design. (6) The evidence should be admitted for
     the limited purpose of rebutting the state of the art defense.
J   I concur. The objection will be overruled.
P   Dr. Gunther, ISN'T IT A FACT THAT in March 1989, you redesigned
     the oven?
W   Yes.
P   AND ISN'T IT CORRECT THAT the part of the oven you redesigned
     was the heating coil?
W   Yes.
P   AND DIDN'T the redesign make an accidental explosion less likely?
W   Yes.
O   Your Honor, I request a limiting instruction.

J   Certainly. Ladies and gentlemen, you've just heard the doctor's testimony that she redesigned the oven shortly after the plaintiff's accident. You are not to use this evidence simply as proof of the defendant's negligence. You are to use the evidence for only one purpose, namely, deciding whether the state of the art would have permitted the defendant to market a safer product.

K. COMPROMISE STATEMENTS

1. STATEMENTS DURING CIVIL SETTLEMENT NEGOTIATIONS

The courts have long favored the out-of-court settlement of legal claims. That attitude has become even more pronounced in recent years; the trial courts are so badly backlogged that it is imperative that we encourage out-of-court settlements. The attitude expresses itself in a doctrine excluding statements made during civil settlement negotiations. The courts reason that if negotiators know that their statements are privileged, their discussions will be more candid and, hopefully, more successful.

Federal Evidence Rule 408 states the norm: "Evidence of (1) furnishing or offering or promising to furnish, or (2) compromising or attempting to compromise a claim which was disputed as to either validity or amount, is not admissible to prove liability for or invalidity of the claim or its amount. Evidence of conduct or statements made in compromise negotiations is likewise not admissible."

Like the subsequent repair doctrine, this doctrine is not an absolute exclusionary rule. In the words of Federal Rule 408, the proponent may not offer the evidence "to prove liability for or invalidity of the claim or its amount." Again, however, the proponent may offer the evidence on other theories of logical relevance. Rule 408 adds: "This rule ... does not require exclusion when the evidence is offered for another purpose, such as proving bias or prejudice of a witness, negating a contention of undue delay, or proving an effort to obstruct a criminal investigation or prosecution."

The party attempting to exclude the evidence should lay this foundation:

1. At the time of the statement, there was a dispute over the existence or extent of civil liability.
2. The party made the statement for the purpose of settling the dispute.
3. The subject-matter of the statement is proper. All jurisdictions protect an offer to settle. However, some jurisdictions protect accompanying statements of fact only if the speaker expressly states that the statements of fact are hypothetical or without prejudice.

The party attempting to introduce the evidence must be ready to make an offer of proof. In the offer of proof, the party should state:

4. What the witness will testify to if the judge permits the party to pursue the line of questioning.
5. The evidence is logically relevant to some issue other than the general question of the claim's validity.
6. The issue the evidence relates to is a disputed question in the case.

The first fact situation is a tort action for personal injuries. The plaintiff, Mr. James Stone, sues the defendant, Ms. Rachel Damer. The plaintiff alleges that the defendant caused a collision and that in the collision, the plaintiff suffered injuries in the amount of $ 100,000. The plaintiff takes the witness stand to testify in his own behalf. On cross-examination, the following occurs. The proponent is the defendant.

P   Mr. Stone, ISN'T IT TRUE THAT in your complaint in this case, you claim that you've suffered $100,000 in damages?
W   Yes.
P   ISN'T IT A FACT THAT on February 17, 1989, you were at my office?
W   Right.
P   ISN'T IT CORRECT THAT while you were there, you offered to settle your whole claim for only $15,000?
O   Your Honor, I object to that question. May we approach the bench?
J   Yes.
O   Your Honor, I object to that question on the ground that it calls for an inadmissible compromise statement. I request permission to voir dire the witness before you rule on my objection. I request that you excuse the jurors.
J   Yes. Ladies and gentlemen of the jury, I am going to ask you to leave the courtroom for a few minutes. The bailiff will accompany you to the deliberation room.
O   Mr. Stone, WHY did you go to the opposing attorney's office on February 17th? (2)
W   I went there to discuss my claim against his client.
O   WHAT was your claim? (1)
W   I took the position that Ms. Damer was at fault in the accident and caused my injuries.
O   WHAT was your belief about the validity of this claim? (1)
W   I thought I was in the right. I thought the claim was valid. As I remember the accident, I had the green light.
O   WHAT did the defendant say about your claim? (1)
W   She denied that she was at fault.
O   WHAT was the purpose of the meeting on February 17th? (2)
W   We wanted to see if we could settle without going to trial.
O   WHY did you want to settle if you thought that your claim was valid? (2)
W   You told me that juries are unpredictable and that sometimes it's better to be conservative and accept less money than you ask for in your complaint. I still thought that I had a good claim, but that's why I was willing to talk about settling.
O   Your Honor, I have no further voir dire questions. The witness' testimony shows that there was a dispute over his claim's validity and that he made his offer in a bona fide effort to compromise. The question I'm

objecting to calls for the settlement offer itself. (3) The question is objectionable.

J   The objection is sustained.

(As in the case of subsequent repair evidence the opponent should consider moving for a mistrial.)

The second fact situation is a contract action. The plaintiff, Mr. John Peterson, sues the defendant, Aramco Construction Company. In its answer, the defendant alleges that the plaintiff did not reasonably mitigate damages; the answer alleges that after the defendant's breach, the plaintiff delayed three months before looking for another contractor. The plaintiff takes the witness stand in his own behalf. The plaintiff has already testified to the contract's formation and the defendant's breach. The plaintiff is the proponent.

P   WHAT happened after the defendant's work crew walked off the site?
W   The next day I contacted Mr. Garner, the defendant's president.
P   WHAT happened when you contacted him?
W   He and I discussed how we might settle my claim against his company.
O   Your Honor, I move to strike the last answer. May we approach the bench?
J   By all means.
O   Your Honor, the answer refers to inadmissible compromise negotiations.
P   Your Honor, may I be heard?
J   Yes.
P   I offer to prove that the witness will testify that the parties began settlement negotiations that day and that the negotiations continued for over two months. (4) The testimony is logically relevant to explain the plaintiff's delay in hiring another contractor. (5) In its answer, the defendant alleged that the plaintiff did not properly mitigate damages. (6) The evidence is admissible for the limited purpose of rebutting the defendant's allegation.
J   Motion denied.
P   Mr. Peterson, permit me to repeat the question. WHAT happened when you contacted Mr. Garner?
W   We discussed settling my claim against his company.
P   HOW long did these discussions last?
W   On and off for over two months. I kept trying to get them back on the project; I wanted a warehouse, not a lawsuit.
O   Your Honor, I request a limiting instruction.
J   Granted. Ladies and gentlemen of the jury, you've just heard testimony about settlement negotiations between the plaintiff and defendant. You are not to use the evidence of the defendant's willingness to negotiate as an admission of liability. You are to use this evidence only for the limited purpose of deciding whether the plaintiff acted with reasonable speed in finding a new contractor to finish the project. The defendant claims that the plaintiff did not. The plaintiff offers these pending settlement negotiations as an explanation for his delay in hiring a new contractor.

2. STATEMENTS DURING PLEA BARGAINING NEGOTIATIONS

The last subsection examined the doctrine excluding statements made during civil settlement negotiations. The reason for that doctrine is that the courts want to encourage out-of-court settlements and save court time. For a similar reason, many jurisdictions recognize a parallel doctrine excluding statements made during criminal plea bargaining negotiations. Federal Evidence Rule 410 places the federal courts among the ranks of the jurisdictions following the doctrine. The latest version of the Rule generally excludes "(1) a plea of guilty which was later withdrawn; (2) a plea of *nolo contendere;* (3) any statement made in the course of any proceedings under Rule 11 of the Federal Rules of Criminal Procedure or comparable state procedure regarding either of the foregoing pleas; or (4) any statement made in the course of plea discussions with an attorney for the prosecuting authority which do not result in a plea of guilty or which result in a plea of guilty later withdrawn."

The jurisdictions following this doctrine usually allow a few exceptions to the general norm. Some permit the prosecutor to use plea bargaining statements to impeach the defendant's testimony. The federal courts take a narrower view. The only exceptions mentioned in the latest version of Rule 410 are that the evidence "is admissible (i) in any proceeding wherein another statement made in the course of the same plea or plea discussions has been introduced and the statement ought in fairness be considered contemporaneously with it, or (ii) in a criminal proceeding for perjury or false statement if the statement was made by the defendant under oath, on the record and in the presence of counsel." The second exception is limited to statements the defendant makes formally while a judge is questioning the defendant under oath, on the record, about a proposed plea.

The defendant attempting to invoke this doctrine must lay this foundation:

1. At a certain time and place, the defendant met with the authorities, that is, the prosecutor, or the police acting with the prosecutor's consent.
2. The defendant subjectively believed that the purpose of the meeting was plea bargaining. Although in the past most courts have required proof of this element to invoke Rule 410, some courts have construed the latest amendment to Rule 410 as dispensing with proof of the defendant's subjective belief. *State v. Fox,* 760 P.2d 670 (Hawaii 1988).
3. The defendant's belief was reasonable. The authorities' statements and conduct reasonably led the defendant to that belief.
4. The defendant made the statement during the plea bargaining session.

5. The subject-matter of the statement was proper. The jurisdictions recognizing this doctrine tend to protect both offers and accompanying statements of fact.

Our fact situation is a medical aid fraud prosecution. The government alleges that the defendant, Mr. George Aston, is a pharmacist and knowingly filled fraudulent prescriptions for doctors receiving medical aid payments from the state. The indictment alleges that the defendant filled excessive prescriptions and prescriptions for fictitious patients. Since this is a white collar crime prosecution, the defendant was not in custody. The government's primary interest was convicting the doctors with whom the defendant conspired. Prior to trial, the defendant makes a motion *in limine* to suppress certain statements he made to the prosecutor during a meeting at the prosecutor's office. Since the defendant was not in custody and there is no evidence of force or threats, the defense counsel cannot argue *Miranda* or the voluntariness doctrine. Rather, the defense counsel rests the motion squarely on the doctrine excluding statements made during plea bargaining negotiations. The defense counsel calls the defendant as a witness in support of the motion. The defendant has already identified himself. The defendant is the proponent.

P   Mr. Aston, WHERE were you on the afternoon of April 3, 1989? (1)
W   I went to the D.A.'s office in downtown Gainesville.
P   WHO else was there? (1)
W   You were there, and the other person present was a Deputy D.A.
P   WHO was that? (1)
W   I think her name was Hester Martin.
P   WHAT was the purpose of this meeting? (2)
W   Plea bargaining. I hoped to get some concessions, maybe even immunity.
P   WHY did you think that was the purpose of the meeting? (2)
W   You told me that before we got there.
P   WHAT, if anything, did Ms. Martin say about the purpose of the meeting? (3)
W   When we got there, she said that she wanted to be honest with me. She said that I was just a small fish and that they were really interested in nailing all the doctors I had filled false prescriptions for. She said that if I came clean, they might give me a break. She even mentioned some sort of immunity.
P   WHAT did you say then? (4), (5)
W   With your permission, I told her about my involvement with the doctors. I said that I'd be willing to repeat those statements in court for full immunity.
P   HOW did Ms. Martin respond to your offer?
W   She said that she'd have to talk it over with her boss, Mr. Ching, before giving us a final answer.
P   WHAT was the final answer?
W   Ms. Martin phoned me at work about three days later. She said that her boss would O.K. some sentence concessions but wouldn't buy immunity.

P   WHAT, if anything, did you say then?
W   I told her that it was too bad because you and I had agreed that I'd talk only if I got immunity.
P   WHAT happened to your plea bargaining with the District Attorney's office?
W   That conversation ended the negotiations.
P   Your Honor, I have no further questions of the defendant. I renew my motion to preclude any reference to my client's statements during the plea bargaining session at the District Attorney's office.
J   I shall grant the motion.

Chapter 8

THE BEST EVIDENCE RULE

A. INTRODUCTION

The last three chapters analyzed rules which exclude logically relevant evidence for policy reasons — either policies relating to jury behavior or extrinsic social policies. The next three chapters also discuss rules which have the effect of barring the admission of logically relevant evidence. However, the doctrines discussed in these chapters exclude relevant evidence for a very different reason, namely, doubts about the reliability of certain types of evidence.

The common law prefers that evidence take the form of a witness walking into court, subjecting himself or herself to cross-examination, and either reciting observed facts or quoting a document produced in the courtroom. In the mind of the common-law courts, that type of testimony is the most trustworthy. Whenever the proponent of evidence attempts to deviate from the norm, the proponent is likely to encounter an exclusionary rule. If the proponent offers testimony about an out-of-court statement rather than calling the declarant as a witness at trial, the proponent may have to surmount the hurdle of the hearsay rule. When the proponent attempts to elicit opinions from the witness rather than statements of observed fact, the proponent may encounter the opinion prohibition. Finally, if the proponent invites the witness to paraphrase a document rather than producing the document in court, the proponent may face a best evidence objection. The proponent may be able to introduce the hearsay, opinion, or paraphrase; but in order to do so, the proponent must establish an exceptional reason for deviating from the preference.

The best evidence rule is illustrative. The best evidence rule excludes secondary evidence of a writing's contents; the rule expresses a preference for the more reliable evidence, the writing itself. Federal Rules of Evidence 1001-08 set out the rule. Briefly, the rule is that when a writing's terms are in issue, the proponent must either (1) produce an original or duplicate or (2) both excuse the non-production of the originals and present an admissible type of secondary evidence. The rule presents five issues: What is a "writing" for purposes of the rule? When are a writing's terms "in issue"? What is an "original" or a "duplicate"? What are the admissible types of secondary evidence? And what are adequate excuses for non-production?

The proponent can usually defeat a best evidence objection. The proponent can do so because the five issues convert into several different bases for overriding the objection. The judge can overrule the objection on the grounds that the article involved is not a "document"; the document's terms are not "in issue"; the document's terms are only collaterally "in issue"; the evidence offered is an "original"; the evidence offered is a "duplicate"; and there is an adequate excuse for the nonproduction of the originals, and the proponent is offering an admissible type of secondary evidence. The following sections illustrate the various bases for defeating best evidence objections.

B. THE OBJECT INVOLVED IS NOT A "WRITING"

The title of the doctrine, "the best evidence rule," is a misnomer. There is no general requirement that the proponent produce or account for the best evidence. The rule's scope is limited to writings; the rationale is that detail is often more important in the analysis of writings. Thus, a more accurate title for the doctrine would be the "original writing rule."

Federal Evidence Rule 1002 contains a broad definition of the rule's scope. Rule 1002 applies the rule to writings, recordings, and photographs. Rule 1001(1) defines writings and records as "letters, words, or numbers, or their equivalent, set down by handwriting, typewriting, printing, photostating, photographing, magnetic impulse, mechanical or electronic recording, or other form of data compilation." Rule 1001(2) defines photographs as "still photographs, X-ray films, video tapes and motion pictures."

However, in some jurisdictions, "writing" has a relatively narrow meaning. For instance, a few jurisdictions do not apply the rule to photographs. Other jurisdictions hold that the rule does not apply to inscribed chattels, articles, or personal property such as tires bearing inscriptions.

The fact situation is a products liability action. The plaintiff, Mr. Konert, brings a tort action against Goodyear Tire Company. He alleges that the defendant negligently manufactured his tire and that the negligent manufacture caused the tire to blow out and thereby cause an accident. The defendant has generally denied liability. The plaintiff calls Mr. Langdale, the police officer who investigated the accident. The witness has already identified himself and generally described the investigation at the accident scene. The officer has stated that he carefully examined the condition of the plaintiff's car. The plaintiff is the proponent.

P   WHAT parts of the car did you inspect?
W   Any part that might have contributed to the accident — the steering wheel, the engine, and the tires.
P   WHAT condition were the tires in?
W   Three were O.K.
P   WHAT was the condition of the fourth tire?

W It had blown out. There was no air in it, and there was a large hole in it.
P HOW large was the hole?
W I'd say that it was easily two inches in diameter.
P WHERE was the hole located?
W On the tread part of the tire.
P WHAT was written on the tire?
W There were size specifications and a tradename.
P WHAT was the tradename on the tire?
O Your Honor, I object to that question on the ground that it calls for secondary evidence.
P Your Honor, may I be heard?
J Yes.
P In this jurisdiction, the best evidence rule does not apply to inscribed chattels such as tires.
J I agree. Objection overruled.
P Let me repeat the question. WHAT was the tradename on the tire?
W It was Goodyear.

C. THE WRITING'S TERMS ARE NOT "IN ISSUE"

In the words of Federal Evidence Rule 1002, the rule applies only when the proponent attempts "to prove the content of a writing...." There are three situations in which a document's terms are "in issue" for purposes of triggering the best evidence rule.

The first situation is the case in which the material facts of consequence automatically place the document's terms in issue. For example, in a forgery prosecution, the terms of the allegedly forged document are automatically in issue; and the same analysis applies in a contract action if the complaint alleges that the agreement was a written contract.

We must distinguish this situation from the situation in which a fact exists independently of the writing but the writing is convenient evidence of the fact. Thus, a witness who observed payment of a debt may testify to that fact without producing the receipt; the receipt is merely convenient evidence of payment. In most jurisdictions, a witness who attended a wedding ceremony may testify to the marriage without producing the marriage certificate. Again, the certificate is convenient evidence, but the wedding is an historical event that occurred independently of the writing.

The second situation is a case in which the witness expressly or impliedly refers to the writing in his or her testimony. Suppose that the proponent attempting to prove the marriage cannot find an eyewitness to the ceremony. The proponent instead calls a deputy county clerk to testify to the contents of the marriage certificate on file. The clerk will expressly or impliedly rely upon the document's contents; the express or implied reference to the document's contents triggers the best evidence rule.

Finally, in some jurisdictions, there are statutes declaring that certain types of documents are "legal proof" of particular facts. For instance, some statutes announce that the marriage certificate is "legal proof" of the marriage. The question of statutory construction is whether the legislature intended the statute to extend the best evidence rule's scope. Some courts have answered that question in the affirmative; they have held that the statute evidences a legislative intent to make the certificate the best evidence even when there is an available eyewitness to the ceremony.

Our hypothetical fact situation is a probate contest. The contestants are challenging the will and claiming by intestate succession. To prove their right to take by intestate succession, they have to show that on March 1, 1965, Joan Merchant married Thomas Kleven. The contestants call Ms. Trudy Guinn, an eyewitness to the marriage. The contestants are the proponents.

P   Ms. Guinn, WHERE were you on March 1, 1965?
W   I was in Chicago, Illinois.
P   WHAT were you doing there?
W   I was attending a wedding.
P   WHOSE wedding?
O   Your Honor, I object to that question on the ground that it calls for secondary evidence; the marriage certificate is the best evidence.
P   Your Honor, may I be heard?
J   Yes.
P   The event of the wedding occurred independently of the certificate; a witness could observe the wedding ceremony without ever seeing the certificate. This eyewitness is prepared to testify without relying on the certificate. Thus, the certificate's terms are not in issue.
J   Objection overruled.
P   Ms. Guinn, let me repeat the question. WHOSE wedding?
W   The marriage of Joan Merchant and Thomas Kleven.
P   HOW can you remember a wedding that occurred almost twenty-five years ago?
W   It sticks in my mind because I was Joan's maid of honor. I knew Joan and Tom well, and Joan asked me to stand up with her.

D. THE WRITING'S TERMS ARE ONLY COLLATERALLY "IN ISSUE"

Even if the writing's terms are technically in issue, the judge may dispense with compliance with the best evidence rule. Sometimes the writing's terms relate to a minor issue in the case, and the judge concludes that it is not worth the time and inconvenience to require the proponent to comply with the best evidence rule. Suppose, for instance, that the opponent wants to impeach the witness with a written prior inconsistent statement. If the opponent is going to use the document solely to impeach the witness, the judge is likely to hold that the document is only collaterally relevant. The opponent could dispense with compliance with the best evidence rule and use a Xerox copy of the written prior inconsistent statement.

Federal Evidence Rule 1004(4) recognizes this limitation on the scope of the best evidence rule. That subsection states that the proponent need not comply with the best evidence rule if "(t)he writing, recording, or photograph is not closely related to a controlling issue." The judge considers the importance of the issue the document relates to. If the judge concludes in his or her discretion that the issue is a minor question in the case, the proponent need not comply with the best evidence rule.

The fact situation is a tort action arising from a hit-and-run accident. The plaintiff, Ms. Difiglia, alleges that the defendant, Mr. Walker, negligently struck her in a crosswalk. The defendant denies that he was the driver. The plaintiff calls Mr. Meese, an eyewitness to the accident. Mr. Meese has just testified that he saw the accident and observed the car's license number. The plaintiff is the proponent.

P WHAT was that license number?

W I'm sorry, but I can't remember offhand.

P WHAT, if anything, might help you remember?

W Well, I made a note of the license number right after the accident. If I could see that note, I could probably remember.

P Your Honor, I request that this be marked plaintiff's exhibit number two for identification.

J It will be so marked.

P Please let the record reflect that I am showing the exhibit to the opposing counsel.

J It will so reflect.

O Your Honor, I am going to have to object to the use of this document to refresh the witness' recollection. It's obvious that this is a Xerox copy and not the best evidence.

P Your Honor, may I be heard?

J Yes.

P I intend to use the exhibit solely to refresh the witness' recollection; I am not going to use the exhibit as substantive evidence of its contents. The exhibit is being used only collaterally.

J Objection overruled.

P I request permission to approach the witness.

J Granted.

P Mr. Meese, I now hand you plaintiff's exhibit number two for identification. WHAT is it?

W It's a copy of the note I just mentioned.

P HOW can you recognize it?

W I recognize my handwriting style.

P WHO prepared the note?

W I did.

P WHEN did you prepare it?

W Right after the accident.

P HOW soon after the accident?

W It was a matter of minutes at most.

P   Please read the exhibit to yourself silently. *(The witness does so.)* Please hand the exhibit to me. *(To the judge)* Please let the record reflect that I am holding the exhibit away from the witness and out of the witness' sight.

J   The record will reflect that.

P   Mr. Meese, you've had an opportunity to read the exhibit to refresh your memory. Now, without relying on the exhibit, HOW well can you remember the license number?

W   Now it's clear in my mind.

P   WHAT was the license number?

W   It was a South Carolina license, FIA 986.

E. THE EVIDENCE OFFERED IS AN "ORIGINAL"

1. THE DOCTRINE

If the object involved is a writing and its terms are in issue, the proponent must comply with the best evidence rule. The simplest method of complying is by offering an original or duplicate. The "original" is usually the first document prepared, the first writing signed, the first tape recording prepared, or the negative of the photograph.

However, it must be borne in mind that the common-law test for originality is legal rather than chronological. Suppose that the case is a threat prosecution. The government alleges that the defendant sent a bomb threat through the mail. The defendant first prepared the threat by typing it. However, the defendant realized that it would be more difficult for a questioned document examiner to identify the paper or typewriter if he mailed a copy rather than the original. Consequently, the defendant Xeroxed a copy of the typed threat and mailed the Xerox copy to the bank. For purposes of the best evidence rule, the Xerox copy is the original. It is a copy in a chronological sense. However, since it is the very writing the defendant mailed to the bank, the copy is the legal original.

As the preceding paragraph indicates, at common law there was usually an original writing — in the singular. The Federal Rules broaden the definition of "original." Rule 1001(3) states that "[a]n 'original' of a writing or recording is the writing or recording itself or any counterpart intended to have the same effect by a person executing or issuing it." Assume, for example, that the purchaser of a car signs a single copy of the contract of purchase and leaves the writing with the seller. The next day the seller decides that the buyer should have her own copy of the writing. For that reason, the seller Xeroxes a copy and mails it to the buyer. Since the Xerox is an exact copy made by reliable, mechanical means and it is intended to have essentially the same effect as the copy earlier signed in ink, both writings would be "originals" in federal practice.

2. ELEMENTS OF THE FOUNDATION

The foundation includes these elements:

1. The witness recognizes the document.

2. The witness specifies how he or she recognizes the document.

3. The witness adds that the document is the original.

3. SAMPLE FOUNDATION

The fact situation is a contract action. The plaintiff, Mr. Levine, alleges that the defendant, Mr. Bratton, breached a written employment contract by discharging Levine without cause. The plaintiff's attorney calls the plaintiff to the stand. The plaintiff has already identified himself and described the parties' oral agreement. The plaintiff is the proponent.

P WHAT did you do after you reached the oral agreement?

W Mr. Bratton's secretary reduced the agreement to writing.

P WHEN did she do that?

W The very afternoon we reached the agreement. Mr. Bratton had standard forms with blanks, so it didn't take the secretary long to get the contract ready for signature.

P Your Honor, I request that this be marked plaintiff's exhibit number one for identification.

J It will be so marked.

P Please let the record reflect that I am showing the exhibit to the opposing counsel.

J The record will reflect that.

P I request permission to approach the witness.

J Granted.

P Mr. Levine, I now hand you plaintiff's exhibit number one for identification. WHAT is it? (1)

W It's the contract I was describing.

P HOW can you recognize it? (2)

W I can tell by its general appearance and especially by the signatures on page five. I certainly know my own handwriting.

P HOW many copies of this did you make? (3)

W Three. We signed one in ink, and two were carbon copies.

P WHICH one is this exhibit — the one in ink or one of the carbon copies? (3)

W This is the one in ink.

P WHEN did you sign this one? (3)

W We signed it first.

P HOW did you sign the carbon copies? (3)

W The signature just pressed through to them and marked them as we signed the one in ink.

P Your Honor, I now offer plaintiff's exhibit number one for identification into evidence as plaintiff's exhibit number one.

O Your Honor, I object to the introduction of the exhibit on the ground that the plaintiff has not accounted for the other documents.

P Your Honor, may I be heard?

J Yes.

P The testimony shows that this exhibit is the original, the very first writing the parties signed. Thus, we've complied with the best evidence rule.

J Objection overruled. The exhibit will be received.

P   I request permission to hand the exhibit to the jurors for their inspection.
J   Permission granted.

F. THE EVIDENCE OFFERED IS A "DUPLICATE"

1. THE DOCTRINE

The proponent can comply with the best evidence rule by offering a duplicate rather than an original. At common law, a duplicate original is as admissible as the original; the proponent may offer a duplicate original without proving any excuse for the non-production of the original. The common law developed a fairly narrow definition of duplicate. The common law insisted that the duplicate be prepared for the same purpose at the same time as the original and executed with roughly the same formalities. Carbon copies signed by the same stroke of the pen as the original are acceptable duplicate originals at common law.

However, the common law balked at accepting subsequently prepared documents as duplicates. The common law refused to accept subsequently prepared documents even if they were prepared by reliable, mechanical means of reproduction. The trend, however, is to include such documents within the definition of duplicate. Federal Rule of Evidence 1001(4) follows that trend. That subsection defines "duplicate" as "a counterpart produced by the same impression as the original, or from the same matrix, or by means of photography, including enlargements and miniatures, by mechanical or electronic re-recording, or by chemical reproduction, or by other equivalent techniques which accurately reproduce the original." So long as the writing is prepared by reliable, mechanical means, it qualifies as a duplicate even if it was prepared much later or for a different reason.

2. ELEMENTS OF THE FOUNDATION

To qualify a document as a duplicate at common law, the proponent must establish the following foundational elements:

1. The witness recognizes the writing.
2. The witness specifies the basis on which he or she recognizes the writing.
3. The writing is a copy of the original.
4. The parties made the copy at the same time as the original.
5. The parties intended the copy to have the same legal effect as the original.
6. The parties executed the copy with roughly the same formalities as the original.

If the proponent is invoking the broader, modern definition of duplicate original, the proponent must lay the following foundation:

1. The witness recognizes the writing.

2. The witness specifies the basis on which he or she recognizes the writing.

3. The writing is a copy of the original.

4. The witness states the time when the copy was made.

5. The witness specifies the reason why the copy was made. In federal practice, this element is unnecessary. However, in some jurisdictions, the writing does not qualify if it was prepared specially for purposes of trial.

6. The copy was made by a reliable, mechanical means of reproduction.

3. SAMPLE FOUNDATIONS

We shall assume that we are continuing the hypothetical involving the employment contract in the last section. The first foundation qualifies a document as a duplicate under the common-law definition. The plaintiff has already stated that the parties reached an oral agreement and had the agreement reduced to writing. The plaintiff is still the proponent.

P   HOW many documents did you prepare?
W   Three.
P   HOW did the documents differ, if at all?
W   We signed the one on top in ink, and the other two were carbon copies.
P   WHERE was the carbon paper? (6)
W   It was between the sheets of white paper.
P   WHEN did you prepare the copies? (4)
W   At the same time as we signed the originals.
P   HOW did you prepare the copies? (5)
W   The secretary typed them by carbon, and then we signed them by carbon at the same time we signed the one on top in ink.
P   WHY did you prepare the copies? (5)
W   So that everyone would have his own copy of the agreement — the original for Mr. Bratton's files, one copy for his general personnel files, and another copy for me.
P   WHAT legal effect did you want the original to have? (5)
W   It was supposed to be our agreement.
P   WHAT legal effect did you want the copies to have? (5)
W   The same effect as the original. Everyone was to have his own copy of the contract.
P   Your Honor, I request that this be marked plaintiff's exhibit number one for identification.
J   It will be so marked.
P   Please let the record reflect that I am showing the exhibit to the opposing counsel.
J   The record will so reflect.
P   I request permission to approach the witness.
J   Granted.
P   Mr. Levine, I now hand you plaintiff's exhibit number one for identification. WHAT is it? (1)

W   It's the contract.

P   HOW can you recognize it? (2)

W   I know it by its general appearance and the signatures at the end of page five. I certainly ought to know my own handwriting style.

P   Again, HOW many documents did you prepare? (3)

W   As I said, an original and two copies.

P   WHICH one is this? (3)

W   It's one of the copies.

P   HOW can you tell? (3)

W   The signature is obviously a carbon impression rather than ink.

P   Your Honor, I now offer plaintiff's exhibit number one for identification into evidence as plaintiff's exhibit number one.

O   Your Honor, I object to the introduction of this exhibit on the ground that it is not the best evidence. The plaintiff has not produced or accounted for the original.

P   Your Honor, may I be heard?

J   Certainly.

P   The testimony shows that this exhibit is a duplicate — an accurate copy made at the same time for the same purpose with roughly the same formalities. As a duplicate, it is just as admissible as the original.

J   The objection will be overruled, and the exhibit will be received into evidence.

P   I request permission to hand the exhibit to the jurors for their inspection.

J   Permission granted.

Now we shall work through the same hypothetical with the modern definition of "duplicate."

P   HOW many documents did you prepare when you signed the contract?

W   Three.

P   HOW did the documents differ, if at all?

W   We signed one in ink, there was a carbon copy, and we made one other copy.

P   WHEN did you prepare the carbon copy?

W   When we signed the original.

P   WHEN did you prepare the other copy? (4)

W   About a week after the signing of the contract.

P   HOW did you prepare this other copy? (5)

W   I ran it off on my Xerox machine at work.

P   WHAT condition was the Xerox machine in when you made the copy? (6)

W   It seemed to be in good, working condition. I didn't have any mechanical difficulties with the machine.

P   WHY did you make this other copy? (5)

W   I just wanted to be on the safe side. I wanted one copy, the carbon, at home and the other, the Xerox, at my office.

P   Your Honor, I request that this be marked plaintiff's exhibit number one for identification.

J   It will be so marked.

P   Please let the record reflect that I am showing the exhibit to the opposing counsel.

J   It will so reflect.

P   I request permission to approach the witness.
J   Permission granted.
P   Mr. Levine, I now hand you plaintiff's exhibit number one for identification. WHAT is it? (1)
W   It's the contract.
P   HOW can you recognize it? (2)
W   I know it by its general appearance and the signatures at the end of page three. I certainly ought to know my own handwriting style.
P   Again, HOW many documents did you prepare? (3)
W   Three — the ink original, one carbon copy, and one Xerox copy.
P   WHICH one is this? (3)
W   It's the Xerox copy.
P   HOW can you tell? (3)
W   It's obviously a Xerox copy rather than an ink or carbon. You can tell by its appearance and the feel of the paper.
P   Your Honor, I now offer plaintiff's exhibit number one for identification into evidence as plaintiff's exhibit number one.
O   I object to the introduction of this exhibit on the ground that it is not the best evidence.
P   Your Honor, may I be heard?
J   Yes.
P   The testimony shows that this exhibit is a duplicate. It is true that it was prepared subsequently; but under the law in this jurisdiction, it can still qualify as a duplicate so long as it was made by a mechanical means of reproduction.
J   The objection will be overruled, and the exhibit will be received into evidence.
P   I request permission to hand the exhibit to the jurors for their inspection.
J   Permission granted.

On the one hand, the Federal Rules expand the definition of "duplicate." On the other hand, in federal practice, a duplicate is not necessarily as admissible as an original. Federal Rule 1003 reads: "A duplicate is admissible to the same extent as an original unless (1) a genuine question is raised as to the authenticity of the original or (2) in the circumstances it would be unfair to admit the duplicate in lieu of the original." The opposing attorney might invoke 1003(1) by presenting evidence that the original document was a forgery; the purported author might deny ever signing such a writing. That evidence sharpens the need to examine the original. Similarly, the opposing attorney could resort to 1003(2) if the copy was incomplete and omitted a potentially important part of the original. In either event, the proponent would have to establish excuses for the non-production of all originals before introducing a duplicate.

G. ADMISSIBLE TYPES OF SECONDARY EVIDENCE

If the object involved is a writing and the writing's terms are in issue, there are two methods of satisfying the rule. The last two sections dealt with the first method: proving that the evidence offered qualifies as an original or duplicate. The second method involves two steps: (1) proving an adequate excuse for the non-production; and (2) offering an admissible type of secondary evidence. There are two admissible types of secondary evidence. The first is an authenticated copy; the witness testifies that the document is an accurate copy of the original. The second is oral recollection testimony; the proponent does not have even a written copy of the original, but the witness can recall the substance of the contents of the original.

1. AN AUTHENTICATED COPY

One permissible type of secondary evidence is an authenticated copy. The witness need not have personally prepared the copy. However, the witness must remember the tenor or contents of the original, read the copy, and finally testify that the exhibit is a true and accurate copy of the original. The elements of the foundation are:

1. On a previous occasion, the witness read the original.
2. The witness still remembers the original.
3. As best he or she can tell, the exhibit is a true and accurate copy of the original.

Our fact situation is a civil tort action. The plaintiff, Mr. Smythe, alleges that the defendant, Mr. Wiggins, is guilty of libel. The complaint alleges that the defendant committed the libel in a letter to Mr. Jackson. The plaintiff calls Mr. Jackson as a witness. Mr. Jackson first testifies that he received the letter in the defendant's handwriting. The plaintiff then establishes an excuse for the non-production of the original letter such as the loss of the letter; the next section describes the foundation for that excuse. Now the proponent, the plaintiff, will attempt to authenticate a Xerox copy of the letter.

P   WHAT did you do when you first received the letter? (1)
W   I read it.
P   HOW carefully did you read it? (1), (2)
W   Very carefully.
P   WHY did you read it carefully? (1), (2)
W   It shocked me. I had to read it several times before I could believe what I saw.
P   HOW many times did you read it? (1), (2)
W   At least three.
P   WHY did you read it three times? (1), (2)
W   Again, it was hard to believe what I read in that letter.
P   HOW well do you remember the contents of the letter? (2)
W   Very well. I can't quote it word for word, but I have a distinct recollection of it.
P   HOW can you remember it so well? (2)
W   Well, it was fairly short; and I read it both carefully and several times.
P   Your Honor, I request that this be marked plaintiff's exhibit number two for identification.

J	It will be so marked.
P	Please let the record reflect that I am showing the exhibit to the opposing counsel.
J	It will so reflect.
P	I request permission to approach the witness.
J	Permission granted.
P	Mr. Jackson, I now hand you plaintiff's exhibit number two for identification. WHAT is it? (3)
W	It's a Xerox copy of the letter I just described.
P	HOW can you recognize it? (3)
W	I recognize the handwriting, the general contents, and some phrases that stick in my mind.
P	HOW accurate is this copy? (3)
W	As far as I can tell, it's verbatim.
P	Your Honor, I now offer plaintiff's exhibit number two for identification into evidence as plaintiff's exhibit two.
O	I object to the introduction of this exhibit on the ground that it is not the best evidence; it's only a secondary copy.
P	Your Honor, may I be heard?
J	Yes.
P	It's true that this is secondary evidence. However, we've established the loss of the original which is an adequate excuse for non-production. In addition, the witness has authenticated the copy.
J	The objection will be overruled, and the exhibit will be received into evidence.
P	Mr. Jackson, would you please read the last paragraph of the letter to the jurors?
W	The paragraph reads: "I heard this juicy rumor about our mutual friend, James Smythe. He evidently slipped $2,000 to Councilman Wild to get a favorable ruling on a zoning application. Old Smythe is a lot slicker — and a lot less honest — than I thought."
P	WHOSE handwriting is that letter in?
W	The defendant's, Marvin Wiggins.
P	I request permission to hand the exhibit to the jurors for their inspection.
J	Granted.

2. ORAL RECOLLECTION TESTIMONY

Even if the proponent does not have a copy, the witness can testify to his or her recollection of the original's contents. Again, the proponent must establish an excuse for non-production. The foundation is quite simple:

1. On a previous occasion, the witness read the original.
2. The witness still remembers the substance of the original's contents.
3. The witness states the substance of the original's contents.

We shall use the same hypothetical to illustrate this type of secondary evidence. Again, assume that the proponent has already established an excuse for non-production of the original letter.

P	WHAT did you do when you first received the letter? (1)

W	I read it.
P	HOW carefully did you read it? (1), (2)
W	Very carefully.
P	WHY did you read it carefully? (1), (2)
W	It shocked me. I had to read it several times before I could believe what I saw there.
P	HOW many times did you read it? (1), (2)
W	At least three times.
P	WHY did you read it three times? (1), (2)
W	Again, it was so hard to believe what I read there.
P	HOW was the letter prepared? Was it printed, written, or typed? (2)
W	It was handwritten.
P	HOW well do you remember the contents of the letter? (2)
W	Very well. I can't quote it word for word, but I have a distinct recollection.
P	HOW can you remember it so well? (2)
W	It was relatively short, and I read it carefully several times.
P	WHAT were the contents of the letter? (3)
W	It talked about a lot of things.
P	WHAT, if anything, did the letter say about Mr. Smythe? (3)
O	Your Honor, I object to that question on the ground that it calls for secondary evidence.
P	Your Honor, may I be heard?
J	Yes.
P	It's true that the witness' recollection is secondary evidence. However, we've established the loss of the original which is an adequate excuse for the non-production of the original. In addition, the witness has testified to recalling the substance of the letter.
J	Objection overruled.
P	Mr. Jackson, let me repeat the question. WHAT, if anything, did the letter say about Mr. Smythe? (3)
W	It said that he had bribed Councilman Wild in connection with a zoning application.
P	WHOSE handwriting was the letter in?
W	The defendant's, Marvin Wiggins.

H. EXCUSES FOR NON-PRODUCTION

As we have seen, if the proponent's evidence does not qualify as an original or duplicate, the proponent must both authenticate the evidence and establish an excuse for non-production. At common law, there was authority that the proponent must excuse the non-production of all originals and duplicates before resorting to secondary evidence. The Federal Rules make it easier to introduce secondary evidence; they typically require an excuse for the non-production of only the originals.

1. THE PROPONENT LOST THE ORIGINAL

Federal Rule of Evidence 1004(1) states that there is an adequate excuse for non-production if "[a]ll originals are lost...." Sometimes the witness can testify directly to the original's loss; for example, perhaps the witness saw the original fall into a sewer. In most cases, however, the proponent will have to rely on circumstantial proof of loss: Although the witness conducted a diligent search for the original, the witness could not locate it. Some jurisdictions impose hard-and-fast rules to determine the search's diligence; the proponent must always search the last known place of custody or contact the last known custodian. However, in most jurisdictions, there are no hard-and-fast rules; the trial judge makes a discretionary determination whether the proponent exercised sufficient diligence to locate the original.

The foundational elements include the following:

1. The witness discovered that the original was lost.
2. The witness then searched for the original.
3. The search was reasonably diligent.
4. Despite the search, the witness could not locate the original.

Our fact situation is the previous hypothetical. The plaintiff will use Mr. Jackson's testimony to establish the excuse for non-production. Mr. Jackson has already testified about receiving a handwritten letter from the defendant.

P   WHAT did you do with the letter after you received it? (1)
W   I put it in my dresser in our bedroom.
P   WHERE is the letter now? (1)
W   I don't know.
P   WHEN did you discover that the letter was missing? (1)
W   I looked for it three weeks ago when you told me we would be going to trial.
P   HOW did you discover that the letter was missing? (1)
W   I went to the dresser, looked through it, and couldn't find the letter.
P   WHAT did you do then? (2)
W   I searched for the letter.
P   HOW did you conduct this search? (3)
W   I went through each drawer in the dresser very carefully.
P   HOW carefully? (3)
W   I went through it item by item and still couldn't find the letter.
P   WHERE else did you search? (3)
W   I looked all around the room.
P   WHERE else did you look? (3)
W   I checked my desk to see if I might have put it there.
P   WHAT else did you do? (3)
W   I asked my wife if she had seen it.
P   WHAT did she say? (3)
W   She said she hadn't seen it. *(Note that her response is being offered for a nonhearsay purpose; the purpose is to prove the effect on the hearer's state of mind. Given the wife's response, it was reasonable for the witness not to search further.)*
P   WHAT did you do then? (3)
W   I stopped searching.
P   WHY did you stop the search? (3)
W   I just couldn't think of anywhere else to look.
P   WHAT was the outcome of your search? (4)

W   I couldn't find it. I just don't know where it got to.

Authentication of the Secondary Evidence

At this point, the proponent authenticates the secondary evidence. See Section G.2, supra. Assume that the proponent authenticates the witness' recollection of the letter's contents.

P   WHAT, if anything, did the letter say about Mr. Smythe?
O   Your Honor, I object to that question on the ground that it calls for secondary evidence.
P   Your Honor, may I be heard?
J   Yes.
P   It's true that the witness' recollection is secondary evidence. However, we've established the loss of the original which is an adequate excuse for non-production. In addition, the witness says he can remember the substance of the letter.
J   The objection will be overruled.
P   Mr. Jackson, let me repeat the question. WHAT, if anything, did the letter say about Mr. Smythe?
W   It said that he had bribed Councilman Wild in connection with a zoning application.
P   WHOSE handwriting was the letter in?
W   The defendant's.

2. THE PROPONENT INNOCENTLY DESTROYED THE ORIGINAL

The early, common-law view was that if the proponent intentionally destroyed the original, the proponent could not introduce secondary evidence of the original's contents. However, modern courts realize that an intentional destruction might have been in perfect good faith. For example, businesses routinely destroy their original records after a number of years; they retain only computer or microfilm copies because they do not want warehouses jammed with voluminous, outdated records. The current test is whether the proponent destroyed the original in bad faith. If the proponent destroyed the original intentionally but in good faith, the secondary evidence is admissible. Federal Evidence Rule 1004(1) adopts this doctrine. The subsection provides that secondary evidence is admissible if "[a]ll originals ... have been destroyed, unless the proponent ... destroyed them in bad faith."

The foundation includes these elements:
1. The witness had the original.
2. The witness destroyed the original.
3. The destruction was accidental, or the witness' intentional destruction of the original was in good faith.

The fact situation is an anti-trust action. Belmar Corporation sues Dutton Corporation for various violations of the federal anti-trust statutes. Belmar alleges that over a ten-year period, it lost $5,000,000 in sales because of Dutton's anti-competitive practices. To show its damages, the plaintiff calls its chief records custodian, Ms. Gerst. Ms. Gerst has already identified herself and testified to her familiarity with Belmar's records policies. The proponent is the plaintiff.

P   WHAT, if any, procedures does Belmar use to record its sales? (1)
W   We first prepare sales memoranda.
P   WHAT is a sales memorandum? (1)
W   It is a permanent record of all the data concerning the sale — customer, product, date, amount, and the like.
P   WHO prepares the memorandum? (1)
W   One of the people in bookkeeping.
P   WHAT do they do with the memorandum? (1)
W   They place it in their files.
P   WHAT happens to the memoranda after they are inserted in the files? (2)
W   They're kept there for two years.
P   WHAT happens after two years pass? (2)
W   They're transferred to a records holding area in our warehouse.
P   WHAT happens to the memoranda after they are stored in the warehouse? (2)
W   They're kept there for another two years.
P   WHAT happens after that two-year period passes? (2)
W   We make microfilm copies of the records and destroy the originals.
P   WHY do you do that? (3)
W   We just don't have enough room to keep the originals. We don't want warehouses stuffed with nothing but records; we need the warehouse space for equipment and merchandise.
P   Ms. Gerst, WHAT were your company's sales in 1982?
W   I don't know offhand.
P   WHERE could you find that data?
W   Either in the sales memoranda or the microfilm entries.
P   WHERE are the sales memoranda for that year? (2)
W   They're gone.
P   HOW do you know that? (2)
W   I searched for them in the warehouse and couldn't find them.
P   WHAT happened to them? (3)
W   In all probability, they were destroyed after sitting in the warehouse for the two-year period. As I said, that is our customary practice.
P   WHEN would they have been destroyed? (3)
W   By my estimates, probably in 1986.
P   WHEN did you first learn of this lawsuit? (3)
W   About a year ago.
P   WHAT year was that? (3)
W   1988.
P   WHAT did you know about this suit in 1986 when you destroyed the sales memoranda? (3)
W   Nothing. I had no notice of the suit at all.

Authentication of the Secondary Evidence

At this point, the proponent authenticates the secondary evidence, the microfilm entries. The proponent marks the microfilm entries as plaintiff's exhibit number three for identification. The witness then describes the reliable equipment and procedures the corporation uses to produce its microfilm copies. Finally, the witness states that she took the copies from the right file cabinet.

P   Your Honor, I now offer plaintiff's exhibit number three for identification into evidence as plaintiff's exhibit number three.

O   Your Honor, I object to the introduction of that exhibit on the ground that the microfilm copies are not the best evidence. The plaintiff intentionally destroyed the originals.

P   May I be heard?

J   Yes.

P   It's true that the microfilm entries are secondary evidence and that the plaintiff intentionally destroyed the original sales memoranda. However, the witness' testimony shows that the destruction was in good faith; the plaintiff did not destroy the originals for the fraudulent purpose of making them unavailable to the defendant.

J   The objection will be overruled, and the exhibit will be received into evidence.

3. THE ORIGINAL IS IN OFFICIAL CUSTODY

If the original is in official custody, the original's non-production is excused. As Federal Rule of Evidence 1005 declares, "(t)he contents of an official record, or of a document authorized to be recorded or filed and actually recorded or filed, including data compilations in any form, if otherwise admissible, may be proved by copy, certified as correct in accordance with Rule 902 or testified to be correct by a witness who has compared it with the original." There are several reasons for this doctrine. First, the removal of the original from official custody might inconvenience other persons who wanted to use the original. Second, the removal would create the risk of the loss of the original. Some jurisdictions restrict the excuse to documents that cannot lawfully be removed from official custody; there must be a statute or regulation prohibiting the removal of the original from official custody. Many jurisdictions broadly apply the excuse to any document in official custody.

There is one peculiar aspect of this excuse. This excuse does not generally authorize the admission of any secondary evidence. Rather, most courts insist that the proponent produce a specific type of secondary evidence, that is, a properly attested copy of the original. Federal Evidence Rule 1005 states this preference for attested or compared copies; the Rule ordinarily requires a copy "certified as correct in accordance with Rule 902 or testified to be correct by a witness who has compared it with the original." The Rule states that the proponent may introduce oral recollection testimony only if "a copy which complies with the foregoing cannot be obtained by the exercise of reasonable diligence...."

The foundation includes the following elements:

1. The original is in official custody.

2. (In some jurisdictions) it would be unlawful to remove the original from official custody.

Our fact situation is a probate contest. The contestants claim by intestate succession. To establish their claim, they must prove the marriage between Joan Merchant and Thomas Kleven. The contestants want to offer the marriage certificate to prove the marriage. We shall work the hypothetical first with live testimony and then with an attesting certificate. In the first variation of the hypothetical, the witness is Mr. John Stern, the deputy county clerk. Mr. Stern has already identified himself and described his duties as deputy county clerk.

P   Your Honor, I request that this be marked contestants' exhibit B for identification.

J   It will be so marked.

P   Please let the record reflect that I am showing the exhibit to the opposing counsel.

J   The record will so reflect.

P   I request permission to approach the witness.

J   Permission granted.

P   Mr. Stern, I now hand you contestants' exhibit B for identification. WHAT is it?

W   It's a copy of a marriage certificate.

P   HOW can you tell that it is a copy?

W   It's obviously a Xerox rather than an ink original.

P   WHERE are the ink originals of marriage certificates kept in this county? (1)

W   In our office.

P   WHERE is the ink original of this certificate kept? (1)

W   In our office.

P   HOW do you know that? (1)

W   I saw it there only a few days ago when I ran off this copy at your request.

P   WHEN can you remove the original certificate from the official files? (2)

W   You can't.

P   WHY not? (2)

W   There's a state statute which prohibits us from permitting the originals to leave our custody.

P   WHAT did you do when I requested that you copy the original marriage certificate in this case?

W   I made this copy.

P   HOW did you make it?

W   I did it by mechanical means, our Xerox machine.

P   WHAT condition was the Xerox machine in?

W   Fine as far as I could tell. I didn't experience any mechanical difficulties when I used it.

P   WHAT did you do with the copy after you made it?

W   I compared it with the original to make sure I had a good copy.

P   HOW did it compare with the original?

W   It was a clear, verbatim copy.

P   Your Honor, I now offer contestants' exhibit B for identification into evidence as contestants' exhibit B.

O   Your Honor, I object to the introduction of this exhibit on the ground that the copy is not the best evidence.

P   May I be heard?

J   Yes.

P   We've shown that the original is in official custody and cannot be removed from that custody; that is an adequate excuse for non-production. We've also authenticated the copy.

J   The objection will be overruled, and the exhibit will be received into evidence.

P   Mr. Stern, would you please read exhibit B to the jurors?

W   Yes. It states, "On this day, March 1, 1965, in Chicago, Illinois, I, the Honorable Judge Louis Welsh, married Miss Joan Merchant and Thomas Kleven in accordance with the laws of the State of Illinois."

P   I request permission to hand the exhibit to the jurors for their inspection.

J   Permission granted.

In the second variation of the hypothetical, the proponent does not use live testimony. Rather, the proponent merely offers a properly attested copy of the original marriage certificate.

P   Your Honor, I request that this be marked contestants' exhibit B for identification.

J   It will so reflect.

P   I now offer contestants' exhibit B for identification into evidence as contestants' exhibit B.

O   Your Honor, I object to the introduction of this exhibit on the ground that it is not the best evidence. On its face, it shows that it is a Xerox copy rather than an original.

P   Your Honor, may I be heard?

J   Yes.

P   It's true that this is a purported copy of the original. However, there is an attached attesting certificate. The certificate is self-authenticating because it is in proper form, and the certificate states that the original is in official custody of the county clerk.

O   Your Honor, in this jurisdiction, that excuse applies only to documents which cannot be removed from official custody.

P   In that respect, I would ask that Your Honor judicially notice Civil Code § 76. That section describes the duties of the county clerks. It states that county clerks must accept marriage certificates for filing and that they may not release the original certificate to any private party.

J   I will grant the request for judicial notice and overrule the objection. The exhibit will be received into evidence.

P   I request permission to hand the exhibit to the jurors for their inspection.

J   Permission granted.

4. THE ORIGINAL IS IN THE POSSESSION OF A THIRD PARTY BEYOND THE REACH OF THE COURT'S COMPULSORY PROCESS

Federal Rule of Evidence 1004(2) reads that there is an excuse for non-production if "[n]o original can be obtained by any available judicial process or procedure." The proponent usually relies on this excuse when the original is in the possession of a third party beyond the reach of the court's compulsory process. Some jurisdictions impose an additional requirement; they insist that the proponent show that he or she could not induce the third party to voluntarily send the document to the place of trial. In federal practice, the proponent must exhaust all compulsory process. According to the Advisory Committee Note to Rule 1004, that requirement "includes subpoena duces tecum as an incident to the taking of a deposition in another jurisdiction." However, the federal rules do not require resort to any extra-legal means such as requests that the custodian voluntarily produce the writing.

The foundation includes these elements:

1. A third party has the original.
2. The third party resides in a certain place.
3. That place is beyond the reach of the court's compulsory process.
4. (In some jurisdictions) the proponent unsuccessfully attempted to persuade the third party to voluntarily send the document to the place of trial, or the circumstances indicate that it would be futile for the proponent to attempt to persuade the third party to do so.

Our fact situation is a civil libel action. The plaintiff, Mr. Smythe, alleges that the defendant, Mr. Wiggins, is guilty of libel. The complaint alleges that the defendant committed the libel in a letter to a Mr. Jackson. The witness is the plaintiff, Mr. Smythe. Mr. Smythe has already identified himself. The plaintiff is the proponent. The place of the trial is Topeka, Kansas.

P   WHERE were you on the afternoon of January 15, 1989?
W   I was visiting Bill Jackson in Morena.
P   WHERE is Morena located? (2)
W   It's in El Dorado.
P   WHAT did you do while you visited Mr. Jackson?
W   We were just talking about some mutual acquaintances.
P   WHICH acquaintances?
W   Several, including the defendant, Mr. Wiggins.
P   WHAT, if anything, did Mr. Jackson say about Mr. Wiggins? (1)
W   He said that Wiggins had just sent him a handwritten letter about me.
P   WHAT did Mr. Jackson do after he told you about the letter? (1)
W   He showed it to me.
P   WHOSE handwriting was the letter in?
W   Clearly the defendant's.
P   HOW do you know that?
W   I've known the defendant for years, and I've seen him sign his name on innumerable occasions.

P WHAT did you do after Mr. Jackson showed you the letter? (4)
W I asked him if I could have it. I told him it made me real angry and I wanted to use the letter to sue the defendant.
P HOW did Mr. Jackson respond to your request for the letter? (4)
W He refused to let me have it. *(Mr. Jackson's statement is being used for a nonhearsay purpose. The statement is an operative fact; it is the refusal which satisfies the fourth element of the foundation.)*
P WHY did he refuse to let you have it? (4)
W He said he didn't want to become involved.
P WHAT other efforts did you make to persuade Mr. Jackson to give you the letter? (4)
W I phoned him several times since returning to Kansas. Each time I asked him to send it to me.
P WHAT was his answer? (4)
W He still insists that he won't send it to me.

Authentication of the Secondary Evidence

At this point, the proponent authenticates the witness' oral recollection. See Section G.2, supra.

P WHAT, if anything, did the letter say about you?
O Your Honor, I object to that question on the ground that the witness' testimony is not the best evidence.
P Your Honor, may I be heard?
J Certainly.
P The testimony shows that a third party, Mr. Jackson, has the original. Mr. Jackson lives in El Dorado, and Your Honor may judicially notice the fact that under our Code of Civil Procedure, Mr. Jackson is beyond the reach of Kansas' compulsory process. You can further notice that unfortunately, El Dorado procedure won't allow us to obtain any process to compel him to turn the document over. Finally, the testimony shows that Mr. Jackson refused to send the original here. The testimony hence establishes an excuse for the original's non-production.
J I will judicially notice that and overrule the objection.
P Mr. Smythe, let me repeat the question. WHAT, if anything, did the letter say about you?
W It said that I had bribed Councilman Wild in connection with a zoning application.
P WHOSE handwriting was the letter in?
W The defendant's.

5. THE PARTY-OPPONENT HAS POSSESSION OF THE ORIGINAL AND FAILS TO PRODUCE IT AFTER NOTICE TO PRODUCE

Federal Evidence Rule 1004(3) recognizes an excuse for non-production if "(a)t a time when an original was under the control of the party against whom offered, that party was put on notice, by the pleadings or otherwise, that the contents would be a subject of proof at the hearing, and that party does not produce the original at the hearing...." Sometimes the proponent has direct evidence of the party-opponent's possession of the original. More often the proponent must rely on circumstantial evidence, tracing the original to the party-opponent.

The other problem facing the proponent is proving that the party-opponent had fair notice the original would be needed at trial. The proponent can sometimes argue that the terms of the pleadings gave the party-opponent implied notice; the implication would be very strong in a contract action based on breach of a written contract. However, to be safe, the proponent should give the party-opponent express notice that the original will be needed at trial.

The foundation includes these elements:

1. The party-opponent has the original.
2. The party-opponent knew that the original would be needed at trial.
3. The party-opponent nevertheless failed to produce the original at trial.

The fact situation is a civil contract action. The plaintiff, Mr. Renfield, alleges that the defendant, Mr. Payntor, warranted that the car the defendant sold plaintiff would get at least 20 miles per gallon on the open highway. The complaint alleges that the defendant breached the warranty because, on the open highway, the car gets only 15 miles to a gallon. The plaintiff takes the stand. The proponent is the plaintiff. The plaintiff wants to testify that before agreeing to buy the car, he wrote the defendant and made it clear that he did not want the car unless it got at least 20 miles per gallon. The plaintiff has identified himself and described his preliminary oral negotiations with the defendant.

P WHAT did you do after your oral discussion with the defendant? (1)
W I thought about the deal and then decided to write the defendant and outline the parts of the deal I was really insistent on.
P WHEN did you write this letter? (1)
W I wrote it on February 14, 1989.
P WHAT did you do with the letter? (1)
W I mailed it to the defendant.
P HOW did you mail it to him? (1)
W I stuck it in an envelope and addressed it to the defendant.
P WHERE did you get the defendant's address? (1)
W From the telephone book.
P WHAT did you do with the letter after you addressed it? (1)
W I stamped it and deposited it in a mailbox.
P WHAT response, if any, did you receive from the defendant? (1)
W I didn't get any written response.
P WHEN, if ever, did you see the letter again? (1)
W Well, when we sat down to sign the final contract, the defendant pulled it out and showed it to me.
P WHEN was the last time you saw the letter? (1)
W The day I signed the contract for the car.
P WHO had the letter? (1)
W The defendant.

P   WHERE were you on the morning of November 17th of this year? (2)
W   I was here at the Courthouse.
P   WHY were you here? (2)
W   We were having a conference in this case.
P   WHO attended the conference? (2)
W   You and I were there. The defendant and his attorney were also there.
P   WHAT happened during the conference? (2)
W   We discussed some aspects of the case.
P   WHAT, if anything, did you tell the defendant during the conference about the letter? (2)
W   I told him that you and I wanted him to bring the letter to trial.
P   WHAT was the defendant's response? (3)
W   He said to forget about the letter. *(This statement is being offered for a nonhearsay purpose. The answer is the party-opponent's refusal, the last foundational element.)*
P   WHAT, if anything, did you tell the defendant today about the letter? (3)
W   I again asked the defendant for the letter.
P   WHAT was his response? (3)
W   He said he didn't have it.
P   WHAT did you tell the defendant in your letter to him?
O   Your Honor, I object to that question on the ground that it calls for secondary evidence. The letter is the best evidence.
P   Your Honor, may I be heard?
J   Yes.
P   The testimony shows that the defendant was the last known custodian of the letter. The testimony also indicates that the defendant knew we wanted the original letter at trial today. That amounts to an excuse for the letter's non-production.
J   The objection will be overruled.
P   Mr. Renfield, let me repeat the question. WHAT did you tell the defendant in your letter to him?
W   I said that unless the car got at least 20 miles a gallon, I didn't want the car at all.

6. VOLUMINOUS OR BULKY RECORDS

Federal Rule of Evidence 1006 declares: "The contents of voluminous writings, recordings, or photographs which cannot conveniently be examined in court may be presented in the form of a chart, summary, or calculation. The originals, or duplicates, shall be made available for examination or copying, or both, to the other parties at a reasonable time and place. The court may order that they be produced in court." Federal Rule 1006 generally codifies the common law.

The foundational elements are:

1. The original entries would be admissible in evidence.
2. The original entries are so voluminous or bulky that it would be inconvenient for the trier of fact to examine them.
3. The witness was qualified to review the records.
4. The witness reviewed the records.

5. The witness' testimony is a summary of the records. If the proponent offers a written summary, it is not merely demonstrative evidence. In federal practice, the summary is substantive evidence. Hence, the summary can be formally admitted and sent to the jury during deliberation.

The fact situation is a civil action to rescind a corporate merger. The Gemini Corporation was to merge into Rohr Corporation. Gemini sues to rescind the merger agreement; the complaint alleges that the contract is voidable because of Rohr's fraud. Specifically, the complaint alleges that the defendant overstated the amount of its yearly sales. The defendant denies that its representations were false. The defendant is attempting to prove the amount of its annual sales. To prove its annual sales, the defendant would probably call two witnesses. The first witness would be the defendant's bookkeeper or records custodian. The first witness would describe the original records and show that they fall within the business entry exception to the hearsay rule. This testimony would lay the first element of the foundation. The witness would conclude his or her testimony by stating that he gave the second witness access to the relevant records.

The second witness is Mr. Beer. Mr. Beer has already identified himself. The defendant is the proponent.

P   WHAT is your occupation? (3)
W   I am a certified public accountant.
P   WHERE do you work? (3)
W   I am self-employed. I own my own C.P.A. firm downtown.
P   HOW long have you been a C.P.A.? (3)
W   Roughly ten years.
P   WHAT is your formal education? (3)
W   I have a Bachelor's, a Master's, and a doctorate.
P   WHAT was your field of study? (3)
W   Accounting.
P   WHAT school awarded you your degrees? (3)
W   Cornell.
P   WHERE were you on April 15th of this year? (4)
W   I went to the offices of Rohr Corporation.
P   WHY did you go there? (4)
W   You asked me to review the corporation's sales records from 1985 to the present.
P   WHAT did you do when you arrived at the corporation's offices? (4)
W   First I met Mr. Gaynor, the head bookkeeper.
P   WHAT did he do?
W   He led me to the office where all the records are kept.
P   WHAT did you do when you arrived at the office? (4)
W   I immediately started reviewing the records to compute the annual sales for each year since 1985.
P   HOW did you do that? (4)
W   I used generally accepted accounting techniques and a calculator to double check my computations.

P HOW many pages of records did you review? (2)

W I couldn't give you a precise number. The number would run into the thousands.

P HOW long did it take you to compute the yearly totals? (2)

W Five workdays.

P HOW long is your workday? (2)

W A solid eight hours a day.

P Mr. Beer, WHAT was the total amount of Rohr Corporation's sales in 1986? (5)

O Your Honor, I object to that question on the ground that it calls for secondary evidence. The best evidence would be the records themselves.

P Your Honor, may I be heard?

J Yes.

P Mr. Gaynor's testimony established that the original records would be admissible. Mr. Beer's testimony shows that the original records are too voluminous to be used in the courtroom. Moreover, last week we offered to let the plaintiff's accountants review the records.

J *(To the opposing attorney)* Is that true?

O Yes, Your Honor.

J I think there's an adequate excuse for non-production. The objection will be overruled.

P Mr. Beer, let me repeat the question. WHAT was the total amount of Rohr Corporation's sales in 1986? (5)

W It was $5,312,400.

Chapter 9

OPINION EVIDENCE

A. INTRODUCTION

Like the best evidence rule, the opinion prohibition is based on doubts about the reliability of a certain type of evidence. The common law has doubts about the trustworthiness of opinions. For that reason, the common law prefers that witnesses restrict their testimony to statements of observed fact. The witness states the primary, sensory data, and the jurors then draw the inferences or conclusions from the underlying data.

The opinion prohibition is a general norm rather than an absolute, categorical rule. There are two situations in which the law sanctions opinion testimony. In the first situation, a lay witness may express an opinion on a subject if the lay witness cannot verbalize all the underlying data and communicate the data to the jury. For example, a witness cannot articulate all the sensory impressions which led the witness to the conclusion that a car was going 45 miles an hour rather than 60. The lay witness' inability to verbalize the underlying data necessitates permitting the lay witness to voice an opinion. Federal Evidence Rule 701 allows this type of lay opinion testimony.

In the second situation, the lay trier of fact lacks the knowledge or skill to draw the proper inferences from the underlying data. If the subject matter is technical or scientific, the lay jurors may lack the expertise necessary to evaluate the hard data; lacking the expert knowledge and skill, they cannot draw reliable inferences or opinions from the facts. In this situation as well, the law sanctions opinion testimony: expert opinion testimony. Federal Evidence Rule 702 authorizes such testimony.

B. LAY OPINION TESTIMONY

As previously stated, Rule 701 governs the admissibility of lay opinion testimony. The Rule reads: "If the witness is not testifying as an expert, the witness' testimony in the form of opinions or inferences is limited to those opinions or inferences which are (a) rationally based on the perception of the witness and (b) helpful to a clear understanding of his testimony or the determination of a fact in issue." In practice, the courts have construed the Rule as authorizing two types of lay opinion testimony: (1) collective fact or shorthand rendition opinions; and (2) skilled lay observer opinions.

1. COLLECTIVE FACT OPINIONS

The commentators have coined various titles for this doctrine; they sometimes call it the collective fact doctrine, and on other occasions they refer to it as the shorthand rendition doctrine. The elements of the doctrine are these: The witness' opinion is based on perceived facts; the opinion is a type of inference that lay persons commonly and reliably draw; and the key to the doctrine — the lay witness cannot verbalize all the underlying sensory data supporting the opinion. This doctrine sanctions opinions on such subjects as height, distance, speed, color, and identity. The trial judge passes on the second and third elements of the doctrine as questions of law. The judge asks himself or herself whether lay persons commonly draw this type of inference and whether it would be practical for the lay witness to articulate all the underlying factual data.

The foundation for the doctrine's first element includes proof that:
1. The witness was in a position to observe.
2. The witness in fact observed.
3. The witness observed enough data to form a reliable opinion.
4. The witness states the opinion.

Our fact situation is a tort action arising from a collision. The plaintiff, Ms. Cook, alleges that the defendant, Mr. Armato, caused the accident by speeding. The accident occurred on November 17, 1989 at the intersection of Haight and Ashbury Streets. The plaintiff calls Mr. Carona as a witness. Mr. Carona has already identified himself. The plaintiff is the proponent.

P   WHERE were you on the morning of November 17, 1989 at approximately ten o'clock? (1)

W   I was standing at the intersection of Haight and Ashbury Streets in San Francisco.

P   HOW were you facing? (1)

W   I was ready to enter the crosswalk, so I was facing the intersection itself.

P   WHAT, if anything, did you see while you were standing there? (2)

W   I saw a red car on Haight Street approaching the intersection.

P   WHAT else did you see? (2)

W   There was a blue car approaching the intersection on Ashbury Street.

P   HOW far was the red car from the intersection when you first saw it? (3)

W   A couple of hundred feet away.

P   HOW long did you have to observe the red car before it reached the intersection? (3)

W   Several seconds. I had a pretty good chance to eyeball it.

P   Do you have an opinion of the red car's speed? (4)

W   Yes.

P   In your opinion, WHAT was the speed of the red car? (4)

W   I'd say 40 miles an hour. It was moving at a pretty good clip.

P   WHAT happened when the red car reached the intersection?

W   It hit the blue car.
P   WHO was the driver of the red car?
W   The fellow sitting at the table over there.
P   WHAT is he wearing?
W   He's wearing a blue suit and a striped tie.
P   Your Honor, may the record reflect that the witness has identified the
    defendant, Mr. Armato?
J   It will so reflect.
P   HOW can you recognize him?
W   After the two cars hit, he got out of the car, and I walked over to see
    what had happened.
P   HOW long did you stay at the accident scene?
W   About an hour. I talked to the parties and then to the police.
P   HOW close were you standing to the defendant?
W   At one time, I was talking to him. He was no more than a foot or two
    away from me.
P   WHAT were the lighting conditions?
W   It was broad daylight.
P   HOW well could you see him?
W   Very well.
P   WHO was the driver of the blue car?
W   That lady over there.
P   HOW is she dressed?
W   She's wearing a green dress and white shoes.
P   Your Honor, please let the record reflect that the witness has correctly
    identified the plaintiff, Ms. Cook.
J   The record will reflect that.
P   HOW can you recognize her?
W   She was also at the accident scene. I had a chance to look at and talk
    with her.

2. SKILLED LAY OBSERVER TESTIMONY

The judge will assume that the witness has enough common, human
experience to be able to estimate distance, time, or height. The judge's
assumption explains why the foundation for collective fact opinions is
so minimal. However, there is a second type of lay opinion testimony
that requires a more extensive foundation. The courts sometimes use
the expression, "skilled lay observer testimony," to describe this second
type of lay opinion. This category includes lay opinions about a person's voice, handwriting style, or sanity. A lay witness cannot express
an opinion identifying someone's voice unless the witness has had repeated opportunities to hear that voice. Similarly, a lay witness cannot
identify a person's handwriting style unless the witness had numerous
occasions to observe that person's writing. Finally, a lay witness cannot express an opinion about a person's sanity unless the witness is
intimately familiar with the person. In each of these situations, if the
witness has had repeated, prior opportunities for observation, the witness qualifies as a skilled lay observer.

The foundation for skilled lay observer testimony includes these elements:

1. The witness is familiar with the person or his or her voice or handwriting style.
2. The witness explains how he or she became familiar.
3. The witness states his or her opinion.

To illustrate this doctrine, we can use the foundation set out in Section B.2 of Chapter 4 on Authentication. As you will recall, the witness is Mr. Bucher. Mr. Bucher did not observe the check's execution, but he is familiar with the author's handwriting style.

P   Your Honor, I request that this be marked plaintiff's exhibit number seven for identification.

J   It will be so marked.

P   Please let the record reflect that I am showing the exhibit to the opposing counsel.

J   It will so reflect.

P   I request permission to approach the witness.

J   Permission granted.

P   Mr. Bucher, I now hand you plaintiff's exhibit number seven for identification. WHAT is it?

W   It seems to be a check.

P   Do you have an opinion as to who signed the check? (3)

W   Yes.

P   In your opinion, WHO signed the check? (3)

W   I'd say that the defendant signed it.

P   WHY do you say that? (1)

W   I recognize his handwriting style on the check.

P   HOW well do you know the defendant's handwriting style? (1)

W   Very well.

P   HOW did you become familiar with his handwriting style? (2)

W   We've been friends for years.

P   HOW many years? (2)

W   About thirteen.

P   HOW often have you seen the defendant sign his name? (2)

W   Tens, maybe hundreds, of times.

P   Your Honor, I now offer plaintiff's exhibit number seven for identification into evidence as plaintiff's exhibit number seven.

J   It will be received.

P   I request permission to hand the exhibit to the jurors for their inspection.

J   Permission granted.

C. EXPERT OPINION TESTIMONY

The Federal Rules of Evidence admit expert opinion testimony in addition to lay opinion testimony. The Rule in point is 702: "If scientific, technical, or other specialized knowledge will assist the trier of fact to understand the evidence or to determine a fact in issue, a witness qualified as an expert by knowledge, skill, experience, training, or education, may testify thereto in the form of an opinion or otherwise."

In reality, the proponent may use an expert witness in three different ways. First, the proponent may use an expert purely as a fact witness. Suppose that the defendant is being prosecuted for rape. The complaining witness testifies that during the rape, she scratched the rapist's face and drew blood. It just so happened that the defendant visited his doctor the day after the alleged rape. The defendant could call his doctor and elicit the doctor's testimony that there were no scratches on the defendant's face. The witness certainly did not have to be an expert to observe the defendant's face, but it is equally clear that the witness is not incompetent to testify to facts solely because he or she is an expert.

Secondly, the proponent may use the expert to teach the jurors scientific or technical principles they need to evaluate the facts in the case. The expert witness explains the principles without applying them to the specific facts of the case; the jurors themselves apply the principles to the facts. This use of expert testimony is quite common. As we previously noted, there is a sharp controversy over the reliability of sound spectrography (voiceprint) evidence. A prosecutor offering sound spectrography evidence must not only have the evidence admitted; more importantly, the prosecutor must persuade the jurors to believe the evidence. The prosecutor might call several speech scientists to testify solely about the validity of the underlying theories of inter-speaker variability and invariant speech; the witnesses might not even refer to the voiceprint examination in that particular prosecution. The witnesses' sole function would be to educate the jurors on the general theories and convince the jurors that the theories are valid.

Finally, the proponent may have the expert express an opinion evaluating the facts in the case. This is probably the most common use of expert testimony. When the proponent uses an expert in this manner, the expert usually employs a general theory or principle to evaluate the facts of the case. After stating his or her qualifications, the expert's testimony follows a syllogistic structure. The expert describes a general explanatory theory (the major premise), states the case-specific facts to be evaluated (the minor premise), and derives an opinion (the conclusion) by applying the major premise to the minor premise. Experienced litigators often conclude the expert's examination by having the expert explain the opinion. The testimony therefore covers five topics: the witness' qualification as an expert, the general theory, the facts of the case, the opinion, and the explanation of the opinion. Each topic requires a foundation. The following subsections analyze the five topics and their respective foundations.

1. THE EXPERT'S QUALIFICATIONS TO FORM THE OPINION

The law permits expert opinion testimony because the expert can draw inferences beyond the capability of lay jurors. The expert can do so because the expert has knowledge or skill the jurors lack. The expert can acquire the knowledge or skill by education, experience, or a combination of education and experience. The expert's background usually includes theoretical education and practical experience.

The foundation for the expert's qualifications can include the following elements:

1. The witness has acquired degrees from educational institutions.
2. The witness has had other specialized training in this field of expertise.
3. The witness is licensed to practice in the field.
4. The witness has practiced in the field for a substantial period of time.
5. The witness has taught in the field.
6. The witness has published in the field.
7. The witness belongs to professional organizations in the field.
8. The witness has previously testified as an expert on this subject.

Our fact situation is a civil personal injury action. The plaintiff, Mr. Nowick, alleges that the defendant, Mr. Johnson, negligently caused the collision in which Mr. Nowick was injured. The complaint alleges that the plaintiff has suffered severe brain injury as a result of the accident. The plaintiff calls Dr. Worth. The plaintiff is the proponent. Dr. Worth has already identified himself.

P   WHAT is your formal education? (1)
W   I have a Bachelor's degree and a medical degree.
P   WHICH undergraduate school did you attend? (1)
W   Arizona State University.
P   WHAT degree did you obtain there? (1)
W   I earned a Bachelor of Science degree.
P   WHAT was your major field of study? (1)
W   Biology.
P   WHICH medical school did you attend? (1)
W   The Johns Hopkins University Medical School in Baltimore.
P   WHAT degree did you obtain there? (1)
W   My M.D.
P   WHAT did you do after you graduated from medical school? (2)
W   I interned at the University of Southern California Medical Center.
P   HOW long was your internship? (2)
W   A year.
P   WHAT did you do after your internship? (2)
W   I became a resident at Gross Hospital in Lexington, Kentucky.
P   WHAT is a residency? (2)
W   You specialize in a certain field and get practical experience.
P   WHAT was your specialty? (2)
W   Neurology, brain problems.
P   HOW long was your residency? (2)
W   Three years.
P   WHEN did your residency end? (2)
W   In 1979.

P WHAT did you do when your residency ended? (3)
W I moved here to Denver and began practicing.
P WHAT did you have to do to practice in Denver? (3)
W I had to become licensed in Colorado.
P WHEN did you obtain your license in this state? (3)
W In 1980.
P WHAT did you do after you obtained your license? (4)
W I began my practice, specializing in neurology.
P HOW long have you practiced in this state? (4)
W Nine years now.
P HOW many clients with neurological problems have you treated? (4)
W I can't name a number. By this time, I've probably treated thousands.
P HOW much of your time do you devote to the practice of medicine? (5)
W About 80% of my working time.
P WHAT else do you spend your time on? (5)
W For one thing, I teach at the University of Colorado Medical School in Boulder.
P HOW long have you taught there? (5)
W For four years now.
P WHAT courses do you teach? (5)
W I teach three upper division courses in the field of neurology.
P WHAT else do you spend your professional time on? (6)
W I try to publish with some frequency.
P WHAT journals have published your articles? (6)
W Some of the leading medical and neurological journals, including the A.M.A. Journal.
P What is the "AMA"?
W I'm sorry. It's the American Medical Association.
P HOW many articles have you published? (6)
W Nine.
P WHAT topics did you discuss in these articles? (6)
W All the articles relate to neurology.
P WHAT professional organizations do you belong to? (7)
W Several, including the American College of Neurological Specialists and the American Board of Neurology.
P HOW do you become a member of the American College? (7)
W You have to have specialized in the neurological field for at least five years.
P HOW do you become a member of the Board? (7)
W There are strict requirements. You not only have to have practiced for several years; you also have to pass oral and written examinations.
P HOW often have you testified in court? (8)
W I'd say at least one hundred cases.
P HOW many times were you permitted to give expert opinion testimony? (8)
W Every time.
P WHAT subjects did you testify on? (8)
W Most of the time I testified on neurology.

2. THE GENERAL THEORY OR PRINCIPLE THE EXPERT RELIES ON

After describing his or her credentials, the expert often states the major premise: The general scientific theory or principle the expert proposes to rely on. If the witness is a psychiatrist, the witness may testify that there is a recognized symptomatology for a particular mental disease or disorder. To be a permissible premise for expert testimony, the theory or principle must pass two tests. One test is stated in Rule 702; the theory or principle must "assist the trier of fact." If the subject is a matter of common knowledge, there is no need for expert testimony.

In most jurisdictions the principle or theory must satisfy a second test: the *Frye* standard discussed in Chapter 4. Under *Frye,* the proponent of scientific testimony must show that the principle in question is generally accepted within the relevant scientific field. Although most of the cases enforcing *Frye* are criminal, *Frye* has also been applied to scientific testimony in civil cases. *In re Agent Orange Prod. Liab. Litig.,* 611 F. Supp. 1223, 1242 (E.D.N.Y. 1985); *Cameron v. Knapp,* 520 N.Y.S.2d 917 (Sup. Ct. 1987). Similarly, while most of the cases applying *Frye* involve instrumental techniques such as polygraphy, other cases extend *Frye* to non-instrumental techniques employed in psychology. *People v. Shirley,* 31 Cal. 3d 18, 34, 641 P.2d 775, 783-84, 181 Cal. Rptr. 243, 252, *cert. denied,* 459 U.S. 860 (1982). *See also People v. Murtishaw,* 29 Cal. 3d 733, 769 n.32, 631 P.2d 446, 467 n.32, 175 Cal. Rptr. 738, 759 n.32 (1981).

To lay this element of the foundation, the proponent should establish that:

1. The expert used a particular theory to evaluate the facts in the case.
2. The theory in question has been experimentally verified.
3. The theory is generally accepted by the majority of experts in the pertinent scientific specialty.

The fact situation is a rape prosecution. The People allege that on October 15, 1988, the defendant Marx raped the complainant, Ms. Jane Whitlow. During her direct testimony, Ms. Whitlow described the rape and identified the defendant as the rapist. On cross-examination, she admitted that although on the day in question she reported the alleged rape to the police, the next day in a conversation with her mother Ms. Whitlow refused to confirm or deny that there had been a rape. As their next witness, the People call Dr. Herbert Dubowski, a licensed psychiatrist. The People propose to elicit Dr. Dubowski's testimony about rape trauma syndrome (RTS) to rehabilitate Ms. Whitlow's credibility. In *People v. Bledsoe,* 36 Cal. 3d 236, 251, 681 P.2d 291, 301, 203 Cal. Rptr. 450, 460 (1984), the California Supreme Court held that the prosecution may not use the fact that the complainant displays RTS symptoms as substantive evidence that there has been a rape. However, the court indicated that RTS evidence could be used for other purposes, such as rehabilitating the credibility of an impeached complainant. *People v. Roscoe,* 168 Cal. App. 3d 1093, 1099, 215 Cal. Rptr.

45, 49 (1985), applied *Bledsoe* and held RTS evidence admissible "to support the victim's credibility." After stating his credentials, Dr. Dubowski testifies:

P   Doctor, WHAT is your specialty? (1)

W   For the past few years, I've concentrated my practice and research in the area of rape trauma syndrome.

P   WHAT is rape trauma syndrome? (1)

W   The theory holds that in most cases, after a rape women cope with that traumatic event in a predictable manner.

P   WHAT manner is that? (1)

W   Their reaction usually progresses through two phases. The initial stage is the acute phase. They try to come to terms with the physical trauma and the immediate psychological impact. They experience disorganization in their lives. They become confused.

P   WHAT do you mean by "confused"? (1)

W   They're indecisive. Even if someone asks them point blank about the rape, out of shame or a sense of morality, they are often reluctant to discuss it. Again, that's the acute phase. That's followed by the long-term phase.

P   WHAT happens during that phase? (1)

W   They begin reorganizing their lives. They may move, change their telephone number, and visit friends and family much more frequently to gain moral support. They often develop phobias. They may have a fear of being alone.

P   WHAT research, if any, have you done on rape trauma syndrome? (2)

W   I was fortunate enough to participate in the original research done on the subject. Before I moved to Dallas, I lived in Boston. That's where Burgess and Homstrom did the first intensive study of this subject.

P   WHEN and WHERE did they conduct that study? (2)

W   Between July 1972 and July 1973, they interviewed all the rape victims admitted to the emergency ward of Boston City Hospital.

P   HOW many persons did they study? (2)

W   About 150 women were included in the data base.

P   WHAT types of women were included in the study? (2)

W   All sorts — they were all races. About 70% were adult, and the rest were minors. In fact, there were three male children included in the study.

P   HOW did the researchers conduct the study? (2)

W   They initially interviewed these people, and they then followed up by studying the changes in the life patterns after the traumatic incident.

P   WHAT findings did the researchers make? (2)

W   In the overwhelming majority of cases, there was a clear pattern.

P   WHAT do you mean by "overwhelming majority"? (2)

W   I mean about 85 to 90% of the cases.

P   WHAT was the pattern? (2)

W   It was the two stages, the acute and long-term phases, that I described a few moments ago.

P   WHAT other research, if any, has been done on rape trauma syndrome? (2)

W   There have been several other studies, including Sutherland and Scherl.

P   WHAT were the findings in those studies? (2)

W   About the same. You can quibble with percentages, but the virtually uniform finding is that in most cases, there is a definite pattern of coping behavior after a rape.

P   Doctor, HOW well accepted is rape trauma syndrome? (3)

W   It's very well accepted in my field.

P   WHAT evidence is there that the syndrome is well accepted? (3)

W   The latest editions of the leading, authoritative treatises on psychiatry all mention the syndrome.

P   WHAT professional organizations are there in your field? (3)

W   One is the APA, the American Psychiatric Association.

P   To WHAT extent has the American Psychiatric Association recognized the existence of rape trauma syndrome? (3)

W   The APA has an official manual, the Diagnostic and Statistical Manual of Mental Disorders. It's now in the third, 1980 edition — DSM III. Actually it's been further revised — DSM III-R. DSM III-R lists post-traumatic stress disorder as a recognized syndrome.

P   WHAT, if anything, does DSM III-R say about rape trauma syndrome? (3)

W   One of the examples of post-traumatic stress disorder in DSM III-R is its application after a rape.

3. THE FACTUAL BASES OF THE EXPERT'S OPINION

The expert should now state the minor premise, the factual data to which the theory will be applied. Federal Evidence Rule 703 governs the bases for an expert's opinion: "The facts or data in the particular case upon which an expert bases an opinion or inference may be those perceived by or made known to the expert at or before the hearing. If of a type reasonably relied upon by experts in the particular field in forming opinions or inferences upon the subject, the facts or data need not be admissible in evidence." Hence, there are three possible bases for an expert's opinion.

a. Facts the Expert Personally Knows

All jurisdictions allow an expert to base an opinion on facts the expert has personal or firsthand knowledge of. For instance, doctors usually base their opinions in part on conditions and symptoms they personally observed during an examination of the patient. The foundation for this basis ordinarily includes these elements:

1. Where the witness observed the fact.
2. When the witness observed the fact.
3. Who was present.
4. How the witness observed the fact.
5. A description of the fact(s) observed.

We shall continue our hypothetical with the neurologist.

P   WHERE were you on the afternoon of July 11, 1989? (1), (2)

W   In my office.

P   WHAT, if anything, happened that afternoon? (3)

W   I conducted an examination of the plaintiff, Mr. Nowick.
P   WHO is Mr. Nowick? (3)
W   He's the gentleman sitting over there at the end of the table.
P   HOW is he dressed? (3)
W   He's wearing the white suit with the gray tie.
P   Your Honor, please let the record reflect that the witness has identified the plaintiff, Mr. Nowick.
J   The record will reflect that.
P   WHO was present during this examination? (3)
W   Just Mr. Nowick, myself, and my nurse, Ms. Cartwright.
P   WHAT happened during the examination? (4)
W   I personally examined the plaintiff for any symptoms of brain damage.
P   HOW did you conduct the examination? (4)
W   I conducted a manual inspection of his cranium and then administered a battery of standard eye and coordination tests.
P   HOW long did this examination take? (4)
W   A good three hours. I conducted a very thorough examination.
P   WHAT, if anything, did you observe during the examination? (5)
W   I saw some symptoms and signs of brain damage.
P   WHAT were the symptoms? (5)
W   For one thing, there was a deep scar on the front, right side of Mr. Nowick's head.
P   HOW deep? (5)
W   Almost ⅛ of an inch into the surface — easily deep enough to cause some damage.
P   WHAT else did you observe? (5)
W   There was a sort of vacancy in the plaintiff's eyes, again possibly indicating brain problems. Finally, the plaintiff exhibited real difficulty in the eye-to-hand coordination tests.

b. Hearsay Reports from Third Parties

There is a split of authority whether the expert may rely on reports from third parties such as other experts if the reports do not fall within any hearsay exception. The traditional view has been that the expert may not do so. However, the Federal Rules follow the trend in the case law that the expert may do so in certain circumstances. Rule 703 allows an expert to rely on a hearsay report "[i]f of a type reasonably relied upon by experts in the particular field in forming opinions or inferences upon the subject ...." Some courts equate "reasonably" with "customarily"; if the judge finds that it is the specialty's practice to consider a particular type of data, the judge must allow the witness to use that type of information as part of the basis for the opinion. However, other courts interpret "reasonably" as giving the trial judge the power to second-guess the specialty's use of that type of data; although the judge should ordinarily defer to the specialty's customary practice, in an extreme case the judge may rule that the specialty's practice is unreasonable. It must be remembered that under either construction of Rule 703, the evidence of the report is not admitted as substantive proof of the report's truth; the report is admitted for the limited purpose of showing the basis of the expert's opinion. The fact that the expert has heard and considered the report is some evidence that the opinion is well grounded. Consequently, upon request, the opponent is entitled to a limiting instruction by the trial judge.

The foundation for this basis includes these elements:

1. The source of the third party report.
2. The content or tenor of the report.
3. It is customary within the specialty to consider that type of report.

Our hypothetical continues:

P   Dr. Worth, in addition to the symptoms you personally observed during your examination of Mr. Nowick, WHAT else have you considered? (1)
W   For one thing, I talked to Mr. Nowick's family physician, Dr. Stiles.
P   WHO is Dr. Stiles? (1)
W   Maynard Stiles is a general practitioner here in town.
P   HOW long has he been in practice here? (1)
W   Maybe fifteen years. He's a well-respected member of our local medical community.
P   WHEN did you talk with him? (1)
W   The day after I examined the plaintiff.
P   WHY did you talk to him? (3)
W   I had to get Mr. Nowick's medical history. Specifically, I wanted to know whether he had that scar or displayed the vacant stare or lack of coordination before his car accident.
P   WHAT is the importance of the medical history? (3)
W   You just can't make an intelligent diagnosis without that.
P   WHAT is the customary medical practice concerning the use of medical history? (3)
W   I followed the custom here. It would be malpractice not to gather the history and consider it in evaluating your diagnosis. Use of the history is good, accepted practice.
P   WHAT did Dr. Stiles tell you about the plaintiff's medical history? (2)
W   He said that prior to the accident, there was no scar on the plaintiff's cranium. Further, prior to the collision, the plaintiff had not exhibited the symptoms of either vacancy of stare or lack of coordination.
O   Your Honor, I request a limiting instruction.
J   Yes. Ladies and gentlemen of the jury, Dr. Worth has just referred to a statement made by a Dr. Stiles. You may not consider Dr. Stiles' statement as proof that before the accident, the plaintiff had no scar or vacant stare or lack of coordination. You may consider Dr. Stiles' statement only for the limited purpose of showing one factor or element Dr. Worth considered in arriving at his opinion.

c. Assumed Facts

Sometimes the testifying expert has neither examined the party nor even talked with an expert who has personally examined the party. The testifying expert may still express an opinion in response to a hypothetical question. In the hypothesis, the proponent specifies the facts he or she wants the expert to assume. The expert then relies on his or her expert knowledge and skill to draw a proper inference from the facts in the hypothesis.

There are two major limitations on hypothetical questions. The first limitation is that in most jurisdictions, the proponent must have already introduced evidence to support a finding that the assumed facts exist. The trial judge may permit the proponent to vary the order of proof and introduce proof of the assumed facts later, but judges are often reluctant to permit the proponent to do so. The second limitation is that in many jurisdictions, the hypothesis must include all the undisputed, material facts. The reason for this limitation is obvious; if the hypothesis is incomplete and omits critical facts, the ultimate opinion will be misleading rather than helpful.

Hypothetical questions can take two forms. In the first form, the proponent specifies the historical facts he or she wants the expert to assume. For example, the proponent could say:

P   Dr. Worth, please assume the following facts as true:
     One, in the accident, the plaintiff sustained a cut three inches in length
     and 1/8 inch in depth on the right, front part of his head.
     Two, the plaintiff bled profusely from that cut.
     Three, immediately after the accident, the plaintiff began experiencing
     sharp, painful headaches in the right, front part of his head.

In the second form, the proponent asks the witness to assume the truth of the testimony of another witness or witnesses. Assume, for instance, that the ambulance attendant, Mr. Phelan, has already testified. During his testimony, Phelan stated that he observed the cut on plaintiff's head, noted the bleeding, and heard plaintiff complain about a headache. The plaintiff now calls Dr. Worth.

P   Dr. Worth, WHERE were you this morning?
W   Here in the courtroom.
P   WHAT were you doing?
W   Listening to the testimony.
P   WHOSE testimony did you listen to?
W   Mr. Phelan, the ambulance attendant, was on the stand most of the
     morning.
P   HOW well could you hear his testimony?
W   Very well. I had no problems hearing what he was saying.
P   Specifically, WHERE were you sitting?
W   In the first row reserved for spectators.
P   HOW often did you leave the room during Mr. Phelan's testimony?
W   I didn't leave; I stayed in the courtroom the whole time.
P   Dr. Worth, please assume the truth of Mr. Phelan's testimony about
     Mr. Nowick's condition immediately after the accident.

Many jurisdictions prohibit the second form of hypothetical question. These courts reason that at the very least, this form is ambiguous; it is difficult for the jurors to determine the specific facts the expert witness is assuming. Moreover, if the proponent invites the expert to assume the truth of several witnesses' testimony and there are any conflicts between those witnesses' testimony, the proponent is really asking the expert to resolve those conflicts. In effect, the proponent is asking the expert to usurp the jury's function. However, many jurisdictions sanction this form of hypothetical question if the assumed testimony is simple and internally consistent.

4. THE STATEMENT OF THE OPINION ITSELF

In the next part of the expert's testimony, the proponent should elicit the ultimate opinion. Some jurisdictions insist that the expert vouch that his or her opinion is "reasonably certain." Other jurisdictions demand a "reasonably probable" opinion. The witness must be willing to testify that he or she has formed the opinion to a reasonable medical or scientific certainty or probability. Still other jurisdictions have abandoned these formal limitations; so long as the opinion is likely to be helpful to the jurors, these jurisdictions allow an expert to state a possibility, probability, or certainty.

The complete foundation for the opinion includes these elements:
1. The witness has formed an opinion.
2. The witness believes that the opinion is a reasonable medical or scientific certainty or probability.
3. The witness states the opinion.

The hypothetical fact situation continues:

P   Dr. Worth, do you have an opinion whether Mr. Nowick suffered brain damage as a result of the accident? (1)
W   Yes.
P   HOW positive are you of your opinion? (2)
W   I'm fairly confident in it. I think that any competent neurologist would reach the same conclusion.
P   WHAT is the degree of your certainty? (2)
W   You can't treat this sort of question as an absolute, but I'm reasonably certain of my conclusion.
P   WHAT is that conclusion? (3)
W   In my opinion, Mr. Nowick has suffered permanent brain damage, located in the right, front part of his cranium, as a direct result of the accident.

5. THE EXPLANATION OF THE OPINION

Evidence law does not require that the expert explain the opinion. However, common sense tells the proponent that unless the expert explains the opinion, the jurors will not be persuaded. The proponent cannot expect the jurors to make a blind act of faith in the expert. As a practical matter, the jury is unlikely to attach much weight to the opinion unless the expert explains his or her reasoning process in plausible, common sense terms. Consequently, the customary practice is for the proponent to invite the expert to explain the opinion. The expert should explain the opinion in general terms and specifically relate the opinion to the bases the expert previously recited. The opinion will be most persuasive if the expert can show the jurors that the opinion is firmly grounded in the facts that are the bases of the opinion.

In short, the foundation for this last part of the expert's testimony consists of two elements:

1. In general terms, the expert explains the opinion.
2. The expert explains the significance of each basis of the opinion. The expert demonstrates how each basis contributes to and supports the opinion.

The hypothetical finally concludes:

P Dr. Worth, WHY did you reach that conclusion? (1)
W The symptoms evidence the existence of brain damage, and the medical history discloses only one possible cause.
P WHAT symptoms are you referring to? (2)
W Well, the scar, the vacancy of gaze, and the lack of eye-to-hand coordination.
P WHAT is the significance of those symptoms? (2)
W The scar is deep enough to indicate a wound that probably would have applied damaging pressure to the brain. The part of the brain located under the scar is the part that controls vision and eye-to-hand coordination. The other symptoms of vacant stare and lack of manual coordination confirm that pressure in fact was applied with resulting damage.
P WHAT medical history are you relying on? (2)
W My consultation with Dr. Stiles and the plaintiff's hospital records.
P WHAT is the significance of the medical history? (2)
W It establishes the causation. The scar was apparently inflicted in the accident. The other symptoms not only didn't exist before the accident; they arose immediately after the accident. The timing is almost conclusive in my mind.

Chapter 10

THE HEARSAY RULE, ITS EXEMPTIONS, AND ITS EXCEPTIONS

A. INTRODUCTION

The hearsay doctrine is the last major exclusionary doctrine based on doubt about the reliability of a type of evidence. The best evidence rule's underlying rationale is a fear of secondary evidence. The opinion rule expresses the courts' doubts about the reliability of opinions. Underlying the hearsay rule is a fear about the reliability of in-court testimony about out-of-court statements when the proponent is attempting to use the statements as evidence in the case. The common law prefers that the third party (the declarant) appear in court and subject himself or herself to cross-examination. The common law assumes that evidence will be more trustworthy if the declarant testifies under oath, in the jury's view, and subject to cross-examination. The opponent may use cross-examination to expose any errors of perception, memory, narration, or sincerity.

Lay persons commonly think that the hearsay rule applies to any out-of-court statement. In truth, the rule has a relatively narrow scope. Evidence constitutes hearsay only if it is (1) an assertive statement (2) by an out-of-court declarant (3) offered to prove the truth of the assertion. Federal Evidence Rule 801 follows this view. The rationale for the rule explains the rule's limited scope. We are interested in the declarant's credibility only when the out-of-court statement is being used to prove the truth of the assertion. In that circumstance, the evidence's value depends on the credibility of the out-of-court declarant. For example, suppose that an in-court witness testifies that an out-of-court declarant said that the defendant's car ran a red light. The plaintiff wants to offer the testimony for the purpose of showing that in fact, the defendant's car ran the red light. For that purpose, the testimony's value depends upon the perception and memory of the out-of-court declarant. The opponent thus needs to cross-examine the out-of-court declarant to test the evidence.

On the other hand, if the proponent does not offer the out-of-court declaration for its truth, the opponent does not need to cross-examine the declarant. If the declaration is logically relevant on some other theory, the evidence's value usually depends on the credibility of the in-court witness. Suppose that the plaintiff has sued a defendant for slander. The plaintiff alleges that the defendant repeated the slanderous statement to X. The plaintiff calls X, the in-court witness, to testify that the defendant made an out-of-court statement that the plaintiff bribed a public official. The plaintiff does not want to offer the statement for its truth; quite to the contrary, if the defendant can show that the statement is true, the defendant has a complete defense to tort liability. The plaintiff wants to show only that at a particular time and place, the defendant made the slanderous statement. The value of X' testimony depends on X' credibility. Did X hear the statement correctly? Does X remember the statement correctly? If X testifies in court, the defendant can test the value of the evidence. Hence, the limitation on the hearsay rule's scope is a corollary of the rule's rationale; the rule is limited to statements offered to prove their truth because then and only then does the opponent need to cross-examine the out-of-court declarant.

Even if a statement falls within the definition of hearsay, the statement may be admissible. There are numerous exemptions from and exceptions to the hearsay rule. Federal Rule 801 sets out the admission exemption, and Federal Rules 803 and 804 contain a lengthy list of exceptions. Section C of this chapter discusses the admission exemption. As that section explains, to bring a statement within the admission exemption, the proponent need not show that the statement was reliable or that there is any necessity for resorting to the statement; all the proponent has to do is to show that the statement should be imputed to the party-opponent. Sections D-J describe a series of hearsay exceptions based primarily on an inference of the reliability of the statement. In contrast, sections L-N address a number of exceptions resting in large part on a showing of necessity; all of these exceptions require proof that the out-of-court declarant is unavailable at the time of trial. Finally, section O of this chapter describes the residual hearsay exception. To invoke this exception, the proponent must demonstrate both reliability and an element of necessity.

Part 1. Hearsay

B. THE DEFINITION OF HEARSAY

As previously stated, the definition of hearsay is narrow. Federal Evidence Rule 801(c) states that "'[h]earsay' is a statement, other than one made by the declarant while testifying at the trial or hearing, offered in evidence to prove the truth of the matter asserted." Rule 801(a) adds that "[a] 'statement' is (1) an oral or written assertion or (2) nonverbal conduct of a person, if it is intended by the person as an assertion." Under the Federal Rules, evidence constitutes hearsay only if three conditions are present: (1) the evidence is an assertive statement or act; (2) the statement was made or the act committed out of court; and (3) the evidence is being used to prove the truth of the assertion. Evidence falls within the hearsay definition only if all three elements are present; if any element is missing, the evidence is not hearsay, and there is no need to search for a hearsay exception. We shall now examine each of the three elements of the hearsay definition.

1. THE EVIDENCE IS AN ASSERTIVE STATEMENT OR ACT

a. Assertive Statements

All courts agree that assertive statements fall within the hearsay definition. If the person makes an oral out-of-court statement or reduces the statement to writing out of court, the statement is hearsay. However, it must be remembered that not all statements are assertive. Grammar tells us that there are four types of sentences: declarative, imperative, exclamatory, and interrogatory. As a practical matter, only declarative sentences ordinarily fall within the hearsay definition; they declare or assert facts, including states of mind. Imperative sentences giving orders, exclamatory sentences, and interrogatory sentences posing questions usually fall outside the hearsay definition. There is little or no need to cross-examine the declarant of an imperative, exclamatory, or interrogatory sentence about perception or memory.

If the proponent is going to offer evidence on the theory that it is a non-assertive statement, the foundation usually includes these elements:

1. Where the statement was made.
2. When the statement was made.
3. Who was present.
4. The tenor of the statement.
5. In an offer of proof outside the jury's hearing, the proponent states that the tenor of the statement is nonassertive.
6. In the same offer of proof, the proponent shows that the nonassertive statement is logically relevant to the material facts of consequence in the case.

Our fact situation is a criminal prosecution. The government charges that Messrs. Cetina and Britton conspired to sell and actually sold heroin. The witness is Ms. Grace. Ms. Grace identifies herself. She then testifies that she is a government informant and infiltrated the meeting of a drug ring. The prosecutor is the proponent.

P   Ms. Grace, WHERE were you on the evening of January 17, 1989? (1), (2)
W   I was at 70 Aberdeen Court in downtown Indianapolis.
P   WHO else was there? (3)
W   The two defendants, Cetina and Britton.
P   WHERE are they now? (3)
W   In the courtroom.
P   Specifically, WHERE in the courtroom? (3)
W   At that table over there.

P   HOW are they dressed? (3)

W   Cetina is wearing a blue suit with red tie. Britton has a brown suit and yellow tie.

P   Your Honor, please let the record reflect that the witness has correctly identified the two defendants.

J   It will so reflect.

P   Ms. Grace, WHAT happened during this meeting? (4)

W   The defendants made some plans.

P   WHAT plans did they discuss? (4)

O   Your Honor, I object to that question on the ground that it calls for incompetent hearsay.

P   Your Honor, may we approach the bench and be heard?

J   Yes.

P   (Out of the jury's hearing) Your Honor, I offer to prove that the witness will testify that the defendant Cetina ordered the defendant Britton to get some bags of heroin out of Britton's car and that Britton did so. (4) Cetina's statement is not hearsay because it is not assertive; the statement is not a declarative sentence but rather an imperative one, ordering Britton to do something. (5) The only thing we're interested in is whether he gave the order. You might say that Ms. Grace is an "ear-witness" to the fact that he gave the order. The statement is logically relevant to prove the existence of a conspiracy between them. (6)

J   The objection will be overruled.

P   Ms. Grace, let me repeat the question. WHAT plans did they discuss? (4)

W   The plans for a drug sale. Cetina ordered Britton to get some bags of heroin out of Britton's car to get them ready for sale.

P   WHAT happened then?

W   Britton left for a couple of minutes and then came back with some bags.

P   WHAT was the appearance of the bags?

W   The bags themselves were transparent.

P   WHAT, if anything, could you see in the bags?

W   There was a white, powdery substance in each bag.

b. Assertive Acts

Sometimes a person intends an act to be a true substitute for speech. For instance, persons sometimes nod or shake their heads in response to questions. In principle, these acts should be treated in the same fashion as verbal hearsay statements; these acts present the same probative dangers of perception, memory, narration, and sincerity. For this reason, all courts agree that like assertive statements, assertive acts fall within the hearsay definition. Federal Evidence Rule 801 (a)(2) is illustrative; that rule includes within the hearsay definition "nonverbal conduct of a person, if it is intended by the person as an assertion."

The following hypothetical illustrates the scope of the hearsay definition. The fact situation is a robbery prosecution. The witness is a police officer. The officer, Patrolman Glancy, has already identified himself. He testifies that he investigated the crime, interviewed the victim, and brought the victim to the police station. Assume that in this jurisdiction, a witness' prior identification of a person is not admissible to bolster the witness' credibility. The proponent is the prosecutor.

P   WHAT happened after you took the victim, Mr. Clayton, to the police station?

W   I talked to him, and then I took him to the lineup room.

P   WHAT is the lineup room?

W   It's the room in the station where we permit victims and eyewitnesses to view suspects. We hope that they can pick the criminal out of the lineup parade.

P   WHAT happened after you took Mr. Clayton into the interview room?

O   Your Honor, I object to that question on the ground that it calls for incompetent hearsay.

P   Your Honor, may we approach the bench and be heard?

J   Yes.

P   Your Honor, the witness is prepared to testify that at the lineup, Mr. Clayton pointed to the defendant. The evidence can't be hearsay because Mr. Clayton didn't say anything. He just pointed.

O   Mr. Clayton's act of pointing is an assertive act; he subjectively intended it to be a substitute for the verbal statement that the defendant was the robber. Assertive acts fall within the hearsay definition.

J   I agree with the defense counsel. Under Rule 104(a), I find that the act was subjectively intended to be the functional equivalent of an assertive statement. The objection will be sustained.

c. Nonassertive Acts

Although the courts agree that assertive statements and acts are within the hearsay definition, they disagree over a third category of evidence: nonassertive acts. A classic English case, *Wright v. Tatham*, contained this fact situation. The issue was a testator's mental capacity. The proponent of the will was attempting to prove that the testator was mentally competent. To prove that, the proponent offered to show that several persons had written serious business letters to the testator. Although the act of writing of the letter incidentally involved assertions in the letters, the act itself was nonassertive; the persons did not subjectively intend their act to substitute for the verbal statement that the testator was competent. The authors of the letters assumed that the testator was competent, and the proponent of the will offered the evidence to show the truth of their assumption and belief. The proponent of the will reasoned that they would not have mailed the testator serious letters unless they believed he was competent; and if they, his close acquaintances, believed him to be competent, he probably was competent. The English court held that the evidence fell within the hearsay definition; the court argued that even though the act was nonassertive, it presented probative dangers of perception and memory. This case was the landmark case for the traditional common-law view that evidence of a nonassertive act is hearsay if (1) the act is apparently actuated or prompted by a certain belief and (2) the proponent offers the evidence to prove the truth of the belief.

The trend in the statutes and case law has been to the contrary. If the person is willing to act on his or her belief, the person's willingness removes most doubts about the person's sincerity; and there is much less justification for including the evidence within the hearsay rule. Federal Rule 801 excludes this evidence, sometimes called Morgan hearsay, from its hearsay definition. The Advisory Committee took the position that the dangers of this type of evidence are "minimal in the absence of an intent to assert and do not justify the loss of the evidence on hearsay grounds."

The following hypothetical illustrates the third category of evidence. We can adapt the basic fact situation in *Wright*. The testator is the decedent, Mr. Marsden. The decedent owned a large car dealership. The proponent of the will is Mr. Wright. Mr. Wright calls Mr. Toscher as a witness. Mr. Toscher owns a janitorial services company. Mr. Wright wants to show that Toscher sent Mr. Marsden a serious business proposal for janitorial services on the decedent's car lot. During closing argument, Mr. Wright's attorney wants to use Toscher's conduct as evidence of Mr. Marsden's competency: Toscher would not have sent Marsden the letter unless he, Toscher, believed that Marsden was mentally competent. Mr. Toscher has already identified himself and stated his line of business.

P   WHERE were you on the morning of April 16, 1989?
W   In my office in downtown Kansas City.
P   WHAT were you doing there?
W   I was getting some bids ready on some new contracts for janitorial services.
P   WHAT is a bid?
W   We offer services to a company at a certain monthly rate. Then they decide whether they want to award the work to us or another company.
P   WHAT did you do after you finished the bids?
W   I mailed them.
P   WHOM did you mail them to?
W   Several people, including the decedent, Mr. Marsden.
O   Your Honor, I move to strike the last question and answer on the ground that they are irrelevant.
P   Your Honor, may we approach the bench?
J   Yes.
P   Your Honor, the evidence shows that Mr. Toscher mailed a serious business proposal to Mr. Marsden. That conduct shows Mr. Toscher's belief in Mr. Marsden's mental competency; he wouldn't have mailed him that sort of letter unless he thought Mr. Marsden was competent.
O   Now I object on the ground that the evidence is hearsay.
P   How can it be hearsay if it's evidence of a nonassertive act?
O   Your Honor, as you know, this jurisdiction subscribes to the traditional view that even a nonassertive act is hearsay if (1) it's actuated by a

belief and (2) it's used to prove the truth of the belief. The opposing counsel has shown he's really interested in Mr. Toscher's belief in Mr. Marsden's competency, and the counsel wants to use the belief as evidence of Marsden's competency.

J   The objection will be sustained.

Assume that this case arose in a jurisdiction following the modern view that nonassertive acts fall outside the hearsay definition. The proper objection would be that the proponent has not laid a proper foundation for skilled lay observer opinion testimony. On the witness stand, a lay person may not express an opinion of another person's sanity unless he or she is intimately familiar with that person. Change the judge's hearsay ruling and continue the hypothetical.

J   Counsel, you overlook the fact that this jurisdiction recently adopted the Federal Rules, excluding nonassertive acts from the hearsay definition.

O   My last objection is that the proponent hasn't shown that the witness knew Mr. Marsden well enough to express an opinion about Marsden's competency. Your Honor, if you admit this evidence, you are in effect permitting Toscher to give opinion testimony about Marsden's competency or sanity. I request permission to take the witness on voir dire.

J   Permission granted.

O   Mr. Toscher, ISN'T IT TRUE THAT you never personally met the decedent, Mr. Marsden?

W   Yes.

O   ISN'T IT A FACT THAT the only letters you ever received from his company were signed by other persons?

W   Yes.

O   ISN'T IT CORRECT THAT you never had a telephone conversation with Mr. Marsden?

W   Yes.

O   ISN'T IT TRUE THAT your only information about Mr. Marsden is what other people told you about him?

W   Yes.

O   Your Honor, I have no further voir dire questions of this witness. I renew my objection that the question calls for improper lay opinion testimony.

J   The objection will be sustained.

2. THE STATEMENT IS OFFERED FOR A HEARSAY PURPOSE

Even if the statement is assertive, the statement is not hearsay unless the proponent offers the statement to prove the truth of the assertion. Offering the statement for that purpose creates the need to cross-examine the declarant about perception or memory. This step in hearsay analysis parallels the second step in best evidence analysis: Just as the best evidence rule does not come into play unless the writing's terms are in issue, a statement is not hearsay unless the proponent offers the statement to prove the truth of an assertion contained in the statement. The statement is deemed hearsay only when the immediate inference the proponent wants to draw is the truth of the assertion on the statement's face. If the proponent can demonstrate that the statement is logically relevant on any other theory, the statement is nonhearsay. When the proponent offers the statement for a nonhearsay purpose, we are primarily interested simply in the fact that the statement was made. The only need to cross-examine is the need to question on the stand the witness who heard the statement made.

When the proponent is going to argue a nonhearsay theory for admitting a statement, the foundation includes these elements:

1. Where the statement was made.
2. When the statement was made.
3. Who was present.
4. The tenor of the statement.
5. In an offer of proof, the proponent states that he or she intends to use the statement for a nonhearsay purpose.
6. In the same offer of proof, the proponent shows that on that nonhearsay theory, the statement is logically relevant.

There are three common nonhearsay uses of evidence. First, the proponent may argue that the statement is circumstantial evidence of the declarant's state of mind. If the declarant's state of mind is logically relevant in the case, the proponent may use the declarant's statements as circumstantial proof of such states of mind as malice, hatred, premeditation, and love. Sometimes the mere fact that a person makes a certain statement gives us insight into that person's frame of mind. Second, the statement may be an operative fact or verbal act in the case. In some situations, legal consequences flow directly from the use of certain words such as the offer in a contract suit or the slander in a tort action. Again the mere fact that the declarant uttered the words is logically relevant; the words themselves have legal consequences. Finally, the proponent can prove the statement to show its effect on the state of mind of the hearer or reader. For example, if it is disputed whether the defendant knew of a certain dangerous condition, it is logically relevant to prove that someone told him of the condition. Quite apart from the truth of the third party's statement, the statement puts the defendant on notice. The following hypotheticals illustrate these various nonhearsay uses.

a. The Statement Is Circumstantial Proof of the Declarant's State of Mind — Mental Output

Our fact situation is a dispute over title to real property. The decedent, Joan Furlow, formerly owned the land. Before she died, she gave her nephew, Garrett Furlow, a deed to the property; she gave him the deed on April 14, 1989. The executor claims that although Ms. Furlow gave Garrett the deed, she did not intend the deed to be immediately effective; and since she did not have the intent required by Real Property law, the deed was ineffective. The nephew calls Ms. Barbara Peterson as a witness. Ms. Peterson identifies herself and states that she knew the decedent for several years. The nephew is the proponent.

P   WHERE were you on April 13, 1989? (1), (2)
W   I was visiting Joan at her house on Dwight Street.
P   WHO else was there? (3)
W   Only the two of us.
P   WHAT happened while you were there? (4)
W   We just had a nice chat.
P   WHAT did you chat about? (4)
W   A lot of things, including Joan's nephew, Garrett.
P   WHAT did Ms. Furlow say about her nephew, Garrett? (4)
O   Your Honor, I object to that question on the ground that it calls for hearsay.
P   Your Honor, may we approach the bench?
J   Yes.
P   Your Honor, I offer to prove that Ms. Peterson will testify that Ms. Furlow said that her nephew was a man in a million. (4) I want to offer that testimony for a nonhearsay purpose, as circumstantial proof of Ms. Furlow's affection for Garrett. (5) The testimony is logically relevant to show that she had donative intent when she gave him the deed the next day. (6)
J   The objection will be overruled. I will admit the evidence for that nonhearsay purpose.
P   Ms. Peterson, let me repeat the question. WHAT did Ms. Furlow say about her nephew, Garrett? (4)
W   She said that he was a man in a million.
O   Your Honor, I request a limiting instruction.
J   Yes. Ladies and gentlemen of the jury, you have just heard Ms. Peterson's testimony about Ms. Furlow's statement. I am admitting the evidence of Ms. Furlow's statement only for the purpose of showing Ms. Furlow's state of mind, her feeling or affection for her nephew.

b. The Statement Is an Operative Fact or Verbal Act

To illustrate this foundation, we shall use a variation of the fact situation in *Hanson v. Johnson,* 161 Minn. 229, 201 N.W. 322 (1924). In that case, the plaintiff Hanson owned a farm that he leased to Schrik. There were a number of large cribs on the farm for storing corn, and Schrik intended to use the farm to raise corn. In our variation of the fact situation, Schrik falls behind in his rent. He then enters into an agreement with Hanson. Under the agreement, Hanson will accept the corn stored in two cribs, five and seven, in lieu of rent due for June and July. When they enter into the agreement at the farm, Schrik says: "It's a deal. The corn in cribs five and seven is yours." Later Schrik obtains a loan from Cattlemen's Bank. He pledges "my corn" as security for the loan. He defaults on the loan. The bank forecloses and sells all the corn on the premises, including the corn in cribs five and seven. Hanson then sues the bank for conversion. Hanson is the witness. He has already identified himself, explained that he was Schrik's landlord, and testifies that Schrik was delinquent on his rent. The plaintiff is the proponent.

P   Mr. Hanson, WHERE were you on the afternoon of July 6, 1988? (1), (2)

W   I was at the farm, the one I rented to Schrik.

P   WHO else was there? (3)

W   Schrik was the only one around. I didn't see his wife or kids.

P   WHY were you there? (4)

W   As I said, he'd fallen behind in his rent. He was supposed to pay at the beginning of the month, and he'd missed the June and July payments. I asked him what he intended to do about the delinquent rent.

P   WHAT happened when you asked him that? (4)

W   He offered me a deal.

O   Your Honor, I move to strike that last answer on the ground that it is hearsay.

P   Your Honor, may we approach the bench?

J   Yes.

P   Your Honor, I offer to prove that Mr. Hanson will testify that Mr. Schrik offered to give my client the corn in two cribs, cribs five and seven, in exchange for the delinquent rent. (4) I want to use the statement for a nonhearsay purpose, namely, to show the offer itself. (5) The words constituting the offer are an operative fact or verbal act; legal consequences flow simply from the fact that Schrik uttered those words. (6)

J   The motion will be denied.

P   Mr. Hanson, let me repeat the question. WHAT happened when you asked him about the delinquent rent? (4)

W   He offered to give me the corn in two cribs in exchange for the late rent.

P   WHAT were his words? (4)

W   As best I recall, he said, "It's a deal. The corn in cribs five and seven is yours."

P   WHAT did you say then? (4)

W   I just said that I accepted the offer, and we shook on it.

c. The Effect of the Statement on the Mind of the Hearer or Reader — Mental Input

Suppose that the plaintiff, Zillman, alleged that the defendant has been negligent in two respects. First, the defendant was speeding. Second, the defendant carelessly drove the car although he knew that the car had bad brakes. Under the second theory, one issue would be whether the defendant knew that the brakes were defective. The plaintiff calls Mr. John Horne. Horne testifies that he manages the auto repair shop near the defendant's house. Horne adds that on January 14, 1989, the defendant dropped off his car for regular maintenance. The plaintiff is the proponent.

P   Mr. Horne, WHERE were you on January 16, 1989? (1), (2)
W   I was at my repair shop.
P   WHO else was there? (3)
W   We had several customers, including the defendant.
P   WHAT happened when the defendant came into the shop? (4)
W   He was there to pick up his car.
P   WHAT happened while he was there? (4)
W   He got the car, and we talked for a while.
P   WHAT did you talk about? (4)
W   Mostly his car.
P   WHAT did you tell him about the car? (4)
O   Your Honor, I object to that question on the ground that it calls for hearsay.
P   Your Honor, may we approach the bench?
J   Yes.
P   Your Honor, I offer to prove that the witness will testify that he told the defendant his brakes were bad. (4) I want to use the witness' prior statement for a nonhearsay purpose, namely, to show its effect on the defendant's state of mind; it gave him knowledge that his brakes were bad. (5) Under our second cause of action, this evidence is logically relevant; our second cause is that the defendant negligently drove the car when he knew it had defective brakes. (6)
J   The objection will be overruled.
P   Mr. Horne, let me repeat the question. WHAT did you tell the defendant about his car? (4)
W   I told him that the brakes were bad and could go out any time.
P   HOW close were you standing to the defendant when you told him that?
W   Only a foot or two away.
P   HOW noisy was the repair shop at the time?
W   It was very quiet.
P   HOW were you facing when you told him about his brakes?
W   I was talking right at him.
P   WHO else was talking to him at the time?
W   No one else. We were the only two talking.
P   HOW did he react when you told him about the bad brakes?
W   He nodded his head, shrugged his shoulders, and got into his car.
O   Your Honor, I request a limiting instruction.
J   Yes. Ladies and gentlemen of the jury, you have just heard the witness' testimony that he told the defendant that the defendant's brakes were bad. You may not consider the witness' testimony as evidence that in fact, the brakes were bad. You may consider the witness' testimony only in deciding whether the next day, the defendant knew the car was defective and acted negligently in driving the car. If other evidence in this case establishes that the brakes were bad, then and only then may you consider the witness' testimony — and then only in deciding whether the next day, the defendant knew the brakes were bad and acted negligently in driving the car.

Of course, to get to the jury, the proponent will have to introduce other, independent evidence that the brakes were defective. The plaintiff could call the repairman who actually worked on the brakes to describe the condition of the brakes. However, it is clear that the plaintiff could use Mr. Horne's testimony for the limited, nonhearsay purpose of proving that the defendant knew of the brakes' hazardous condition.

3. THE STATEMENT WAS MADE OR THE ACT PERFORMED BY A PERSON STILL CONSIDERED AN OUT-OF-COURT DECLARANT

Assume that the proponent is offering testimony about an out-of-court statement for the truth of the assertion. Offering the evidence for that purpose creates an acute need to cross-examine the declarant about his or her perception, memory, and other testimonial qualities. However, suppose that the declarant becomes a witness at trial. If so, the opposing attorney can cross-examine the person both about the person's in-court testimony and about the earlier statements. The person's current availability seemingly satisfies the need for cross-examination. Does the person's current availability for cross-examination remove the earlier statements from the definition of hearsay?

The traditional view is "once an out-of-court declarant, always an out-of-court declarant." If the person was not on the stand when he or she made the statement, it is immaterial that the person later becomes a witness and subjects himself or herself to cross-examination. Consider this example. On Monday, the person tells a friend that the person saw the defendant's car run the red light. On Tuesday, that same person becomes a witness in the suit between plaintiff and defendant. The person testifies that he or she saw the defendant's car run the red light. To increase the impact of the testimony, the plaintiff's attorney attempts to elicit the person's testimony that Monday the person told the friend the same story. If the proponent attempts to use the statement on Monday as substantive proof of the defendant's fault, the statement is hearsay; although the person is now the witness, the person was not on the witness stand when the person made the statement.

Several commentators, including Morgan, argued that the definition of hearsay should not include prior statements made by witnesses now on the stand and subject to cross-examination. These commentators begin with the premise that the primary purpose of the hearsay rule is to protect the opponent's right to cross-examine. They then argue that the opportunity to cross-examine is adequate even if the opportunity is delayed until trial; on Tuesday, the opponent can cross-examine the witness about Monday's statement. These commentators conclude that if the person is now a witness available for examination in court, the person should no longer be considered an out-of-court declarant; and the hearsay rule should not apply to the witness' prior statements. To date, only one jurisdiction, Kansas, has adopted this view.

There is a compromise view gaining a growing number of adherents. The compromise view is that if the witness' prior statement is otherwise admissible for a nonhearsay purpose (as a prior identification to bolster, as a prior inconsistent statement to impeach, or as a prior consistent statement to rehabilitate), the statement should be admitted as substantive evidence. Federal Evidence Rule embraces the compromise view. Rule 801(d)(1) exempts certain prior statements of the witness from the hearsay definition and permits their use as substantive evidence: "A statement is not hearsay if ... the declarant testifies at the trial or hearing and is subject to cross-examination concerning the statement, and the statement is (A) inconsistent with the declarant's testimony, and was given under oath subject to the penalty of perjury at a trial, hearing, or other proceeding, or in a deposition, or (B) consistent with the declarant's testimony and is offered to rebut an express or implied charge against the declarant of recent fabrication or improper influence or motive, or (C) one of identification of a person made after perceiving the person ...." This compromise view reflects two beliefs. First, its supporters believe that there is substantial merit in Morgan's position. Second, they frankly believe that limiting instructions are largely ineffective; although the judge tells the jurors to use the prior statement for the limited purpose of bolstering, impeaching, or rehabilitating, many jurors will use the statement as substantive evidence of the assertion. These two beliefs lead the supporters of the compromise view to admit prior statements as substantive evidence when the statements are otherwise admissible, usually on a credibility theory.

In a jurisdiction wholeheartedly embracing Morgan's view, the foundation for the prior statement is simple. The foundation includes these elements:

1. Where the prior statement was made.
2. When the statement was made.
3. Who was present.
4. The present witness made the prior statement.
5. The tenor of the statement.

The fact situation is a tort action arising from a collision. The plaintiff, Mr. Kionka, contends that on January 17, 1989, the defendant caused the accident by speeding. Mr. Kionka calls Ms. Gerst as a witness. She identifies herself, states that she observed the two cars, and expresses her opinion that defendant's car was going 60 miles an hour. Her direct examination continues. The proponent is the plaintiff.

P   WHERE were you on January 18, 1989? (1), (2)
W   I went down to the police station on Mission Boulevard.
P   WHY did you go there?
W   The officer at the accident scene told me to stop by and give a statement the next day.

P   WHAT happened when you arrived at the police station? (3)
W   I met Officer Grouton, the traffic sergeant.
P   WHAT, if anything, did you tell him about the accident? (4), (5)
O   Your Honor, I object to that question on the ground that it calls for hearsay.
P   Your Honor, may we approach the bench?
J   Yes.
P   Your Honor, the witness is present in court and available for cross-examination. In this jurisdiction, in that situation, the witness' prior statements are no longer considered hearsay.
J   Correct. The objection will be overruled.
P   Ms. Gerst, let me repeat the question. WHAT, if anything, did you tell Officer Grouton about the accident? (4), (5)
W   I said I thought the defendant caused the accident because he was speeding about 60 miles an hour.

In a jurisdiction following the compromise view, the proponent would have to show that the prior statement is admissible on a nonhearsay theory. The proponent would have to lay a complete foundation for prior identification, prior inconsistent statement, or prior consistent statement. Chapter 5 outlines those foundations. Suppose that on February 14, 1989, Ms. Gerst told a friend that she thought the defendant was going only 40 miles an hour. In a compromise jurisdiction, the defendant could use Ms. Gerst's prior inconsistent statement as substantive evidence; no limiting instruction would be given. The hypothetical continues, and the defendant now attempts to prove the prior inconsistent statement during Ms. Gerst's cross-examination. The defendant is the proponent.

P   ISN'T IT A FACT THAT on February 14, 1989, you had a conversation with your friend, Charles Gill, at your house?
W   Yes.
P   ISN'T IT CORRECT THAT during the conversation, you told him that the defendant was going only 40 miles an hour?
W   Yes.
O   Your Honor, I request a limiting instruction.
J   What type of limiting instruction?
O   An instruction that the jurors may consider Ms. Gerst's statement only in so far as it reflects on her credibility.
P   Your Honor, may we approach the bench?
J   Yes.
P   Your Honor, I do not think that a limiting instruction is needed.
O   The defendant is obviously introducing this statement as a prior inconsistent statement to impeach; it can't be used as substantive evidence of the defendant's speed.
P   Your Honor, under our Evidence Rules, if a witness' prior statement is admissible for a nonhearsay purpose such as impeachment and the witness is available for cross-examination, the hearsay rule no longer applies. Since Ms. Gerst is available for cross-examination, I can use her prior inconsistent statement both to impeach and as substantive evidence.

J   I agree. I shall not give the jurors a limiting instruction.

Note that Federal Rule 801(d)(1)(A) stops short of wholeheartedly embracing the compromise view. Under that subsection, it is not enough that the statement be otherwise admissible as a prior inconsistent statement. To ensure that the statute would not violate the confrontation clause, Congress wrote into the statute the additional requirement that the statement have been made under oath at a prior formal proceeding such as a grand jury hearing. In short, even if a statement qualifies as a prior inconsistent statement under Rule 613, the statement might not be admissible as substantive evidence under Rule 801(d)(1)(A).

Part 2. The Admissions Exemption Requiring a Showing of Neither Reliability Nor Necessity

C. THE EXEMPTION FOR ADMISSIONS OF A PARTY-OPPONENT

If the statement falls within the definition of hearsay, the proponent of the statement must find an applicable hearsay exemption or exception. One of the most frequently used exemptions is that for the admissions of a party-opponent. For example, in a tort action the plaintiff can prove the defendant's out-of-court statements acknowledging fault; from the plaintiff's perspective, the defendant's statements are admissions of the party-opponent. The same hearsay exemption permits prosecutors to introduce defendants' confessions acknowledging guilt.

Although the common law treats the admission doctrine as a hearsay exception, the admission doctrine differs from most hearsay exceptions. Commentators have had some difficulty explaining the admission doctrine. Unlike most hearsay exceptions, admissions do not have to have a circumstantial guarantee of trustworthiness; although the admission is obviously disserving at the time of trial, the admission is admissible even if it was self-serving when made. Nor is there any need to show a necessity for resorting to the hearsay; the opposing party may be available and perfectly willing to testify about the subject-matter of the earlier statement. The truth of the matter is that the admission doctrine is a product of the adversary litigation system; the opponent can hardly complain that he or she does not have an opportunity to cross-examine himself or herself. The opponent can always take the stand to deny or explain the statement. Because of the unique rationale for this exception, some commentators do not even classify admissions as hearsay. Thus, Federal Evidence Rule 801(d)(2) exempts admissions from the hearsay definition and admits admissions as nonhearsay.

Although the commentators and courts disagree over the question whether admissions should be classified as hearsay, there is general consensus on the foundational elements of the various types of admissions. There are three basic kinds of admissions: personal, adoptive, and vicarious. The basis of the classification is the reason for which we attribute the statement to the party-opponent. In the case of personal admissions, we attribute the statement to the party-opponent because we find the statement in his or her own words or acts. In the case of adoptive admissions, a third party makes the statement, but we impute the statement to the party-opponent because the opponent manifests agreement with the statement. The opponent thereby "adopts" the statement. Finally, in the case of vicarious admissions, again a third party makes the statement, but the party-opponent does not manifest agreement. Rather, we attribute the statement to the party-opponent because of the legal relationship such as agency between the third party and the party-opponent. We shall now examine the foundations for these various types of admissions in detail.

1. PERSONAL ADMISSIONS

All jurisdictions admit the party-opponent's own personal admissions in civil and criminal cases. Federal Evidence Rule 801 (d)(2)(A) sanctions the admission of personal admissions. It permits the proponent to introduce a statement when "(t)he statement is offered against a party and is ... the party's own statement, in either an individual or a representative capacity ...." Personal admissions are liberally admissible; the phrasing of the admission can be highly opinionated, and the admission need not even be based on personal knowledge.

a. In Civil Cases

In civil cases, the foundation for personal admissions is very simple. The foundation includes these elements:
1. The witness heard a declarant make a statement.
2. The witness identifies the declarant as the present party-opponent.
3. The statement is inconsistent with the position the party-opponent is taking at trial. (Although the appellate courts usually phrase this requirement negatively and insist upon inconsistency, in practice trial judges apply the requirement affirmatively; trial judges ask whether the statement is logically relevant to an issue the proponent has a right to prove in the case. The phrasing of the question eliciting the statement usually ensures the statement's logical relevance; the question inquires "about" a specific topic.)

Our fact situation is a civil tort action. The case arose from a collision on May 19, 1989. The plaintiff, Ms. Langdale, alleges that the defendant, Mr. Maire, caused the collision by speeding. The speed limit in this section of town is 25 miles an hour. The plaintiff calls the investigating officer, Patrolman Hightower. The witness has already identified himself and testified that he went to the accident scene. The proponent is the plaintiff.

P   WHAT did you do when you arrived at the scene of the collision?
W   I investigated the accident.
P   HOW did you investigate the accident? (1)
W   I viewed the debris and interviewed the persons involved.
P   WHOM did you interview? (2)
W   Ms. Langdale and Mr. Maire.
P   WHERE is Mr. Maire now? (2)
W   In the courtroom.
P   Specifically, WHERE in the courtroom? (2)
W   He's sitting at the table.
P   HOW is he dressed? (2)
W   In a green suit and blue tie.
P   Your Honor, please let the record reflect that the witness has correctly identified the defendant.
J   It will so reflect.
P   Officer Hightower, WHAT did the defendant say about the accident? (3)
O   Your Honor, I object on the ground that the question calls for hearsay.
P   Your Honor, may I be heard?
J   Yes.
P   The statement is hearsay, but it falls within the exception for admissions of a party-opponent. (In federal court, the proponent would say, "The statement is exempt from the hearsay rule because it is the admission of a party-opponent" or "The statement is not hearsay because it is the admission of a party-opponent.")
J   The objection will be overruled.
P   Let me repeat the question. WHAT did the defendant say about the accident? (3)
W   He said he was really sorry about it because he thought he caused it by going too fast.
P   HOW fast did he say he was going? (3)
W   He said maybe 40 miles an hour.

b. In Criminal Cases

The foundation for a criminal defendant's confession is more complex than the foundation for admissions in civil cases. The foundation is more complex because in a criminal case, the prosecutor must comply with constitutional requirements as well as common-law hearsay requirements. The prosecutor must first demonstrate that the confession was voluntary; the fifth and fourteenth amendment due process clauses bar the admission of involuntary confessions. In addition, if the defendant was in custody, the prosecutor must demonstrate that the police administered proper *Miranda* warnings; *Miranda* imposes requirements in addition to traditional voluntariness. Finally, the prosecutor must prove that the defendant properly waived his *Miranda* rights. Thus, the complete foundation includes these elements:

1. The witness heard a declarant make a statement.
2. The witness identifies the declarant as the present defendant.
3. Any confession was voluntary.
4. The police administered proper *Miranda* warnings to the defendant.
5. The defendant waived his or her rights.
6. The statement is inconsistent with the position the defendant takes at trial; the statement is logically relevant to some issue the prosecution has a right to prove at trial. If the defendant pleads not guilty, the defendant requires the prosecution to prove all the elements of the crime. By pleading not guilty, the defendant takes the general position that all the facts alleged are false.

Our fact situation is a prosecution for robbery. The defendant is Mr. Walters. The prosecution calls Officer Gannon as a witness. Officer Gannon identifies himself and then testifies that he is assigned to the robbery detail of the Lincoln, Nebraska Police Department. The proponent is the prosecutor.

P Officer Gannon, WHERE were you on the afternoon of January 20, 1989?
W I was at our downtown station on duty in the robbery detail office.
P WHAT happened that afternoon?
W Some other officers brought in someone for questioning.
P WHO was that person? (2)
W James Walters.
P WHERE is James Walters now? (2)
W Here in the courtroom.
P Specifically WHERE in the courtroom? (2)
W He's sitting right there.
P HOW is he dressed? (2)
W He's attired in a brown shirt and green pants.
P Your Honor, please let the record reflect that the witness identified the defendant.
J It will so reflect.
P WHAT happened after the officers brought Mr. Walters in? (3)
W I took him to the interrogation room.
P WHAT happened then? (3)
W I began questioning him.
P WHAT promises did you make to him during the questioning? (3)
W None.
P WHAT force did you use during the interrogation? (3)
W None. I never touched him.
P WHAT threats did you make? (3)
W I didn't make any. I didn't threaten him or his family in any way.
P WHAT requests did he make during the questioning? (3)
W He asked for a cigarette, for coffee, and to go to the bathroom — that sort of thing.
P HOW did you respond to his requests? (3)

W I granted them. I gave him cigarettes and coffee. I let him go to the bathroom. I tried to make him as comfortable as possible.

P WHAT, if anything, did you say to Mr. Walters? (4)

W I read him his rights.

P HOW did you read him his rights? (4)

W I read them verbatim from a warning card.

P Your Honor, I request that this be marked prosecution exhibit number three for identification.

J It will be so marked.

P Please let the record reflect that I am showing the exhibit to the opposing counsel.

J It will so reflect.

P I request permission to approach the witness.

J Permission granted.

P Officer Gannon, I now hand you prosecution exhibit number three for identification. WHAT is it? (4)

W It's the warning card I just referred to.

P HOW can you recognize it? (4)

W I initialed it, and I had the defendant initial it as well. I see the initials and the date we wrote in pencil on the card.

P HOW did you use the card during the questioning? (3)

W I read from it verbatim to make certain I gave the suspect the correct warnings.

P Your Honor, I now offer prosecution exhibit number three for identification into evidence as prosecution exhibit three.

J It will be received.

P Officer Gannon, please read prosecution exhibit three.

W It says: "You have a right to remain silent. Anything you say can and will be used against you in a court of law. You also have a right to an attorney. You have a right to consult an attorney before any questioning. You have a right to have an attorney present during any questioning. If you cannot afford an attorney, one will be appointed to represent you."

P WHAT happened after you read Mr. Walters these rights? (5)

W I asked him whether he understood his rights.

P WHAT was his answer? (5)

W He said he did.

P WHAT happened then? (5)

W I asked him whether he wanted an attorney.

P WHAT was his response?

W He said no.

P WHAT happened then? (5)

W I asked him whether he was willing to talk about the robbery.

P WHAT was his response? (5)

W He told me about the robbery.

P WHAT did he say about the robbery? (6)

W He said he had held up the McDonald's on 4th Street, and he was very sorry he had done it. He said he needed money for rent, and he couldn't figure out any other way to get it.

Many jurisdictions impose an additional requirement for the admission of confessions; these jurisdictions require corroboration. In these jurisdictions, apart from the defendant's confession, there must be independent evidence that a crime was committed. For example, in a robbery case, the store owner would have to testify that he found his locks broken and discovered money or merchandise missing. The corroboration need not show the identity of the perpetrator of the crime; it need show only that a crime was committed. The prosecutor ordinarily presents the corroborating evidence first and then calls the witness who will testify about the defendant's confession to the crime.

2. ADOPTIVE ADMISSIONS

In personal admissions, the party-opponent himself or herself says or writes the statement constituting the admission. In adoptive admissions, a third party says or writes the statement. The party-opponent then manifests assent to the statement in some fashion. In the words of Federal Evidence Rule 801(d)(2)(B), the party "manifest(s) an adoption or belief in its truth ...." When a criminal defendant signs a confession typed by a secretary at the police station, the defendant is manifesting assent to the contents of the writing. A party-opponent can manifest assent expressly or impliedly, even by silence.

a. Express Adoption

The foundation includes these elements:
1. A declarant made a statement.
2. The declarant made the statement in the party's presence.
3. The party heard and understood the statement. The declarant's statement is thus offered for a nonhearsay purpose — to show its effect on the state of mind of the party.
4. The party made a statement which expressed agreement with the declarant's statement.

Most jurisdictions treat these foundational facts as Rule 104(b) issues. Hence, for example, the proponent need only present sufficient evidence to create a permissive inference that the party-opponent heard the declarant's statement. The jury ultimately decides whether the party opponent heard the statement.

To illustrate this doctrine, we shall use a tort action involving a hit-and-run accident. On July 1, 1988, the plaintiff, Waylen, was crossing a street in downtown Iowa City when a car struck her and fled the scene. The plaintiff's complaint alleges that the driver of the car was the defendant, Brad Benton. Benton works as a salesperson at an electronics store in Iowa City. The defendant denies any involvement in the accident. In his pretrial deposition, he claimed that he was on vacation in Mexico on the date of the accident. The plaintiff is the proponent. The plaintiff calls Mr. George Nickmeyer as her next witness. Nickmeyer testifies that he is the manager of the store where Benton works.

P   Mr. Nickmeyer, WHAT are your duties as manager?

W   I'm generally in charge of everything — purchasing, finance, personnel, you name it, and I do it at the store. It's a pretty small operation.

P   Please tell us more about your personnel responsibilities.

W   It's a big area. I make sure that everyone is signed up for fringe benefits, medical plans, and the like. I also keep track of work days and vacations. We don't have an old-fashioned time clock.

P   HOW do you keep track of vacation days? (1)

W   I keep a personal log of when people work and when they're off. Then at the end of each month I prepare a summary for each employee and have them verify its accuracy.

P   HOW do you do that? (2), (3)

W   I hand them the statement. At the end of each month, everyone checks by my office to inspect their work and vacation statement. They read it, and then they sign it.

P   Your Honor, I request that this be marked Plaintiff's exhibit #1 for identification.

J   It will be so marked.

P   Please let the record reflect that I am showing the exhibit to the opposing counsel.

J   The record will so reflect.

P   Permission to approach the witness?

J   Granted.

P   Mr. Nickmeyer, I now hand you Plaintiff's exhibit #1 for identification. WHAT is it? (1), (4)

W   It's Brad Benton's statement for the month of July 1988.

P   HOW do you recognize it? (1)

W   I was the one who prepared it; I recognize the contents and the form. In addition, I see Brad's signature at the bottom. He's worked for me for over three years.

P   HOW many times have you seen the defendant sign his name? (4)

W   I can't give you a precise number, but I've probably seen him do it dozens of times during that period. Like I said, the employees come by at the end of every month to sign these statements right in my presence.

P   HOW was this form prepared? (2), (3), (4)

W   I always do it the same way. I don't want any hassles with them over their vacation time. I call them into the office or they stop by on their own, read the statement while I'm present, and then put their John Hancock on it.

P   Your Honor, I now offer Plaintiff's exhibit #1 for identification into evidence as Plaintiff's number one.

O   Your Honor, I must object on the ground that this is inadmissible hearsay. There's obviously an inadequate foundation for a business entry.

P   Your Honor, may I be heard?

J   Yes.

P   I'm not offering this exhibit as a business entry. I'm offering it as an adoptive admission. Mr. Nickmeyer prepared the form, but his testimony shows that the defendant had an opportunity to read and check it before signing it. By signing it, the defendant manifested his assent to the accuracy of the form. The form lists July 1, 1988 as a workday for the defendant — not a vacation day. (4)

J   Objection overruled. The exhibit will be received.
P   Mr. Nickmeyer, let me direct your attention to the extreme, left-hand margin of the exhibit. WHAT is listed on that margin?
W   That margin lists each day of the month.
P   Now let me direct your attention to the middle column of the form and the column on the extreme right-hand margin. WHAT do those columns represent?
W   The middle column is for checkmarks indicating workdays. The column on the right is for vacation days. If someone works a particular day, I place a checkmark in the middle of the form. If they're on vacation, I place the check in the right-hand column.
P   Please look at the columns for July 1st, 1988.
W   O.K.
P   WHERE is the checkmark for July 1st — in the middle or on the right-hand margin?
W   It's in the middle.
P   Again, WHAT does the middle column represent?
W   Workdays.
P   Your Honor, I now request permission to circulate the exhibit to the jurors for their inspection.
J   Certainly.

b. Implied Adoption by Silence — "Tacit Admission"

Sometimes, if a person stands silent in the face of an accusation, we may infer the person's assent to the accusation from his or her silence. Thus, there can be an implied adoption by silence; the courts sometimes refer to this doctrine as "tacit admission." The foundation includes these elements:

1. The declarant made a statement.
2. The statement was an accusation against the party-opponent.
3. The declarant made the statement in the party's presence.
4. The party heard and understood the statement.
5. The party had the opportunity to deny the statement.
6. The party either remained silent or made an evasive or equivocal reply.
7. Under similar circumstances, a reasonable innocent person would have immediately denied the accusation.

Our fact situation is another tort case arising from a collision. The plaintiff, Mr. Girard, alleges that the defendant, Ms. Ratner, caused the accident by disregarding a stop sign. The investigating officer was Highway Patrolman Kuns. The plaintiff calls Patrolman Kuns. He has already identified himself and testified that he responded to the accident scene. The plaintiff is the proponent.

P   WHAT did you do when you responded to the scene?
W   I immediately sought out the two drivers.
P   WHO were the drivers?
W   Your client, Mr. Girard, and Ms. Ratner.
P   WHERE is Mr. Girard now?

W   At the table over there.
P   HOW is he dressed?
W   He's wearing a gray business suit and blue tie.
P   Your Honor, please let the record reflect that the witness has identified the plaintiff.
J   It will so reflect.
P   WHERE is Ms. Ratner now?
W   At the other table there.
P   HOW is she dressed?
W   She has on a pink dress and red shoes.
P   Your Honor, please let the record reflect that the witness has also identified the defendant.
J   It will so reflect.
P   WHERE did you find the plaintiff and defendant at the accident scene?
W   They were standing on the northeast corner of the intersection.
P   HOW close were they to each other?
W   Right next to each other.
P   WHAT were they doing?
W   They were talking.
P   WHAT were they talking about?
W   The accident.
P   WHAT, if anything, did Mr. Girard tell the defendant about the accident? (1), (2)
O   Your Honor, I object to that question on the ground that it calls for hearsay.
P   Your Honor, may we approach the bench?
J   Yes.
P   I offer to prove that Mr. Girard told the defendant she had run a stop sign and that she adopted the statement by remaining silent. I am using Mr. Girard's statement for a nonhearsay purpose; I am not offering the statement itself for its truth. I simply want to prove that the plaintiff made the statement and the defendant then adopted it.
O   There's been no foundation for an adoptive admission yet.
J   I will admit the statement subject to a motion to strike.
P   Officer Kuns, let me repeat the question. WHAT, if anything, did Mr. Girard tell the defendant about the accident? (1), (2)
W   He told her that she had caused the accident by running a stop sign. He said she was as blind as a bat.
P   WHAT language was Mr. Girard speaking in? (4)
W   English.
P   HOW close was Mr. Girard to the defendant when he made that statement? (3)
W   Two feet away at most. As I said, they were standing talking.
P   HOW much noise was there when Mr. Girard made the statement? (4), (5)
W   It was pretty quiet. The traffic congestion had died down.
P   HOW many other people were talking to the defendant at the time? (4), (5)
W   No one else.
P   WHOM was Mr. Girard facing when he made the statement? (4), (5)
W   He was looking right at Ms. Ratner.
P   HOW was she facing? (4), (5)
W   She was facing him.

P   WHAT was Mr. Girard's tone of voice when he made the statement? (5), (7)
W   He was obviously excited.
P   WHAT threats did Mr. Girard make against the defendant at the time? (5), (7)
W   None. He was upset, but he wasn't threatening or anything like that.
P   WHAT gestures did Mr. Girard make? (5), (7)
W   He was animated, but he wasn't making a fist or pointing a finger in Ms. Ratner's face. He was just exasperated.
P   WHAT was the defendant's facial expression immediately after Mr. Girard made the statement? (7)
W   She looked worried.
P   WHERE did she look? (4), (5), (7)
W   Right after he made the statement, she looked down and away from the plaintiff.
P   WHAT, if anything, did the defendant say then? (6)
W   Nothing.
P   WHAT was her response to Mr. Girard's statement that she had run the stop sign? (6)
W   None. She didn't say anything in response to his remark.

3. VICARIOUS ADMISSIONS

a. In Civil Cases

In vicarious admissions, the basis for imputing the statement to the party-opponent is the party's relationship with the declarant. A principal debtor's statement may be admitted against a surety, the statements of a predecessor in title against the present titleholder, and the statements of an agent against the principal. The foundation consists of demonstrating the relation between the declarant and the party-opponent. Once the relation has been demonstrated, the declarant's statements are vicariously admissible against the party-opponent. There is a division of authority over the question of whether vicarious admissions must be based on personal knowledge.

Most vicarious admissions in civil cases are statements made by agents and admitted against the agent's principal. The traditional view is that the declarant must have been a spokesperson for the principal. It is not sufficient that the declarant was an agent or employee of the party-opponent. The declarant must have been a special type of agent, authorized to make statements on the principal's behalf. In the words of Federal Evidence Rule 801(d)(2)(C), "the statement" was made "by a person authorized by the party to make a statement concerning the subject." In these jurisdictions, the foundation includes the following elements:

1. The declarant was an agent of the party-opponent.
2. The party-opponent authorized the declarant to make the particular statements.

3. The statement is inconsistent with a position the party-opponent is taking at trial; the statement is logically relevant to an issue the proponent has a right to prove at trial.

The fact situation is a suit against an insurance company. Delta Corporation sues Grant Insurance Company. The complaint alleges that the defendant insured the plaintiff against fire; a fire occurred on the plaintiff's premises and caused $100,000.00 in damages; but the defendant has wrongfully refused to compensate the plaintiff. The policy excluded any fire which the plaintiff's employee negligently started. In discovery, the defendant obtained a copy of a report the plaintiff's safety investigator, Mr. Grant Richards, prepared. The report includes the finding that one contributing cause of the fire was some careless welding by plaintiff's employees; the welder negligently cut into a furnace and permitted flames to escape. During its case-in-chief, the defendant calls Mr. Richards. In many jurisdictions, the defendant could treat him as an adverse witness and conduct the direct examination as cross-examination and use leading questions. For our purposes, we shall restrict the defense attorney to non-leading questions. The defendant is the proponent. Mr. Richards has already identified himself.

P   WHERE do you work? (1)
W   I work for Delta Corporation in Albuquerque.
P   HOW long have you worked for them? (1)
W   Seven years, give or take a few months.
P   WHAT is your job with Delta Corporation? (2)
W   I am a safety and accident investigator.
P   HOW long have you held that position? (2)
W   The last five years.
P   WHERE were you on November 13, 1989? (2)
W   At our plant in Santa Fe.
P   WHAT were you doing there? (2)
W   I was investigating the fire that had occurred the day before.
P   HOW long did you spend investigating the fire? (2)
W   The whole day.
P   WHAT did you do when you finished the investigation? (2)
W   As is my normal practice, I prepared a report of the investigation.
P   Your Honor, I request that this be marked defense exhibit F for identification.
J   It will be so marked.
P   Please let the record reflect that I am showing the exhibit to the opposing counsel.
J   It will so reflect.
P   I request permission to approach the witness.
J   Permission granted.
P   Mr. Richards, I now hand you defense exhibit F for identification. WHAT is it? (2)
W   It's my report on the fire.
P   HOW can you recognize it? (2)

W   I recognize my handwriting on the last page. I also generally recall the report's contents.

P   Again, WHAT are your duties for Delta Corporation? (2)

W   As I said before, I'm the safety and accident investigator.

P   In general terms, WHAT is the subject of this particular report?

W   It relates to the fire I investigated as part of my duties.

P   WHY did you prepare this particular report? (2)

W   It's part of my job. In fact, the vice-president for operations ordered me to get that report finished and submitted as soon as possible.

P   Your Honor, I now offer defense exhibit F for identification into evidence as defense exhibit F.

J   It will be received.

P   Mr. Richards, please turn to page 18 of exhibit F and read finding #4 to the jury. (3)

W   The report reads, "Another contributing factor may have been our own employees' carelessness. Some of our welders were evidently working next to furnace #3 on the second floor. Some eyewitness reports indicated that the welders accidentally cut into the furnace, releasing the flames that started the fire."

Many jurisdictions limit this doctrine to statements made to third parties outside the business organization. In this hypothetical, the document was an internal report; Richards submitted the report to his superiors in the corporation. Those jurisdictions would exclude the report. Even in those jurisdictions, the report would be admissible if Richards prepared the report for a third party outsider such as a government safety agency. The trend is to abandon this limitation. Federal Evidence Rule 801(d)(2)(C) follows the trend and would permit the admission of Richards' report as a vicarious admission.

The emerging view is that the party-opponent need not have authorized the particular statement; the declarant need not be a spokesperson. Under the emerging view, it is sufficient that the declarant was an agent of the party-opponent and the statement relates to the agent's employment duties. Federal Evidence Rule 801(d)(2)(D) opts for this view. That Rule authorizes the admission of "a statement by the party's agent or servant concerning a matter within the scope of the agency or employment, made during the existence of the relationship." Under this view, the only foundational elements are:

1. The declarant was an agent of the party-opponent.
2. The declarant made the statement while he or she was an agent.
3. The statement related to the agent's employment duties. The proponent first elicits testimony about the agent's employment duties. The proponent then asks the agent "about" a topic related to the duties.
4. The statement is inconsistent with a position the party-opponent is taking at trial; the statement is logically relevant to an issue the proponent has a right to prove at trial.

Our fact situation is a tort action arising from a collision. Ms. Henning, the plaintiff, alleges that Carrington Company's driver, Mr. Julius, negligently caused the accident. The only named defendant is the company, Carrington. During the plaintiff's case-in-chief, she calls Mr. Julius as a witness. As in the previous hypothetical, many courts would permit the proponent to treat the witness as hostile and conduct the direct examination as if it were cross-examination. However, for teaching purposes, our proponent will use non-leading questions. Mr. Julius has already identified himself.

P   WHERE do you work? (1)
W   I work for the Carrington warehouse here in Billings.
P   HOW long have you worked there? (1)
W   Eight years.
P   WHAT are your duties? (1)
W   I'm a driver. I haul our deliveries all over the United States. I do mostly intrastate moves, but I occasionally do cross-country moves.
P   Mr. Julius, WHERE were you on the afternoon of October 13, 1988? (2)
W   I was driving along Highway 84 headed for Colorado.
P   WHO were you working for that day? (2)
W   My regular employer, Carrington.
P   WHAT happened that afternoon? (2)
W   I was involved in an accident with a Ms. Henning. *(Here the proponent would elicit facts about the collision itself.)*
P   WHAT happened immediately after the accident? (3)
W   I talked to the police officer who investigated the accident.
P   WHAT was his name? (3)
W   I think his name was Patrolman Blue.
P   WHAT, if anything, did you tell him about your speed just before the collision? (3), (4)
O   Your Honor, I object to that question on the ground that it calls for hearsay.
P   Your Honor, may we approach the bench?
J   Yes.
P   Your Honor, I offer to prove that the witness will admit he said he was going 70 miles an hour. My theory of admissibility is that Mr. Julius' statement about his speed is a vicarious admission against his employer.
O   Carrington hires drivers to drive rather than to act as spokespersons.
P   As you know, Your Honor, this jurisdiction recently adopted the Federal Rules of Evidence. Rule 801 authorizes the admission of agents' statements so long as they relate to the agent's employment duties. This statement relates to the speed at which Mr. Julius was driving.
J   The objection will be overruled.
P   Mr. Julius, let me repeat the question. WHAT, if anything, did you tell Patrolman Blue about your speed just before the collision? (3), (4)
W   I told him I thought I was going about 70 miles an hour. I was a little behind schedule, and I was trying to make up time.
P   WHAT is the posted speed limit on the stretch of highway where the collision occurred?
W   55 miles an hour.

b. In Criminal Cases

The criminal counterpart of the exception for agents' statements is the co-conspirator doctrine. Federal Evidence Rule 801 (d)(2)(E) states the doctrine. That Rule excepts "a statement by a co-conspirator of a party during the course and in furtherance of the conspiracy." The foundation includes these elements:

1. There was a conspiracy.
2. The conspiracy was in progress when the declarant made the statement. The conspiracy continues at least until the conspirators attempt to commit the crime. If the crime is a theft offense, the conspiracy also continues until the conspirators divide the proceeds of the theft. However, in most jurisdictions absent an express agreement, the conspiracy does not continue while the individual conspirators try to evade arrest and prosecution.
3. The declarant was a co-conspirator.
4. The declarant made the statement in furtherance of the conspiracy. The declarant furthers the conspiracy by attempting to recruit new conspirators or updating current conspirators on the state of their plans. If the declarant has already been arrested, his or her confession is usually not deemed to promote the conspiracy.
5. The defendant was a member of the conspiracy. The defendant need not be a member of the conspiracy when the declarant makes the statement; if the defendant later joins the conspiracy, the defendant is deemed to ratify the earlier statements.

In *Bourjaily v. United States,* 483 U.S. 171 (1987), the Supreme Court announced that in deciding whether the prosecution has established all the foundational elements, under Rule 104(a) the trial judge may consider the content of the proffered statement itself.

To lay the foundation, the prosecutor usually calls an informer or a conspirator who has turned state's evidence. Our fact situation is a prosecution for conspiracy to sell cocaine. The defendant is Mr. George Sherr. The indictment alleges that the defendant conspired with Mr. James Blanton. The prosecution calls Mr. Donald Peterson as a witness. The prosecutor hopes to use Mr. Peterson's testimony to prove the intent to sell. The witness has already identified himself. The prosecution is the proponent.

P   WHAT is your occupation?
W   I am a police officer, a member of the Tucson Police Department.
P   WHAT are your duties?
W   I specialize in undercover work for the Narcotics Division.
P   HOW long have you done that type of work?
W   For the last three years.
P   WHERE were you on the evening of September 3, 1988? (1)
W   I was at James Blanton's house near the City Hall in Tucson.
P   WHO else was there? (1), (3), (5)

W   It was just me, Blanton, and the defendant.

P   WHAT happened while you were there? (1)

W   Blanton showed me some bags containing a drug. Both Blanton and the defendant referred to it as cocaine.

P   WHAT happened after Blanton showed you the bags? (1)

W   I pretended to get high on some marijuana; and while I was doing that, Blanton and the defendant discussed their plans for getting more cocaine.

P   WHAT plans did they discuss? (1)

W   Blanton said he had a contact in Mexico for good cocaine; and the defendant said he could fly down, pick up the cocaine, and smuggle it back across the border.

P   WHEN did they say they would carry out these plans? (2)

W   Over the next couple of months.

P   WHAT happened after they discussed their plans?

W   The defendant took me home.

P   WHAT happened the next day? (2)

W   I met Blanton for lunch.

P   WHAT happened during the lunch? (4)

W   Blanton invited me to help the defendant and him carry out their plans.

P   HOW did he want you to help him? (4)

W   He said he wanted me to hide some bags of cocaine in my apartment. He said he thought it would be a good idea to divide up his cache rather than storing it in only one place.

P   HOW did you respond? (4)

W   I said that I wanted to make certain there was something in it for me.

P   WHAT, if anything, did Blanton say then? (4)

O   Your Honor, I object to that question on the ground that it calls for hearsay.

P   Your Honor, may we approach the bench?

J   Yes.

P   Your Honor, I offer to prove that the witness will testify that Blanton said he and the defendant were going to sell the cocaine and make enough money to pay the witness $10,000.00. The testimony is directly relevant to prove the intent to sell. Since Blanton was the defendant's co-conspirator, Blanton's statement is vicariously admissible against the defendant.

J   The objection will be overruled.

P   Mr. Peterson, let me repeat the question. WHAT did Mr. Blanton say when you said you wanted to make certain there was something in the proposal for you? (4)

W   He said that he and the defendants weren't simply piling up the cocaine supply for their personal use. He told me that they intended to sell the cocaine. He was certain that they would make enough money to pay me $10,000.00 for the use of my apartment.

Part 3. Hearsay Exceptions Based Primarily on a Showing of Reliability

As we saw in the last section, a proponent offering a statement as the admission of a party-opponent need not establish the reliability of the statement or any necessity to resort to the statement. In contrast, many hearsay exceptions require a showing of reliability. These exceptions fall into two categories. In one category, the exception is usually a spinoff of the old *res gestae* doctrine; and there is an inference of sincerity on the part of the declaration. Sections G through J of this chapter focus on the exceptions falling into this category. The second category includes primarily documentary statements. There is something about the process of generating the writing which creates an inference of the reliability of the statement. Sections D through F of this chapter discuss those hearsay exceptions.

D. BUSINESS ENTRIES

1. THE DOCTRINE

At common law, business entries are exceptionally admissible. Federal Evidence Rule 803(6) restates the modern doctrine: "A memorandum, report, record, or data compilation, in any form, of acts, events, conditions, opinions, or diagnoses, made at or near the time by, or from information transmitted by, a person with knowledge, if kept in the course of a regularly conducted business activity, and if it was the regular practice of that business activity to make the memorandum, report, record, or data compilation, all as shown by the testimony of the custodian or other qualified witness, unless the source of the information or the method or circumstances of preparation indicate lack of trustworthiness. The term 'business' as used in this paragraph includes business, institution, association, profession, occupation, and calling of every kind, whether or not conducted for profit."

In the case of business entries, the circumstantial guarantee of trustworthiness is that since the entry is routine, the business' employees have developed habits of precision in gathering and reporting the data. The employees' habits help to ensure the reliability of the report. There is also necessity for resorting to the hearsay report. If a business conducts hundreds or thousands of similar transactions during a year, it is doubtful whether any employee will remember the particular transaction recorded in the entry. Even if an employee remembers, the employee's memory is likely to be incomplete or hazy. Thus, the business entry is probably the most reliable evidence available.

2. ELEMENTS OF THE FOUNDATION

Some commentators have suggested that the Federal Rules of Evidence "collapse" the traditional, common-law elements of the business entry foundation into a single requirement for a general showing of reliability. However, most commentators and courts still assume that the proponent must establish the following foundational elements:

1. The report was prepared by a person with a business relationship with the company. It is ideal if the person is an employee of the

company. However, the person might also work for a parent, subsidiary, or affiliated company.

2. The informant (the ultimate source of the report) had a business duty to report the information. This requirement is traceable to the leading case of *Johnson v. Lutz,* 253 N.Y. 124, 170 N.E. 517 (1930). There the court held that a report is not prepared in the course of business unless all the persons contributing to the report have a business duty to do so. In that case, the business entity was the police department. The parts of the police report reflecting bystanders' statements did not qualify as business entries, since the civilian bystanders were not employees of the police department. The informant's business duty is one of the guarantees of the report's trustworthiness.

3. The informant had personal knowledge of the facts or events reported.

4. The written report was prepared contemporaneously with the facts or events.

5. It was a routine practice of the business to prepare such reports.

6. The report was reduced to written form.

7. The report was made in the regular course of business. The expression, "regular course of business," at least requires that the entry be related to the nature of the business. For instance, a sales slip is obviously related to the nature of a retail merchandise business. *Palmer v. Hoffman,* 318 U.S. 109 (1943) adds another level of meaning to "regular course of business." The lower courts and commentators have construed *Palmer* as meaning that reports specially prepared for litigation are not made "in the regular course of business." If the trial judge finds that the business entry is in reality a special litigation report, the judge has discretion to exclude the entry as being suspect and unreliable.

8. The entry is factual in nature. Rule 803(6) relaxes this requirement by expressly allowing the admission of "opinions ... or diagnoses."

The witness need not have personal knowledge of the entry's preparation. In fact, the witness rarely has such knowledge. The witness is ordinarily the business' records custodian or librarian. The witness testifies to his or her connection with the business and then describes the habitual method with which the business prepares and maintains its reports. The proponent lays the foundation for such habit by following the procedure outlined in Section C of Chapter 6. The habit evidence has sufficient probative value to support a finding that the business followed that procedure on the occasion in question.

3. SAMPLE FOUNDATION

The fact situation is a contract suit. The plaintiff is Armor Corporation. Its complaint alleges that it delivered 500 stereophonic speakers to Hyatt Corporation and that the defendant wrongfully failed to pay for the speakers. The defendant filed an answer, generally denying the complaint's allegations. The plaintiff wants to introduce a Delivery Sheet, stating that its employees delivered the 500 speakers to the defendant. The plaintiff calls Mr. James Merton as a witness. Mr. Merton has already identified himself. The plaintiff is the proponent.

P   WHERE do you work?
W   I am the records librarian for Armor Corporation.
P   HOW long have you held that position?
W   About six years.
P   WHAT are your duties as records librarian?
W   I establish company-wide procedures for preparing records. I ensure that the records that are prepared are properly filed, and I'm finally in charge of records retirement and destruction.
P   Your Honor, I request that this be marked plaintiff's exhibit number three for identification.
J   It will be so marked.
P   Please let the record reflect that I am showing the exhibit to the opposing counsel.
J   It will so reflect.
P   I request permission to approach the witness.
J   Permission granted.
P   Mr. Merton, I now hand you plaintiff's exhibit number three for identification. WHAT is it?

Authentication

The complete foundation would include proof of the document's authenticity. See Sections B and C of Chapter 4.

Best Evidence

The complete foundation will also include proof of compliance with the best evidence rule. See Chapter 8.

Hearsay

P   WHO prepared this document? (1)
W   Well, it seems to have been prepared by Bob Grant.
P   HOW do you know that? (1)
W   I recognize his handwriting style. I've seen his writing on hundreds of occasions.
P   WHO is Bob Grant? (1)
W   He's one of our delivery personnel.
P   As a delivery man, WHAT are Mr. Grant's duties? (2)
W   He picks up merchandise in our warehouse in Scranton, makes sure that it gets to the customer, and prepares the paperwork on the delivery.
P   WHICH of your employees are authorized to prepare the paperwork? (3)
W   Only the delivery person in charge of that particular delivery. That's the employee who fills out the delivery report or sheet.
P   WHEN does the delivery person make out the report? (4)

W   He's supposed to make it out as soon as they make the delivery. At the very latest, they make it out when they get back to our office.

P   HOW often do your employees prepare these reports? (5)

W   Every time they make a delivery. I'd say that they send us 50 to 80 of those delivery sheets each week.

P   WHAT form does the report take? (6)

W   It's a standard, written report we call a Delivery Sheet. Like the one we have here, exhibit number three or whatever the number is.

P   WHY do you require that the delivery personnel prepare these reports? (7)

W   There are all sorts of business reasons for the reports — accounting, inventory, taxes. You just can't run an efficient, profitable business establishment unless you keep very, very close tabs on your deliveries.

P   WHAT does the delivery person do with the report after he prepares it?

W   He hands it to someone in our office.

P   WHAT does your office do with it?

W   We store it in a separate file, including all the Delivery Sheets for that week.

P   WHERE did you find plaintiff's exhibit number three for identification?

W   In the file for that week's Delivery Sheets.

P   WHEN did you remove it from that file?

W   Just this morning before trial.

P   Your Honor, I now offer plaintiff's exhibit number three for identification into evidence as plaintiff's exhibit number three.

O   Your Honor, I object to the exhibit's introduction on the ground that the exhibit is incompetent hearsay.

J   The objection will be overruled, and the exhibit will be received.

P   Mr. Merton, please read the circled part of the exhibit to the jury.

W   That part reads, "January 18 — delivered 500 stereo speakers to Hyatt Corp."

P   Your Honor, I request permission to submit the exhibit to the jurors for their personal inspection.

J   Permission granted.

E. OFFICIAL RECORDS

1. THE DOCTRINE

The second major documentary exception to the hearsay rule is the official record doctrine. Just as business employees presumably are careful in gathering and recording information for their employers, public employees presumably are diligent in gathering and recording information for their employer, the government. For this reason, the common law and the Federal Rules admit official records as well as business entries. Federal Evidence Rule 803(8) states the basic doctrine: "The following are not excluded by the hearsay rule, even though the declarant is available as a witness: Records, reports, statements, or data compilations, in any form, of public offices or agencies, setting forth (A) the activities of the office or agency, or (B) matters observed pursuant to duty imposed by law as to which matters there was a duty to report, or (C) in civil actions and proceedings and against the Government in criminal cases, factual findings resulting from an investigation made pursuant to authority granted by law, unless the sources of information or other circumstances indicate lack of trustworthiness."

Section D of Chapter 4 discusses the authentication of official records. As that section noted, the proponent of an official record rarely presents live, sponsoring testimony to authenticate the record. In most instances, live testimony is similarly unnecessary to lay the foundation for the official record exception to the hearsay rule. Two doctrines make the live testimony unnecessary. The first doctrine is judicial notice. The judge will ordinarily judicially notice the statute, regulation, or custom requiring that the public official prepare the record. Next, if the attested copy is fair on its face (complete with no erasures), the document's face creates a permissive inference that the officials followed the proper procedures in preparing the particular record.

2. ELEMENTS OF THE FOUNDATION

At common law, a complete foundation for the official record hearsay exception includes these elements:

1. The record was prepared at or near the time of the fact or event recorded. Some cases and statutes no longer explicitly require this element. Federal Evidence Rule 803(8) is illustrative; its language does not impose this requirement. In jurisdictions dispensing with this element, the only requirement is that the entry be properly prepared. If, long after the original event, the official discovers an error in the record and follows prescribed procedures for making a corrected entry, the corrected entry will qualify as an official record.
2. The record is in official custody.
3. The record is open to public inspection. The early, English cases impose this requirement. Many jurisdictions have dispensed with this element; in these jurisdictions, it is sufficient that the record is in official custody.
4. The record was properly prepared. The official must substantially comply with the procedures prescribed for the report's preparation.
5. The preparer was a public official.
6. The official had a duty to record the fact.
7. The official had personal knowledge of the fact.
8. The entry is factual in nature. Rule 803(8)(c) relaxes this requirement "in civil actions and proceedings against the Government in criminal cases...." That subsection allows the admission of "factual findings resulting from an investigation made pursuant to authority granted by law...." Some lower courts construed this

language as permitting the admission of findings about events even when the investigating officer lacked firsthand knowledge of the event. The Supreme Court adopted that construction in *Beech Aircraft Corp. v. Rainey*, 109 S. Ct. 439 (1988).

3. SAMPLE FOUNDATIONS

We shall first illustrate the admission of an official record without live testimony. The fact situation is a quiet title action. The plaintiff, Mr. Thelan, and the defendant, Mr. Garrett, both claim title to the same parcel of land in Miami, Florida. Both claim from the same grantor, but Mr. Thelan contends that he recorded his deed first. Mr. Thelan proposes to offer a properly attested copy of the recordation of the deed in the County Clerk's office. The plaintiff is the proponent.

P   Your Honor, I request that this be marked plaintiff's exhibit number four for identification.

J   It will be so marked.

P   Please let the record reflect that I am showing the exhibit to the opposing counsel.

J   It will so reflect.

P   I now offer plaintiff's exhibit number four for identification into evidence as plaintiff's exhibit number four.

O   Your Honor, I object to the introduction of the exhibit on the ground that the exhibit is hearsay.

P   Your Honor, may we approach the bench?

J   Yes.

O   Your Honor, this record is an assertive out-of-court statement, and the plaintiff is obviously going to use it for its truth, namely, the date of the recordation of his deed. The exhibit is incontestably hearsay.

P   That's true, but the record falls within the official record exception to the hearsay rule.

O   There's been no foundation for that exception. No sponsoring witness has come forward to lay the foundation.

P   Live testimony is unnecessary. Your Honor, you can judicially notice Civil Code section 1477 which requires the County Clerk to record deeds relating to land in the County. Moreover, the attached copy is fair on its face; it's complete, and there are no erasures or unexplained marks. The face of the document creates an inference that the public official properly carried out his duties.

J   I agree. The objection will be overruled, and the exhibit will be received.

P   Your Honor, I request permission to read the exhibit to the jury.

J   Permission granted.

P   Ladies and gentlemen, I am about to read this exhibit to you. The exhibit purports to be a Xerox copy of a page from the records of the Dade County Clerk. The exhibit reads, "Date of recordation — January 13, 1987, grantor — Paul A. Peterson, grantee — John D. Thelan, parcel number — 17,886." Your Honor, I now request permission to hand the exhibit to the jurors for their inspection.

J   Permission granted.

In the next hypothetical, we shall use live testimony. The plaintiff, Mr. Schmitt, has sued the defendant, the State of Missouri. Mr. Schmitt sustained personal injuries when his car left a Missouri highway and crashed. Mr. Schmitt alleges that the degree of slope in the curve where he lost control of his car was too sharp. His expert will testify that for that type of road, any slope greater than 17 degrees would represent negligent design and engineering. Mr. Schmitt wants to introduce a Missouri Department of Transportation report, listing the degree of slope on the curve as 19 degrees. Mr. Schmitt calls Mr. Justin as a witness. Mr. Justin has already identified himself. The plaintiff is the proponent.

P   WHAT is your educational background?
W   I have bachelor's and master's degrees in civil engineering from the University of Missouri.
P   WHERE do you work? (5)
W   I am a civil engineer for the Missouri Department of Transportation.
P   WHAT is the Department of Transportation? (5)
W   It's an official department of our state government.
P   HOW long have you worked there? (5)
W   The past seven years.
P   Your Honor, I request that this be marked plaintiff's exhibit number six for identification.
J   It will be so marked.
P   Please let the record reflect that I am showing the exhibit to the opposing counsel.
J   It will so reflect.
P   I request permission to approach the witness.
J   Permission granted.
P   Mr. Justin, I now hand you plaintiff's exhibit number six for identification. WHAT is it?
W   It's a report I prepared on the curve on Missouri Highway 10 seven-tenths of a mile south of the Columbia turnoff.
P   WHERE have you been this morning?
W   Right here in the courtroom.
P   WHAT stretch of road have the witnesses this morning been talking about?
W   The same curve I surveyed in this report.
P   WHEN did you make this survey? (1)
W   In early 1988.
P   WHY did you make the survey? (6)
W   The regional office decided to conduct a safety inspection of the area, and the local supervisor ordered me to do the field work.
P   WHO actually inspected the curve? (7)
W   I did personally.
P   WHO actually prepared the report? (7)
W   I did. Well, to be exact, I dictated it. A secretary typed it, and then I reviewed and signed it.
P   HOW long after the survey did you prepare the report? (1)
W   The very next day. I always follow that practice with surveys.

P   WHAT procedures are you supposed to follow in conducting this type of survey and preparing the report? (4)

W   The practice is that you both drive the road and walk it with appropriate surveying equipment. You take detailed notes and then have them immediately transcribed.

P   WHAT procedure did you actually follow? (4)

W   I did it by the book. As far as I know, I complied with all the required steps.

P   WHERE is this report ordinarily kept? (2)

W   In my office files at the Department's local office.

P   WHO can inspect the report? (3)

W   It's generally open to the public.

P   Your Honor, I now offer plaintiff's exhibit number six for identification into evidence as plaintiff's exhibit number six.

O   Your Honor, I object to the introduction of the exhibit on the ground that the exhibit is hearsay.

P   Your Honor, may we approach the bench?

J   Yes.

P   Your Honor, I concede that the exhibit is hearsay, but I submit that I've laid a complete foundation for the official record exception to the hearsay rule.

O   In general, that's true. However, an additional requirement is that the entry offered be factual. Page 10 of the report has a lot of conclusory opinions. I want to know whether the plaintiff's counsel intends to read that page to the jury.

J   (To the proponent) What is your intention?

P   I want the witness to read one of the measurements listed on page seven.

O   Very well, I have no objection to that.

J   Then the exhibit will be received, and you have permission to have the witness read that portion of page seven to the jury. I won't let the exhibit go to the jury because it contains inadmissible opinion.

P   Mr. Justin, please read the first measurement on page seven to the jurors.

W   The report reads, "While at the scene, I measured the slope of the curve. I determined the angle to be 19 degrees."

F. PAST RECOLLECTION RECORDED AND PRESENT RECOLLECTION REFRESHED OR REVIVED

1. PAST RECOLLECTION RECORDED

The next documentary hearsay exception is the past recollection recorded doctrine. Suppose that the witness on the stand cannot recall a particular fact or event. The witness' inability to recall supplies necessity for resorting to hearsay evidence. If at the time of the event, the witness had made a record of the fact or event, the record would be a reliable substitute for the witness' present recall. The recognition of this necessity and reliability led to the development of the past recollection recorded doctrine.

Federal Evidence Rule 803(5) states the doctrine succinctly: "A memorandum or record concerning a matter about which a witness once had knowledge but now has insufficient recollection to enable the witness to testify fully and accurately, shown to have been made or adopted by the witness when the matter was fresh in the witness' memory and to reflect that knowledge correctly."

If the proponent can show that the exhibit satisfies the doctrine, the real evidence is the document. In many jurisdictions, since the real evidence is the document, the judge formally admits the document and permits it to be submitted to the jury. Other courts take a different position. They reason that the document is the functional equivalent of oral testimony and that it would place undue emphasis on that evidence to permit the jury to examine the document. This reasoning partially persuaded the draftsmen of the Federal Rules of Evidence. Federal Rule 803(5) provides that "[i]f admitted, the ... record may be read into evidence but may not itself be received as an exhibit ...."

The foundation for this hearsay exception includes these elements:

1. The witness formerly gained personal knowledge of the fact or event recorded.

2. The witness subsequently prepared a record of the facts. All courts accept the foundation if the witness personally prepared the record. Most courts accept the record if a third party prepared it but the witness verified it while the events were still fresh in the witness' memory. Some courts also accept cooperative past recollection recorded; witness #1 gives an accurate oral report to witness #2, and witness #2 testifies that he or she accurately transcribed the oral report. The cooperative theory necessitates that both witnesses appear at trial and testify.

3. The witness prepared the record while the events were still fresh in his or her memory. The courts have interpreted Rule 803(5) as liberalizing this timing requirement. In *United States v. Patterson,* 678 F.2d 774 (9th Cir. 1982), the court found a declarant's memory sufficiently fresh despite a ten month time lapse.

4. The witness can vouch that when he or she prepared the record, the record was accurate. Ideally, the witness will recall the very occasion on which he or she prepared the document. Alternatively, the witness may testify that he or she habitually records that type of information and that their habit is to record the information carefully. A police officer assigned to the traffic detail could give that type of testimony about measurements at accident scenes. Finally, in some jurisdictions, it is acceptable if the witness at least recognizes his or her handwriting on the document. In this last situation, in reality the witness is vouching for his or her own honesty; they are really testifying that they are an honest person and would not knowingly record false data.

5. At trial, the witness cannot completely and accurately recall the facts even after reviewing the document. The early view was that the witness had to completely forget the event. Most modern courts are of the view that it is sufficient if the witness' memory is partial or hazy. In the words of Federal Rule 803(5), the witness cannot remember "fully and accurately."

On the one hand, Rule 803(5) can be interpreted as permitting the formal admission of the exhibit. On the other hand, the rule forbids physically submitting the exhibit to the jurors for their inspection. *Maggapinto v. Reichman,* 607 F.2d 621 (3d Cir. 1979) (construing similar language in Rule 803(18)).

Our fact situation is a bank robbery prosecution. The government charges that Mr. Gary Vincent robbed the First National Bank in downtown Phoenix. The witness is Ms. Jane Millot. Ms. Millot has already identified herself. She has testified that she works as a teller at the First National Bank. The prosecution is the proponent.

P   Ms. Millot, WHERE were you on the morning of February 14, 1989? (1)
W   I was at work at the bank.
P   WHAT happened that morning? (1)
W   The bank was robbed.
P   HOW were the robbers dressed? (1)
W   They all had masks on. That's why I can't identify any faces.
P   WHAT happened immediately after the robbers took the money? (1)
W   They made their getaway.
P   HOW did they make their getaway? (1)
W   In a white car parked in front of the bank.
P   WHAT was the car's license number? (1), (5)
W   I can't remember. I saw it, but I can't remember it now.
P   WHAT, if anything, might help you remember? (2)
W   I made a note on a slip of paper I had at the time.
P   WHAT did you note on this slip of paper? (2)
W   The license number of the getaway car.
P   WHO prepared this slip? (3)
W   I did it myself.
P   WHEN did you prepare this slip? (3)
W   Right after the car got away.
P   HOW many minutes passed between the time the car left and the time you wrote on the slip? (3)
W   One or two. Not any more than that. I had the slip of paper and a pen in the pocket of my dress.
P   HOW clear was your memory of the license number when you wrote the number down? (3), (4)
W   I don't remember making any mistakes. I looked at it carefully, and it seemed O.K. at the time.
P   Your Honor, I request that this be marked prosecution exhibit five for identification.
J   It will be so marked.
P   Please let the record reflect that I am showing the exhibit to the opposing counsel.

J   It will so reflect.
P   Ms. Millot, I now hand you prosecution exhibit five for identification. WHAT is it?
W   It's the slip of paper I mentioned.
P   HOW can you recognize it?
W   I recognize my handwriting.
P   Please read the exhibit silently to yourself. *(Pause.)* Have you done so?
W   Yes.
P   Now please hand it to me. *(The witness does so.)* Your Honor, please let the record reflect that I am holding the exhibit away from the witness and out of her view.
J   It will so reflect.
P   Ms. Millot, you've had a chance to read the exhibit and refresh your memory. Now, without relying on the exhibit, WHAT was the car's license number? (5)
W   I still can't remember apart from the exhibit.
P   WHY can't you remember? (5)
W   I have a bad memory for numbers. I can't honestly say that I now remember the license number.

In jurisdictions prohibiting the introduction of the exhibit:

P   Please read the slip of paper to the jury.
W   It reads, "USC 247."
P   WHAT does that stand for?
W   That's the license number of the getaway car.

In jurisdictions permitting the introduction of the exhibit:

P   Your Honor, I now offer prosecution exhibit number five for identification into evidence as prosecution exhibit five.
J   It will be received.
P   Ms. Millot, please read the exhibit to the jurors.
W   It reads, "USC 247."
P   WHAT does that stand for?
W   It's the license number of the getaway car.

2. PRESENT RECOLLECTION REFRESHED OR REVIVED

In past recollection recorded, even after viewing the document, the witness cannot recall the relevant fact or event. Suppose that viewing the document refreshed the witness' recollection. Then the witness may testify from his or her revived recollection. The courts use the expressions, "present recollection refreshed" or "present recollection revived" to describe the use of exhibits to refresh present memory. Under this theory, the real evidence is the witness' oral testimony, and the exhibit serves only as a memory aid or jogger. A few courts apply the foundational requirements for past recollection recorded to documents used to refresh recollection. However, most courts draw a clear distinction between the two doctrines and permit the proponent to use any document to refresh recollection. Some courts even broadly permit the proponent to use photographs or songs to revive a witness' memory.

Federal Rule of Evidence 612 governs this practice in federal courts: "Except as otherwise provided in criminal proceedings by section 3500 of title 18, United States Code (the Jencks Act), if a witness uses a writing to refresh memory for the purpose of testifying, either

—

(1) while testifying, or
(2) before testifying, if the court in its discretion determines it is necessary in the interests of justice,

an adverse party is entitled to have the writing produced at the hearing, to inspect it, to cross-examine the witness thereon, and to introduce in evidence those portions which relate to the testimony of the witness."

If the jurisdiction does not apply the past recollection recorded requirements to present recollection revived, the foundation for present recollection refreshed or revived is quite simple:

1. The witness states that he or she cannot recall a fact or event.
2. The witness states that a certain writing or object could help refresh his or her memory. Most jurisdictions do not require this showing as a formal element of the foundation, but many trial attorneys think that it is good practice to have the witness first mention the writing or object.
3. The proponent tenders the writing or object to the witness.
4. The proponent asks the witness to silently read the writing or study the object.
5. The witness states that viewing the document or object refreshes his or her memory.
6. The witness then testifies from revived memory.

On this theory, the evidence is the witness' oral testimony, and the proponent does not formally offer the writing or object into evidence. For purposes of making a good record, many trial judges prefer that the proponent at least mark the writing or object as an exhibit for identification.

We can use the same robbery hypothetical to illustrate present recollection refreshed. In this variation of the hypothetical, Ms. Millot has a better memory for numbers.

P   WHAT was the getaway car's license number? (1)
W   I can't honestly remember right now.
P   WHAT, if anything, might help you remember? (2)
W   I wrote the number down on a slip of paper.
P   Your Honor, I request that this be marked prosecution exhibit number five for identification.
J   It will be so marked.
P   Please let the record reflect that I am showing the exhibit to the opposing counsel.

J   It will so reflect.
P   I request permission to approach the witness.
J   Granted.
P   Ms. Millot, I now hand you prosecution exhibit number five for identi-
     fication. (3) WHAT is it? (2)
W   It's the slip of paper I mentioned.
P   HOW can you recognize it? (2)
W   I ought to know my own handwriting style.
P   Please read the exhibit silently to yourself. (4) *(Pause.)* Have you done
     so?
W   Yes.
P   Now hand it to me. *(The witness does so.)* Your Honor, please let the
     record reflect that I am holding the exhibit away from the witness and
     out of her view.
J   It will so reflect.
P   Ms. Millot, you've had a chance to read the exhibit to refresh your
     memory. Now without relying on the exhibit, can you remember the
     license number? (5)
W   Yes.
P   WHAT was the license number? (6)
W   USC 247.

Many experienced trial attorneys use this combination of past recollection recorded and present recollection refreshed. As soon as a witness states that he or she cannot recall a fact or event, the proponent
lays elements one through four of the past recollection recorded foundation. The proponent then tenders the writing to the witness in an
attempt to revive present recollection. If the attempt is successful, the
witness testifies from present, refreshed memory. If the attempt is
unsuccessful, the witness' inability to recall lays the last element of the
past recollection recorded foundation. Whichever response the witness
gives, the proponent elicits the desired testimony.

G. EXCITED OR STARTLED UTTERANCES

1. THE DOCTRINE

In the last three sections, we analyzed documentary hearsay exceptions resting primarily on a showing of reliability. In each case, the
showing is based on testimony describing the trustworthy manner in
which the document was generated. The next four sections address
other hearsay exceptions recognized principally because of an inference of reliability. In these exceptions, however, the inference of reliability has a different basis; each exception in this category is a variation of the old *res gestae* doctrine and rests on an inference of the
declarant's sincerity. This category includes excited utterances,
present sense impressions, declarations of bodily condition, and statements of mental condition.

The exception for excited utterances illustrates the common rationale of the exceptions in this category. A startling event occurs, an observer becomes excited, and the observer then makes a spontaneous statement about the event. The statement's spontaneity is the circumstantial guarantee of the declarant's sincerity. Federal Evidence Rule 803(2) describes the doctrine in this fashion: "The following are not excluded by the hearsay rule, even though the declarant is available as a witness: ... A statement relating to a startling event or condition made while the declarant was under the stress of excitement caused by the event or condition."

2. ELEMENTS OF THE FOUNDATION

The foundation for an excited utterance includes the following elements:

1. An event occurred. Most jurisdictions, including the federal courts, do not require any independent, corroborating evidence that the event occurred; these courts accept the declarant's assertion of the event's occurrence at face value. A minority of jurisdictions requires independent evidence as part of the foundation. However, even in these jurisdictions, the quantum of required corroboration is usually slight. For example, if the declaration refers to an assault on the declarant and, at the time, the declarant's clothing was dirty and disheveled, the declarant's appearance might be sufficient corroboration that the assault occurred.

2. The event was startling, or at least stressful. This element is the objective guarantee of the statement's sincerity. The nature of the event was likely to inspire nervous excitement.

3. The declarant had personal knowledge of the event. The declarant must have been a participant in or observer of the event. Again, the courts apply this element laxly. In some cases, the declarants have been unidentified bystanders. The courts have admitted the bystanders' excited statements so long as the time and place of the statement suggest that the bystander actually observed the event. Thus, if a person made a statement a few minutes after an accident and at the same intersection where the accident occurred, the court well might assume that the declarant observed the accident.

4. The declarant made a statement about the event. At the end of the foundational questioning, the proponent usually asks the witness whether the out-of-court declarant made a statement "about" the event. The federal courts seem to be relaxing this requirement. In *United States v. Napier*, 518 F.2d 316 (9th Cir. 1975), a kidnapping victim was injured and became unconscious. Weeks later she saw a newspaper article containing a photograph of the defendant. She immediately stated, "He killed me, he killed me."

The court admitted the statement as evidence of the defendant's identity as the kidnapper.

5. The declarant made the statement while he or she was in a state of nervous excitement. This element is the subjective guarantee of the statement's sincerity.

3. SAMPLE FOUNDATION

Our fact situation is a tort action arising from a collision at an intersection. The plaintiff was driving a blue car. The defendant was driving a red car. The issue is which car was facing and ran a red light. The plaintiff calls Mr. Reynolds as a witness. Mr. Reynolds has already identified himself. The plaintiff is the proponent.

P   WHERE were you on the afternoon of March 13, 1989? (1)
W   I was in downtown Jefferson City at the intersection of Cedar Street and Sixth Avenue.
P   WHY were you there? (1)
W   I just happened to be walking my dog.
P   WHAT, if anything, happened at the intersection while you were there? (1), (2)
W   There was a collision.
P   HOW noisy was the collision? (1), (2)
W   It was an awful, shattering sound.
P   HOW many bystanders were there? (1)
W   I'd say that there were about 20 people in the immediate vicinity.
P   WHAT was their reaction to the collision? (2)
W   We were all shocked. It happened so fast, and the noise was so loud. And as soon as we looked, we could see that some people were injured and bleeding. It was just an awful sight.
P   WHO else besides yourself was in the crowd of bystanders? (3)
W   There were a number of people mingling around, but there was one guy in particular who stuck in my mind.
P   WHAT was his name? (3)
W   I never got his name.
P   WHAT did he look like?
W   He was a male Caucasian, maybe 30 or 35.
P   WHERE was he at the time of the collision? (3)
W   Standing right next to me.
P   HOW was he facing? (3)
W   He was looking right into the intersection. He was evidently waiting for the light to change to walk across.
P   WHAT was his condition right after the collision? (5)
W   He was just like the rest of us — shocked and frightened.
P   WHAT was his facial expression? (5)
W   He had his mouth open — I guess he was dumbfounded at first.
P   WHAT was his tone of voice? (5)
W   He was shouting in a loud voice.
P   WHAT were his gestures? (5)
W   He was pointing at the wreck and gesturing wildly.
P   WHAT, if anything, did he say about the accident? (6)

O   Your Honor, I object to that question on the ground that it calls for hearsay.

P   Your Honor, may I be heard?

J   Yes.

P   Although the statement is hearsay, it pretty clearly falls within the excited utterance exception.

J   I agree. The objection will be overruled.

P   Mr. Reynolds, let me repeat the question. WHAT, if anything, did this man say about the accident? (4)

W   He said that the fellow in the red car had gone right through the red light and caused the collision.

H. PRESENT SENSE IMPRESSIONS OR CONTEMPORANEOUS STATEMENTS

1. THE DOCTRINE

The spontaneity of the statement is the basic rationale for the excited utterance exception. The statement's contemporaneity can also serve as proof of the declarant's sincerity; the fact that the declarant makes the statement at roughly the same time the event occurs is some evidence of the statement's reliability. A growing number of courts accept the contemporaneous statement or present sense impression doctrine as a separate hearsay exception. The federal courts joined ranks with those courts when Congress enacted Federal Evidence Rule 803(1): "The following are not excluded by the hearsay rule, even though the declarant is available as a witness: ... A statement describing or explaining an event or condition made while the declarant was perceiving the event or condition, or immediately thereafter."

The present sense impression doctrine differs from the excited utterance doctrine in three important respects. First, the timing requirement is more rigorous under the present sense impression doctrine. To qualify as a contemporaneous statement, the declaration must usually be made within minutes after the event. If the declarant is still excited or in pain, an excited utterance can be made hours after the event. Second, the event need not be startling to prompt a present sense impression statement. The guarantee of trustworthiness is contemporaneity rather than nervous spontaneity. Finally, in some jurisdictions such as California, contemporaneous statements are limited to statements describing or explaining the declarant's own conduct. A declarant may make an excited utterance about any startling, external event; but in a minority of jurisdictions, a present sense impression must relate to the declarant's own conduct. In these jurisdictions, the statement must describe, explain, or qualify the declarant's acts.

2. ELEMENTS OF THE FOUNDATION

The foundation for present sense impression includes these elements:

    1. An event occurred. As in the case of excited utterances, there is a

split of authority whether the proponent must present independent, corroborating evidence that the event occurred.
2. The declarant had personal knowledge of the event.
3. The declarant made the statement during or very shortly after
the event.
4. The statement relates to the event. As previously stated, a minority of jurisdictions follows a more restrictive approach. These jurisdictions insist that the declaration relate to the declarant's own
conduct.
5. In a minority of jurisdictions, the witness on the stand must have
observed the same event — the percipient witness limitation. This
element ensures that a witness is available to verify or contradict
the declaration. The modern statutes codifying the present sense
impression doctrine usually omit this requirement. For example,
the text of Federal Evidence Rule 803(1) makes no mention of this
requirement. However, some commentators have pointed out that
the Adversary Committee Note to Rule 803 cites many of the
older writings about the present sense impression doctrine advocating the percipient witness limitation.

3. SAMPLE FOUNDATION

To illustrate this doctrine, we can use the same hypothetical as in
Section G. In this variation of the hypothetical, the proponent deletes
the questions designed to show the declarant's nervous excitement.

P   WHERE were you on the afternoon of March 13, 1989? (1), (5)
W   I was in downtown Jefferson City at the intersection of Cedar Street
and Sixth Avenue.
P   WHY were you there? (1), (5)
W   I just happened to be walking my dog there.
P   WHAT, if anything, happened at the intersection while you were
there? (1), (5)
W   There was a collision.
P   HOW far were you from the collision when it occurred? (1), (5)
W   I was about 30 feet from the point of impact. That's just a rough esti-
mate.
P   HOW were you facing? (1), (5)
W   I was waiting for the light to change, so I was looking right into the
intersection.
P   HOW clear was your line of sight to the collision? (1), (5)
W   It was clear. I don't think there were any cars obstructing my view.
P   HOW much of the collision did you see? (1), (5)
W   Just about the whole thing. I saw the cars approaching the intersection
and actually collide.
P   HOW many other bystanders were there? (2)
W   I'd say that there were about 20 people in the immediate vicinity.
P   WHO were the bystanders? (2)

W   I didn't know any by name, but one guy in particular stuck in my mind.
P   WHAT did he look like? (2)
W   He was a male Caucasian, maybe 30 or 35.
P   WHERE was he at the time of the collision? (2)
W   He was standing right next to me.
P   HOW was he facing? (2)
W   He was looking right into the intersection. He was evidently waiting for the light to change to walk across.
P   WHAT did he do after the collision? (3)
W   He was pointing to the wreck, and we talked about the collision.
P   WHEN did you and this bystander talk about the collision? (3)
W   Right after it.
P   HOW many minutes elapsed between the collision and your discussion of the collision with this bystander? (3)
W   It may have taken us a minute or two to get over the shock of what we had witnessed, but it was no longer than that.
P   WHAT, if anything, did this bystander say about the accident? (4)
O   Your Honor, I object to that question on the ground that it calls for hearsay.
P   Your Honor, may I be heard?
J   Yes.
P   I will concede that the question calls for hearsay, but the record shows that any statement by the bystander qualifies as a present sense impression or contemporaneous statement.

In most jurisdictions

J   The objection will be overruled.
P   Mr. Reynolds, let me repeat the question. WHAT, if anything, did this bystander say about the accident? (4)
W   He said that the fellow in the red car had gone right through the red light and caused the collision.

In the minority of jurisdictions restricting present sense impressions to statements describing the declarant's own conduct

O   It's true that the statement was roughly contemporaneous with the event. However, as Your Honor knows, this jurisdiction limits present sense impressions to statements describing the declarant's own conduct. The bystander was describing an external event, the collision, rather than his own conduct.
J   Objection sustained.

I. DECLARATIONS OF STATE OF MIND OR EMOTION

1. OFFERED TO PROVE STATE OF MIND OR EMOTION

One of the most difficult things for a trial attorney to prove is a person's state of mind. The attorney must usually rely on circumstantial proof such as conduct which evidences a certain state of mind.

However, sometimes a person openly declares his or her state of mind. Because of the difficulty of proving state of mind, the courts have been especially eager to admit any evidently sincere declarations of state of mind or emotion. These declarations often give us the best insight into the declarant's state of mind or emotion. Thus, the courts have developed a general rule that these declarations are admissible; if a person declares his or her then existing state of mind or emotion, the declaration is admissible to prove the existence of that state of mind or emotion. Federal Evidence Rule 803(3) provides: "The following are not excluded by the hearsay rule, even though the declarant is available as a witness: ... A statement of the declarant's then existing state of mind (or) emotion ...."

Ideally, the declarant will make the statement at the pivotal time under the substantive law. For example, under Real Property law, the grantor must have the intent to pass title when he hands the deed to the grantee. If at the very instant he hands the deed to the grantee, the grantor states that he intends to pass title, the statement is certainly admissible. What if the grantor makes such a statement shortly before or shortly after the manual delivery of the deed? The courts still admit the statement on the theory of continuity of state of mind; the time lapse between the statement and the critical event is so short that we may assume that the declarant's state of mind was the same at both times.

The foundation for this doctrine is simple. The proponent need only establish the normal foundation for an event:

1. Where the statement was made.
2. When the statement was made. The declarant must make the statement at or near the pivotal time under the substantive law.
3. Who was present.
4. Who made the statement.
5. The tenor of the statement.

Our fact situation is a quiet title action. The plaintiff, Ms. Sheila Morris, has brought suit against the defendant, Ms. Marilyn Winters. Ms. Morris claims title from the original titleholder, Mr. Forest Morris, her grandfather. She claims that on December 25, 1988, her grandfather gave her a deed to the property as a Christmas present. The plaintiff calls Mr. Thomas Morris, her brother, as a witness. The plaintiff is the proponent.

P   WHERE were you on December 25, 1988? (1), (2)
W   I was at our family Christmas party at Camden.
P   WHO else was there? (3)
W   All the close relatives, including Grandfather and my sister, Sheila.
P   WHAT, if anything, unusual happened during the party?
W   As an unexpected Christmas gift, Grandfather handed Sheila a deed to our land in Vermont.

P   WHAT, if anything, did he do when he handed her the deed? (4)
W   Well, he did say something.
P   WHAT did he say? (5)
W   He said that he wanted her to have the land because, ever since she
     was a little girl, she had loved to vacation there.

In the next variation of the hypothetical, the grantor makes the
statement shortly before delivery of the deed.

P   WHERE were you on December 25th, 1988? (1), (2)
W   I was at our family Christmas party at Camden.
P   WHO else was there? (3)
W   All the close relatives, including Grandfather and my sister, Sheila.
P   WHAT, if anything, unusual happened during the party?
W   As an unexpected Christmas gift, Grandfather handed Sheila a deed to
     our land in Vermont.
P   WHAT, if anything, did he say about the deed during the party? (5)
O   Objection, Your Honor. That question calls for hearsay.
P   Your Honor, may we approach the bench?
J   Yes.
P   Your Honor, I offer to prove that the witness will say the grandfather
     said he wanted Sheila to have the land. The witness will also testify
     the grandfather made this statement only an hour before handing the
     deed to Sheila. The time lapse is so short that we may assume that the
     grandfather's state of mind was the same at both times.
J   The objection will be overruled.
P   Mr. Morris, let me repeat the question. WHAT, if anything, did your
     grandfather say about the deed during the party? (5)
W   He said he wanted Sheila to have the land because, ever since she was
     a little girl, she had loved to vacation there.
P   WHEN did your grandfather say that? (4)
W   A little while before he handed the deed to her.
P   Specifically, HOW many minutes or hours before he handed her the
     deed? (4)
W   About an hour — maybe a little less.

2. OFFERED TO PROVE SUBSEQUENT CONDUCT

In Subsection 1, we use declarations of state of mind when state of
mind itself is in issue. There is another use for state of mind declarations. Suppose that the declaration is a statement of present plan,
intention, or design: "I plan to ...," "I intend to ...," or "I am going to
...." These declarations indicate that the declarant currently plans to
engage in subsequent conduct. Moreover, the fact that the declarant
expressed that intent increases the probability that the declarant subsequently performed the planned act. Federal Evidence Rule 803(3)
also sanctions this use of state of mind declarations; it expressly authorizes the admission of statements of "intent, plan, ... (or) design ...."
The foundation is the same as in Subsection 1:
1. Where the statement was made.
2. When the statement was made.

3. Who was present.

4. Who made the statement.

5. The tenor of the statement.

The fact situation is a burglary prosecution. The government alleges that the defendant, Mr. Michael Waylen, burglarized a drug store in Tulsa on August 17, 1989. The defendant has raised an alibi defense. The defendant testified that he was with his girlfriend in Oklahoma City on the day of the burglary. His girlfriend testified to the same effect. Now the defendant calls Mr. John Farmer as a witness. Mr. Farmer has already identified himself. The defendant is the proponent:

P   Mr. Farmer, WHERE were you on the evening of August 15, 1989? (1), (2)

W   I was at a party at a friend's here in Tulsa.

P   WHO else was at the party?

W   A lot of people, including the defendant, Michael Waylen.

P   WHERE is the defendant now? (3)

W   He's in the courtroom.

P   Specifically, WHERE in the courtroom? (3)

W   He's sitting at that table.

P   HOW is he dressed? (3)

W   He's wearing a gray sweater and black pants.

P   Your Honor, please let the record reflect that the witness has identified the defendant.

J   It will so reflect.

P   Mr. Farmer, WHAT happened during the party? (4)

W   It was just a quiet party. I drank a little and talked with some friends.

P   WHOM did you talk with? (4)

W   I had a nice long talk with Michael, the defendant.

P   WHAT did you talk about? (5)

W   A lot of things, especially his plans for the future.

P   WHAT, if anything, did the defendant say about his immediate plans? (5)

O   Your Honor, I object to that last question on the ground that it calls for self-serving hearsay.

P   Your Honor, may we approach the bench to be heard?

J   Yes.

P   Your Honor, I offer to prove that the witness will testify that the defendant said he intended to visit his girlfriend in Oklahoma City the weekend of the alleged crime. The defendant's statement falls within the hearsay exception for declarations of present state of mind.

J   The objection will be overruled. You may proceed.

P   WHAT, if anything, did the defendant say about his immediate plans? (5)

W   He said that that weekend he was going to visit his girlfriend, Norma, in Oklahoma City.

P   WHICH weekend was he referring to? (5)

W   He mentioned the weekend of August 17 and 18.

Assume that a murder victim made a statement that she presently intended to meet the defendant at a particular location. Later the victim's body is found at that location. Under this exception, the victim's statement is certainly admissible to prove that she carried out her plan and went to that location. Is the statement also admissible as evidence that the defendant met her at that location? The courts have divided over that question. If the jurisdiction holds that the statement is inadmissible for that purpose, the judge must either redact the reference to the defendant or give the jury a limiting instruction about the proper use of the statement.

J. DECLARATIONS OF BODILY CONDITION

1. PRESENT BODILY CONDITION

The courts are almost as willing to admit evidently sincere statements of bodily condition as they are to admit statements of mental condition. Federal Rule 803(3) specifically authorizes the admission of statements of "pain and bodily health ...." Ordinarily, if a declarant proclaims his or her present bodily sensation or condition, the declaration is admissible. However, many courts exclude statements made to a physician who was consulted solely to qualify the physician to testify at trial.

The foundation includes these elements:

1. Where the statement was made.
2. When the statement was made.
3. Who was present.
4. Who made the statement.
5. Whom the statement was made to. The statement can be made to a lay person or a physician. The traditional, common-law view is that the statement may not be made to a physician consulted solely for purposes of trial testimony. However, the Federal Rules abandon that view.
6. The tenor of the statement. The statement must refer to the person's present bodily condition.

This fact situation will illustrate the doctrine. The plaintiff, Ms. Joan Gillette, brings a product liability action against Miller Pharmaceuticals. The plaintiff alleges that the defendant sold her defective medication and that the medication caused her serious internal injuries. Her complaint prayed for $5,000 for pain and suffering. At the trial, she called Mr. Leonard Wright as a witness. Mr. Wright identifies himself and states that he is a physician. The plaintiff is the proponent.

P   Doctor Wright, WHERE were you on the afternoon of January 28, 1989? (1), (2)

W   In my office.

P   WHO else was there? (3)

W   The plaintiff, Ms. Gillette.

P   WHERE is the plaintiff now? (3)

W   In this courtroom.

P   Specifically, WHERE in the courtroom? (3)

W   She's sitting at that table to your right.

P   HOW is she dressed? (3)

W   She's wearing a white blouse and a green skirt.

P   Your Honor, please let the record reflect that the witness identified the plaintiff.

J   It will so reflect.

P   WHAT happened while the plaintiff was at your office? (3)

W   I examined her.

P   WHAT, if anything, did she say to you about her physical condition during the examination? (4), (5), (6)

O   Your Honor, I object to that question on the ground that it calls for hearsay.

P   Your Honor, may we approach the bench?

J   Yes.

P   I concede that the question calls for hearsay. However, I offer to prove that the witness will testify that the plaintiff said she was then in terrible pain. That statement qualifies as a declaration of present bodily condition.

O   Your Honor, I request permission to take the witness on voir dire before you rule on my objection.

J   Permission granted.

O   Doctor Wright, ISN'T IT TRUE THAT you didn't give the plaintiff any medicine during this examination?

W   Yes.

O   ISN'T IT A FACT THAT the plaintiff never asked you for medication? (5)

W   Yes.

O   ISN'T IT TRUE THAT you never prescribed any treatment for her? (5)

W   Yes.

O   AND ISN'T IT CORRECT THAT the plaintiff told you that she was consulting you so that you could testify at this trial? (5)

W   Yes.

O   Your Honor, I renew my objection. It's clear that Dr. Wright is a physician consulted solely for purposes of testimony. The hearsay exception is inapplicable.

J   The objection will be sustained.

2. PAST BODILY CONDITION

A majority of jurisdictions now admit statements of past bodily condition as substantive proof in limited circumstances. The Federal Rules commit the federal courts to this view. Federal Evidence Rule 803(4) states: "The following are not excluded by the hearsay rule, even though the declarant is available as a witness: Statements made for purposes of medical diagnosis or treatment and describing the medical history, or past or present symptoms, pain, or sensations, or the inception or general character of the cause or external source thereof insofar as reasonably pertinent to diagnosis or treatment."

In the jurisdictions admitting declarations of past bodily condition, the foundation usually includes these elements:

1. The declarant made the statement to a proper addressee. Many jurisdictions limit this exception to statements made to physicians. The Federal Rules do not contain that limitation. The Advisory Committee's Note to Rule 803 states that the exception encompasses statements made to "hospital attendants, ambulance drivers, or even members of the family."

2. The declarant made the statement for a treatment motive. Most jurisdictions subscribing to this exception require that the declarant have a significant treatment motive; it is insufficient if the declarant is consulting a physician to testify at trial. The Federal Rules opt for a more liberal view. The Rules permit the statement's admission if the declarant sought "diagnosis or treatment." A diagnosis for purpose of trial is sufficient. The Advisory Committee Note expressly repudiates the "[c]onventional doctrine ... exclud(ing) from the hearsay exception, as not within its guarantee of truthfulness, statements to a physician consulted only for the purpose of enabling him to testify."

3. The subject-matter of the statement was proper. Most jurisdictions recognizing the exception limit its scope to statements of past bodily condition. Once again, the Federal Rules adopt a broader view. Rule 803(4) also authorizes the admission of statements of "the inception or general character of the cause or external source" of a physical condition. The Advisory Committee's Note contains this explanatory language: "Statements as to fault would not ordinarily qualify under this latter language. Thus a patient's statement that he was struck by an automobile would qualify but not his statement that the car was driven through a red light." Thus, a general reference to an external cause is admissible, but a statement specifically attributing fault to a person will probably be excluded.

Our fact situation is a personal injury action. The plaintiff, Ms. Norton, alleges that she sustained severe internal injuries after drinking some of the defendant's medicine. The defendant is Shaevers Drug Company. The plaintiff wants to introduce a hospital record. The record contains the following entry in section #15 Medical History: "The patient stated she experienced intense pain after drinking from a bottle of cough medicine." The plaintiff calls Mr. Florence as a witness. Mr. Florence identifies himself, states that he is University Hospital's records librarian, and lays a proper business entry foundation for the hospital record itself. The exhibit has already been marked for identification as plaintiff's exhibit number four. The plaintiff is the proponent.

P   Now, doctor, permit me to direct your attention to this section on exhibit #4 for identification, the section labeled #15. WHAT is that section?

W   That's the case history part of the patient's record.
P   WHAT is case history?
W   The patient's past medical history.
P   WHO took this medical history? (1)
W   Dr. Morrell, one of our internists.
P   HOW do you know he took it? (1)
W   I recognize his signature and handwriting style.
P   WHO normally takes the history? (1)
W   The intern.
P   WHEN does the intern ordinarily take the history from the patient? (2)
W   As soon as the patient arrives at the first processing station.
P   WHY does the intern take the history? (2)
W   It's often critical to diagnosis and treatment. The case history helps you make a much more informed evaluation of the patient's condition.
P   WHAT, if anything, does the intern usually tell the patient about the purpose of taking the case history? (2)
W   Some patients are very resentful of prying, and we always tell them that we are taking the history to give them better treatment. We tell them we need to know everything about their medical past.
P   Now, doctor, without disclosing to the jury the precise entry on the exhibit, WHY would this particular entry have been included in the patient's case history? (2)
W   Well, it describes how the patient suffered the injuries. The treating doctor has to have that sort of data to do a professional, competent job.
P   Your Honor, I now offer plaintiff's exhibit number four for identification into evidence as plaintiff's exhibit number four.
O   Your Honor, I object to the introduction of the exhibit on the ground that it is hearsay. In fact, it is double hearsay.
P   Your Honor, may we approach the bench?
J   Yes.
P   Your Honor, even double hearsay is admissible if each statement falls within a hearsay exception. The first statement, the hospital record itself, qualifies as a business entry.
J   Are we in agreement on that point?
O   Yes, Your Honor.
P   The second statement, of course, is my client's statement reflected in section #15 of the report. I feel that it qualifies as a statement of past bodily condition. My client made the statement to a physician for a treatment motive. In this jurisdiction, statements of past condition and external cause are admissible.
J   The objection will be overruled, and the exhibit will be received.
P   Doctor Florence, would you please read section #15 to the jury?
W   It reads: "The patient stated she experienced intense pain after drinking from a bottle of cough medicine." (3)

Part 4. Hearsay Exceptions Based on a Showing of Unavailability

The preceding seven sections analyze hearsay exceptions recognized primarily because of an inference of the reliability of the hearsay statement. Other exceptions, though, depend to a greater degree for their recognition on a showing of necessity for resorting to the hearsay.

These exceptions require proof of the declarant's unavailability at the time of trial. The following section discusses the test for unavailability in federal practice. Sections L through N then describe three hearsay exceptions requiring proof of unavailability as part of their foundation.

K. THE UNAVAILABILITY OF THE DECLARANT AT TRIAL

At common law, the exceptions requiring proof of unavailability emerged at different times and developed varying tests for unavailability. Some exceptions demanded proof of the declarant's death, while others were satisfied by proof that the declarant was beyond the reach of compulsory process. The drafters of the Federal Rules elected a single, uniform definition of unavailability. Federal Rule 804(a) sets out that definition:

"Unavailability as a witness" includes situations in which the declarant —

(1) is exempted by ruling of the court on the ground of privilege from testifying concerning the subject matter of the declarant's statement; or

(2) persists in refusing to testify concerning the subject matter of the declarant's statement despite an order of the court to do so; or

(3) testifies to a lack of memory of the subject matter of the declarant's statement; or

(4) is unable to be present or to testify at the hearing because of death or then existing physical or mental illness or infirmity; or

(5) is absent from the hearing and the proponent of statement has been unable to procure the declarant's attendance (or in the case of a hearsay exception under subdivision (b)(2), (3), or (4), the declarant's attendance or testimony) by process or other reasonable means.

A declarant is not unavailable as a witness if exemption, refusal, claim of lack of memory, inability, or absence is due to the procurement or wrongdoing of the proponent of a statement for the purpose of preventing the witness from attending or testifying.

Under Rule 804(a) there are numerous methods of demonstrating the prior witness' unavailability. In the first three subsections of Rule 804(a), the witness is technically unavailable but actually present at hearing #2. Under Rule 804(a)(1), the witness is deemed unavailable if the witness "is exempted by ruling of the court on the ground of privilege from testifying concerning the subject matter of the declarant's statement." The prior witness from hearing #1 actually takes the stand in hearing #2, but the witness properly refuses to testify on the ground of privilege. Under 804(a)(2), the witness is considered unavailable if he or she "persists in refusing to testify concerning the subject matter of the declarant's statement despite an order of the court to do so." Here the witness does not have a legitimate ground for refusing to answer; but if the witness refuses to answer notwithstanding a court order to answer, as a practical matter the witness is unavailable. Under Rule 804(a)(3), the witness is unavailable if the witness "testifies to a lack of memory of the subject matter of the declarant's statement." Here too the witness is physically present, but as a practical matter the witness' testimony is unavailable. When the proponent is relying on one of these three grounds to show unavailability, the proponent need ensure only that the witness' refusal or failure to recall is reflected on the record. The proponent should ask point blank about the topic of the prior testimony: "WHAT was the color of the defendant's car?" If the witness responds "I refuse to answer" or "I cannot remember," there is a sufficient showing of unavailability.

Rule 804(a)(4) declares that the prior witness is unavailable if the witness "is unable to be present or to testify at the hearing because of death or then existing physical or mental illness or infirmity." If the witness is now dead, the proponent may introduce a properly attested death certificate. The death certificate qualifies as an official record. If the witness is ill, under Rule 104(a), the jurisdiction may permit the proponent to prove the illness by a physician's affidavit, declaration, or letter. Otherwise the proponent may have to call the physician at hearing #2 to prove the illness of the prior witness. The proponent would have to lay the expert opinion testimony foundation outlined in Section C of Chapter 9: the physician's qualifications, the physician's major premise, the basis of the expert's opinion, the ultimate opinion that the former witness is now too ill to appear and testify, and the expert's explanation of the opinion. (Remember that in determining the existence of preliminary facts under Rule 104(a), the trial judge need not follow the technical exclusionary rules such as hearsay.)

Finally, Rule 804(a)(5) announces that the former witness is considered unavailable if the witness "is absent from the hearing and the proponent of a statement has been unable to procure the declarant's attendance ... by process or other reasonable means." This subsection applies in two situations.

The first situation is the case in which the proponent simply cannot locate the former witness. The proponent could use a process server's testimony to establish the former witness' unavailability.

P   WHAT is your name?
W   Michael Senet.
P   WHERE do you live?
W   At 1440 Alsworth Street here in Alexandria.
P   HOW long have you lived there?
W   For the past five years.
P   WHAT is your occupation?
W   I am a process server.
P   WHERE do you work?

W   I work for the Speedy Process Service Company downtown.

P   HOW long have you worked there?

W   Three years.

P   HOW long have you been a process server?

W   Three years.

P   Mr. Senet, WHERE were you on the morning of January 17th of this year?

W   I stopped by your office.

P   WHY did you visit my office?

W   You had phoned and asked me to pick up a subpoena.

P   WHO was the subpoena for?

W   John Milton.

P   WHAT was his address?

W   Both the subpoena and the telephone directory listed his address as 40 Oxford Street, Apartment 201.

P   WHAT did you do after you picked up the subpoena?

W   I went directly to the address given.

P   WHAT happened when you arrived there?

W   I inquired whether he still lived there.

P   WHAT was the result of your inquiry?

O   Your Honor, I object to that question on the ground that it calls for hearsay.

P   Your Honor, may we approach the bench?

J   Yes.

P   Your Honor, I offer to prove that this witness will testify that the manager said Mr. Milton had moved. I want to use the testimony for a nonhearsay purpose, its effect on the process server's state of mind. The issue is whether the process server acted reasonably and diligently. We have to judge his diligence in light of the information about Mr. Milton he was given by other persons such as the apartment manager.

J   The objection will be overruled.

P   Mr. Senet, let me repeat the question. WHAT was the result of your inquiry at Mr. Milton's apartment?

W   The manager said he had moved.

P   WHAT was Mr. Milton's new address?

W   Unfortunately, he did not leave a forwarding address.

P   WHAT did you do then?

W   Over the next few days I contacted other companies and agencies that might have Milton's new address.

P   WHICH companies and agencies did you contact?

W   To list just some, I talked to people at the telephone company, the gas company, the electricity company, and the welfare department.

P   WHAT was the result of your contact with these companies and agencies?

W   It was negative. None of them knew where I could locate Mr. Milton.

P   HOW many hours did you spend talking to people at these companies and agencies?

W   Over the period of days, I'd estimate I spent at least ten full hours trying to hunt him down.

P   Mr. Senet, WHERE is Mr. Milton now?

W   I'm afraid that I have no idea.

The second situation is the case in which the former witness is in another jurisdiction. In some states, it is sufficient to show that the former witness is now beyond the reach of compulsory process. In the case of dying declarations and declarations against interest, the proponent must not only show that there was no compulsory process to compel the declarant's attendance at trial; the proponent must also show that he or she could not depose the deponent before trial. At hearing #2, the judge can, of course, judicially notice the constitutional and statutory provisions setting out the territorial limits of the court's compulsory process. In other states, the proponent must show not only that the former witness is now beyond the reach of compulsory process; the proponent must also show that the proponent unsuccessfully attempted to persuade the former witness to voluntarily attend hearing #2 or that any attempt would probably be futile. Federal Rule 804(a)(5) expressly requires the proponent to attempt to use "other reasonable means."

Suppose that Mr. Watson has sued Ms. Belson for personal injuries resulting from a traffic accident. At the first trial of the case, Mr. Green testified on behalf of the plaintiff. Mr. Green was a passing acquaintance of the plaintiff and happened to be in the plaintiff's car at the time of the accident. The trial resulted in a judgment for plaintiff, but the defendant appealed. After the trial, Mr. Green moved from California to Minnesota. On appeal, the court reversed the judgment and remanded for a second trial. At trial #2, the plaintiff wants to use Mr. Green's former testimony. The plaintiff himself takes the stand to establish Mr. Green's unavailability.

P   WHO were your witnesses at the first trial in this case?
W   Myself, Officer Halston, and a Mr. Ted Green.
P   WHERE does Mr. Green live now?
W   In St. Paul, Minnesota.
P   HOW do you know that?
W   For one thing, I've received letters from him postmarked St. Paul, Minnesota.
P   HOW do you know the letters came from Mr. Green?
W   I recognized his handwriting.
P   HOW did you recognize his handwriting?
W   I'm familiar with it. We worked together for several years, and I saw his handwriting on numerous occasions.
P   WHY else do you think he now lives in Minnesota?
W   I tried to contact him by telephone. I went through the operator in St. Paul and eventually reached him.
P   HOW do you know you were speaking with Mr. Green?
W   I recognized his voice just as I recognized his handwriting.
P   WHERE is Mr. Green today?
W   I don't know for sure.
P   WHERE was he when you last spoke with him?
W   In St. Paul.
P   WHY isn't he here?

W   He refused to come.
P   HOW do you know that?
W   I asked him to come during our last telephone conversation, and he said he was too tied up with his business to come.
P   WHAT efforts have you made to persuade him to attend this trial?
W   I phoned him several times. I even volunteered to pick up the tab for his airline ticket. He just won't cooperate.

L. DECLARATIONS AGAINST INTEREST

1. THE DOCTRINE

Admissions of a party-opponent are disserving to the declarant's interest at the time of trial; the admission is inconsistent with some position the party-opponent is defending at the time of trial. So long as the statement is disserving at that time, it is admissible even if it was highly self-serving when made. Declarations against interest contrast with admissions in several respects. Declarations against interest are admissible only if at the time of the statement, the declarant believed the statement was contrary to his or her interest. The declarant's belief is the guarantee of the reliability of declarations against interest. Moreover, declarations against interest are admissible only if at the time of trial, the declarant is unavailable. The declarant's unavailability supplies the necessity for resorting to the hearsay. In the case of admissions, the party-opponent is usually available and present at trial. Finally, the declarant of an admission must be the party-opponent while any person can make a declaration against interest.

Federal Rule 804(b)(3) states the doctrine: "The following are not excluded by the hearsay rule if the declarant is unavailable as a witness: A statement which was at the time of its making so far contrary to the declarant's pecuniary or proprietary interest, or so far tended to subject the declarant to civil or criminal liability, or to render invalid a claim by the declarant against another, that a reasonable person in the declarant's position would not have made the statement unless believing it to be true."

2. ELEMENTS OF THE FOUNDATION

The foundation for this hearsay exception includes the following elements:

1. The declarant subjectively believed that the statement was contrary to his or her interest. Even at common law, the belief of the hypothetical, reasonable person could be used as circumstantial evidence of the subjective belief of the declarant. On its face, Federal Rule 804(b)(3) refers only to the objective reasonableness test; and some federal courts have read the statute literally.
2. The interest was a recognized type of interest. All jurisdictions recognize pecuniary and proprietary interest, and most jurisdic-

tions have expanded those categories to admit any statement that would subject the declarant to civil liability. Most jurisdictions now recognize penal interest, and roughly a fourth of the states admit statements contrary to social interest.

3. The declarant is unavailable at the time of trial.

4. In some jurisdictions, if the defense offers a third party's confession to the crime the defendant is charged with on the theory that the confession is a declaration against interest, there must be corroboration that the third party committed the crime. As Federal Evidence Rule 803(b)(3) declares, "A statement tending to expose the declarant to criminal liability and offered to exculpate the accused is not admissible unless corroborating circumstances clearly indicate the trustworthiness of the statement." To eliminate a potential equal protection challenge to the statute, one court has read in the same corroboration requirement when the prosecution offers a declaration against interest against a defendant.

3. SAMPLE FOUNDATION

Our fact situation is a robbery prosecution. The government alleges that the defendant, Mr. Charles Bosley, robbed the Midland Stereo Store in New Orleans on February 17, 1989. The defense theory is that Mr. Gregory Bennett actually committed the robbery. During the defense case-in-chief, the defense called Bennett to the stand. Bennett refused to answer any questions about the robbery. His refusal would render him "unavailable" in most jurisdictions. As his next witness, the defendant calls Mr. William Store. Mr. Store has already identified himself. The defendant is the proponent.

P   WHAT is your occupation?
W   I am a member of the New Orleans Police Department.
P   HOW long have you held that position?
W   For about eight years.
P   WHERE were you on the morning of February 19, 1989?
W   I was on duty at the Dupont Street station.
P   WHAT happened while you were on duty that morning?
W   Some patrolmen brought in a suspect for questioning.
P   WHO was the suspect?
W   A Gregory Bennett.
P   WHEN was the last time you saw Mr. Bennett?
W   A few moments ago.
P   WHERE was he then?
W   He was on the witness stand. He's the witness who just left the stand.
P   WHAT happened after the patrolmen brought in Mr. Bennett?
W   As is my custom, I first informed him of his rights.
P   WHAT rights did you tell him about? (1), (2)
W   I told him he had a privilege against self-incrimination and a right to counsel.

P WHAT was his condition when you informed him of his rights? (1)

W He seemed O.K. He was alert, and there didn't seem to be anything physically wrong with him.

P HOW did he react when you informed him of his rights? (1)

W He seemed concerned.

P WHAT did you do after you informed Mr. Bennett of his rights? (1)

W I asked him if he understood his rights.

P HOW did he respond? (1)

W He said he understood them, and then he gave me some factual information I wanted.

P WHAT did you do after you spoke with Mr. Bennett? (4)

W I attempted to verify some of the facts Mr. Bennett had told me.

P WHAT facts? (4)

W He told me about the location of some of the stolen property, some receivers and speakers.

P WHAT did Mr. Bennett say about the location of the stolen property? (4)

W He said that several of the stolen receivers and speakers were in his apartment.

P WHAT steps did you take to verify his statement? (4)

W With his consent, I visited and searched his apartment.

P WHAT did you find in his apartment? (4)

W I found his personal effects. In addition, I found several receivers and speakers. I checked the serial numbers against the list supplied by Midland Stereo. The numbers matched.

P Mr. Store, during your questioning of Mr. Bennett, WHO did he say robbed the Midland Stereo Store on February 17, 1989?

O Your Honor, I object to that question on the ground that it calls for hearsay.

P Your Honor, may we approach the bench?

J Yes.

P Your Honor, I offer to prove that the witness will testify that Mr. Bennett confessed to the robbery my client is charged with. In light of the warnings Officer Store gave Bennett, Bennett must have realized his confession was contrary to his penal interest. There is corroboration that Bennett was involved in the robbery; some of the stolen property was found in his apartment. Finally, Bennett's refusal to answer makes him unavailable.

J The objection will be overruled.

P Officer Store, let me repeat the question. WHO did Mr. Bennett say robbed the Midland Stereo Store?

W He said that he did.

M. DYING DECLARATIONS

1. THE DOCTRINE

Another type of evidently sincere statement that is exceptionally admissible is a dying declaration. At early common law, the courts admitted the decedent's dying declarations in homicide prosecutions. The courts reasoned that there was a peculiar need for dying declarations in homicide prosecutions; the courts feared that if they excluded the victim's dying declaration, the murderer might go free. The circumstantial guarantee of the trustworthiness of dying declarations is the declarant's sense of impending death; at the point of death, the declarant should not have any reason to lie, and there is the theistic belief that the decedent will not want to face the Creator with a last lie on his or her lips. At common law, the necessity for admitting the hearsay is that at the time of trial, the declarant was dead.

The most arbitrary limitation on the common-law doctrine was its restriction to homicide prosecutions. Some jurisdictions now admit dying declarations in any type of criminal prosecution. Other jurisdictions admit such declarations in any type of case, civil or criminal. Congress decided to adopt a compromise view. When it enacted Federal Evidence Rule 804(b)(2), Congress declared that "[T]he following are not excluded by the hearsay rule if the declarant is unavailable as a witness: ... In a prosecution for homicide or in a civil action or proceeding, a statement made by a declarant while believing that the declarant's death was imminent, concerning the cause or circumstances of what the declarant believed to be [his or her] impending death." The most radical aspect of the Federal Rule is its abandonment of the requirement that the declarant be dead at the time of trial. The Federal Rule requires that at the time of trial, the declarant be "unavailable," as that term is defined in Rule 804(a). However, it is no longer necessary to prove the declarant's subsequent death.

2. ELEMENTS OF THE FOUNDATION

The common-law doctrine included the following foundational elements:

1. The case is a prosecution for homicide or a crime including homicide as an element. As we previously noted, many jurisdictions now admit dying declarations in other criminal prosecutions and civil actions. To determine whether this element is present, the trial judge looks to the indictment, information, or complaint; the charging pleading specifies the offense the defendant is on trial for.

2. The declarant is the victim named in the charging pleading. The witness must identify the declarant. The trial judge then examines the charging pleading to determine whether the declarant is the named victim. The consequence of this rule was that a declaration by decedent #2 was inadmissible in a prosecution for killing decedent #1 even if the defendant killed them at the same time and by the same blow. Many jurisdictions, including the federal courts, have abandoned this requirement.

3. At the time of the statement, the declarant had a sense of impending death. The declarant had abandoned all hope and concluded that certain death was imminent. The declarant sometimes voices

his or her belief. The proponent may rely on such circumstances as the nature of wound, the administration of last rites, and statements made by third parties to the declarant.

4. At the time of trial, the declarant is dead. Under the Federal Rules, it is sufficient if the declarant is unavailable.

5. The statement relates to the event inducing the declarant's dying condition. The proponent usually asks "about" the cause of death. The statement may not describe previous quarrels or fights between the declarant and the defendant.

6. The statement is factual in nature. The early common law limited dying declarations to statements of observed fact. Modernly, the courts have relaxed the application of the opinion prohibition to dying declarations. The courts now admit conclusory statements such as the defendant killed the declarant "intentionally" or "without provocation."

3. SAMPLE FOUNDATION

The fact situation is a homicide prosecution. The indictment alleges that the defendant, Mr. James Ireland, murdered Ms. Grace Shafer. The indictment thus supplies the first element of the foundation. The prosecution calls Mr. William Turner as a witness. Mr. Turner has already identified himself. The prosecutor is the proponent.

P   Mr. Turner, WHAT is your occupation?
W   I am a physician.
P   WHERE are you licensed to practice medicine?
W   In three states, including here in New Hampshire.
P   WHERE were you on the morning of February 22, 1989?
W   I was in my office.
P   WHAT happened that morning?
W   I received an emergency call.
P   WHAT was the nature of the call?
W   Someone was hurt very badly, and they needed immediate medical attention.
P   WHAT did you do after you received this call?
W   I jumped in my car and drove to 1444 Garnet Street.
P   WHAT did you find there?
W   I found several police surrounding a very badly injured person.
P   WHO was that person? (2)
W   A Ms. Grace Shafer.
P   HOW do you know that? (2)
W   She identified herself, and I also checked the ID that she had in her purse.
P   WHAT condition was she in? (3)
W   Very bad. She had several stab wounds.
P   HOW many stab wounds? (3)
W   Five in her chest.
P   HOW deep were the wounds? (3)
W   Some were several inches deep.

P   HOW much blood was she losing? (3)
W   She was bleeding profusely.
P   WHERE was she bleeding? (3)
W   All over the chest area.
P   WHAT did you do after you discovered these wounds? (3)
W   I helped her as best I could; and when I realized that she was dying, I tried to make her as comfortable as possible.
P   WHAT, if anything, did you tell her about her condition? (3)
O   Your Honor, I object to that question on the ground that it calls for hearsay.
P   Your Honor, may we approach the bench?
J   Yes.
P   Your Honor, I offer to prove that the witness will testify he told Ms. Shafer that she was dying. I want to use that statement for a nonhearsay purpose, namely, to show its effect on her state of mind. His statement helped produce a sense of imminent death in her mind. That is part of the foundation for the dying declaration I ultimately want to offer.
J   The objection will be overruled.
P   Doctor Turner, let me repeat the question. WHAT, if anything, did you tell Ms. Shafer about her condition? (3)
W   I was honest with her. She asked, and I told her she was dying.
P   HOW did she respond? (3)
W   She looked frightened. Then she sighed very deeply.
P   WHAT happened then? (3)
W   She asked that I contact a Catholic priest. She said that she wanted to receive the last rites of her church before she died.
P   WHAT happened then? (3)
W   The priest arrived and administered the sacrament. Then the priest and I accompanied her to the hospital.
P   Doctor, WHERE is Ms. Shafer now? (4)
W   She's dead.
P   HOW do you know that? (4)
W   She died in the ambulance on the way to the hospital.
P   WHAT, if anything, did she say about the cause of her death before she died? (5), (6)
W   She said someone had stabbed her with an ice pick.
P   WHO did she say stabbed her? (5), (6)
W   She said it was Jim Ireland.

N. FORMER OR PRIOR TESTIMONY

1. THE DOCTRINE

The next exception we shall consider is former testimony. As we noted in Section A of this chapter, the primary rationale for the hearsay rule is that opponent has not had an opportunity to test the hearsay by cross-examination. What if the opponent had an opportunity to test the hearsay by cross-examination in a prior trial? Does that opportunity satisfy the hearsay rule and justify admitting the prior testimony in the present proceeding? Most courts have answered that question in the affirmative.

Federal Rule of Evidence 804(b)(1) states the doctrine: "The following are not excluded by the hearsay rule if the declarant is unavailable as a witness: Testimony given as a witness at another hearing of the same or a different proceeding, or in a deposition taken in compliance with law in the course of the same or another proceeding, if the party against whom the testimony is now offered, or in a civil action or proceeding, a predecessor in interest, had an opportunity and similar motive to develop the testimony by direct, cross, or redirect examination."

The most controversial aspect of the doctrine has proven to be the requirement that the parties to the two hearings be identical. Early common law insisted upon complete identity of parties; the parties to hearing #2 were parties to hearing #1, and there were no additional parties at either hearing. The common law quickly realized that the complete identity requirement was unnecessarily strict; so long as the present parties were parties to hearing #1, the courts generally concluded it was immaterial that there were additional parties to either hearing.

The courts then developed the modern "same party" view: The prior testimony is admissible *against* a party to hearing #2 if that party was a party to hearing #1. The courts focus on the party the testimony is now offered against, and they inquire whether that party had a fair opportunity to develop the facts at hearing #1 by direct or cross-examination. If the opponent had a fair opportunity to do so, it should not make any difference that the present proponent of the former testimony was not a party to hearing #1. The opponent had a prior opportunity to test the evidence, and that opportunity satisfies the purpose of the hearsay rule. Suppose that several passengers are injured when an airplane crashes during landing. In hearing #1, passenger A sues the airline and introduces the testimony of a safety engineer. During hearing #1, the airline can test and attack the engineer's testimony. Subsequently passenger B sues the airline. If the engineer dies prior to hearing #2, passenger B may use the record of the engineer's prior testimony against the airline. The "same party" view is the prevailing view in contemporary criminal cases.

In civil cases, most jurisdictions also recognize the "privity" view. Once again, the court begins its analysis by focusing on the party the testimony is now offered against. However, in the next step of analysis the court poses this question: Was the party the evidence is now offered against a party to hearing #1 *or* in technical privity with a party to hearing #1? The testimony is admissible against the party in hearing #2 if that party was a party to hearing #1 or in technical privity with a party to hearing #1. Since Federal Rule 804(b)(1) uses the expression "predecessor in interest," some courts have construed the rule as codifying the "privity" view for civil cases.

Some courts and legislatures have taken a step beyond the "same party" and "privity" views; they recognize the "similar party" view. They still begin their analysis by focusing on the party to hearing #2 that the former testimony is offered against. However, they then pose a different question. Under the prevailing view, the pivotal question is whether that party had an opportunity in hearing #1 to probe the testimony. Under this new view, the question is whether there was *a* party to hearing #1 who had a similar motive to probe the testimony. The present opponent need not have had that opportunity; it is sufficient if there was a similarly situated party, a party with a motive and interest similar to that of the present opponent. To illustrate this view, we can revisit the last hypothetical. Suppose that in hearing #1, the airline had offered the testimony of a safety engineer against passenger A. The engineer dies before passenger B sues. Under this new view, at hearing #2 between passenger B and the same airline, the airline could use the engineer's testimony against passenger B. It is true that passenger B was not a party to hearing #1. However, passenger A was a party, and the two plaintiffs' motive and interest are sufficiently similar. We can assume with fair assurance that passenger A attacked the engineer's testimony as vigorously as passenger B would have. This new view is still a distinct minority position, applied in only civil cases.

2. ELEMENTS OF THE FOUNDATION

1. Hearing #1 was a fair, adversary hearing.
    a. The witness testified under oath.
    b. The opponent had an opportunity to cross-examine the witness.
    c. If the hearing was a critical stage in a criminal prosecution, the defendant was afforded the right to counsel.
2. There is substantial identity of issues between the two hearings.
3. There is substantial identity of parties between the two hearings. Subsection 1, *supra,* describes the split of authority on the test for substantial identity of parties.
4. At hearing #2, the witness is unavailable.

In many cases, the proponent will need two witnesses. One witness will establish the unavailability of the prior witness. The second witness will then describe the prior witness' testimony. The second witness may have been a spectator at hearing #1 who simply remembers the substance of the prior testimony; the witness need not be able to recite the testimony verbatim. Or the second witness may be the court reporter who describes the testimony with or without relying on notes. Finally, the proponent may entirely dispense with live testimony if the jurisdiction permits the authentication of the documentary record of hearing #1 by the court reporter's attesting certificate. In such a jurisdiction, the transcript is self-authenticating. The judge examines the transcript to determine whether the foundational elements are present.

3. SAMPLE FOUNDATION

Assume that the proponent has already established the declarant's unavailability. In the following hypotheticals, the proponent is laying the other elements of the foundation.

We shall first illustrate the testimony of a spectator who happens to remember the substance of the witness' testimony at hearing #1. Our fact situation is a homicide prosecution. The government charges that Mr. John Gentile murdered his wife. An eyewitness to the killing, Mr. John Walton, testified at the preliminary hearing. Walton died after the hearing and before the trial. The prosecution has already proven Walton's unavailability by introducing a properly attested death certificate. Now the prosecutor calls Ms. Pamela Martin to lay the other elements of the foundation. The prosecutor is the proponent. Ms. Martin has already identified herself.

P   Ms. Martin, WHERE were you on the afternoon of March 12, 1989?
W   I was in another courtroom in this building.
P   WHAT were you doing there?
W   I was a spectator at a court proceeding.
P   WHY were you there?
W   I had read a lot about the case in the papers, and I was interested in watching it.
P   WHAT proceeding did you see the afternoon of March 12, 1989? (2), (3)
W   It was the preliminary hearing in this case.
P   WHO was there attending the hearing? (3)
W   For one, the defendant himself, Mr. Gentile.
P   WHERE is Mr. Gentile now? (3)
W   He's in the courtroom right now.
P   Specifically, WHERE in the courtroom? (3)
W   Over there at the end of that table.
P   HOW is he dressed? (3)
W   He's wearing a blue suit, white shirt, and red tie.
P   Your Honor, please let the record reflect that the witness has identified the defendant.
J   It will so reflect.
P   WHAT happened at this hearing you attended on March 12th? (1)
W   They called witnesses to testify.
P   WHAT did they do when they first called the witnesses to the stand? (1a)
W   They would swear them.
P   WHO questioned the witnesses? (1b)
W   Usually the prosecutor would start, and then the defense counsel would ask questions.
P   WHO asked questions on behalf of the defendant? (1c)
W   An attorney. I honestly can't remember her name.
P   WHO were the witnesses that day?

W   There were three who stand out in my mind.
P   WHO were they?
W   A police officer named Strait, a doctor, and an eyewitness. The eyewitness was on the stand most of the day.
P   WHO was the eyewitness?
W   His name was John Walton.
P   HOW long was he on the stand?
W   About three hours.
P   HOW much of his testimony did you hear?
W   All of it.
P   HOW often did you leave the room while he was on the stand?
W   I didn't. I wanted to hear all of it. It was really exciting.
P   HOW well could you hear Mr. Walton while he testified?
W   Very well. I didn't have any problem hearing him.
P   HOW loudly was he speaking?
W   In a normal voice, but his voice carried well.
P   HOW close were you sitting to him while he was on the stand?
W   About 15 feet away. I was in the very first row for the spectators.
P   HOW well do you remember his testimony?
W   Very well. I was really enthralled. As I said, it was real exciting.
P   WHAT did he say during his testimony?
O   Your Honor, I object to that question on the ground that it calls for hearsay.
P   Your Honor, may we approach the bench?
J   Yes.
P   Your Honor, I concede that the testimony will be hearsay. However, it falls within the former testimony exception. The witness' testimony shows that there was oath, cross-examination, and counsel at the preliminary hearing. Since it was the preliminary hearing in this case, there's obviously identity of issues and parties. Finally, the death certificate shows that the former witness is now unavailable.
J   The objection will be overruled.
P   Ms. Martin, let me repeat the question. WHAT did Mr. Walton say during his testimony?

The proponent should now elicit all the important facts Walton previously testified to.

We shall now illustrate the use of a properly attested or certified transcript of the former testimony. To do so, we shall continue the same hypothetical. In this variation of the hypothetical, there is a documentary transcript of the preliminary hearing. We shall assume that the rule in this jurisdiction is that if the court reporter attaches a proper certificate to the transcript, the transcript is self-authenticating. Again, please assume that the prosecutor has already introduced Mr. Walton's death certificate.

P   Your Honor, I request that this be marked prosecution exhibit seven for identification.
J   It will be so marked.
P   Please let the record reflect that I am showing the exhibit to the opposing counsel.

J   It will so reflect.

P   I now offer prosecution exhibit number seven for identification into evidence as prosecution exhibit seven.

O   Your Honor, I object to the introduction of the exhibit on the ground that the exhibit is hearsay.

P   Your Honor, may we approach the bench?

J   Yes.

P   Your Honor, I concede that the exhibit is hearsay; but it is a properly certified transcript, and it falls within the former testimony exception.

O   Where is the foundation for the former testimony exception?

P   The transcript purports to be the record of the preliminary hearing in this case; there is obviously identity of issues and parties. I've already introduced Mr. Walton's death certificate, showing his unavailability. Page 2 of the transcript shows that the defendant had counsel at the hearing, page 16 shows that Mr. Walton was sworn before he testified, and page 142 shows that the defense had an opportunity to cross-examine Mr. Walton.

J   I agree. The objection will be overruled, and the exhibit will be received.

P   Your Honor, I request permission to read pages 22-53 to the jurors. I shall read the questions, and my clerk will take the witness stand and read the answers.

J   Permission granted.

Part 5. The Residual Hearsay Exceptions Based on Showings of Reliability and Necessity

O. THE RESIDUAL HEARSAY EXCEPTIONS

1. THE DOCTRINE

The list of hearsay exemptions and exceptions in Sections B-N of this chapter is incomplete. In the first place, the Federal Rules enumerate other hearsay exceptions. For example, Rules 803(13) and 804(b)(4) create exceptions for certain statements about family history. Rules 803(14)-(15) set out exceptions relating to documents affecting property interests. Rule 803(16) recognizes an exception for ancient documents, 803(17) another exception for market reports, and 803(22) still another exception for judgments.

However, the list is incomplete in a second, more fundamental sense. The Rules explicitly confer residual discretion on the trial judge to admit hearsay that falls outside the enumerated exceptions. The discretion is granted in Rules 803(24) and 804(b)(5). Rule 803(24) reads:

The following are not excluded by the hearsay rule, even though the declarant is available as a witness:

(24) Other exceptions. — A statement not specifically covered by any of the foregoing exceptions but having equivalent circumstantial guarantees of trustworthiness, if the court determines that (A) the statement is offered as evidence of a material fact;

(B) the statement is more probative on the point for which it is offered than any other evidence which the proponent can procure through reasonable efforts; and (C) the general purposes of these rules and the interests of justice will best be served by admission of the statement into evidence. However, a statement may not be admitted under this exception unless the proponent of it makes known to the adverse party sufficiently in advance of trial or hearing to provide the adverse party with a fair opportunity to prepare to meet it, the proponent's intention to offer the statement and the particulars of it, including the name and address of the declarant.

During the mid 1970's and early 1980's, most courts applied the residual exceptions conservatively. However, since the mid 1980's, the courts have been more receptive to invocations of the residual exceptions. One of the battlegrounds has been the admissibility of transcripts of the grand jury testimony of deceased witnesses. Since even the target of the grand jury investigation does not have a right to cross-examine at the hearing, the grand jury testimony cannot be admitted as former testimony under Rule 804(b)(1). If the testimony is going to be admitted, it must be introduced, if at all, under 804(b)(5). There are now several decisions admitting grand jury testimony on that theory.

2. ELEMENTS OF THE FOUNDATION

Under the residual exceptions, the proponent must lay the following foundation:

1. The proponent gave the opposition adequate, advance notice of the tenor of the hearsay statement and the proponent's intention to offer the statement at trial.

2. The statement was reliable. It is ideal if the proponent shows that there was little possibility of insincerity or of error in the declarant's perception, memory, or narrative ability. The courts tend to place the greatest stress on the factor of the declarant's sincerity; if there is a common sense reason to believe that the declarant was speaking sincerely, that factor cuts strongly in favor of admitting the statement. The proponent can show that there was a factor present giving the declarant a positive motivation for sincerity, as in the case of the nervous excitement making startled declarations admissible. Alternatively, the proponent can show that there was a factor present creating a disincentive for lying, as in the case of the disserving quality of declarations against interest.

3. There is some necessity for resorting to the hearsay. At the very least there should be the relative necessity required by Rule 803(24)(B) and 804(b)(5)(B): The out-of-court statement is more likely to be reliable than any testimony now available from the

same source. The case is stronger when the necessity is absolute, that is, unavailability satisfying 804(a).

3. SAMPLE FOUNDATION

The hypothetical fact situation is a vehicular manslaughter prosecution. The prosecution alleges that the defendant Nelson was speeding, ran a red light, and struck a pedestrian named Garner. Garner died as a result of the injuries he sustained. A month after the accident the grand jury conducted an investigation into the accident and indicted Nelson. An eyewitness, Mr. West, testified at the hearing. At the hearing, West identified the defendant's car and testified positively that the defendant ran the red light. West died unexpectedly after the hearing and before trial. The prosecution has made a motion *in limine* in the nature of a motion to admit the transcript of West's grand jury testimony. Under the rules of court in this jurisdiction, at these hearings the judge receives affidavits rather than hearing live testimony. The following is the oral argument on the motion:

J   I'm prepared to hear argument on the motion. Ms. Prosecutor, are you ready to proceed?

P   Certainly, Your Honor. Your Honor, let me say at the outset that the government realizes that we cannot offer Mr. West's testimony under 803(1); the defendant didn't have an opportunity to cross at the grand jury hearing, and we therefore can't offer the transcript as former testimony.

However, the government believes very strongly that this is an appropriate case for admitting the testimony under the residual exception, Rule 804(b)(5).

To begin with, we've complied with the advance notice requirement. (1) We served notice of this motion on the defense more than two weeks ago. There is a copy of the service in the court file. To make sure that the defense understood exactly what we intended to offer, we attached a Xerox copy of the relevant pages of the transcript to the notice of motion.

Next, there is evident necessity for resorting to this evidence. (3) Mr. West was one of only three, surviving percipient witnesses to the accident. One of those witnesses is the defendant, and we have no idea of whether he will testify at trial. The other eyewitness, Ms. Neys, admits that she was somewhat distracted when she witnessed the accident; she was walking with her daughter, and her daughter had just tripped and fallen when the car struck Mr. Garner. Mr. West was the only impartial eyewitness who had a good view of the accident. We've filed with the court Mr. Garner's attested death certificate.

Finally, Mr. West's testimony certainly passes muster under the reliability requirement. (2) He had excellent perceptual ability and a good opportunity to view the accident. (2) We've submitted the affidavit of Dr. Norgard, Mr. West's optometrist. The affidavit points out that Mr. West's vision was perfect. We've also submitted the affidavit of Ms. Garcia. She was standing next to Mr. West when he witnessed the accident. Unfortunately, she was turned to look at a store window, but her affidavit states that Mr. West was looking straight in the direction of the accident.

Neither is there any question about the quality of Mr. West's memory. (2) The grand jury hearing occurred less than a month after the accident. In her affidavit, Mr. West's mother states that Mr. West had an excellent memory. Her statement is a proper lay opinion under Rule 701.

There can't be any question about his narrative ability. (2) As you can see from reading the transcript yourself, your Honor, the testimony was presented in simple, lay terms; and there couldn't have been any confusion about the meaning of the terms Mr. West used. Referring again to his mother's affidavit, Mr. West was not only a college graduate; he had been an English minor.

Finally, there is every reason to believe that his grand jury testimony was sincere. (2) He testified under oath at the hearing that he neither was related to nor previously knew either the victim or the defendant. His mother's affidavit corroborates that. Consequently, he had no reason to be biased in this case. Further, his mother's affidavit states that she spoke with him just before he went downtown to testify. She quotes him as saying that he realized that a grand jury hearing was "serious business" and he would "do my best" to help the grand jury understand what happened. His statements qualify as declarations of state of mind under Rule 803, and they are admissible to show his subjective sincerity at the time of the grand jury hearing.

Based on these arguments, your Honor, the government asks you to grant our motion *in limine.*

J   Mr. Defense Attorney, would you like to be heard?

O   I certainly would, Your Honor. I'll be brief.

First, we don't believe that this is a proper use of Rule 804(b)(5). On pages two and three of our memorandum of law, we've noted the many cases stating that Congress intended the residual exceptions to be used sparingly. Even more to the point, page four of the memo lists the cases specifically holding that the exception does not apply to grand jury transcripts. We urge you to follow those cases.

Second, even assuming arguendo that the rule could be construed that broadly, it would violate the confrontation clause. We've never had an opportunity to cross-examine this declarant. The jury has never had an opportunity to assess this person's demeanor. There hasn't been confrontation in any meaningful sense.

For both reasons, this motion should be denied.

J   Ms. Prosecutor, do you have any response?

P   Yes, your Honor. I'll also try to be brief.

The government acknowledges that there are cases urging a narrow interpretation of the residual exceptions and even cases specifically rejecting grand jury transcripts offered under the exceptions. However, we'd ask you to note that all the cases cited in the defense memorandum were decided in the late 1970's. On page three of our memorandum, we conceded that until the early 1980's, the trend in the case law was toward a narrow interpretation of the residual exceptions. However, pages four through seven of our memorandum cite more recent decisions. After carefully considering the legislative history of the residual exceptions, those decisions adopt a more expansive interpretation of the residual exceptions, and several cases now admit grand jury transcripts.

Like the defense's statutory construction argument, the defense's constitutional argument is flawed. Especially when there's necessity as in this case, the linchpin of confrontation analysis is reliability. The confrontation clause doesn't freeze the hearsay doctrine. New hearsay exceptions can evolve and be recognized if they admit only reliable hearsay. Although the defense counsel has argued against the admission of Mr. West's testimony, he hasn't cited one, solid reason to doubt Mr. West's perception, memory, narrative ability, or sincerity. On this state of the record, the interests of justice require granting the government's motion.

J   I agree. The motion to admit will be granted.

Chapter 11

SUBSTITUTES FOR EVIDENCE

A. INTRODUCTION

The previous 10 chapters analyze the legal restrictions on the process of admitting evidence during a trial. However, there are substitutes for conventional evidence: The parties may stipulate to certain propositions, the judge may judicially notice a proposition, or the jurors themselves may be taken outside the courtroom to view a scene or object that is relevant to the case. This chapter discusses the limitations on those substitutes.

B. STIPULATIONS

1. THE DOCTRINE

It is very common for the parties to stipulate before or during a trial. A stipulation can save both parties time, and by stipulating in the jury's presence, a party can attempt to create the impression in the jurors' minds that he or she is a reasonable, fair person.

There are several types of stipulations. For example, the parties may stipulate to continuances. However, we are concerned primarily with two types of evidentiary stipulations. The first is a stipulation of fact; the parties agree that a certain fact existed or that a certain event occurred. If the parties enter a stipulation of fact, neither party can ordinarily introduce evidence to contradict the stipulated fact. The second type of stipulation is a stipulation of expected testimony; the parties agree that if a particular person were present in court as a witness, the person would give certain testimony. The parties are not stipulating that the testimony is truthful or correct; the parties may introduce evidence to contradict what the person would testify to. The parties are agreeing upon only what the person's testimony would be if the person appeared and testified in court.

The procedure for introducing stipulations varies. Some judges commonly permit the attorneys to recite oral stipulations. Other judges prefer that the parties reduce their stipulation to writing. Written pretrial stipulations obviously reduce the possibility for disagreement at trial over the content of the stipulation.

The final procedural question is whether the judge accepting the stipulation must personally question the parties. May the judge accept the attorneys' assurances that the parties assent? In civil actions, the judges routinely do so.

The answer is more complex in criminal cases. In *Boykin v. Alabama,* 395 U.S. 238 (1969), the Supreme Court held that since a defendant waives certain constitutional rights by pleading guilty, the trial record must reflect that the defendant knowingly waived the rights. In many cases, the defendant stipulates to a trial on the basis of the preliminary hearing transcript. This practice is sometimes called a "slow (guilty) plea." Even if the defendant does not stipulate to the truth of all the facts recited by the prosecution witnesses at the preliminary hearing, the defendant is entering into a stipulation of expected testimony; the defense is agreeing that if the same witnesses appeared at trial, they would give the testimony they gave at the earlier hearing. The argument was made that since this practice is practically a guilty plea, the courts should apply *Boykin* by analogy. A minority of state and federal courts have accepted the analogy. For example, in *United States v. Brown,* 428 F.2d 1100 (D.C. Cir. 1970), in which the defendant raised an insanity defense, the court commented: "[W]here a defendant in a criminal case seeks to waive trial on all issues except insanity, the trial judge should address the defendant personally in determining whether the waiver is made voluntarily with understanding of the consequences of the act." The California Supreme Court imposed similar requirements in *Bunnell v. Superior Ct.,* 13 Cal. 3d 592, 531 P.2d 1086, 119 Cal. Rptr. 302 (1975).

2. ELEMENTS OF THE FOUNDATION

The procedure for entering a stipulation includes these steps:
1. One attorney announces to the judge that there has been a stipulation.
2. The judge then inquires of the other attorney whether there has been a stipulation.
3. The second attorney answers in the affirmative.
4. The proponent of the stipulation establishes the tenor or content of the agreement. If the stipulation is oral, the proponent simply states the nature of the agreement on the record. If the stipulation is in writing, the proponent introduces the writing.
5. When required, the judge personally questions the party or parties before accepting the stipulation. The judge ensures that the party understands the nature and consequences of the stipulation.

After the judge accepts the stipulation, the judge informs the jury of the stipulation and instructs the jury on the legal effect of the stipulation.

3. SAMPLE FOUNDATIONS

The first fact situation is a suit for breach of contract. The plaintiff, Marshall Industries, alleges that on January 10, 1989, it entered into a contract with the defendant, Rowl Company. The complaint alleges that under the terms of the contract, Rowl Company promised to excavate a site, lay a foundation, and build a two-story shopping center for the plaintiff. In its answer the defendant raises the affirmative defenses of impossibility and financial impracticability. The answer alleges that a week after beginning excavation, the defendant discovered a subsoil condition that made it prohibitively expensive for it to do the promised construction work. The proponent is the plaintiff.

P   Your Honor, I would like to announce that the parties in this case have reached a stipulation as to their actual knowledge of the existence of the subsoil condition that the defendant discovered in March 1989. (1)

J   (To the defense attorney) Is that true? (2)

O   Yes, Your Honor. (3)

J   What is the nature of this stipulation? (4)

P   We have stipulated that before the defendant's discovery of the layer of granite in March 1989, none of the employees of either the plaintiff or the defendant had actual, subjective knowledge that the layer of granite existed.

J   (To the defense attorney) Is that the tenor of the stipulation?

O   Yes.

J   And both of your clients consent to this stipulation?

P   Yes.

O   Yes, Your Honor.

J   Has this agreement been reduced to writing?

P   No, Your Honor.

O   No — it's an oral stipulation.

J   Very well. If that is the case, I shall accept the stipulation of fact. Ladies and gentlemen of the jury, the plaintiff and the defendant have just entered into an agreement or stipulation. All parties agree that before the defendant discovered the layer of granite at the construction site in March 1989, none of the employees of the plaintiff or defendant had actual, subjective knowledge that the granite was there. Will both parties state for the record that I have correctly described the stipulation for the jury?

O   Certainly, Your Honor.

P   I concur.

J   And ladies and gentlemen of the jury, because of the stipulation, you will not hear any evidence on that issue. However, I am instructing you that you are simply to assume the truth of the stipulated fact. All right, let's proceed with the evidence.

The second fact situation is a criminal prosecution for theft. The People allege that the defendant, Mr. David Miles, stole $1,700 from a local Vons Department Store. An acquaintance of the defendant saw him leave the department store in a furtive, hurried fashion immediately after the alleged theft. Unfortunately for the prosecution, that person is now vacationing in Florida. Rather than forcing the witness to return or seeking a continuance, the parties enter into a stipulation of expected testimony. On this occasion, the parties decided to reduce the stipulation to writing before trial.

STIPULATION OF EXPECTED TESTIMONY

It is hereby stipulated between the People and the defense, with the defendant's express consent, that if Robert Prothero, 766 Somerset Street, Daly City, California, were present in court and sworn as a witness, he would give the following testimony:

I know the defendant, David Miles. We have been members of the same labor union for the past three years. I can recognize him by sight. On the afternoon of July 28, 1988, as I was walking by the entrance to the Vons Department Store on H Street in downtown Millbrae, I saw the defendant exit the store. As soon as he stepped outside, he looked both ways — up and down the street. He seemed to be nervous. Then he stuck his hand in his right pants pocket; there was a big bulge in the pocket. As soon as he removed his hand from his pocket, he began running away from the store.

/s/ Deputy District Attorney

/s/ Defense Counsel

/s/ Defendant

Dated: November 1, 1988

The parties now offer the stipulation at trial. The prosecutor is the proponent. Since the parties are not stipulating to a trial on the preliminary hearing transcript, *Brown* does not apply directly. However, the judge decides to conduct an abbreviated *Brown* inquiry.

P   Your Honor, I want to announce that the parties in this case have reached a stipulation as to the expected testimony of an unavailable witness. (1)
J   (To the defense counsel) Is that true? (2)
O   Yes, Your Honor. (3)
J   What is the stipulation? (4)
P   Your Honor, I request that this be marked People's exhibit number four for identification.
J   It will be so marked.
P   Please let the record reflect that I am showing the exhibit to the opposing counsel.
J   It will so reflect.
P   I now offer People's exhibit number four for identification into evidence as People's exhibit four.
J   (To the defense counsel.) Is this the stipulation?
O   Yes, Your Honor.

J   Mr. Miles, please hold the exhibit in your hands while I ask you a few questions. (5)

D   Yes, sir.

J   Have you ever seen this document before? (5)

D   Yes.

J   When? (5)

D   My attorney showed it to me when he asked me to sign it.

J   Are you familiar with the contents? (5)

D   Yes.

J   Is that your signature on the bottom of the page? (5)

D   Yes.

J   Has your lawyer advised you that you do not have to enter into this stipulation? (5)

D   Yes. He told me that.

J   Has your lawyer informed you that you have a right to insist that the prosecution produce Mr. Prothero at this trial? (5)

D   Yes.

J   Do you realize that if Mr. Prothero appeared at this trial, he would have to testify under oath? (5)

D   Yes.

J   Do you understand that if he testified at trial, he would have to testify in view of the jury? (5)

D   Yes.

J   Do you realize that if he testified at trial, you would have an opportunity to cross-examine him? (5)

D   Yes.

J   Do you understand that you are losing these rights by agreeing to this stipulation? (5)

D   Yes, sir.

J   Has your counsel advised you that even if you stipulate to Mr. Prothero's testimony, you can introduce evidence to rebut or contradict what Mr. Prothero says? (5)

D   Yes.

J   Has your counsel told you that even if you stipulate to Mr. Prothero's testimony, your counsel can make objections on evidentiary grounds to the testimony? (5) (*As a practical matter, there will rarely be evidentiary objections after the entry of the stipulation; the parties usually eliminate any objectionable material during the bargaining over the content of the stipulation.*)

D   Yes.

J   Do you consent to this stipulation? (5)

D   Yes.

J   Well, then the stipulation will be accepted. The exhibit will be received.

P   Your Honor, I request permission to read the exhibit to the jurors.

J   Permission granted.

P   Both parties, the People and defense, have agreed and stipulated that if Mr. Robert Prothero, 766 Somerset Street, Daly City, California, were present in court, he would give the following testimony: "I know the defendant, David Miles. We have been members of the same labor union for the past three years. I can recognize him on sight. On the afternoon of July 28, 1988, I was walking by the entrance to the Vons Department Store on H Street in downtown Millbrae. I saw the defendant exit the store. As soon as he stepped outside, he looked both ways — up and down the street. He seemed to be nervous. Then he stuck his hand in his right pants pocket; there was a big bulge in the pocket. As soon as he removed his hand from his pocket, he began running away from the store."

O   Your Honor, will you please instruct the jury about the stipulation?

J   Yes. Ladies and gentlemen of the jury, the prosecutor has just read a stipulation of expected testimony. The parties have agreed as to what the testimony of Mr. Prothero would be if he appeared here and testified under oath. The stipulation does not admit the truth of the testimony, and it does not add anything to the weight of Mr. Prothero's testimony. The defense may attack, contradict, or explain Mr. Prothero's testimony. In deciding how much weight to attach to Mr. Prothero's testimony, you may consider the fact that you have not had an opportunity to personally observe his demeanor.

C. JUDICIAL NOTICE

1. THE DOCTRINE

Like the stipulation technique, judicial notice is an alternative to the presentation of formal evidence. The judge relieves the parties of the duty to present evidence by noting a fact and informing the jury of the fact's existence. What types of facts may be judicially noticed? Federal Evidence Rule 201(b) answers that to be judicially noticeable, a fact must be "either (1) generally known within the territorial jurisdiction of the trial court or (2) capable of accurate and ready determination by resort to sources whose accuracy cannot reasonably be questioned." The Rule typifies the modern common law of judicial notice; the Rule recognizes two separate, independent bases for judicial notice: (1) The fact is a matter of common knowledge within the court's territorial jurisdiction; and (2) the fact is a readily verifiable certainty.

The procedure for judicial notice varies from jurisdiction to jurisdiction. Many courts permit attorneys to orally request judicial notice during trial. Other courts prefer that the attorneys submit judicial notice requests in writing before trial. Perhaps the emerging view is that the procedure depends on the basis for judicial notice the party is invoking. If the party claims that the fact is a matter of common knowledge, the request can be informal. If the knowledge of the fact is widespread in the territorial area, the judge and attorneys should know the fact; and a formal hearing would be a waste of time. On the other hand, if the party claims that the fact is a readily verifiable certainty, the request should be written and supported by documentary material. For example, if the party requests judicial notice of a scientific principle, the party should submit at least documentary proof of the principle's validity. Courts usually relax the hearsay rule when the parties are litigating the propriety of judicial notice; the judge often permits the parties to use affidavits, declarations, and letters that would usually be considered inadmissible hearsay. In federal practice, the parties may do so by virtue of Rule 104(a).

2. SAMPLE FOUNDATIONS

The first fact situation illustrates the first basis for judicial notice, matter of common knowledge. The fact situation is a tort action arising from a traffic accident. The plaintiff, Ms. Garnet, alleges that the defendant, Mr. Simmons, was speeding and carelessly struck her as she was crossing the street. The plaintiff has already called Mr. James Farnsworth as a witness. Mr. Farnsworth testifies that he observed the accident. He testified that the defendant's car struck the plaintiff at the intersection of F and Girard Streets in downtown Bismarck. Mr. Farnsworth also expresses his opinion that the defendant was driving 35 miles an hour just before the accident. Mr. Farnworth leaves the witness stand, and the following occurs. The plaintiff is the proponent.

P   Your Honor, I now request that you judicially notice two facts.

J   What are the facts?

P   The first is that in this state, the speed limit in any business district is 25 miles an hour. The second is that the intersection of F and Girard Streets in downtown Bismarck is part of our business district. Both facts are matters of common knowledge in this area.

J   I agree.

P   Would you please instruct the jury about the judicially noticed facts?

J   Yes. Ladies and gentlemen of the jury, I am now judicially noticing two facts. The first fact is that in the State of North Dakota, the speed limit in any business district is 25 miles an hour. The second fact is that the intersection where this accident occurred — F and Girard Streets — is in Bismarck's business district. Since these facts are matters of common knowledge, I am authorized to note these facts without requiring formal evidence from the parties. You are to accept these facts and assume them to be true even though you will not hear any evidence on these facts.

The second fact situation illustrates the second basis for judicial notice, verifiable certainty. The second situation is a continuation of the first. The plaintiff ultimately wants to offer the testimony of Officer Newton Ripley. Officer Ripley had his police car parked near the intersection when the accident occurred. His police car was equipped with a radar speedmeter. The speedmeter clocked the defendant's car at 36 miles an hour just before the accident. As Section J in Chapter 4 points out, part of the foundation for an offer of scientific evidence is proof of the theory's validity and the instrument's reliability. Since the radar speedmeter is a scientific instrument, the plaintiff must lay those two elements of the foundation in our hypothetical. However, since those facts are readily verifiable certainties, the plaintiff need not present live testimony; the plaintiff can use judicial notice to supply the first two elements of the scientific evidence foundation. Before trial, the plaintiff could obtain this affidavit.

STATE OF NORTH DAKOTA

CITY OF BISMARCK

} AFFIDAVIT

I, the undersigned, being duly sworn, depose and say that:

1. My name is Glenda Schneider. I reside at 7144 Frontier Boulevard, Bismarck, North Dakota.

2. I teach Electronics at the University of North Dakota. I have taught that subject there for the past seven years. I have a B.S., a Master's, and a Doctorate in that field from Michigan State University.

3. The underlying theory of the radar speedmeter is the Doppler shift principle. The principle is that if a beam of microwaves of known frequency strikes an approaching or receding object, the beam changes frequency. The change in frequency is proportional to the speed of the object. This theory has been experimentally verified by hundreds of experiments throughout the world. It is accepted as a valid theory by all experts in the field.

4. The radar speedmeter applies the Doppler shift principle. The speedmeter consists of a transmitter and a receiver. The transmitter generates and sends out the beam of microwaves. The receiver measures the frequency change after the beam strikes an object and bounces back to the car containing the radar speedmeter. Like the underlying theory, the radar speedmeter instrument has been subjected to numerous experiments. The conclusion of the experiments is that if the speedmeter is in proper, working order and operated properly, the instrument will accurately measure speed to within a few hundredths of a mile per hour. At one time or another speedmeters have been used by law enforcement agencies in every state in the United States. Experts in my field almost universally accept the reliability of radar speedmeters.

/s/ Glenda Schneider

On September 17, 1989, before the undersigned, a Notary Public for the State of North Dakota, personally appeared Glenda Schneider, known to me to be the person whose name is subscribed to the within instrument, and acknowledged that she executed the same.

/s/ Mildred Adams
Notary Public
My license expires October 17, 1992

In addition to using affidavits from experts, the party can sometimes use an affidavit from a professional school librarian. The librarian's affidavit is attached to Xerox copies of the title page and the pertinent pages from a learned treatise in the scientific field. The librarian's affidavit states the librarian's position, lists the credentials of the author of the treatise, and finally asserts that the treatise is a standard, authoritative text in its field. The party then uses the excerpts from the treatise to establish that the principle's validity or the instrument's reliability is a verifiable certainty.

The plaintiff would use the affidavit at trial in this fashion. As soon as the judge granted the first request for judicial notice, the plaintiff could make this request before calling Officer Ripley as a witness. The plaintiff is still the proponent.

P   Your Honor, I have one last request for judicial notice.

J   What is that?

P   May we approach the bench?

J   Yes.

P   Your Honor, I request that you judicially notice the validity of the theory underlying radar speedmeters and the general reliability of speedmeters. Both facts are verifiable certainties.

J   (To the opposing attorney) Did you have advance notice that the plaintiff was going to make this request?

O   Yes, Your Honor. He gave me notice a week ago.

P   Your Honor, I request that this be marked plaintiff's exhibit number nine for identification.

J   It will be so marked.

P   Please let the record reflect that I am showing the exhibit to the opposing counsel.

J   It will so reflect.

P   I now offer plaintiff's exhibit number nine for identification into evidence as plaintiff's exhibit number nine.

J   (To the opposing attorney) Have you seen this exhibit before?

O   Yes. The plaintiff's attorney gave me a copy about a week ago.

J   Do you have any objection?

O   Yes, Your Honor. This affidavit is gross hearsay.

P   Your Honor, at this point we're litigating the propriety of judicial notice. In this jurisdiction, under Rule 104(a), the hearsay rule doesn't apply to your determination whether these facts are verifiable certainties.

J   You're right. The objection will be overruled, and the exhibit will be received.

P   The exhibit establishes that the validity of the underlying principle and the reliability of the instrument are verifiable, scientific certainties. For that reason, judicial notice is appropriate.

J   I will grant your request.

P   I request that you inform the jury of these facts.

J   Yes. Ladies and gentlemen of the jury, I am now going to judicially notice two more facts. One fact is the validity of the theory underlying radar speedmeters. As you may know, the police in this jurisdiction use radar speedmeters to measure the speed of cars. The technical theory underlying speedmeters has been accepted by scientists. Secondly, the speedmeter itself is a reliable instrument if it's in working order and operated correctly. You are to assume the validity of the theory and the general reliability of the instrument. I understand that we are about to hear some testimony about a radar speedmeter clocking of the defendant's car. I want to make it clear that I am not deciding whether this speedmeter was in good, working condition or whether the officer used the correct procedures. You will have to listen to the testimony and make those decisions. I am instructing you only that you must assume the validity of the scientific principle and the general reliability of speedmeters even though you won't hear any evidence on these topics.

The above hypothetical assumes a civil action. In a civil action, Federal Rule 201(g) permits the judge to direct the jury to assume the existence of the noticed fact. However, Rule 201(g) prescribes a different rule for criminal cases: "In a criminal case, the court shall instruct the jury that it may, but is not required to, accept as conclusive any fact judicially noticed."

D. JURY VIEWS

1. THE DOCTRINE

Sometimes the attorneys want the jurors and judge to view an object or location that cannot feasibly be brought into the courtroom. In most cases, the attorney will be content to offer either a witness' oral description of the object, a diagram of the object, or a photograph. However, in some cases, the object is so complex and plays such a pivotal role in the case that the attorney wants the trier of fact to personally observe the object or location. This procedure is known as a jury view.

In most jurisdictions, the sense impressions the trier of fact gathers during a view do not qualify as substantive evidence in the case. However, there is a minority view. California Evidence Code § 140 defines "evidence" as including "things presented to the senses that are offered to prove the existence or nonexistence of a fact." The California Law Revision Commission comment explains that § 140 includes jury views. Hence, the information the trier of fact gains during a jury view constitutes independent evidence under the Code.

2. ELEMENTS OF THE FOUNDATION

The proponent of a jury view usually makes a pretrial motion for a view and submits affidavits or declarations in support of the motion. The declarations should show that:
1. Certain property exists.
2. The property is logically relevant to the pending case.

3. It is impossible or inconvenient to bring the property into the courtroom.
4. The features of the property are so complex or detailed that an oral description, diagram, or photograph would be inadequate.
5. The property is in substantially the same condition as at the time of the relevant event. If the property has changed materially, the judge usually exercises discretion by denying the motion. If the property has changed markedly, a view might mislead the jury. When there is potential for misleading the jury, Rule 403 cuts against granting the motion.

3. SAMPLE FOUNDATION

The fact situation is a personal injury action arising from a collision in February 1988 on a winding, rural road in Yolo County. The plaintiff moves for a jury view of the section of road where the collision occurred. In support of the motion, the plaintiff submits two declarations. Both declarations refer to the same section of road mentioned in the pleadings. For that reason, both declarations lay the first three elements of the foundation. The date of the hearing on the motion is August 1, 1989.

DECLARATION[1]

1. My name is George Wasterson. I live at 1444 Court Street, Woodland, California.
2. I am a professional photographer. I am the proprietor of the Wasterson Photography Studio, 1456 Court Street, in Woodland. I have owned that company for 15 years. While I was on active duty in the United States Army between 1965 and 1972, I received formal training in photography. I have since taken seven photography classes at California State University in Sacramento.
3. On July 1, 1989, an attorney, Ms. Eileen Richards, contacted me by phone. She asked me to meet her at the intersection of Rural Route 4 and Range Road outside the city limits of Woodland. (1), (2), (3) I met her there later that afternoon.
4. While we were at the intersection, Ms. Richards explained to me that she represented the plaintiff in a civil action arising from a collision at the intersection. She also explained that she was interested in showing the jurors the 200 yards of Range Road immediately to the west of the intersection with Rural Route 4. She asked whether I could photograph or videotape that section of road.

---

1. California Code of Civil Procedure § 2015.5 permits the use of a declaration in lieu of an affidavit.

5. I carefully inspected the two hundred yards of road in question. I walked the stretch of road twice and drove it twice. I then advised Ms. Richards that in my professional opinion, neither still photographs nor a videotape would be adequate. The section of road in question is not only winding; the road is also uneven — any car traveling that section of road is constantly riding up and then down and then up again. Even if I took 100 still photographs and submitted them to a jury, the stills would not adequately convey to the jury the sense of traveling down that stretch of road. In addition, since the road is both curvy and uneven, even a videotape would convey only a limited sense of perspective of a driver on that stretch of road. I declare under penalty of perjury that the above statements are true and correct.

Executed this 14th day of July, 1989, in Woodland, Yolo County, California.

_____

/s/ George Wasterson

_____

DECLARATION

1. My name is Doris Kingman. I reside at 723 Range Road in Yolo County, California. I have lived at that residence for the past 37 years.

2. I am intimately familiar with the intersection of Range Road and Rural Route 4 outside Woodland in Yolo County. It is the intersection closest to my house. I have driven through that intersection thousands of times.

3. I can recall the condition of the 200 yards of Range Road immediately to the west of the intersection with Rural Route 4 as of February 1988. I generally remember the condition of the road and the foliage on both sides of the road. I inspected that area again today. To the best of my recollection, the condition of the foliage and road today is substantially the same as the condition in February 1988.

I declare under penalty of perjury that the above statements are true and correct.

Executed this 29th day of July, 1989 in Woodland, Yolo County, California.

_____

/s/ Doris Kingman

Index